Venice

Damien Simonis

D1510791

LONELY PLANET PUBLICATIONS
Melbourne • Oakland • London • Paris

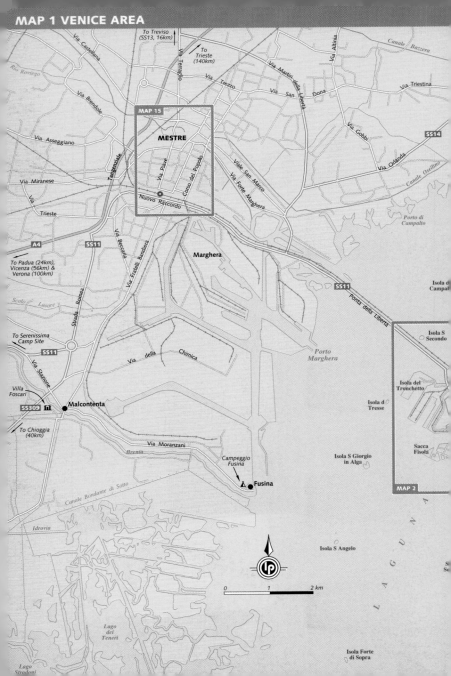

MAP 1 VENICE AREA

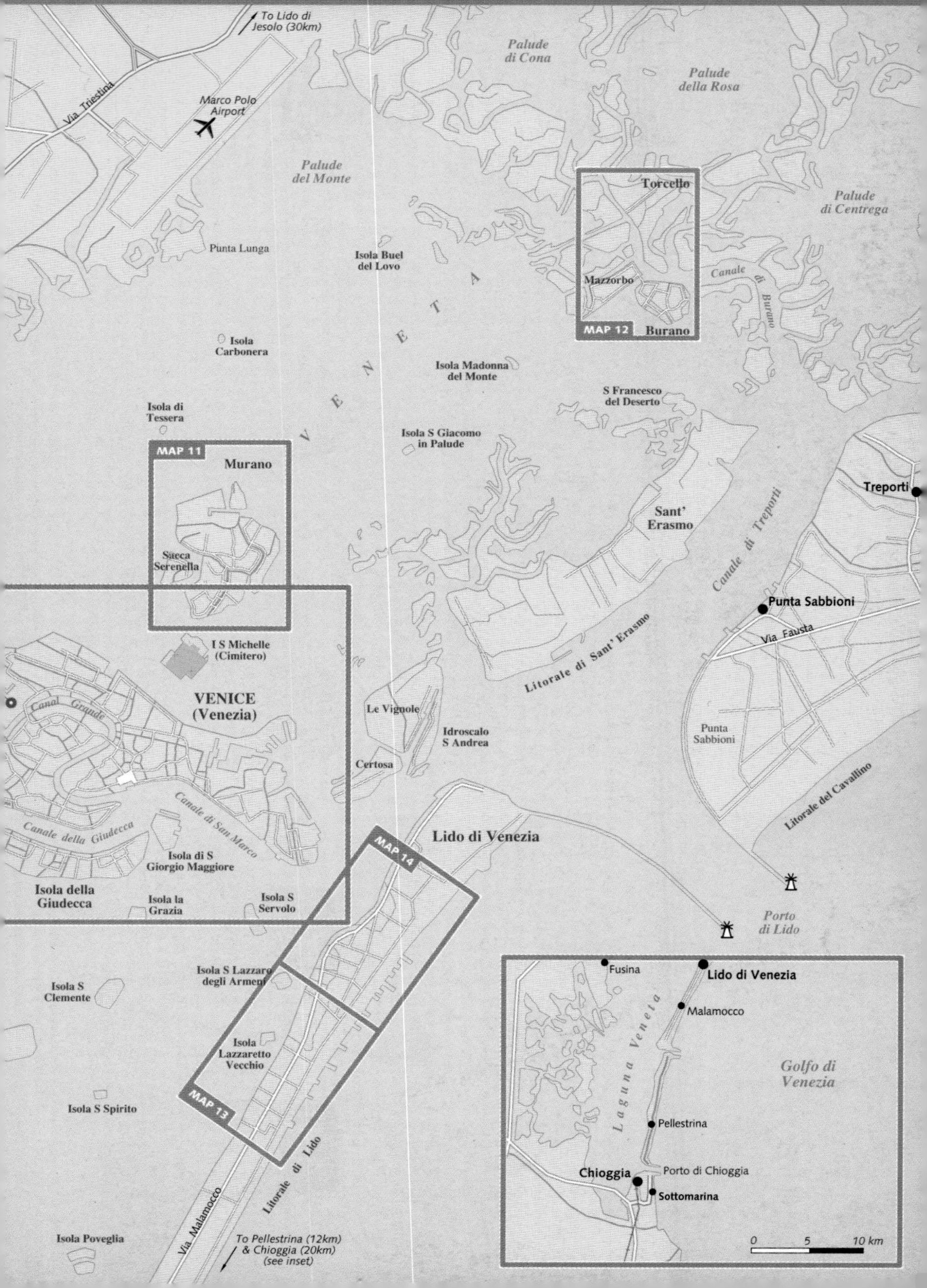

To Lido di
Jesolo (30km)

Via Triestina

Marco Polo
Airport

*Palude
di Cona*

*Palude
della Rosa*

*Palude
del Monte*

Torcello

*Palude
di Centrega*

Punta Lunga

Isola Buel
del Lovo

Mazzorbo

Canale di Burano

Isola
Carbonera

MAP 12

Burano

Isola Madonna
del Monte

L A G U N A

Isola di
Tessera

Isola S Giacomo
in Palude

S Francesco
del Deserto

Treporti

MAP 11

Murano

V E N E T A

Sant'
Erasmo

Canale di Treporti

Sacca
Serenella

Punta Sabbioni

Via Fausta

I S Michelle
(Cimitero)

VENICE
(Venezia)

Le Vignole

Punta
Sabbioni

Canal Grande

Idroscalo
S Andrea

Litorale di Sant' Erasmo

Certosa

Canale della Giudecca

Canale di San Marco

Isola di S
Giorgio Maggiore

MAP 14

Lido di Venezia

Litorale del Cavallino

Isola della
Giudecca

Isola la
Grazia

Isola S
Servolo

Isola S
Clemente

Isola S Lazzaro
degli Armeni

Fusina

Lido di Venezia

*Porto
di Lido*

Malamocco

*Golfo di
Venezia*

Isola
Lazzaretto
Vecchio

MAP 13

Laguna Venezia

Isola S Spirito

Pellestrina

Isola Poveglia

Via Malamocco

Litorale di Lido

To Pellestrina (12km)
& Chioggia (20km)
(see inset)

Chioggia

Porto di Chioggia

Sottomarina

0   5   10 km

Venice
1st edition – April 2000

Published by
Lonely Planet Publications Pty Ltd A.C.N. 005 607 983
192 Burwood Rd, Hawthorn, Victoria 3122, Australia

Lonely Planet Offices
Australia PO Box 617, Hawthorn, Victoria 3122
USA 150 Linden St, Oakland, CA 94607
UK 10a Spring Place, London NW5 3BH
France 1 rue du Dahomey, 75011 Paris

Photographs
Many of the images in this guide are available for licensing from
Lonely Planet Images.
email: lpi@lonelyplanet.com.au

Front cover photograph
The view across to Isola di San Giorgio Maggiore from Piazzetta San
Marco (Olivier Cirendini)

ISBN 0 86442 786 7

text & maps © Lonely Planet 2000
photos © photographers as indicated 2000

Printed by The Bookmaker Pty Ltd
Printed in China

Contents – Text

PLACES TO EAT — 182

ENTERTAINMENT — 198

SHOPPING — 204

EXCURSIONS — 211

LANGUAGE — 233

GLOSSARY — 240

INDEX — 251

MAP SECTION — 257

MAP LEGEND — back page

METRIC CONVERSION — inside back cover

The Author

Damien Simonis

With a degree in languages and several years' reporting and sub-editing on Australian newspapers (including the *Australian* and the *Age*) behind him, Sydney-born Damien left Australia in 1989. He has since lived, worked and travelled extensively throughout Europe, the Middle East and North Africa. Since 1992, Lonely Planet has kept him busy writing for *Jordan & Syria*, *Egypt & the Sudan*, *Morocco*, *North Africa*, *Italy*, *Spain*, *Canary Islands* and *Barcelona*. As well as this edition of *Venice*, he has written *Florence* and *Tuscany*. At last report he was heading back to Spain, where among other things he is working on Lonely Planet's new guide to Madrid. He has also written and snapped for other publications in Australia, the UK and North America. When not on the road, Damien resides in splendid Stoke Newington, deep in the heart of north London.

From the Author

The staff at the tiny APT office at Stazione di Santa Lucia were very helpful – but really, they deserve a bigger workspace! Thanks, also, to Christine Stroyan at Lonely Planet in London for being a fine and patient editor.

Further thanks are due to the people in the Arca, L'Arlecchino, Distilleria Poli, Distilleria Nardini and Rizzi stores for allowing me to photograph their wares.

I remain constantly indebted to my friends in Milano. They seem to have the welcome mat out no matter what happens. Anna Cerutti, in particular, has been more than generous – *ci vediamo in istituto*! Daniela Antongiovanni and Sergio Bosio – *vi abbraccio forte forte*.

Stefano Falletti gave me a couple of useful tips on eating in Venezia, for which *grazie. Non vedo l'ora di fare un'altro giro in barca!*

Alberto Stassi, ex-Milano, had the misfortune of being moved to Padova for work. The good thing is, we were able to get together and shoot the breeze on more than one occasion.

Although our meetings came late in my stay, I would like to say *grazie* to several people in Venezia too. Kristin Flood, Irina Fraguia, Roberta Guarnieri, Bernhard Klein and Federica Centulani were all willing to hand out tips, or at least gather for a prosecco or two. Michela Scibilia, if only I had met you – 'the key' – and Daniele earlier! *La prossima volta sarà!*

Un abrazote for Osvaldo of the 'frisbee club', wherever you may be – thanks for drawing me briefly into the whirlwind of the Biennale arty party circuit! And in that vein, cheers to Christabel, Rob and Deirdre, with whom several drinks were drunk in fine style!

3

Another person to whom I am indebted is Franco Filippi, the sharpness of whose knowledge of Venezia is matched only by his love of the subject. I must also thank Marina, of the Locanda Remedio, who not only shared her enthusiasm for her local history but also was my bridge to Franco.

Frances Hawkins of Venice in Peril in London graciously helped update information on work being done to restore monuments in the city.

And finally, cheers to Roberto, at Ai Postali – I wish I had had more time to hang around the bar!

This Book

Damien Simonis researched and wrote this 1st edition of *Venice*.

From the Publisher

This edition of *Venice* was edited in Lonely Planet's London office by Christine Stroyan, with assistance from Katie Cody and Clay Lucas in the Melbourne office. It was proofed by Tim Ryder and Christine. Angie Watts drew the Venice city and regional maps, laid out the book and designed the colour pages, and Sara Yorke drew the Excursions maps. Ed Pickard assisted with the mapping and David Wenk produced the climate chart. Angie designed the front cover, Jim Miller did the back-cover map and Nicky Caven drew the illustrations. The photographs were supplied by Lonely Planet Images. The index was compiled by Angie Hipkin and Quentin Frayne produced the Language chapter. Finally, thanks are due to Imogen Franks for extra research and to Damien, who, despite a hectic schedule of his own, remained patient and supportive throughout the project.

Foreword

ABOUT LONELY PLANET GUIDEBOOKS

The story begins with a classic travel adventure: Tony and Maureen Wheeler's 1972 journey across Europe and Asia to Australia. Useful information about the overland trail did not exist at that time, so Tony and Maureen published the first Lonely Planet guidebook to meet a growing need.

From a kitchen table, then from a tiny office in Melbourne (Australia), Lonely Planet has become the largest independent travel publisher in the world, an international company with offices in Melbourne, Oakland (USA), London (UK) and Paris (France).

Today Lonely Planet guidebooks cover the globe. There is an ever-growing list of books and there's information in a variety of forms and media. Some things haven't changed. The main aim is still to help make it possible for adventurous travellers to get out there – to explore and better understand the world.

At Lonely Planet we believe travellers can make a positive contribution to the countries they visit – if they respect their host communities and spend their money wisely. Since 1986 a percentage of the income from each book has been donated to aid projects and human rights campaigns.

Updates Lonely Planet thoroughly updates each guidebook as often as possible. This usually means there are around two years between editions, although for more unusual or more stable destinations the gap can be longer. Check the imprint page (following the colour map at the beginning of the book) for publication dates.

Between editions up-to-date information is available in two free newsletters – the paper *Planet Talk* and email *Comet* (to subscribe, contact any Lonely Planet office) – and on our Web site at www.lonelyplanet.com. The *Upgrades* section of the Web site covers a number of important and volatile destinations and is regularly updated by Lonely Planet authors. *Scoop* covers news and current affairs relevant to travellers. And, lastly, the *Thorn Tree* bulletin board and *Postcards* section of the site carry unverified, but fascinating, reports from travellers.

Correspondence The process of creating new editions begins with the letters, postcards and emails received from travellers. This correspondence often includes suggestions, criticisms and comments about the current editions. Interesting excerpts are immediately passed on via newsletters and the Web site, and everything goes to our authors to be verified when they're researching on the road. We're keen to get more feedback from organisations or individuals who represent communities visited by travellers.

> Lonely Planet gathers information for everyone who's curious about the planet – and especially for those who explore it first-hand. Through guidebooks, phrasebooks, activity guides, maps, literature, newsletters, image library, TV series and Web site we act as an information exchange for a worldwide community of travellers.

Research Authors aim to gather sufficient practical information to enable travellers to make informed choices and to make the mechanics of a journey run smoothly. They also research historical and cultural background to help enrich the travel experience and allow travellers to understand and respond appropriately to cultural and environmental issues.

Authors don't stay in every hotel because that would mean spending a couple of months in each medium-sized city and, no, they don't eat at every restaurant because that would mean stretching belts beyond capacity. They do visit hotels and restaurants to check standards and prices, but feedback based on readers' direct experiences can be very helpful.

Many of our authors work undercover, others aren't so secretive. None of them accept freebies in exchange for positive write-ups. And none of our guidebooks contain any advertising.

Production Authors submit their raw manuscripts and maps to offices in Australia, USA, UK or France. Editors and cartographers – all experienced travellers themselves – then begin the process of assembling the pieces. When the book finally hits the shops some things are already out of date, we start getting feedback from readers, and the process begins again ...

WARNING & REQUEST

Things change – prices go up, schedules change, good places go bad and bad places go bankrupt – nothing stays the same. So, if you find things better or worse, recently opened or long since closed, please tell us and help make the next edition even more accurate and useful. We genuinely value all the feedback we receive. Julie Young coordinates a well-travelled team that reads and acknowledges every letter, postcard and email and ensures that every morsel of information finds its way to the appropriate authors, editors and cartographers for verification.

Everyone who writes to us will find their name in the next edition of the appropriate guidebook. They will also receive the latest issue of *Planet Talk*, our quarterly printed newsletter, or *Comet*, our monthly email newsletter. Subscriptions to both newsletters are free. The very best contributions will be rewarded with a free guidebook.

Excerpts from your correspondence may appear in new editions of Lonely Planet guidebooks, the Lonely Planet Web site, *Planet Talk* or *Comet*, so please let us know if you *don't* want your letter published or your name acknowledged.

Send all correspondence to the Lonely Planet office closest to you:

Australia: PO Box 617, Hawthorn, Victoria 3122
UK: 10A Spring Place, London NW5 3BH
USA: 150 Linden St, Oakland CA 94607
France: 1 rue du Dahomey, Paris 75011

Or email us at: talk2us@lonelyplanet.com.au

For news, views and updates see our Web site: www.lonelyplanet.com

HOW TO USE A LONELY PLANET GUIDEBOOK

The best way to use a Lonely Planet guidebook is any way you choose. At Lonely Planet we believe the most memorable travel experiences are often those that are unexpected, and the finest discoveries are those you make yourself. Guidebooks are not intended to be used as if they provide a detailed set of infallible instructions!

Contents All Lonely Planet guidebooks follow roughly the same format. The Facts about the Destination chapter or section gives background information ranging from history to weather. Facts for the Visitor gives practical information on issues like visas and health. Getting There & Away gives a brief starting point for researching travel to and from the destination. Getting Around gives an overview of the transport options when you arrive.

The peculiar demands of each destination determine how subsequent chapters are broken up, but some things remain constant. We always start with background, then proceed to sights, places to stay, places to eat, entertainment, getting there and away, and getting around information – in that order.

Heading Hierarchy Lonely Planet headings are used in a strict hierarchical structure that can be visualised as a set of Russian dolls. Each heading (and its following text) is encompassed by any preceding heading that is higher on the hierarchical ladder.

Entry Points We do not assume guidebooks will be read from beginning to end, but that people will dip into them. The traditional entry points are the list of contents and the index. In addition, however, some books have a complete list of maps and an index map illustrating map coverage.

There may also be a colour map that shows highlights. These highlights are dealt with in greater detail in the Facts for the Visitor chapter, along with planning questions and suggested itineraries. Each chapter covering a geographical region usually begins with a locator map and another list of highlights. Once you find something of interest in a list of highlights, turn to the index.

Maps Maps play a crucial role in Lonely Planet guidebooks and include a huge amount of information. A legend is printed on the back page. We seek to have complete consistency between maps and text, and to have every important place in the text captured on a map. Map key numbers usually start in the top left corner.

Although inclusion in a guidebook usually implies a recommendation we cannot list every good place. Exclusion does not necessarily imply criticism. In fact there are a number of reasons why we might exclude a place – sometimes it is simply inappropriate to encourage an influx of travellers.

Introduction

For 1000 years the Repubblica Serenissima (Most Serene Republic) – or La Serenissima – as Venice is known to its own, led a dynamic, proud and independent existence. Woven together like a fine piece of Burano lace from a myriad malaria-infested islets, the city came to be one of the canniest and longest-lasting mercantile sea powers in history. Until Napoleon waltzed in in 1797, the Venetian Republic had probably come closer than any other European polity to the modern concept of democracy. Its doges were elected (though admittedly not by universal suffrage), religious and racial tolerance (at least to a greater degree than elsewhere) were considered common sense and few of its dominions ever felt the need to rebel, even when the city clearly did not have the means to resist.

Venice was and remains a sore point with the rest of Italy (and beyond), a source of envy and irritation at the same time. Throughout its history, rivals as varied as the popes, Milan, Genoa, Padua, Imperial Spain and the Turks sought to break the haughty masters of the Adriatic. Often they came close. Nowadays, other Italians consider the city as stuck-up as ever.

Whether anyone likes it or not, Venice is unique, and not only for its watery home. Here East met West, witnessed time and again in the city's art and architecture. The city's builders seem to have delighted in variety as they draped it in an ever-thickening patchwork mantle of monumental splendour. From the great mosaics of Basilica di San Marco and Torcello to the sobre Gothic majesty of the Frari, from the simplicity of Romanesque to the discipline of Palladio, from the sensuality of Veneto-Byzantine to the extremes of baroque, the concentration of architectural gems is astonishing.

The same is true of its art. From the time Venetian painting took off, with the Bellini family in the 15th century, the march past of greats from the Venetian school seems infinite. Although some of their works are scat-tered in galleries far from home, the number of masterpieces by, among others, Tiepolo, Tintoretto, Veronese and Titian still to be seen in the city is the equivalent of death by chocolate for art lovers.

However, there is more to Venice than history, art and architecture. Exploring the islands of the lagoon, each of them vastly different from the main spectacle, is essential to getting a wider view of what makes up the whole. Look, too, behind the facade. Were Thomas Mann, author of the most famous novel about Venice, *Death in Venice* (1912), alive today, he might well pen Death *of* Venice. The proud city of the winged lion is slowly expiring. International organisations fight to preserve its monuments and engineers debate how to stem Adriatic floods. Press coverage of the battle to clean the lagoon of toxic waste excreted by the mainland petrochemical industry alternates with alarmed reports on building subsidence and rotting foundations. Everyone, from the mayor of Venice to ministers in Rome, from art historians in Britain to architecture buffs in the USA, expounds unendingly about the need to do *something*.

Maybe they have missed the point. The lifeblood of a city is not its palaces and churches. It is its people. And the people of Venice are voting with their feet. Since the 1950s, the population has more than halved. Housing is too expensive, transport too complicated, jobs too scarce. Talk to people and you get the uncanny feeling you are on a sinking ship. One day it may truly be just a theme park open daily from eight till late.

For the moment though you can still feel the pulse, and Venice has returned from the brink of extinction before – who knows what rabbit it may pull out of the hat this time? This city defies its admirers and detractors alike. It is, above all, elusive. The tides rise and fall every six hours, pushing the water first this way then that along the canals – more than just a 'sight', Venice seems to be time and motion itself.

Facts about Venice

HISTORY

To transport yourself back to the origins of La Serenissima (the Venetian Republic) – the damp early days of refugees who chose the dubious swampy safety of the Venetian lagoon over the hazards of the lawless Italian mainland – get out of Venice. The grand *palazzi*, the busy canals, the splendid squares – none of this existed in the beginning. Strike out for the distant scrub-covered flats of Torcello, in the north of the lagoon, where the first mainlanders sought haven as the edifice of empire and the rule of law on the mainland crumbled before the barbarian invasions at the beginning of the Dark Ages. That's how it began.

Origins

For some, history begins only with the Roman Empire, but of course Caesar and co were preceded by several thousand years of comings and goings. In the Veneto, the region of which Venice (Venezia) is today the capital, all sorts of theories abound as to the origins of its inhabitants prior to Roman conquest.

Increasingly, historians seem convinced that the Veneti were of Celtic origin. Educated guesstimations have eastern tribes moving west into north-eastern Turkey from the Caspian and Aral Seas around 1500 BC. From there, some tribes are then said to have moved on, settling on the mainland of what is today the Veneto, while others went on to Brittany, in France. The next stage supposedly came after the fall of Troy in 1183 BC. Another wave of migrants left Turkey and joined their confreres in the Veneto. It was the Veneti who founded towns like Padua (Padova), Vicenza, Treviso and Belluno.

As Rome's grip on the north tightened in the wake of the Punic Wars, Padua took on the role of capital of the Veneti in their dealings with the emerging superpower. By the time Caesar was off invading Gaul, in around 50 BC, the Veneto territory had been incorporated into what was soon to consider itself the Roman Empire as the province of Venetia. And thus it remained for more than four centuries.

Twilight of the Gods

When Emperor Theodosius died in AD 395, the lumbering wreck of the Roman Empire was already on the skids. From now on, it was effectively divided in two. Rome (Roma) remained the capital of the western half, while Constantinople (present-day Istanbul) assumed a parallel role in the east.

Already the 4th century had been marked by increasing disorder, plagues, poverty and growing pressure from 'barbarian' tribes beyond the frontiers of the empire. The 5th century opened in a particularly ominous fashion for the Italian peninsula with the Visigothic invasion led by Alaric in 402. He entered Italy through Venetia, sacking the bishopric of Aquileia and pillaging at leisure along the way. The first waves of refugees from the coastal towns and even further inland opted to seek haven on the islands of the Venetian lagoon. When Alaric was tossed out of Italy, they mostly returned to rebuild their homes.

After Alaric more Visigoths, Goths, Germans, Suevi and, perhaps the most fearsome of all, Attila's Huns descended upon various parts of the empire. Attila's incursion into Venetia in 452 in particular had the refugees swarming back to the islands. As with Alaric, they rightly assumed that a pillaging army with little knowledge of the sea would leave them alone while in pursuit of bigger fish (as it were). By now, however, some could see the writing on the wall. The good old days of the Pax Romana were over and no-one could guarantee safety on the mainland. Increasingly, the refugees opted to stay on the islands. The nascent island communities elected tribunes and in 466 met in Grado, on a lagoon south of Aquileia. There they formed a loose federation and established a degree of self-rule.

Little evidence supports the traditional 'foundation' date of 25 March 421.

In the meantime, the Western Roman Empire crumbled. Britain, Spain, Gaul and North Africa, the latter long the granary of Imperial Rome, had all fallen or were about to fall into barbarian hands by 476, when the last, ineffectual emperor, Romulus, capitulated to the German Odoacer. Odoacer in turn was replaced by the Ostrogoth Theodoric, who proclaimed himself king in 493 and installed himself in Ravenna – previously the preferred bolt hole of fearful Roman emperors.

Early Days, the Eastern Empire & the Lombards

Theodoric seems to have kept on good terms with the small island population of the lagoons north of Ravenna. Their maritime skills came in handy for transporting supplies to Ravenna and it appears the islanders were already becoming enterprising local traders.

Theodoric no doubt had more pressing concerns anyway. In 535, the eastern emperor Justinian, as leader of the successor to the Roman Empire, decided it was time to turn the tide, and recovering Italy became his top priority. Venetia (very roughly equivalent to the modern Veneto region), the islands and Ravenna were all thus bound into the Eastern, or Byzantine, Empire, by 540. So long as the islanders provided sea transport when needed, they rubbed along tolerably well with their distant imperial masters. In any event, the latter allowed the Venetians to run their affairs much as before under their own elected tribunes.

Meanwhile, Constantinople pursued the conquest of Italy. All was proceeding much as had been hoped until HQ decided to relieve the key commander in the field, Narses, of his duties. The ensuing squabble opened the way for the last great barbarian invasion. This time it was the Lombards, invited by Narses, and when they entered northern Italy in 568 they meant to stay. As they swept across the Po plains, refugees made for the islands in unprecedented numbers. Aquileia was again sacked.

The new migrants settled primarily on Torcello, which would for some time remain the commercial centre of the islands, as well as Malamocco (the southern end of what today is known as the Lido), Chioggia and Rivoalto. The latter, subsequently known as Rialto (high bank), was no more than the highest of a small huddle of islets in the middle of the Venetian lagoon. Other island settlements, such as Caorle, Grado and Heraclea, the latter built at the mouth of the Piave river, grew up on lagoons farther to the north-east. In 639 the last mainland town in Venetia, Oderzo, fell to the Lombards. All that the empire retained of Venetia was the lagoon islands.

A Doge Is Born

The next imperial move of interest came in the early 700s, when Emperor Leo III decreed that icons should be smashed and banished throughout the empire. Apparently icon-worship was becoming a problem in the east, but in Italy the locals were incensed by this affront to their own common sense and uprisings took place in cities up and down the peninsula.

It appears the Venetian lagoon communities were not immune to the spirit of rebellion. They named a certain Orso Ipato as their Dux, or leader, in 726. Dux in Venetian dialect comes out as *doge* – and in this figure (another 117 followed) would reside the office of head of the Venetian state for the ensuing millennium. Various tales and legends surround the story of the creation of the first doge. It is equally possible the Dux was simply a military nomination by Constantinople. Some hold that Orso was preceded by two other doges, beginning with Pauluccio Anafesto in 697.

At any rate, the lagoon communities of Venetia continued to belong to the Byzantine sphere of influence, even after the Lombards took Ravenna in 751. No sooner had they achieved this than the Franks, on the invitation of the pope, descended into northern Italy and quickly replaced them as the area's overlords. The fact that none of these interlopers reached the islands led the Venetian islanders to claim, however spuriously, direct descent of their people and institutions from those of the Roman Empire.

The islands remained unmolested, but internal intrigues kept them busy enough. Doge Orso and many of his successors found it hard to resist the temptation of turning an elected office into a hereditary one. It became common practice for a doge to associate his sons with himself in the exercise of power. Those sons were then frequently elected as doge. Theoretically, the doge was kept in check by two counsellors and the Arengo, a general assembly of the people. In practice, most of the doges in the first centuries of what came to be known as the Repubblica Serenissima (Most Serene Republic) behaved as autocrats, paying only minimal heed to the counsel of their peers. Some paid for such arrogance with deposition and occasionally their lives, for political murder (Orso himself was assassinated) and coups were a common trait of early Venetian electoral politics.

By the time the Frankish king Charlemagne had elevated himself to Holy Roman Emperor in 800, the Venetian communities were deeply divided into at least three factions: pro-Byzantine, republican and now pro-Frankish. When the latter called upon Pepin (Charlemagne's son) to occupy Venetia and the lagoons, the remaining islanders united to stop the assault, although Grado and mainland towns fell. The outcome was a peace treaty signed by Charlemagne and the Eastern Empire in 810. In return for Constantinople's recognition of him as Holy Roman Emperor, Charlemagne abandoned claims to the Duchy of Venetia (as the Venetian Republic was also known), which remained anchored in the Byzantine sphere of influence. It was the only part of Italy to be officially allotted to the East (although parts of southern Italy remained in Byzantine hands for several centuries to come) and the decision effectively sealed off the emerging republic from the events that would take mainland Italy down a very different road.

Emergence of the Republic

The hero of the battle against Pepin was Agnello Partecipazio, from the tranquil island of Rivoalto. He was elevated to doge in 809 and the cluster of islets around Rivoalto became the focus of community development. They were virtually impregnable to all who did not know how to navigate the deep-water channels that crisscross the lagoon, and were an obvious improvement on the previous administrative capital, Malamocco (on the Lido), which Pepin had come too close to destroying.

It was in this, the 9th century, that the Venetian lagoon settlements began to come into their own. Their commercial and naval fleets were already the most powerful in the Adriatic and Venetian ships were already trading as far away as Egypt.

At home, Partecipazio had a fortress built on what would later be the site of the Palazzo Ducale. To the east, a church to San Zaccaria was going up at Byzantine expense. As the islands of Rivoalto were too small, too few and often too waterlogged for sustained settlement, land was drained and canals cleared. Most impressive of all, the land mass was extended by driving great clusters of wooden piles into the muddy depths as foundations – a system still in use in the 20th century.

Body Snatchers

As Byzantine power slowly waned, the nascent republic assumed greater autonomy, all the while paying homage to Constantinople, at least in name.

What the republic needed was a symbol to distinguish it from its official patrons. Legend had it that the evangelist St Mark (San Marco) had once visited the lagoon islands and been told by an angel that his body would rest there. A band of Venetian merchants apparently decided to make true the prophecy and in 828 spirited the saint's corpse out of Alexandria, Egypt. To house the holy relics the doge ordered construction of a new basilica, which would rise next to the Palazzo Ducale. Thus was the lagoon community's Byzantine-imposed patron saint, San Teodoro (St Theodore), unceremoniously replaced by St Mark.

Over the course of the century, the Venetian Republic slowly increased in strength, always navigating carefully between the empire of the west (which one way or another controlled much of Italy) and that of the east. The northern Adriatic was considered a Venetian lake.

By the end of the century, local administration had been centred in Rivoalto (at the core of what, by the 12th century, would be known instead as Venezia). A new series of bishoprics, independent but loyal to the Republic, was established to counteract any leverage from Rome through the see of Aquileia. A board of *giudici* (judges) was also set up to curb abuses of power by the doge. The office was, after all, supposed to be electoral and the political system in some way democratic.

Phoenix from the Flames

The 10th century was, however, characterised by the growing tendency of the doges to rule as monarchs. Never was this clearer than in the case of the fiery Pietro Candiano IV. By 976 he had so incensed the people by his self-aggrandisement that the mob burned most of Venice down as they cornered Candiano in the flaming wreckage of the Palazzo Ducale and, with a stroke of the sword, sent him to his maker. It was, indeed, a bad century. Only seven years after Candiano's death, factional fighting and bloodletting led one family to betray the city to Holy Roman Emperor Otto. Had he not died young in the same year, Venice might well have been absorbed into the empire.

Things began to look up with the election of Pietro Orseolo as doge in 991. Orseolo was one of the most gifted leaders the Republic ever had. By careful diplomacy he won the medieval equivalent of most-favoured-nation status in Constantinople and in much of the Holy Roman Empire. Constantinople went further before the century was out, virtually opening up all of the Orient (the lands east of the Mediterranean) exclusively to Venetian merchants. Putting trade before all other considerations, Orseolo also courted Muslim capitals from Damascus to Cordova (Córdoba).

The last years of the 11th century brought two momentous events. In 1094, the third

With This Ring I Thee Wet

Pietro Orseolo's successful campaigns to subdue the Dalmatian coast and hamstring piracy from that corner earned him the title of Dux Dalmatiae. So chuffed were he and the nobles of Venice by their success that in 998 they ordained that the events should be celebrated every year on Ascension Day.

The doge, accompanied by the bishops, nobles and other important citizens, would sail out to the Lido on the ducal galley, the Bucintoro, and carry out a brief ceremony. 'Oh Lord, keep safe your faithful mariners from storms, sudden shipwreck and the perfidious machinations of wily enemies.'

The ceremony developed in pomp and circumstance over the years and in time came to be known as the Sposalizio del Mar, the Wedding with the Sea. It became customary for the doge to cast a ring into the waves just in front of the Chiesa di San Nicolò (at the northern end of the Lido) as part of this ritual, although few now believe the story that the pope himself donated a gold ring for the occasion in 1177. The ceremony at sea was followed by a solemn mass in the Chiesa di San Nicolò.

and (to this day) final Basilica di San Marco was consecrated. This gaudy display of Byzantine ostentation, designed no doubt to reflect exuberantly the wealth of its faithful, was in a sense a public declaration to the world that Venice had arrived.

The following year, Pope Urban II called the First Crusade. Ostensibly aimed at liberating the Holy Lands from the Muslims, the exercise seems to have been more an early European version of employment creation for frustrated knights and bounty-hunting adventurers of all classes. While they raped and ransacked their way across a horror-struck Byzantine Empire, before moving on to sack Jerusalem and exterminate its Muslim and Jewish inhabitants, Venice looked on. The city's rulers were unwilling to get too involved in an exercise that could easily have damaged its highly developed trade relations with the Near East.

Between Byzantium & Barbarossa

In the first years of the 12th century, Venice did send fleets to Palestine to shore up the efforts of the mainly Frankish Crusaders on land, but only in return for trade concessions.

The Republic could not fail to notice the emergence of rival sea powers such as Pisa and Genoa (Genova) and perhaps this spurred it on to establish the Arsenale, a fortified zone on the eastern Castello end of the lagoon city. It was the kernel of what would later emerge as Europe's first great shipyard, where commercial and fighting ships could be constructed more efficiently than hitherto imaginable. Venice was going to need every last one of them. Initially, however, it was more like a naval storage and repair centre.

Venetian participation in the First Crusade, however limited, spoiled relations with Constantinople. Although they continued to cooperate during the first decades of the century in attempts to curb growing Norman-Sicilian power, the damage had been done. In 1171 Emperor John Comnenus staged an assault on the newly formed Genoese colony in Constantinople, blaming it on the long-established and wealthy Venetian community, who were promptly clapped into irons. The Venetian response was swift and disastrous. A fleet set sail bent on war, but Doge Vitale Michiel II made the mistake of accepting a proposal of talks. They dragged on so long his inactive fleet collapsed as the crews were ravaged by plague, a disease they carried back home.

Things sometimes have to get worse before they can get better. And they did. The Holy Roman Emperor Frederick Barbarossa had come to the throne in 1152 determined to recreate a single Roman empire, grinding under his heel the northern Italian cities, Rome and the pope, Norman-controlled southern Italy and the Eastern Empire. It was an ambitious programme that by the late 1160s had produced mixed results, among them the creation of the Greater Lombard League to oppose him. Venice had seen itself with little choice but to join the league.

So, in 1172 Venice was technically at war with the two biggest powers in Europe and deeply divided internally. Doge Michiel had been lynched on his return with his plague-decimated fleet, most of which had been wiped out (much of it burned to contain the plague). The coffers were empty and the citizenry were fighting the disease brought home by the surviving seamen.

Checks & Balances

The failure of Vitale Michiel was in part attributed to his refusal to listen to counsel. Refusing to listen was going to be harder from now on. A constitution and a series of bodies to protect it were now put into place.

From the beginning, the base of the pyramid of power had been the Arengo, or Assemblea Generale – an assembly of all the people (albeit always dominated by the wealthier families). If only because of the growing population, such assemblies were hardly ever called by the 12th century, except to rubber-stamp the choice of doge. (By the mid-15th century the Arengo was abolished altogether.)

Now the Venetian equivalent of a parliament was formalised: at the base was the Maggior Consiglio (Great Council), made up of members of Venice's powerful and moneyed families. Technically at least, the approval of its 480 elected members was needed for any decision of moment. By 1340 it would have more than 1200 members (although in earlier years the number sank as low as 210).

The Maggior Consiglio elected the doge. Once elected, the doge had to sign a *promissione*, a legal contract defining the limits of his power. Initially little more than a formality, the document had become a serious check to the doge's freedom of action by the mid-13th century. Its content changed from one election to the next, but in effect ruled out profiting financially from office, acceptance of gifts, communication with other heads of state without the knowledge of the Maggior Consiglio, and other activities potentially at variance with the welfare of the state.

The Quarantia (Forty) was responsible for elaborating economic policy, while the

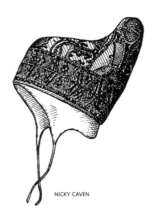

NICKY CAVEN

The *zogia*, or ducal cap, was placed on a new doge's head at his investiture ceremony

60-member Senato (Senate) dealt with lesser affairs. The decisions of either (which on occasion worked jointly) were ultimately supposed to be ratified by the Maggior Consiglio. With time, the Quarantia would evolve into the supreme judicial organ of the state.

The Quarantia elected three heads *(capi)* who were equivalent in status to the *consiglieri ducali*, the doge's counsellors. Six of the latter were elected, one for each of the six *sestieri* of central Venice (municipal divisions created in 1171 for the raising of taxes for a disastrous rescue effort of its jailed citizens in Constantinople). Terms lasted for a maximum of one year and consiglieri could not stand again until two years had elapsed since the end of their previous term.

The consiglieri and the three capi della Quarantia met under the auspices of the doge to elaborate the bulk of policy, distributing tasks to the Quarantia and Senato. These 10 men together were known as the Signoria (Signory). With the passing of time, more and more sub-committees evolved to deal with particular issues, often made up of *savii*, or sages.

Elsewhere in the lagoon, each island or settlement (such as Chioggia) had its own statute but was subordinate to the central government.

In spite of the complexities of this system of accountability, the doge was the one official elected for life. Within the Signoria, a long-lived doge would see his counsellors come and go, but he remained in the chair.

Supreme Referee

In 1177 Venice was agreed upon as the stage for one of history's great acts of reconciliation. Emperor Frederick Barbarossa and Pope Alexander III met here to conclude a peace treaty that meant considerable humiliation for the emperor but great publicity for Venice. Naturally, the Venetians managed to win trade concessions from the empire in return for having provided its good offices.

And so it was, under the watchful eye of Doge Sebastiano Zaini, that Barbarossa knelt before the pope and kissed his ring in a sign of submission. The spot where this occurred is marked in the floor of the narthex before the central entrance into the Basilica di San Marco. With this kiss, peace was restored in Italy and the German-based Holy Roman Empire again fell into line with the papacy.

Revenge of the Venetian Blind

A couple of decades later, the pope was again calling for a holy crusade to strike at the Muslims in the Holy Land. When Doge Enrico Dandolo agreed to head the greatest armada yet put to sea in the service of God, few of the participants in this, the Fourth Crusade, could have known what he had in mind.

In fact, everyone involved in the negotiations of 1201 seems to have had something to hide. At any rate, Dandolo, who had lost his sight many years before, drove an extraordinary bargain: Venice would provide a fleet to carry 30,000 men (an unheard of number for such an undertaking) at a cost of 84,000 silver marks – approximately double the yearly income of the king of England at the time.

Word soon got out that the Crusaders would head for Egypt, not the Holy Land, for strategic reasons, something that displeased many potential Crusaders. In the end, only one-third of the proposed forces turned up in Venice the following year and their leaders couldn't pay. Venice had kept its side of the bargain. Did the wily 80-year-old Dandolo predict this situation? To compensate for non-payment, he suggested the Crusaders help Venice out with a few tasks of its own on the way to Palestine. The most important of these involved a detour to Constantinople.

The events of 1171 and 1172 had not been forgotten, and when the Christian fleet sailed up before Constantinople's mighty sea walls, its intentions as yet undeclared, the city's inhabitants must have had an uneasy sensation. The Venetian plan involved putting a pretender, Alexius the Younger, on the Byzantine throne. He in turn promised to join the Crusade and restore Church unity (breached in the schism of 1054) by submitting the Orthodox Church to Roman control. It appears other Western leaders promised themselves rich spoils from an attack on Constantinople too.

After the first assault, in July 1203, Alexius was put on the throne, but reneged on his promises. And so the Venetians led a second seaborne attack from the Golden Horn the following April, this time sacking the city completely. The booty, including the four bronze horses that adorned the Hippodrome and would end up gracing the Basilica di San Marco, seemed boundless. A puppet Frankish emperor was installed on the Byzantine throne and the doge of Venice became 'Lord of a Quarter and a Half-Quarter of the Roman Empire' – Venice's three-eighths of the spoils.

La Serenissima was not interested in taking lands from which to extract tribute. Rather, it sought secure bases from which to protect and expand its trade. Three-eighths of Constantinople would for 60 years be under direct Venetian control. The maritime republic carefully chose other ports in the Greek isles, the most important of them being the whole island of Crete.

Enrico Dandolo, for some the greatest doge to have lived, had managed to extract from this so-called Crusade more benefits for his city than anyone could have imagined. He died in a subsequent campaign

in the now defunct Constantinople and was buried in the city in whose capture and sack he had been instrumental. The Eastern Empire later recovered its independence, but remained a cripple among the world's powers. Its capital had been devastated, its treasures plundered or destroyed. It is hardly surprising that it would later cave in to the green banner of Islam under the Ottoman Turks. What *is* remarkable is that Constantinople would hold out against them until its final fall in 1453.

Merchant Empire

By the early years of the 13th century, Venice was at the head of a thriving and expanding commercial empire. The city's direct control of the Adriatic Sea was now undisputed. All trading vessels had to pass through La Serenissima and pay customs. With subject cities and bases up and down the eastern coast of the Adriatic, dotted about the Greek mainland and on Crete, Rhodes and Cyprus, as well as Constantinople and along the Black Sea coast, the banner of San Marco flew all over the eastern Mediterranean.

Ever a city of shrewd businessmen, Venice had always been careful to maintain good trade relations with Egypt as well as the Christian-controlled coastal cities of Palestine. The market places around the Rialto teemed with produce from as far away as China – spices, silk, cotton and grain were all unloaded there for transport farther on into the Italian hinterland and beyond the Alps to Germany and France.

Venice was not a feudal city. Its most noble families were generally also wealthy traders. In these early days of empire, the men who captained Venice's trading ships usually came from those trading families. Pretty much all the members of the various councils that ruled the Republic had done their time abroad.

Wars with Genoa

Venice's rapid expansion in the wake of the Fourth Crusade had not gone unremarked by the city's competitors, among whom Genoa was by far the prime rival. In the course of the 13th century, Genoa's presence in Palestine, the Black Sea and elsewhere in the eastern Mediterranean was a constant source of concern to Venice. The first scuffle between them came in the wake of riots between the Genoese and Venetian quarters in the Christian enclave of Acre, in Palestine. This ended in a rather ignomini- ous naval defeat for Genoa off the coast of Acre in 1258.

Three years later, Venice's luck began to look distinctly pear-shaped. In Constantinople, the Byzantines, with Genoese connivance, overthrew the Latin emperor. Suddenly Venice's possessions and trade routes were threatened.

Polos Apart

July 1261 was a disastrous year for Venice. Not only had it lost control of a trade nerve-centre in Constantinople, but Venetian merchants suddenly found themselves debarred from the trading centres of the Black Sea. The new regime in Constantinople declared open season on Venetian traders, labelling them as pirates. When captured, they routinely had their eyes put out and noses lopped off.

During the preceding years, the Mongols had consolidated an empire stretching from China to the Black Sea, incorporating Persia and Iraq. On the Black Sea, Western traders dealt with the Khan's local representatives, the Golden Horde. Among these traders were the Polo brothers, Nicolò and Matteo. By 1261 they were operating deep inside the Crimea and decided to venture farther. Whether or not they knew what had happened in Constantinople is unclear, but they couldn't have timed their departure better.

Local warring between various Mongol khans had blocked the roads south, so they went to Bukhara, in Turkestan, where they stayed for three years – time enough to learn Mongol and Persian. Getting into Persia continued to appear impossible, so they went deeper into the unknown and ended up at the court of Kublai Khan. According to some accounts they were in Beijing (the winter residence); others talk of the Khan's summer residence, Shang-tu (better known to westerners as Xanadu). The Polos were sent back to Italy in 1269 with a request to the pope for a hundred learned men to teach the Mongols the ins and outs of Christianity and the 'seven arts' – whatever they were.

In 1271 the Polos set off again, this time with two missionaries who quickly high-tailed it back to Italy. Nicolò also brought along his 20-year-old son, Marco.

For the next few years the Polos trundled around the Orient making a stash in the jewellery business. It took several years of travel overland from the Gulf of Iskenderun in what is now Turkey to China, but eventually they made it to Shang-tu. Once there, Marco entered the service of the Khan and travelled extensively in China for the following 17 years.

When the Polos finally decided to return home, not everything went terribly well, for they were robbed of much of their fortune in Trebizond (Trabzon in modern Turkey). According to the Polo legend, no-one even recognised them when they finally made it back to Venice.

Marco's tales of adventure were the talk of the town, but sceptics began to consider them rather tall and they came to be known as *il milione* (the million).

In 1299 Marco ended up in a prison in Genoa after being captured during one of Venice's innumerable sea spats with its eternal rival. Here he met a scribbler by the name of Rustichello, to whom he dictated memoirs of his years in the East. Perhaps anticipating the disbelief of some of his readers, he called it *Il Milione*. Freed in 1300, Marco returned to Venice and settled down to a quiet life. His book, known as *The Travels of Marco Polo* in English, has been the subject of constant speculation ever since his death in 1324.

In 1284 the pope issued an interdict, a kind of excommunication en masse, on Venice for refusing to back a Crusade against the Aragonese, who had taken Sicily from the French Charles d'Anjou. The following year, the city was shaken by an earthquake and then flooded, while Venetian forces suffered several military reverses in Istria and Dalmatia. Relations with Italian cities including Padua, Bologna and Ancona were deteriorating. The Venetians must have been wondering what else could possibly go wrong when Acre fell to the Muslims in 1291, delivering another heavy blow to Venetian trade.

At this point, Venice decided something had to be done to curb Genoa, whose trade in everything from Indian spices to Russian slaves and furs through Black Sea ports was booming. From this point until they signed a peace treaty in 1299, their navies pursued each other around the Mediterranean with growing fury but little definitive success. Venice came off worst in several encounters, especially at the battle of Curzola (Korc) on the Dalmatian coast, where the Republic lost 65 out of 95 vessels and the Genoese took 5000 prisoners (among them Marco Polo). The peace treaty was little more than a pause in what would be a long, tiring and bitter conflict.

A Brave New Order

A series of reforms around the end of the 13th century and early into the next fixed the course of Venice's internal political life until the demise of the Republic in 1797. Franchise laws, known as the Serrata del Maggior Consiglio (Closing of the Great Council), effectively restricted access to the Maggior Consiglio or higher office to a caste of established and noble families. Money alone did not constitute nobility. By 1323 membership of the Maggior Consiglio had become permanent and hereditary.

Some crumbs were left to the rising middle class of *cittadini* (citizens). The biggest of them was the office of Gran Cancelliere, or Lord High Chancellor, effectively the head of the civil service and superior in rank to the Senators. The Gran Cancelliere could only be appointed from among the ranks of cittadini, never from the aristocracy.

More important developments were afoot, however. In 1308 Venice found itself embroiled in a hopeless war against the pope and a host of allies over possession of the Po city of Ferrara. Another papal interdict and blockade did considerable damage to Venetian interests – all over the Mediterranean, the city's citizens were arrested, goods seized and vessels attacked by anyone who cared to take a swipe at the Republic.

Ultimately, Venice was compelled to back down, but in the meantime discontent had led several old aristocratic families to plot the overthrow of the doge, Pietro Gradenigo, in 1310. The plot failed (see the boxed text 'Knocking Rebellion on the Head' in the Things to See & Do chapter), and in its wake the Consiglio dei Dieci was set up to monitor the security situation. Meant to last a few months, it ultimately became a kind of CIA-cum-cabinet. From this time forth, the Consiglio, whose members were elected in rotation from the Maggior Consiglio, wove an intelligence network in the city and throughout Europe unequalled by any of the Republic's rivals. In the Palazzo Ducale you can still see a couple of *bocche di denunce*, a kind of letter box where informants could leave anonymous tip-offs for the Consiglio to pursue.

Years of Plenty

The first half of the 14th century was marked by comparative calm, except for a brief war against the Scaliger family, who from Verona had come to control Vicenza, Padua, Treviso, Parma and Lucca. Venice found plenty of allies willing to put an end to this dangerous expansion, and by the end of it all Venice had acquired its first mainland territories, land up to and including Treviso.

The implications were important. For the first time, Venice could secure its own supplies of basic staples for a population that now numbered around 200,000 (almost three times the population today). On the other hand, the maritime republic would never again be able to remain aloof from the intrigues of mainland politics.

Trade was improving all the time. The invention of the compass and the introduction of the rudder on boats had greatly improved seamanship. Commercial vessels were larger and voyages more frequent. The removal of a Moroccan blockade of the Straits of Gibraltar had opened the way to more regular trading with Flanders and England.

Black Death

In the hurly-burly of medieval Europe, you could be sure peace was a fragile business. Rivalry between Venice and Genoa had persisted, but before they could even begin to grapple with one another in a satisfactory fashion, their merchant vessels had brought back from the Black Sea one of the most miserable imports imaginable.

The nasty little rats on board the vessels of 1348 were carrying the Black Death. The effect on Venice was as horrific as anywhere, with as many as 600 people dying a day. Up and down the canals the barges plied their sorry trade: 'Corpi morti! Corpi morti!' (the local equivalent of 'Bring out your dead!'), the steersmen cried. Three-fifths of the city's population perished. Genoa fared just as badly and the disease spread across all of Europe.

The two powers barely paused to absorb this horrible blow. Skirmishes took place regularly and in late 1354 the Venetian fleet was virtually wiped out in a surprise raid in the Greek islands.

In the following years, Venice found itself fighting numerous unpleasant wars with Padua, the Hungarians and the Austrians. The upshot of all this was the loss of all its Dalmatian possessions. Great as these setbacks were, however, they would seem minor compared with the threat that now overshadowed the city's very existence.

The War to End All Wars with Genoa

In 1372 an incident in Cyprus sparked the last and most devastating of La Serenissima's duels with Genoa. It took a while to wind up to its climax, but in August 1379 a Genoese invasion fleet appeared off the Lido. On Genoa's side were ranged Padua

and Hungary, busy devastating the Venetian mainland territories, while Visconti-ruled Milan sided with Venice.

Admiral Pietro Doria's first objective was Chioggia, which fell to his combined sea and land assault with Hungarian troops marched across from Padua. In Venice, a popular hero, Vettor Pisani, took overall command. The city worked day and night to build new ships and defences on and around the islands, especially on the Lido, San Giorgio Maggiore and Giudecca. Incredibly, Doria opted to starve out Venice – a decision that served only to grant the city precious time. Pisani, in fact, turned the tables by laying siege to Chioggia, but his forces were inadequate and all of Venice prayed for the return of Carlo Zeno's war fleet, which had been sent out long before the siege to patrol the Mediterranean. His appearance on the horizon at the beginning of 1380 spelled the end for the Genoese.

Venice had averted disaster, but victory only became apparent in the next century, as the Republic returned to prosperity while Genoa slumped into a century of decline.

The Fall of Constantinople

By the time the Turks marched into Constantinople on 29 May 1453 and so snuffed out what remained of the Byzantine Empire, Venice had in most respects reached the apogee of its power.

Since the Battle of Chioggia, the Republic had largely managed to keep out of major naval conflicts. From 1424, with things relatively quiet elsewhere, Venice threw itself headlong into a campaign of land conquest that brought decades of sporadic warfare with Milan. In the end, La Serenissima was left master of a land empire stretching from Gorizia in the east to Bergamo in the west, but the state coffers were dangerously empty.

Overall, however, things looked good. The Republic had regained sovereignty over the many Dalmatian coastal bases that it had earlier lost to Hungary, while in the Mediterranean it maintained control over a number of Greek islands and mainland bases – not least among them Crete (direct control of Cyprus was still some years off). Despite some nasty clashes, relations with the rapidly expanding Ottoman Turkish Empire generally remained cordial.

Trade flourished. Spices, sugar, silks, cotton and slaves came from the East. From northern Europe, Venice sent wood and iron to the Orient, while with England and Flanders it carried on a lucrative three-way trade in wines, wool and finished textiles. At home, the great buildings of Piazza San Marco as we now know them neared completion.

In the years immediately after the capture of Constantinople, Venice still found cause to hope the event would make no difference to it. As Greek refugees poured into Venice and confirmed its reputation not only as the most Eastern of Western cities, but also as one of the most tolerant (the Orthodox population was given its own church), La Serenissima's ambassadors hammered out new commercial treaties with the victorious Sultan Mehmet II.

But Christian Europe had been given a warning, reinforced by the Turkish campaigns in the Balkans, where the Serbs and Albanians were slowly crushed beneath the wheels of a seemingly unstoppable and none-too-pleasant fighting machine.

For a while Venice managed to kid itself about the Turks' intentions, but the scales fell from its eyes in 1470. By then, most of mainland Greece was in Turkish hands – only the various Venetian outposts had been spared. One of the most important was Negroponte, or Khalkis as it is now called (the ancient Chalcis on the island of Euboea). Its fall after a three-week siege and the inexplicable inaction of a Venetian fleet sent to relieve it came as a heavy blow. The next 10 years brought more bad news, with the loss of several more Greek-island outposts and the Turks advancing in the Balkans. They even raided the Friuli area. They say the fires raging in destroyed villages could be seen from the Campanile in Piazza San Marco.

The biggest problem through all this period was Western disunity. Venice, exhausted by continual warfare against an infinitely more powerful foe, gratefully signed a peace treaty in 1479 with Sultan Mehmet.

This counted for little. In 1499 Venice lost its two remaining key ports in mainland Greece – Modone (Methoni) and Corone (Koroni), in the Peloponnese peninsula (also known then as the Morea).

A Lousy Start to a Century

The last days of the 15th century brought still more bad news. The Portuguese navigator Vasco da Gama had returned to Lisbon, having reached India by sailing around the Cape of Good Hope in Africa. Suddenly, the Mediterranean seemed irrelevant. All the riches of the East could now be brought directly to Lisbon and from there sold on to northern Europe – avoiding the uncertainties of desert caravans and the certainty of expensive taxes added to the prices of goods by Middle Eastern potentates and the Venetians.

Pessimists were already predicting the end for Venice when things took yet another turn for the worse.

League of Cambrai

The lead-up to the formation of the League of Cambrai is a typically convoluted example of European politics. Suffice to say that Pope Julius II had decided that Venice was too powerful a state in Italy and drummed up support from France, the Holy Roman Empire (in the person of the Hapsburg ruler of Austria, Maximilian), Spain and several Italian city-states. In return for cutting Venice to pieces, all were promised rich territorial rewards. In April 1509 French forces marched on Venetian territory.

The initial campaigns boded ill for Venice – within less than a year most of its mainland empire was in enemy hands. Only the Friuli area and Treviso still flew the banner of San Marco. Not since the Battle of Chioggia had Venice stood so close to the precipice.

No-one would have made bets on Venice's recovery at that point, but the shifting sands of Italian politics changed matters repeatedly. All the participants in the League of Cambrai changed sides with monotonous regularity, so that by 1516, when the war finally sputtered to an end, Venice was left with almost all the territory it had begun with, including the cities of Padua, Vicenza, Verona, Brescia and Bergamo.

But something fundamental had changed. In 1519 Charles V ascended the Hapsburg throne and would later be the last sovereign to be crowned Holy Roman Emperor by the pope. His domains spread from Austria to Spain, into which latter country was pouring the newly found wealth of the Americas. Francis I was king of France and Henry VIII of an increasingly self-confident England. The Turks had taken Cairo and were moving rapidly across North Africa. In the emerging world order of nation states and global empires, Venice, whose coffers had been bled dry by all the warring, was distinctly small fry.

Battle of Lepanto

More than ever, Venice knew it had to tread a subtle and, at times, almost impossible line to ensure survival against the unquestionably greater powers around it. So, as Charles V took his empire into repeated conflicts with France and the pope, Venice kept a polite distance from all concerned.

For some years the Republic was able to avoid trouble from Turkey too, which was otherwise engaged in Eastern Europe (Vienna came within an ace of falling to Suleiman the Magnificent in 1529). But it was only a matter of time. In 1537 Suleiman tried and failed to take the stoutly defended Corfu. Frustrated, he quickly swallowed up a series of small Venetian-run Greek islands and two remaining bases in the Peloponnese. Venice was not strong enough to take on the Ottoman Empire alone and its repeated calls for united Christian action came to little.

The subsequent lull was followed by another hammer blow, although one that the Venetians must have seen coming. Suleiman invaded Cyprus, an island governed rather unhappily by Venice. La Serenissima appealed again for Western help, to little avail. A large fleet of Venetian ships was joined by other ships under the standards of the Vatican and Spain, but the latter's distrust of Venice was stronger than its desire to stem the Ottoman tide.

In the end, the island's defenders held out heroically against overwhelming odds while the relief fleet dallied and finally, deciding there was no hope, simply turned around to head home. The slaughter and violence carried out by the Turks after the fall of Famagusta in the island's east was unusually barbarous, even by the standards of the day (see the boxed text 'The Infamy of Famagusta' in the Things to See & Do chapter).

Revenge was not long in coming. This time, even Spain saw that something had to be done and formed a solemn league with Venice and the Vatican. They vowed to assemble a fleet every year and return to the fight until 'the Turk' was destroyed. In 1571 a huge allied fleet led by Don John of Austria (much of it provided by Venice) appeared off Lepanto, in Greece, where the main Turkish fleet was quartered.

The ensuing battle was the last great encounter between rowed galleys and was a resounding victory for the Christian powers. But Venice's plea to press home the advantage and continue the campaign in the Mediterranean went unheeded. A new fleet put to sea in 1572, but without the same resolve. Having achieved nothing, Venice saw that the league was meaningless and sued for peace with Constantinople. Spain and the Vatican, predictably, denounced the Venetians. As the only power directly threatened by the Turks and with support from other Western nations so shaky, Venice had little choice. Lepanto had been a stunning but ultimately hollow naval victory.

The watchword in the remaining years of the century was caution. Venice had by now embarked on the most illustrious period of its diplomatic career. In other words, from here on its single greatest weapon with which to defend some measure of prosperity and independence would be lots of fast talking. Plague in 1576 wiped out one-third of the population and seriously weakened the already wobbly state finances, so warring with anyone was out of the question. For good measure, the Palazzo Ducale and a host of art treasures were destroyed in a fire the following year.

Decline

As the 17th century dawned, Venice was embarked on slow decline. Although not as immediately disastrous as initially thought, the rounding of the Cape of Good Hope a century earlier had changed much. A great deal of the spice trade now went through Lisbon, and northern European cartels buying in bulk were undercutting Venetian prices. Now the Dutch and English were becoming bolder too, and before long the Dutch would assume control of the Atlantic trade with the East.

Mediterranean trade had not, for all this, been truncated. Atlantic piracy, especially towards the end of the 16th century, often made supplies through the eastern Mediterranean more reliable. Increasingly, however, Venice's position had been eroded. Not only had it lost most of its Mediterranean bases, but under the Ottomans its trading privileges were gradually rolled back. In earlier centuries, Venice's only real rival had been Genoa. Under the Turks, Greek, Jewish, Armenian and other local traders came to supplant the Venetians. Towards the end of the 16th century, even the French (or Italians with French passports) were rapidly acquiring a higher profile by virtue of their alliance with Constantinople against the Hapsburgs.

At home, quite simply, the core was going soft. In a state that had managed to preserve its institutions through thick and thin over the centuries – in a way that had won the admiration and envy of people all over Italy and beyond – signs of decay were appearing. Corruption was on the rise and the Consiglio dei Dieci increasingly overstepped its constitutional brief. Renier Zen, several-times member of the Consiglio dei Dieci and self-appointed reformer, mounted a long campaign in the 1620s to compel the doge and the leading institutions of the state to respect more closely the laws of the land and so at least dampen corruption. His calls had great popular appeal but in the end went unheeded.

The city's well-heeled nobs wallowed in luxury. Meanwhile, in the face of the great nations and empires around it, Venice had neither the will nor the manpower to equip great enough fleets, let alone armies, to match those of their competitors.

This was not to say that the Republic couldn't carry off the occasional victory. In 1606 Pope Paul V faced down La Serenissima with an interdict on the city in an argument over temporal and spiritual authority. Led by the greatest thinker Venice ever produced, Paolo Sarpi, the Republic serenely repudiated the arguments of the Vatican and won support from around Europe – much of it by now Protestant. It was a silly argument in one sense, but the pope was compelled to back down. Never again would the papacy be able to impose its will on nations through fear of spiritual castigation. What was a minor victory for Venice represented a lasting blow to the papacy's temporal power.

Venice's policy of maintaining neutrality wherever possible helped turn it into a den of espionage. A rather absurd Spanish conspiracy of 1618 to seize the city from the inside was merely one example among many of the plotting that characterised life in the city.

The Consiglio dei Dieci, in its role as the state's security service, had plenty to do in these years of intrigue. Its spy network within and beyond the Republic was one of the most effective in the world. Given Venice's delicate position in the balance of world affairs, it needed to be. In the case of the 1618 plot, the Consiglio, once it had been informed and gathered intelligence, quietly dispatched about 300 conspirators. The Consiglio worked fast and without ceremony. Trials, torture and executions were all generally carried out in secret. That said, compared with its neighbours to the east and west, Venice remained a haven of tolerance and comparative democracy.

Although Venice was forced into a couple of minor skirmishes in Italy, it managed to stay out of the Thirty Years War altogether. But an old enemy was about to rattle the Republic yet again. In 1645 the Turks landed a huge invasion force on the island of Crete and launched what turned out to be a 25-year campaign to conquer the island. Defence of the main town, Candia, was dogged and the Venetians won a surprising number of engagements at sea. However, unaided by any of the other Christian powers, the island was lost from the beginning. With its surrender expired Venice's presence beyond the Adriatic.

One Last Hurrah
In 1683 the Turks were again at the gates of Vienna, but this time they were cut to pieces. Euphoric at the victory, the Hapsburg forces and their Hungarian, Polish and German allies set off in swift pursuit across Hungary. Other Christian forces poured into the Balkans. Venice was asked to join in the fray and the following year a fleet under Francesco Morosini set out with a mercenary army under a Swedish general.

By the end of 1687, after a series of summer campaigns, Venice seemed to have returned to the days of the Fourth Crusade. Almost all of the Morea (the Peloponnese peninsula) was back in Venetian hands. Athens, too, fell in a siege, during which the invaders managed to blow up most of the Parthenon, which the Turks had converted into a munitions dump. By the Treaty of Karlowitz, Venice ended up with the Morea and various other conquests, but Athens and everything north in Greece was handed back to the Turks.

Administering the Morea turned out to be more trouble than it was worth and in any case, the Turks were soon back. They broke the treaty in 1715 and within a few months had recaptured most of the peninsula. The following year they tried again to invade Corfu and failed. The Austrians were by then on the march in the Balkans. The ensuing Treaty of Passarowitz, signed in 1718, was La Serenissima's last. Venice was left in control of its mainland empire, which included Brescia, Bergamo, Cremona, Verona, Vicenza, Padua, Treviso and the Friuli area. In addition, it had Istria, Dalmatia, parts of coastal Albania, Corfu and a spattering of other Ionian islands.

The Finest Drawing Room in Europe
Venice had become irrelevant. If La Serenissima lasted until the arrival of Napoleon at the gates in 1797, it was as much due to luck and the simple fact that the big players in Europe had other fish to fry.

Venice reverted to its by now increasingly familiar policy of determined neutrality. The War of the Austrian Succession, the Seven Years War and numerous other European conflicts passed, if not unnoticed, at least unheeded in the Republic. As the years floated by, the Republic's navy shrank to a shadow of its former self. In any case, the shipbuilders of the Arsenale and their techniques had long since been eclipsed by their counterparts in England, France and the Netherlands.

No longer master of the Adriatic, the Republic had also come to realise it could not oblige foreign shipping to unload in Venice and pay customs duties. What's more, the Hapsburg-held port of Trieste and the papacy's Ancona had been made free ports.

The only way to respond was to abandon protectionism and open Venice up to free trade – mostly in local goods from around the Adriatic and as far south as Greece. Business was pretty brisk until the end of the Republic, but for many years now trade had been seen as beneath the nobility. The great commercial families that had made Venice's wealth and provided many of its most illustrious characters had long lost interest in the sea. They neither traded nor had any desire to endure the rigours of naval life. These tasks they left mostly to the minority communities resident in Venice, such as the Greeks and Armenians. The nobles, or at least those who had not become impoverished, looked instead to their estates on the mainland.

Impoverishment of many inactive noble families was causing its own problems. Numbers in the Maggior Consiglio were in constant decline and to stem the tide it had become habitual to sell membership of the nobility. The new rich members weren't always welcome, but there was little choice. In any event, by the 18th century, rule of Venice was effectively in the hands of a narrow oligarchy of 42 families.

News of the French Revolution hit Venice with much the same force as it did the rest of Europe. But while the monarchical powers of Europe talked of alliance and left France friendless and isolated, nothing could persuade the Venetian Republic to shift from its policy of neutrality.

Events moved swiftly and by 1795 Napoleon was in Italy giving chase to the Austrians. Both the Austrians and French violated Venice's neutrality. Back in the lagoon, the leaders of La Serenissima debated back and forth how to deal with this menace. In the end, they followed a course tantamount to suicide. Napoleon's campaign took him through Lombardia to Verona and then north in pursuit of the Austrians. Just when he decided to crush Venice is unclear, but as the doge and his counsellors bowed and scraped in an attempt to keep the dashing French general sweet, Napoleon offered up the Republic to Austria as the price of a temporary peace.

On 12 May 1797, with Napoleon's guns ranged along the lagoon and ready, if necessary, to pound Venice into submission, the panicking Maggior Consiglio, which could not manage a quorum, voted the Republic out of existence. Napoleon apparently thought of Venice as the 'finest drawing room in Europe', and now it was his.

The Aftermath

For around six months, the Republic lived as a puppet 'democracy' under the French. In January 1798 Venice and most of the Veneto, along with Istria and Dalmatia, passed into Austrian hands. As Napoleon swept across Europe, Venice became just another playing piece to be shunted around among the great powers.

In 1805 Napoleon incorporated Venice into his Kingdom of Italy. It would be too simplistic to write off what followed as 10 years of oppression. The city's administration was tidied up in line with French precepts. Plans were laid for urban renewal, the laying out of public gardens, the building of a road connection to the mainland and the rehabilitation of the port. On the down side, the expropriation, and in many cases downright looting, of churches, convents and religious schools deprived the city of many of its artistic treasures.

It all came to an end in 1815, when Austria was awarded Venice (along with much of the rest of northern Italy) by the Congress of Vienna.

Trieste was the Austrians' gateway to the sea, so Venice was largely neglected in the early years of Austrian hegemony. Nevertheless, the city was made a free port in 1829. In the 1830s bulwarks were built to protect the three entrances to the lagoon from high tides. The resulting narrower entrances were dredged and deepened for shipping. By 1846 Venice was linked to Milan by rail (although the train station was not inaugurated until 1865). Dredging work near the station meant that merchant ships could unload right by the trains destined to transport goods into Italy.

The Austrians never managed to endear themselves to the Venetians, who in 1848 joined the long list of rebels who rose up against the established order across Europe. The Republic was again proclaimed and the city held out until August of the next year.

Italy United

The movement for Italian unification spread quickly through the Veneto and, after several rebellions, Venice was finally united with the Kingdom of Italy in 1866.

During the last decades of the 19th century, the city was a hive of activity. Increased port traffic was coupled with growing industry. Canals were widened and deepened and pedestrian zones laid out in the city centre. Tourism began to take off around the turn of the century, as the fine hotels along the Grand Canal began to come into their own. And by 1922, La Biennale, or the Esposizione Internazionale d'Arte (International Art Expo), was firmly in place as an added attraction.

Under Mussolini, the road bridge linking Venice with the mainland was built parallel to the railway bridge, and this event in essence marked the shift of business and industry to what is now 'greater' Venice: Mestre and Marghera. Years later they would bear the brunt of Allied bombing campaigns during WWII, while the Arsenale continued to be used as a naval dockyard. It still is, although its importance is negligible. Venice came out of WWII pretty much unscathed.

Venice since WWII

Marghera, industrialised since 1920, was extended southward into reclaimed land in the course of the 1960s and 1970s. The creation and expansion of petrol refineries and metallurgy, chemical and plastics industries brought thousands of jobs to Venice – and plenty of problems too. For more on these see Ecology & Environment later in this chapter.

The threat to Venice from the sea became abundantly clear to anyone who had not already seen it when floods crashed into the city in 1966. To date, they were the most disastrous demonstration of what could be the city's fate if steps are not taken to protect it. International organisations were set up in the wake of the flooding to collect funds intended to be spent on projects to protect the city and also to save and restore its monuments (see the boxed texts 'Acque Alte', later in this chapter, and 'Saving Venice', in the Things to See & Do chapter). But the more than 30 years since the 1966 floods have been a lamentable history of prevarication and corruption in Venice. No-one can be sure just how much money intended for projects to save Venice from sinking has instead ended up lining the pockets of politicians, bureaucrats and lobbyists.

In November 1998, as Venice again experienced heavy flooding (now an all too regular feature of the city's life), the 20-year debate on whether or not to build floating barriers looked set for a final decision. But left-wing mayor Massimo Cacciari, a respected figure who has been mayor since 1993, sided with the Greens, who insist further environmental impact studies are needed. The barrier's backers say the city will soon be peopled only by tourists watching the city sink. Cacciari has been accused of being more worried about keeping the Greens in his coalition sweet.

Meanwhile, Cacciari is one of many politicians advocating a process of federalisation of the Italian state – he would like to see Venice and the Veneto with a greater degree of autonomy vis-a-vis the central government in Rome. He is not the only one, although approaches vary. Lega Nord, a separatist movement born in the 1980s and led by the controversial Umberto Bossi, won considerable support for a while in Venice. In the 1990s it lost ground to the breakaway Liga Repubblica Veneta and a succession of other minor groups. The main difference between Lega and Liga is, surprisingly, that the latter is more open to dialogue with mainstream centre-right parties than Bossi and co.

GEOGRAPHY

The role of geography has been critical in the development of Venice. For hundreds of years, the city's greatest defence was its unique position in the middle of a lagoon. Now, the one-time guarantor of Venice's survival seems bent on the inexorable eradication of the city.

The territory of the Comune di Venezia extends over 457.5 sq km, of which 267.6 sq km are lagoon waters, canals and so on. On the mainland, the city's boundaries take in 134 sq km. The *centro storico* (old city) is just 7.6 sq km of land, while the remaining islands together total 49.9 sq km.

It is tempting when gazing across the lagoon to think of it as a simple extension of the sea. No impression could be more mistaken. The Adriatic forces its way into the lagoon through three *bocche* (mouths) that interrupt the bulwark of narrow sandbanks strung north to south in a 50km arc between the mainland points of Jesolo and Chioggia.

The lagoon was formed by the meeting of the sea with freshwater streams running off from several Alpine rivers. It is like a great shallow dish, crisscrossed by a series of navigable channels. These were either the extension of river flows or ditches created by the inflow of sea water. One of the deepest is the Grand Canal (Canal Grande), which runs through the heart of the city. It is thought to have been an extension of the Brenta river (which has since been diverted south) or another river – human intervention has been so constant that by now it is all but impossible to say with any certainty. Other channels have been dredged and deepened since WWII to allow huge oil tankers to pass through to Porto Marghera.

No-one knew the lagoon better than the Venetians – whenever invaders threatened (such as in 1379–80, during the Battle of Chioggia), the Venetians would pull up buoys marking the course of navigable channels and so pretty much close access to the city. The channels are marked today by lines of wooden pylons *(bricole)*.

More than 40 islands and islets dot the lagoon. The better-known ones include the Lido, Pellestrina, Murano, Burano and Torcello. The tinier ones have served as convents, quarantine stations, hospitals and cemeteries. Today, some belong to the city of Venice, while others are privately owned. Some, such as San Michele, are easily accessible, while others have been pretty much abandoned to decay.

The 7.6 sq km of Venice today were not always there. The islands that together formed Rivoalto were once a fraction of the area now covered. The very shallowness of the lagoon allowed the next step. Along the edge of the deeper channels, the inhabitants began to expand their tiny islands. They did this by creating platforms on which to build new structures. Pine pylons were rammed into the muddy lagoon floor, topped then by layers of Istrian stone. The action of the sea water on the wood caused a process of mineralisation that hardened the structure, while the upper stone layers were impervious to the tides. It was an ingenious solution and the method has remained pretty much the same down to the present day.

CLIMATE

Summer is probably the worst time of year to be in Venice – average daytime temperatures hover around 27°C but can go considerably higher. High humidity also makes for rather sticky weather, and the combination of heat haze with air pollution makes it highly unlikely you'll be able to espy the Alps from any point in the city. Prevailing winds (the sirocco) are from the south and hot.

In spring the weather is often crisp and clear and the temperatures pleasant. That

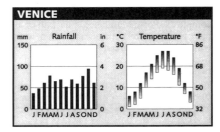

said, quite a lot of rain falls in May and into June. Even in August the chances of rain are high.

The first half of winter sees heavy rainfall, with flooding (see the boxed text 'Acque Alte' in the next section) most likely in November and December. On bad days the city and lagoon are enveloped in mist (which some find enchanting), but every now and then you get lucky and the sky clears. Temperatures can drop quite low, though snow is relatively rare.

ECOLOGY & ENVIRONMENT

Venice is under siege. For the most part, public attention on the city's ailments has focussed on flooding and the chilling cry: 'Venezia sprofonda!' (Venice is sinking!)

While the growing threat from Adriatic tides washing up against the city was dramatically brought home by the disastrous floods of 1966, the hue and cry over this issue has tended to obscure other, more complex problems that ultimately are just as dangerous to the city's future.

The narrow issue of tidal flooding and the wrangling over a project designed to put a brake on it are dealt with in the boxed text 'Acque Alte', along with the related issue of subsidence (sinking).

Pollution

Heavy industry has brought other problems. The establishment and expansion of the petroleum and chemical plants in Marghera was designed to breathe life into the Venetian economy. This it did – but at a price.

Human, agricultural and industrial waste is all cheerfully dumped into the lagoon off Venice, the islands and the mainland, the biggest offender by far being the industrial complex at Porto Marghera: about half of all the cyanide, heavy metals and other toxic waste that winds up in the lagoon comes from Marghera's plants. The effects on life in the lagoon are already of concern, but the waste and air pollution are also corroding Venice's buildings. Although funds have been allocated for the reduction of lagoon pollution, city officials admit that little progress has been made so far.

The passage of supertankers across the lagoon to Porto Marghera presents another disaster waiting to happen. Cleaning up an oil spill in the lagoon would be fraught with difficulty. The shallow waters would impede access for emergency vessels and the chemical techniques usually used could not be applied here because of the threat they would pose to vegetation and fish life in the lagoon. Ten million tonnes of oil are transported across the lagoon each year. There has been talk of cutting this down or stopping the transport of oil altogether, but so far the talk has been largely unaccompanied by action.

A Delicate Balance

Sea water itself is causing damage, and herein lies a particular rub. Ever since the foundation of the Republic, Venetians have continually intervened to maintain a degree of stability in the lagoon (maintaining and dredging canals and so on), which is around 6000 years old.

The very survival of the lagoon relies on a delicate and rarely stable ebb and flow of sea and fresh water. River water brings sediment into the lagoon, some of which accumulates along canals and elsewhere to form sand banks (*velme*). Some of these sand banks are then consolidated by hardy vegetation able to survive whether submerged or not. These *barene* serve as extra internal bulwarks against the potential rage of tides. The main islands of the lagoon were probably formed this way.

On the other hand, too much sediment would fill the lagoon. The regular sea tide is essential to take away the surplus.

Until the 16th century, human intervention in the lagoon was minimal, aiming to do little more than maintain channels and stability. Then, however, interference became more drastic. The flow of fresh river water was diverted away from the lagoon to reduce the build up of sediment and the course of many channels was altered. This century a concerted campaign of land reclamation has wiped out vast areas of the lagoon.

That is nothing, however, compared with what has happened since the end of WWII. The digging of the Canale dei Petroli (Petrol Canal) in the 1960s to allow oil tankers into Porto Marghera created a new problem. It is deeper than the natural channels and allows too much sea water into the lagoon. Tidal movements are therefore faster and more violent.

People are busy making things worse in other respects too. The use of dragnets to harvest clams is ripping up great swathes of rich vegetation from the lagoon floor. That vegetation held in a reasonable amount of sediment, which in turn held up the influx of sea water. The barene are under threat: fun-lovers zipping around in motorboats at weekends help erode the sandbanks.

All these elements constitute an incursion into the lagoon's natural defences against the sea, leading to what the Italians call the *marinizzazione* of the lagoon – its 'seafication'. With less to hold up outward flows, far more sediment is leaving the lagoon than coming in – it is estimated that the lagoon is losing a million cubic metres of sediment a year.

Another charming side-effect of the clam harvesting is the replacement of the lagoon-bed vegetation with rootless algae. The lagoon and its coast have suffered repeatedly from such algae plagues in recent years – they're not pleasant on the nose.

On the subject of the nose, the digging of the Canale dei Petroli had another unexpected result. As the even ebb and flow of the tide has been altered by human activity, it no longer acts as efficiently in one of its traditionally vital tasks – flushing out the lagoon. While at deeper levels sediment is being carried out to sea, at the surface all the waste dumped into the lagoon tends increasingly to remain there.

Acque Alte

Venice can be flooded by high tides during winter. Known as *acque alte*, these mainly occur between November and April, flooding low-lying areas of the city such as Piazza San Marco. Serious floods are announced several hours before they reach their high point by 16 sirens throughout the city and islands. In some areas you can see the water rising up over the edge of the canal, although most of it actually bubbles up through drains.

Although the floods rarely last more than a few hours, the rise can happen with surprising speed and so leave you stranded. The best thing to do is arm yourself with a pair of gumboots *(stivali di gomma)*. Raised walkways *(passerelli)* are set up in Piazza San Marco and other major tourist areas of the city (you can pick up a brochure with a map of the walkways at the tourist office).

Floods are measured against average sea level. Officially, *acqua alta* begins at 0.8m above average level. The sirens go off if it is expected to hit 1.1m. At this level, about 11.5% of the city is under shallow water. If the flood level exceeds 1.2m, you can be in trouble, as even the walkways are no use then. At this level, about 35% of the city's pavements are covered. Add 10cm and 70% of the town is under. At 1.4m a state of emergency would be declared, with most of the city under water. The November 1966 flood level was 1.94m. Floods above 1.2m are pretty rare. On average flooding at 1.4m happens once every five years. The 1.3m mark has been reached twice every three years since 1966. Floods of the catastrophic 1966 level are considered unlikely more than once in 180 years.

Venice's flooding problems are caused and compounded by numerous factors. The ebb and flow of the Adriatic tides is actually essential to the survival of the lagoon (see A Delicate Balance earlier in this Ecology & Environment section), but their effect on the city can be exacerbated by other factors. To the normal daily rhythm of two high tides is added the lunar push and pull at the new moon and full moon. Winds from the south (sirocco) can sometimes whip up waves, while the north wind (bora) causes problems for Chioggia. High and low pressure systems alsoaffect tides.

The very shape of the Adriatic Sea, a little like a washtub, can see northward-bound waves bouncing at the top end of the sea and then spilling back southward, washing into the lagoon. Extra fresh water draining off the mainland can add to the problem. And, of course, in the long term, the greenhouse effect can only be expected to worsen matters, increasing the overall average sea level of the Adriatic.

Sinking

To make things worse, as has been often observed, Venice is, or at least was, sinking. It has been estimated that the city has 'sunk' 23cm this century. Of that total, 9cm are due to the rising sea level, so that actual subsidence has probably been in the order of 14cm. That was in part due to natural long-term giving way of the lagoon floor, but more importantly to the excessive pumping of subterranean water – mostly for industrial purposes – in Porto Marghera. That practice has now been largely stopped and, as ground water again builds up, subsidence may well give way to heave, the opposite phenomenon.

Searching for Solutions

Ever since the disaster of 1966, experts, committees and politicians have scratched around for a solution. The single most popular approach to dealing with Venice's problems has been to attack the tides.

Acque Alte

Of the many plans put forward, the one that first won Italian government approval in the 1980s was based on an experimental moveable dike. The idea is to build mechanical walls into the sea bed at the three entrances into the lagoon, known as the *bocche di porto* (the 'port's mouths' from north to south are called Lido, Malamocco and Chioggia). The walls, weighed down with water, would lie flush with the sea bed until threatening high tides were on the way. At the flick of a switch, the watery ballast would be expelled from the walls, which would then rise up and keep the Adriatic out of the lagoon until the tide subsided. The plan has come to be known, incorrectly, as Mose (from the Modulo Sperimentale Elettromeccanico, a prototype in the lagoon). The word happens to mean Moses.

NICKY CAVEN

"Nice day for a swim, don't you think?"

Ever since the 1980s, the arguments have raged back and forth over the long-term effectiveness of the plan and its impact on the fragile lagoon environment. After finally getting approval from various commissions in 1998, it was again stopped in December of that year when left-wing and Green politicians in Venice said the US$2.5 billion plan required further study. Exasperated by this, Paolo Costa, a Venetian and former public-works minister, declared: 'We do not need more doctors at the bedside.' He claimed that the city would be submerged by the end of the next century.

The Greens countered that the funds for the project (which would require up to US$10 million worth of maintenance annually) would be better spent cleaning up chemical and oil pollution in the lagoon and dredging silted-up canals (see A Delicate Balance earlier in this Ecology & Environment section).

Other alternative palliatives are also on the table. A programme to raise the level of pedestrian areas is already under way. This is not a novelty. The extreme lowness of some doorways is testimony to earlier municipal projects to raise the walkways.

Nevertheless, the pro-Moses camp says that, however imperfect, the project would buy precious time for Venice. And so Chioggia's town council approved the project in February 1999, leading the Venetians to rethink again – this time putting the final decision back to the year 2000. In the meantime, the proposal is to be tinkered with and resubmitted for an environmental impact study.

Well might Lord Byron have sighed: 'Oh Venice, Venice, when thy marble walls are level with the waters there shall be a cry of nations o'er thy sunken halls.'

All the fuss over the Moses dike project to stem the Adriatic flood-tide threat is seen by its opponents as a costly diversion from other real problems that, they say, could ultimately have an equally, if not more, devastating effect on the city. Merely blocking high tides, they say, is not the answer. The lagoon itself has to be helped to rebuild its own defences.

GOVERNMENT & POLITICS

Venice is the capital of the region known as the Veneto (one of 20 in Italy), which extends west to Verona and the Lago di Garda and north into the Alps.

The Veneto is further subdivided into seven provinces, of which the area around Venice – Venezia – is one (provinces are named after the main town in each). The other provinces are: Belluno, Padua, Rovigo, Treviso, Verona and Vicenza.

Since 1927, the *comune*, or municipality, of Venice has comprised the islands of the lagoon (including Murano, Burano, Torcello, the Lido and Pellestrina), as well as Mestre, Marghera and Chioggia on the mainland. Locals often divide the lot into three general areas: *terraferma* (mainland), *centro storico* (Venice proper, including Giudecca) and the *estuario* (all the remaining islands).

Traditionally, Venice itself is divided into six *sestieri*: San Marco, Castello, Cannaregio, Dorsoduro, Santa Croce and San Polo. Nowadays, the territory of the comune is divided up into 13 *quartieri*. The sestieri and the island of Giudecca (which is part of the Sestiere di Dorsoduro for administrative purposes) are grouped into the first two of these 'quarters'. The remaining 11 cover the islands and mainland parts of the comune.

The present *sindaco* (mayor), Massimo Cacciari, has been in the driver's seat since 1993. A left-wing professor of philosophy, he rules a loose coalition that includes I Verdi (the Greens). He commands an unusual degree of respect among the citizens of Venice (who had no hesitation in re-electing him in 1997), but has taken some flak over the Moses plan to stem tidal flooding and the scandals surrounding the 1996 fire that destroyed the city's opera house, La Fenice (see

the boxed text 'Faltering Phoenix' in the Entertainment chapter).

ECONOMY

The ignominious fall of Venice in 1797 had its economic fallout. Although the port was not completely neglected under Austrian rule and a rail link was established with Milan, the city sank into something of a morass. While the north-western triangle of Italy embarked on a programme of industrialisation in the 1880s, the north-east remained fundamentally rural. Well after the end of WWI, more than 60% of the workforce was agricultural. The Veneto remained largely neglected until after WWII.

Industrialisation came mainly with the creation and expansion of Marghera and its port (Porto Marghera). In the following decades the port and the metallurgy, chemical and petrol industries became major employers, not just in Venice, but for the whole region. By the late 1980s, only 7% of the population worked in agriculture, while 40% was in manufacturing and 53% in services. At 4.5 million, the whole Veneto region contains around 7.5% of the country's population, but contributes 12% of exports.

Tourism plays a pivotal role in the life of the Veneto, and above all in Venice. The Veneto as a whole contributes 13% of all Italy's tourist revenue. In 1997, 1.4 million tourists visited Venice, staying an average of 2.3 days. In addition, it is guessed that as many as 15 million day-trippers (people who don't stay overnight and leave no statistical trace) pour in. The majority are Americans, followed by Italians and Japanese.

Of the lagoon's remaining traditional industries, glass-making is perhaps the one with the highest profile. Although clearly directed at the tourist trade, some of the work coming out of Murano's glass factories remains of the highest quality.

Venice's once-proud shipbuilding industry had already wilted to virtually nothing by the time the Republic fell in 1797.

POPULATION & PEOPLE

The population of the Veneto region is 4.5 million. The region's largest centres are

Venice (including the mainland), Padua and Verona, each with more than 200,000 inhabitants. The rest of the populace is spread out across a sea of smaller towns and countryside.

The Comune di Venezia comprises 292,500 people. In the centro storico, only 68,200 people are still resident. The exodus has been slow but constant. It began in part as the mainland areas of Mestre and Marghera expanded and offered greater chances of employment. Constant talk (and little action) of Venice's sinking feeling must have had an effect too. Back in the 1950s, more than 170,000 lived in the lagoon city, and at various points in its long history the total nudged 200,000.

Demographically, the place seems condemned. Talk to the average Venetian about his or her city and it is hard not to detect a note of despair. Said one: 'Venetians have the feeling that nothing is done for them. Those who have made lots of money just buy up houses and keep them empty or rent them out to tourists. And the little people find they have to go.'

And as people leave, so shops and businesses collapse for want of local custom. All that remain are *pizzerie* and *gelaterie* (ice-cream parlours) for day-trippers. 'Here there used to be 50 little shops – fruiterers, bakers, butchers, delicatessens,' our friend sweeps his hand across his neighbourhood. 'Now there is nothing. All those families have had to leave.'

The remaining islands are home to 45,200 people, leaving almost two-thirds of the people within the city boundaries on the mainland.

EDUCATION

The Università Ca' Foscari officially came into being in 1968, although it had already been turning out graduates for 100 years. It began as Italy's first school of commerce. For more details, see Universities in the Facts for the Visitor chapter.

Illiteracy is barely an issue in the Veneto. The national Italian average of 97% literacy can be accepted as a standard reading for this part of the country.

ARTS

Venice was by tradition a city of practical people – merchants interested above all in the business of trade. This is not to say that the city and its people were indifferent to more aesthetic pursuits – periods of uncontested greatness in fields such as painting are proof enough of a substantial creative streak in the Venetians. Less visible arts, such as literature, seem to have excited them considerably less, however.

Architecture

Of the early centuries in the life of Venice no visible sign remains today. The earliest surviving architectural testimony to the Republic's long history dates from the 11th century.

Veneto-Byzantine East was West, and for that matter vice versa. That Venice stood apart from the rest of the Italian peninsula is never more clear than in the city's monuments and art. The obvious starting point is not in Venice proper at all, but rather on the island of Torcello. Here, the Cattedrale di Santa Maria Assunta is a singular lesson in a cross-cultural experiment. Essentially following the Byzantine style we can see in the basilicas of Ravenna, its builders also seem to have been influenced by the Romanesque developments to the west, in Padua, and beyond in the Lombard plains.

The term 'basilica' dates back to pre-Christian Roman times, when many major public buildings, from markets to courts, were constructed in this style. The basic plan is of a covered hall flanked by two columned aisles. When Emperor Constantine (AD 280–337) founded his new capital at Constantinople, he initiated an extensive church-building program. Two basic types emerged: the long, rectangular, three-aisled style already described and used mainly for public worship, and so-called 'centralised' churches. These latter were circular, square or octagonal and had more a commemorative role.

The cathedral is typical of the original standard basilica plan. There is no transept, although even in Constantine's time they had been employed in some churches.

Perhaps the main giveaway feature is the iconostasis separating the central nave from the presbytery – a prime feature of Eastern Orthodox churches – in this case made up of six thin columns.

Although what we see today is largely the rebuilt church of 1008, a few parts date back to the 7th (main apse) and 9th centuries (side apses). Other than the apses, little remains to remind us of the original church founded in 639 AD.

The real treasures are inside. Craftsmen from Ravenna came here to create some of the finest mosaics ever. The 12th- to 13th-century mosaic of the *Madonna col Bambino* (Madonna and Child) in the semi-dome of the central apse is one of the most exquisite examples of Byzantine handiwork. Some art historians rate it more highly than anything done in Constantinople itself.

The use of mosaics dates from Roman times, when the well-to-do covered the floors and walls of public and private buildings with geometric designs or images of people, beasts and events. Remnants of them can be seen in places like Pompeii and as far away as ancient Roman sites in Syria and Tunisia.

Under the Byzantine Empire the custom was continued, but tastes changed. In Venice, the use of a gold background became the norm. Nowhere is that clearer than in the dazzling decor of the city's star attraction, the Basilica di San Marco.

This also started off as a three-nave basilica when founded in the 9th century to house the remains of the city's newly promoted patron saint. Later, two wings were added to create a Greek-cross form, again a Byzantine idea (and based on the Church of the Holy Apostles in Constantinople). To the casual observer, the clearest sign of its Eastern form are the five domes – add a couple of minarets and change the surrounding scenery and you could almost think yourself in Istanbul.

Less visible from the outside, but still another characteristic that separates San Marco from Western churches, is the narthex (or atrium) wrapped around the front and side of the church up to the arms of the cross.

The kaleidoscope of mosaics inside the basilica is described in more detail in the Things to See & Do chapter. Suffice to say that, once again, the tradition is evidently Byzantine – the entire place is seemingly covered with these glittering tapestries of tiny tiles. The creation of mosaics requires glass, and the glass-makers who established themselves in Venice at the same time as the mosaicists soon set up an important local industry on the island of Murano. Their handiwork came to be among the most sought after in the world, ranging from the practical to the most exquisitely decorative.

Medieval Venice was largely a city of wood. Apart from the grand churches, only a handful of buildings were constructed of brick and/or stone. The Byzantine touch can still be made out in a few buildings, mostly trading houses, from the 12th century. The Ca' Farsetti and Palazzo Loredan are good examples, retaining features such as the two-storey loggias, with their graceful rounded arches. To a lesser extent, you can make out the same style in the lower floor of the Ca' da Mosto. Even the Fondaco dei Turchi, much altered in the 19th century, clearly cries out its Veneto-Byzantine origins.

Romanesque The architectural expression of Europe's reawakening, this style that swept across Western Europe made less of an impact on Venice. Much of what was built in Romanesque style was later demolished and replaced.

A reasonable example of it is the Chiesa di San Giacomo dell'Orio, in Santa Croce. Here, you can see all the classic elements of the style. The Romanesque church tended to be squat and simple, with up to three apses. Decoration was minimal and the semi-circle dominant. Doorways and windows, in the church as well as in the square-based and equally squat bell towers, were capped by semi-circular arches. Architectural or sculptural ornament was otherwise virtually absent from most Romanesque buildings.

The pretty cloisters at the Museo Diocesano d'Arte Sacra, just behind (east of) the Palazzo Ducale, are a perfect specimen of Romanesque simplicity.

Several Romanesque bell towers, such as that of the Chiesa di San Geremia (near the train station), are scattered about the city. Time and again they were left intact even as the churches of which they were part were replaced or heavily restructured.

Closer inspection of several monuments also reveals that the influence of Romanesque, while subtle, was perhaps more pervasive than often thought. Churches such as Murano's Chiesa dei SS Maria e Donato and Torcello's Santa Maria Assunta, readily identified as Veneto-Byzantine, contain Romanesque elements.

Gothic In the 13th century Gothic winds began to prevail in Venice, although the Byzantine aesthetic continued to inform artistic and architectural thinking for a good time to come. One way of identifying Venetian Gothic is by looking at the windows. Where you see them in clusters, with their tops tapering to a point, you can be reasonably sure the building you are looking at is Gothic (or perhaps a remake!). Bobbing along the Grand Canal, in particular, you will hardly fail to notice the many mansions built in this style. It is, however, a very Venetian twist on the theme – the shape of the windows is a hallmark of Venetian design.

Of the city's great Gothic monuments, the Palazzo Ducale stands out. It is a remarkable creation and representative of the unique turn the style took in Venice (known as 'florid Gothic'). What you see is a mixed result of building started in the early 15th century, with several extensions and then reconstruction after fires in the late 16th century. Palladio wanted to demolish it then and start from scratch. Luckily for us, the Republic's conservative rulers wanted to replicate what had stood before the blaze. The graceful porticoed facades facing the Bacino di San Marco and the square are given a translucent quality by the use of white Istrian stone and pink Verona marble. Otherwise, the decoration is restrained. Less so on the side facing the Basilica di San Marco. The carving on the Porta della Carta and Arco Foscari are fine examples of the intricacy reached in Gothic sculpture.

The two greatest Gothic churches in Venice were, however, built earlier than this, at the height of the style's sway. Santa Maria Gloriosa dei Frari (or Frari for short) was built in over a century from 1338 to 1443, while the Chiesa dei SS Giovanni e Paolo (aka Zanipolo) was completed in 1368. Both are magnificent edifices on a Latin-cross plan. Work on the decoration of both lasted long after construction was complete and reflects changing tastes. The Frari, a tower of elegance in brick, eschews almost completely the twisting lace-like external decoration typical of French and German Gothic. SS Giovanni e Paolo is partly decorated in marble and shows signs of the transition to the Renaissance.

Many architects at work in Venice were Lombards. Mauro Codussi (also known as Coducci), from Bergamo, was responsible for the imposing facade on the Chiesa di San Zaccaria (1483), although much of the florid Gothic flavour (see the apse) is the work of another architect, Antonio Gambello. Codussi also designed the Palazzo Vendramin-Calergi and Palazzo Corner-Spinelli on the Grand Canal. In all of his buildings, the transition away from Gothic to a more classic approach is a clear harbinger of the arrival of the Renaissance in architectural thinking.

Renaissance The Renaissance cracked over Italian and then European society like a dam burst. Revelling in the rediscovery of the greats of classical literature, philosophy, science and art, artists, thinkers and writers embarked on a frenzied study of the ancient and an impatient search for the new. This was also reflected in architecture. Rejecting the clerical haughtiness of the Gothic and the Eastern rigidity of the Greek and Byzantine, architects of this new age put classical models to their service in a quest for harmony and rationality.

If Gothic churches soared high into the heavens, reminding people of their smallness compared with the Almighty, Renaissance grandeur spread laterally, luxuriating in the powers of the human mind and the pleasure of the human eye. While tall

Gothic spires might be topped by the cross, a building such as the Libreria Sansoviniana is low, flat-roofed and topped by statues. It is a house of learning.

Of course, it is not as simple as that. Among the identifying signs in Venetian Renaissance building is a proclivity for spacious rounded arches on all levels (usually two, sometimes three storeys). Fluted half-columns often feature on the upper storey, but otherwise ornamentation is generally restrained. The classical triangular pediment borne up by columns is another common touch, never seen more clearly than at the front of Andrea Palladio's Chiesa di San Giorgio Maggiore.

Three of the city's master architects were from out of town. Jacopo Sansovino (1486–1570), whose real name was Tatti, was born in Florence and lived and worked there and in Rome. Michele Sanmicheli (1484–1559) came from a little closer to home, Verona, but he, too, was drawn to Rome. The sack of that city in 1527 spurred them both to pack their bags. Sansovino moved to Venice and Sanmicheli back home. Both remained from then on in the service of the Republic. Palladio (1508–80) was from Padua – more about him later.

Sanmicheli's most important contribution to La Serenissima was the Palazzo Grimani (1557–59). The Republic's leaders kept him busy engineering defence works for the city and Venice's scattered possessions.

It was, however, Sansovino who dominated the scene in Venice. To him was entrusted the task of revamping the city's look and he had a hand in 15 buildings, among them: the Zecca (the Mint), the Loggetta (Piazza San Marco), the Palazzo Dolfin-Manin on the Grand Canal, the Ca' Grande and the Chiesa di San Francesco della Vigna. Perhaps the most prominent testimony to Sansovino's work in Venice is his Biblioteca di San Marco (or Libreria Nazionale Marciana), opposite the Palazzo Ducale (see above). It also goes by the name of Libreria Sansoviniana, in memory of its creator.

Quite a deal older than the others, Pietro Lombardo (1435–1515) was another out-of-towner. While he was chiefly a sculptor (see Sculpture later in this section), his latter years were occupied principally with building. One pleasing result was the Chiesa di Santa Maria dei Miracoli (1489). A few years earlier he was also involved in the building of the Palazzo Dario, a cheerfully imaginative edifice topped by characteristically Venetian funnel chimneys. His Scuola di San Marco (1487–90) is a monumental but playful affair. In its fine marble facade, rounded arches, striking statuary and trompe l'oeil trickery compete for the eye's attention.

A unique Renaissance item is the Palazzo Contarini del Bovolo, built in 1499 by Giovanni Candi (died 1506). The gracious arches of the time are much in evidence, but the draw here is the inspired external spiral staircase.

Palladio Although he was active in Venice, the greater concentration of Palladio's work is in and around Vicenza. Palladio's name has a far greater resonance for a wide audience than any of his contemporaries, such as Sansovino, largely because his classicism was later taken as a model by British and American neoclassicists. The White House in Washington DC owes much to Palladio.

It is for his villas in the Venetian hinterland that Palladio is best known. Of them, La Villa Rotonda (just outside Vicenza) is among the most famous. These villas were built for those well-to-do Venetians who had turned their backs on the sea and sought to consolidate their position on the mainland. They were conceived with a double role in mind – pleasure dome and control centre over agricultural estates.

Steeped in the classicism of Rome that had inspired a great deal of Renaissance architecture, Palladio produced buildings rich with columns, triangular pediments and occasionally a central dome (La Rotonda). Palladio's version of Renaissance architecture has often been described as 'archaeological' due to his unswerving recourse to antiquity for inspiration. For more on the villas, see the Excursions chapter.

Palladio was made Venice's official architect on the death of Sansovino in 1570. His single greatest mark on the city was the Chiesa di San Giorgio Maggiore, on the island of the same name. Even in the distance, seen from Piazza San Marco, its majesty cannot fail to impress the observer. It was preceded by his equally significant Chiesa del Redentore, on Giudecca, built as an offering to God in the hope of the city's deliverance from the plague.

It is probably no accident that Palladio received commissions to work his particular magic in these two relatively isolated corners of the city. Bereft of surroundings of any significance, these grand churches, with their weighty columns, high domes and strong classical facades, command respect – and are best contemplated at a distance. Part of their majesty lies in the rigorous eschewal of superfluous ornament. Inside San Giorgio Maggiore, the eye rests on an interplay of rounded arches buttressed by columns and pilasters – there is virtually no decoration.

The grandness of his churches does not by any means imply that Palladio's was a sluggish, ponderous style. His playfulness within the classical traditions that informed his thinking is perhaps best observed in Vicenza. The Palazzo della Ragione, in the heart of that city, is laced with great open porticoes that create an altogether different sensation, one of lightness within the dignity of a grand structure.

Palladio died before finishing many of his projects, including San Giorgio Maggiore. For their completion we are largely indebted to Vincenzo Scamozzi (1552–1616), who faithfully carried out their designer's plans. Scamozzi did his own thing too. He designed the Procuratie Nuove in Piazza San Marco (completed by Baldassare Longhena).

Baroque The 17th century in the Venetian building industry was dominated by Baldassare Longhena (1598–1682). A master of baroque, which took to florid ornament in seeming reaction to what some plainly considered the austerity of the Renaissance,

Longhena cannot be said to have fallen for the most extreme of its decorative excesses.

His masterpiece is the Chiesa di Santa Maria della Salute, the great dome of which dominates the southern end of the Grand Canal. An octagonal church, its classical lines are a reminder of Palladio, but the sumptuous external decoration, with phalanxes of statues and rich sculpture over the main entrance, shows where Longhena is headed. To see where he ended up you only need to look at the facade of the Chiesa dell'Ospedaletto, north-east of Piazza San Marco. You will see his imprint all over the city, even in the Ghetto, where he had a hand in the design of the two larger synagogues (the Schole Levantina and Spagnola).

Antonio Gaspari (c. 1670–1730) was one of several less-outstanding architects to follow in Longhena's footsteps, albeit at a distance. He had a hand in the Ca' Pesaro.

18th Century Venice's last century of independence was something of a twilight period, although architectural activity, leaning by now towards neoclassicism, bubbled along. The style, to some minds a bit of a poor relation to the more inventive Renaissance investigation of the classical genre, was popular throughout Europe. One of the senior names of the period was Giorgio Massari (1686–1766). Inspired by Palladio, his more lasting works included the Chiesa dei Gesuati, the Palazzo Grassi and the completion of Ca' Rezzonico on the Grand Canal.

Giannantonio Selva (1753–1819) carried the neoclassical torch into the next century and the days of Napoleon. He is best remembered for the Teatro della Fenice (completed in 1792), damaged by fire in 1936 and then destroyed the same way in 1996.

To the Present Palladio frequently found himself up against the conservative habits of the town fathers. His plans for the Palazzo Ducale and for a new Rialto bridge were overruled.

The attitude persists to this day, but not necessarily with the same happy results. A design for a magnificent building on the

Grand Canal by Frank Lloyd Wright, and Le Corbusier's plans for a hospital in the area of the ex-Macello Comunale in Cannaregio are among many to have received the thumbs down. Frank Gehry hopes to create a 'Venice Gateway' at the San Marco airport but no decision has been taken.

This is not to say that absolutely nothing has been done. Probably the best known of Venice's modern architects was Carlo Scarpa (1906–78). He designed the entrance to the IUAV in Santa Croce and over the years redesigned the inside of several museums, including the Gallerie dell'Accademia, the Museo Correr and Palazzo Querini-Stampaglia. He also worked on pavilions for the Biennale in Castello from 1948 to 1978. Others to contribute to the Biennale include Studio BBPR, Francesco Cellini and James Stirling. Stirling's book pavilion is said to be the only example of British architecture in Italy.

Painting

Artists are a peripatetic lot. A wealth of paintings by Venice's most gifted can be found in the city. But a great deal of their work was either produced in other cities or has found its way to distant collectors' homes and galleries.

Medieval Painting In addition to the treasure chest of mosaics (see Veneto-Byzantine in the preceding Architecture section), some fairly pedestrian fresco painting was also used in Venetian churches – fragments remain in churches such as San Giovanni Decollato, San Nicolò dei Mendicoli, SS Apostoli and even San Marco.

Il Trecento Painting's first real name in Venice was Paolo Veneziano (c. 1300–62). In his earlier days it appears he was open to some exciting innovations in painting (Giotto was at work in nearby Padua in the first years of the 14th century). An example is *Incoronazione della Vergine* (Coronation of the Virgin), now in the National Gallery of Art in Washington. Later on, however, he reverted to Byzantine type. Gold backgrounds predominated and his figures were

bloodless and didactic. The *Madonna col Bambino* (Madonna and Child) is a perfect example. The almost expressionless face of the Virgin Mary and the Christ child inside the almond are typical Eastern touches. This and a couple of other of his works can be seen in the Gallerie dell'Accademia. He also painted the cover of the Pala d'Oro in the Basilica di San Marco.

Others to toe the Byzantine line were Lorenzo Veneziano and Nicoletto Semitecolo. You can see some of Lorenzo's work, which shows a little more life than that of Paolo, in the Gallerie dell'Accademia. Semitecolo worked a good deal of the time in Padua, where he left behind works in the Duomo and the Chiesa degli Eremitani.

Gothic With Gentile da Fabriano (c. 1370–1427) came a turning point in Venetian art. Gentile had the travel bug and worked in many Italian cities, but if anyone can be said to have brought the so-called International (or Late) Gothic style to the lagoon city, it was probably him. He worked on several frescoes in the Palazzo Ducale (itself a remarkably eclectic Gothic celebration – see the preceding Architecture section) that were subsequently lost. Without him, the work of people like Pisa's Pisanello (c. 1380–1455) would have been unthinkable. Venetian painters directly inspired by Da Fabriano include Jacobello del Fiore (died c. 1439) and Michele Giambono (died c. 1462), both of whom are represented in the Gallerie dell'Accademia. Some Giambono works can also be seen in the Museo Correr.

Early Renaissance You might have already guessed that, one way or another, Venice tended not to be in the artistic vanguard. Rather, influences from the outside (at first from the East, later from the West in the form of Gothic) served to stimulate local artists to contemplate the next step. It was little different in the transition from Gothic to the Renaissance (Il Rinascimento to the Italians).

Getting Noticed With the Renaissance came great change in the artist's station. In earlier periods (such as the Romanesque period in Western Europe and the contemporary period of Byzantine art in Venice and the East), artists generally remained anonymous. This began slowly to change in the Gothic period, but it was really only with the Renaissance that artists began to claim, and receive, individual recognition and even acclaim for their work.

In practice, the distinction we might make today between 'art' and 'craft' only now began to make itself felt, although painters continued to operate workshops in much the same way as the glass-blowers of Murano, or other craftsmen. But while glass-blowers remained largely anonymous (at least to later generations), the illustrious names of the Renaissance would remain forever branded in history's long memory.

Rising Tide The starburst of creativity that flowed forth from Renaissance Florence sooner or later had to wash over the lagoon defences to Venice. Padua, just 37km distant, served as a conduit for this artistic tide. If Paolo Uccello (who did a stint in Venice), Donatello and Filippo Lippi (both of whom worked long in Padua) and others formed the Florentine vanguard, Padua's Andrea Mantegna (1431–1506) was the connection between them and Venice. He never worked in Venice, but Venetian artists came to know him and his work.

Two Venetians straddling the abyss between Gothic and the Renaissance were Jacopo Bellini (c. 1396–c. 1470) and Antonio Vivarini (c. 1415–c. 1480). Both headed what would prove to be potent artistic families and presided over prolific workshops. (The business of painting was, in many respects, similar to any other artisanal craft. People ordered paintings and frescoes and workshops produced them – paintings attributed to masters were in fact often carried out by apprentices under the master's supervision.) You can see works by both artists in the Gallerie dell'Accademia. Vivarini left behind some works in the Frari too.

Bellini and Vivarini both clearly injected a growing sense of movement, emotion and depth into their work, but it was Mantegna who took the great steps and arrived with both palette and brush firmly entrenched in the latest fashion. He embraced the use of perspective to create a sense of three dimensions and the depiction of the full array of human feelings.

All three artists knew each other and Vivarini worked for a while in Padua. It was his younger brother, Bartolomeo (c. 1432–99), who picked up the baton from Mantegna and ran with it. Altarpieces by him can be seen in the churches of the Frari, San Giovanni in Bragora and SS Giovanni e Paolo, as well as the Gallerie dell'Accademia.

Carlo Crivelli (c. 1430–c. 1494) was born in Venice and attended both the Bellini and Vivarini workshops. He too ended up under the spell of Mantegna's work in Padua, but in 1457 was exiled and ended up in Le Marche. His work is at times a curious blend of the new Renaissance ethos and vestiges of a more Gothic rigidity. His *Madonna della Passione* (in Castelvecchio, in Verona) is a good example.

The Bellini Boys A switch came with Jacopo Bellini's sons Giovanni (1432–1516) and Gentile (1429–1507). The latter had a crystal-clear eye for detail, evident in works like *Processione a Piazza San Marco* (Procession to Piazza San Marco; one of three by him in the True Cross cycle on view in Sala 20 of the Gallerie dell'Accademia). He was something of a specialist portraitist in his early career, too – he was even sent to Constantinople in 1479 to do Sultan Mehmet II's profile (now in London's National Gallery).

It was his little brother, however, who shone out above all his contemporaries. Giovanni went beyond what he had learned from Mantegna and his entire career was marked by a constantly renewed search for innovation. The central figures in his more mature works betray the link with Mantegna by their great clarity, standing out from their landscape backdrops, however sweeping. But Bellini extracts greater variety in tone and colour, creating a softness and meditative quality largely missing in the harsher Mantegna. He moves further away from the allegorical stamp that still greatly dominated art at this stage. Later on in his career he began to experiment more with oil paint rather than tempera (powdered pigments mixed with egg yolk and water), which would eventually be displaced by the new medium.

A great number of Giovanni Bellini's works are scattered around Italy, Europe and the USA, but you can see some in the Gallerie dell'Accademia, Museo Correr and elsewhere. His *Pala di San Zaccaria* (1505), in the church of the same name, is a monumental work that shows he was not lost for answers to his younger rivals.

A New Generation Among these latter were Vittore Carpaccio (1460–1526), Cima da Conegliano (c. 1459–c. 1517), Giorgione (1477–1510), from Castelfranco, and Lorenzo Lotto (c. 1480–1556).

Carpaccio was fascinated by Venetian court life and the pageantry of the city in his times, but his best-known works are narrative cycles painted for the Venetian schools (Sant'Orsola, San Giorgio degli Schiavoni, Albanesi, Santo Stefano). Check out his *Storie di Sant'Orsola* (History of St Ursula), nine works in all, in the Gallerie dell'Accademia – perhaps more interesting for the observer today is the fantastical depiction of the Venetian-style background against which the story of the saint unfolds.

Cima da Conegliano was active in Venice from the 1480s. His work is a little more rigidly classical and less innovative than that of some of his contemporaries. Some is on view in the Gallerie dell'Accademia.

Giorgione, on the other hand, was quite another character. Although he is thought to have been a student of Bellini and may have met Leonardo da Vinci during the latter's stay in 1500, he did not follow the usual route of joining one of the art workshops to make his living. He dabbled seriously in poetry and music. In his paintings, which cover a wide range of subjects, he breaks new ground in his manipulation of light and colour. *La Tempesta* (The Storm), in the Gallerie dell'Accademia, shows him painting without having first drawn his subject –

a striking step into new territory at the time. Titian would later become his student and partner.

Lorenzo Lotto spent a good deal of his life moving around between Venice, Treviso, Bergamo and Le Marche. His was a vast palette, ranging from religious works through to portraits, but he never quite got the recognition that was perhaps his due and he died in poverty. In Venice he left a few pieces behind, such as the *Elemosina di Sant'Antonio* (St Anthony's Alms) in the Chiesa dei SS Giovanni e Paolo. The *Ritratto del Giovane Gentiluomo nel Suo Studio* (Portrait of a Young Gentleman in His Studio) is a striking painting now on view in the Gallerie dell'Accademia.

Other lesser artists worth looking out for are Marco Basaiti (c. 1470–c. 1530), Giovanni Mansueti and Antonio da Negroponte, who came to Venice from one of its colonies (Negroponte) in the second half of the 15th century. Some of their works are on display in the Gallerie dell'Accademia.

Late Renaissance Venice might have been a little slow to catch on to the flowering of artistic invention that came with the Renaissance, but the age of the Bellini brothers was but a launch pad for still greater achievement in the lagoon city.

Titian the Titan One reading of Lotto's departure from Venice in 1542 was that the town wasn't big enough for him and his closest rival, Titian (c. 1490–1576), known in Italian as Tiziano Vecellio.

Titian is an all-time great, a 'sun amidst the stars', as one admirer put it. Born at Pieve di Cadore into a family of artists, he was a pupil of Giovanni Bellini. In his early years he worked with Giorgione and experts have had great difficulty in working out which of the two did what in the early years of the 16th century. They first collaborated on frescoes at the Fondaco dei Tedeschi, all since lost except for some fragments that are now on display in the Ca d'Oro. Even after Giorgione's death in 1510, Titian continued for a while to work under the spell of his former master.

Titian's was a poetic approach to painting, full of verve and high drama. By 1514, when he completed his allegorical *Amor Sacro e Profano* (Sacred and Profane Love, now in Rome's Galleria Borghese), Titian had established himself as one of the leading artists of his time. Confirmation came in 1518 with the unveiling of his monumental *Assunta* (Assumption) in the Chiesa di Santa Maria Gloriosa dei Frari. Hanging in a place of honour above the high altar, it was quickly seen as a work of genius.

It was barely the beginning. Titian's fame spread across the peninsula and Europe. Commissions came from left and right, keeping him busy until his final days. His oeuvre falls broadly into three categories: portraiture, religious paintings and mythological subjects. His images of the great and the good are legion. The Hapsburg emperor Charles V was so enamoured of his likeness that he knighted the artist – a rare honour. He also made sure his son and successor, Philip II, was immortalised by the genius' brush. Pope Paul III, the dukes of Urbino and Francis I of France were also among his many subjects.

Considering his output, not an awful lot of Titian's works can be seen in Venice. Apart from the Frari, they can be found in the churches of Santa Maria della Salute, the Gesuiti and San Salvatore. Those works alone are demonstration enough of the movement, humanity and often startling colour that distinguish his works. In the Gallerie dell'Accademia are his last strokes on *Pietà*, intended for his burial chapel but actually finished after his death by Palma il Giovane.

Tintoretto It seems churlish to speak of the likes of Tintoretto (1518–94; his real name was Jacopo Robusti) and Veronese (1528–88; aka Paolo Caliari) as though they were in any way 'lesser' painters. Masters of the late Renaissance Venetian school, they had the 'misfortune' to be at work at much the same time as Titian, who would have been a hard act to follow anywhere or any time.

Tintoretto was, however, a proud and successful painter who established a singular reputation. His children carried on the business of his workshop after his death. He is now regarded as the greatest of all Mannerists in Italy, going beyond Michelangelo's lead in this respect and right up there with El Greco in Spain. Mannerism is one of those twilight phases in the history of art, falling between the splendours of the late Renaissance and the excesses that would come with baroque in the 17th century. It is characterised in painting by a yearning to break with convention and a certain wilful capriciousness in the use of light and colour and the depiction of human figures.

In El Greco's work, the move away from the Renaissance could not be clearer. In the case of Tintoretto, it is more subtle and restrained. He was heavily influenced by Michelangelo and may have visited Rome. In his earlier stages at least, Tintoretto makes some remarkably similar choices to those of El Greco in terms of colour (a predominance of muted blues and crimsons). El Greco studied in Venice in 1560, so the two may well have had some shared experience.

Tintoretto was fascinated by architecture and sculpture, reflected in his love for creating three-dimensional panoramas much in the style of a stage set. A telling example is his *Crocifissione* (Crucifixion), in the Sala dell'Albergo, in the Scuola Grande di San Rocco. Another is the *Trafugamento del Corpo di San Marco* (Stealing of St Mark's Body) in the Gallerie dell'Accademia.

The latter painting shows as clearly as any that he was also a dab hand with the swift brushstroke, which lent an effervescence to his figures that further removes him from earlier Renaissance standards. In contrast, he is decisive in his use of light, or rather the lack of it. A great many of his later paintings seem buried in darkness, with shafts of light used to illuminate only the key characters and scenes.

The place to gorge yourself on the best of late Tintoretto is the Scuola Grande di San Rocco. He dedicated the last 23 years of his life to bedecking it with more than 50 paintings. In the Palazzo Ducale he is also well represented. His *Paradiso*, in the Sala del Maggior Consiglio, is a work of extraordinary complexity. We have to assume, given the amount he had on his plate with the San Rocco project, that much of the material in the Palazzo Ducale was overseen by Tintoretto but executed by his workshop. Some fine pieces by him are also housed in the Gallerie dell'Accademia.

Veronese Paolo Veronese was also busy in the Palazzo Ducale. Born in Verona (hence the sobriquet), he spent the last 30 years of his life in Venice, which likes to claim him as one of its own. His first jobs there were decoration in the Palazzo Ducale and the ceiling of the Libreria Nazionale Marciana across the square. He is, above all, remembered for the grandeur and sheer colourful spectacle of many of his frescoes and paintings. Initially influenced by the trend towards Mannerism, he was later increasingly attracted by certain aspects of architecture; he decorated Palladio's Villa Maser and was pushed towards a more serene harmony in the composition of scenes by the latter's interpretations of classical building.

He also liked to have all sorts of characters in his paintings, something that brought him uncomfortably close to the Holy Inquisition. His *Ultima Cena* (Last Supper), done for the Dominicans in the Chiesa dei SS Giovanni e Paolo, included some figures the Inquisitors found rather impious, including a dog and a jester. It is unlikely Veronese's defence of freedom of artistic expression won the day. The Inquisition was not viewed kindly by the leaders of La Serenissima and so it decided on the face-saving solution of proposing another title for the painting, *Convito in Casa di Levi* (Feast in the House of Levi). It can be seen today in the Gallerie dell'Accademia.

Among the masterpieces of his later years are *Virtù* (Virtue) and *Allegorie di Venezia* (Venetian Allegories), in the ceiling of the Sala del Collegio (Palazzo Ducale), and the *Trionfo di Venezia* (Venice's Triumph) in the Sala del Maggior Consiglio. They are riots of festive colour. Interestingly, in the last works of his life, he tended to tone down the colour, slipping back into softer hues more in line with Venetian tradition (itself surely influenced by the natural light prevailing in the lagoon city).

In his lifetime Veronese was assisted by his brother Benedetto and later his two sons, Gabriele and Carletto, who maintained the family business after his death.

Bringing up the Rear Other artists of this epoch worth bearing in mind include Palma il Vecchio (1480–1528), originally from Cremona, and his grandson Palma il Giovane (1544–1628). Various works have been attributed to the former, but the young one was more prolific. He finished Titian's final work, the *Pietà*.

Another busy family were the Da Pontes, also known as the Bassano because they were born in Bassano del Grappa (of liquor fame). Francesco Bassano il Vecchio worked in the first half of the 16th century. Four of his descendants stayed in the family trade: Jacopo (1517–92), Francesco Bassano il Giovane (c. 1549–92), Leandro (1557–1622) and Gerolamo (1566–1621). Of the lot, Jacopo stands out. Although fully a part of the Venetian school, he actually lived most of his life in Bassano. A handful of his works is on display at the Gallerie dell'Accademia.

A Sorry Century The 17th century brought the age of baroque in European art. It has been getting bad press from one quarter or another ever since. A celebration of curvaceous and gaudy over-embellishment, it is not so simple to judge whether works produced in this and the first half of the following century fall into the category of baroque or of rococo (see the following section).

Compared with earlier glory days, the directory of important artists in Venice at this time makes brief reading. Sebastiano Ricci (1659–1734), from Belluno, and his nephew Marco (1676–1730) were both successful, winning commissions from all over Europe. They travelled and worked extensively in England, where many of their paintings remain.

Last Flash of Glory The 18th century was marked by the steady decline of the once-proud Venetian Republic. In the sphere of the arts, a handful of greats kept the flag flying before the end finally came.

Rococo & the Tiepolos Gian Battista Piazzetta (1683–1754) paved the way into the new century – the Republic's last. This rococo painter had a particular eye for the manipulation of light and chiaroscuro effects. In his later career he dedicated more effort to the depiction of secular scenes and figures. In 1750 he founded the art school that would eventually become the Accademia di Venezia.

Venice's greatest artist of the century and one of the uncontested kings of rococo was Giambattista Tiepolo (1696–1770). He lived most of his life in the lagoon city and preferred to send his foreign commissions to their purchasers by coach than execute them *in situ*. Two exceptions were his stay in Würzburg, Germany, in the 1750s and his move to Madrid in 1762, where he remained until his death in spite of the stuffy nobility's ambivalent reaction to his work there, above all in Madrid's Palacio Nacional.

Tiepolo initially followed Piazzetta's lead and indulged in furious chiaroscuro games, relying on them to convey the passions of his subjects. He soon abandoned the method, preferring to infuse his work with vigorous colour. Among his early masterpieces are the cycle of biblical stories and the *Caduta degli Angeli Ribelli* (Fall of the Rebel Angels), painted in the Palazzo Arcivescovile (Archbishop's Palace) in Udine in 1726.

Commissions poured in, from Milan, Bergamo (he decorated the Cappella Colleoni there), Germany, Sweden and Russia. You can see some of his work in the Chiesa dei Scalzi, the Gesuati and Ca' Rezzonico. The Gallerie dell'Accademia has a fair smattering.

His son Giandomenico Tiepolo (1727–1804) worked with him to the end, returning to Venice after his father's death. Some caricatures of his now housed in the Ca' Rezzonico presage the Spaniard Goya and the Frenchman Daumier.

The Big Picture Antonio Canal, better known as Canaletto (1697–1768), became the leading figure of the so-called *vedutisti* (landscape artists), quite a different genre

NICKY CAVEN

Canaletto (1697–1768) painted some of the most famous scenes of Venice of all time.

from his rococo contemporaries. It is hardly surprising that he went down that road, given his background as a set painter for opera and theatre.

His almost painfully detailed *vedute* (views) of Venice, filled with light, were a kind of rich-man's postcard. Many of the well-to-do visitors to 18th-century Venice took home with them such a souvenir. Canaletto was backed by the English collector John Smith, who lived most of his life in Venice, bringing Canaletto a steady English clientele. This led to a 10-year stint in London, where Canaletto was also busy with the brush. His success with foreigners was such that few of his paintings can be seen in Venice today.

As Canaletto approached his twilight years and his output dwindled, Francesco Guardi (1712–93) stepped in to fill the gap in the market. He had earlier worked with his elder brother, the Vienna-born Giovanni Antonio Guardi (1699–1760), on religious and other paintings. As Francesco's success in the *veduta* field grew, the Republic increasingly turned to him to paint official records of important events, such as the visit of Pope Pius VI.

Although in his early landscapes his reliance on Canaletto's example is all too clear, he soon developed a dreamier, hazier style. Instead of a painstaking documentation of the city's many faces, which in any case was no longer in vogue either in Venice or abroad, Guardi opted for a more interpretative approach, his buildings almost shimmering in the reflected light of the lagoon. Popular with foreign art-buyers, Guardi's paintings are to be found scattered in galleries and private collections around the world. One of the few of his major works in Venice is the *Incendio di San Marcuola* (Fire at San Marcuola), in the Gallerie dell'Accademia.

Quite a different story is that of Rosalba Carriera (1675–1757), one of the few Venetian women to achieve success as a painter. As a portraitist she was much in demand not only in her home city but, thanks in part to the efforts of John Smith, across Europe.

19th & 20th Centuries Even before the fall of La Repubblica Serenissima in 1797, the art scene had decayed, much as everything else had. It may seem a little brutal, but the end of the 18th century essentially also meant the end of Venetian art.

A handful of dim lights flickered in the sombre artistic void. Ippolito Caffi (1809–66) was a landscape artist of talent, while Francesco Hayez (1791–1882) embarked on his career in Venice but ended up spending most of his working life in Milan. He began in a strict neoclassicist vein, but as the century wore on succumbed to the more sentimental feelings of the times and their artistic reflection, Romanticism.

Federico Zandomeneghi (1841–1917) received his formal education at the Accademia di Venezia, but he didn't exactly set the art world on fire. In any case he ended up in Paris, where socialising with Impressionists did little to alter substantially the realist nature of his work, such as it is.

Gino Rossi (1884–1947), whose career took him from Symbolism to a growing interest in Cubism, was one of Venice's biggest names in the first half of the 20th century. He frequently exhibited at the city's pre-WWI art expos in the Ca' Pesaro.

One of the few noteworthy names to emerge since WWII is Emilio Vedova (born 1919). Setting out as an Expressionist, he joined the Corrente movement of artists, who opposed the trends in square-jawed fascist art. Their magazine was shut down in 1940. In postwar years Vedova veered more towards the abstract. Some of his works can be seen in Rome's Galleria Nazionale d'Arte Moderna.

Among young artists hard at work today is Udine-born Mauro Eraldo, whose work has had some success in Italy and abroad (mainly the USA). Mestre-based Tiziana Piccioni has a highly personal style, proudly declaring she has stayed clear of all art schools. Rossella Girardini also lives on the mainland, in Marghera. A lot of her work has Venice as its subject. She has followed the Croatian naive school – inspired by painters like Zacero and Generalic.

Sculpture

Sculpture and its creators did not achieve such prominence in Venice as in other Italian cities. There may be several reasons for this, but it is not to say sculptors were not active here. It's just that their work, usually in the form of adornment of the city's great houses and public buildings, has remained mostly anonymous.

Romanesque to Renaissance While the mosaic was the dominant Byzantine element in decoration from the 11th to the 13th centuries, sculptors were not idle. The interior of the Basilica di San Marco was fully laden with sculpture and the main entrance represents one of the finest of the few displays of Romanesque sculpture in the city.

Some of the best Gothic sculpture in Venice is the tombs of the doges Michele Morosini and Marco Corner in the Chiesa dei SS Giovanni e Paolo. The latter was done by a Pisan, Nino Pisano (c. 1300–68).

As the Renaissance blossomed in Venice, sculpture remained something of a poor cousin next to the outpourings on walls, ceilings and canvas. Again, the funerary statues of doges are among the most important single pieces. The Lombard Pietro Lombardo (1435–1515) spent most of his working life in Venice. Among his more notable efforts are the monuments to three of Venice's leaders: Pasquale Malipiero, Nicolò Marcello and Pietro Mocenigo, all in the Chiesa dei SS Giovanni e Paolo. Pietro's sons Antonio and Tullio carried on the family business. Antonio tended to follow in papa's footsteps, but Tullio was a little more independent. His more interesting sculptures are no longer in Venice.

To the Present Day A handful of notable sculptors were at work in the 17th century, including Orazio Marinali (1643–1720) and Andrea Brustolon (1660–1732), the latter in particular known for his wood and furniture carving.

Closing the 18th century was Antonio Canova (1757–1822), the most prominent sculptor to emerge in late-18th-century Italy. He was born in Possagno, near Treviso, and debuted in Venice, but by 1780 he had shifted to Rome, where he ended up doing most of his work. A few of his early forays, such as *Dedalo e Icaro* (Dedalus and Icarus), remain in Venice, in the Museo Correr. If you really want to get an idea of his work, head for Possagno itself (see the Excursions chapter).

Literature

The Early Days As already hinted, Venice's literary heritage is not among the most brilliant in Italy. Relatively few Venetians have received more than passing recognition in the pantheon of national greats.

One of the first writers to cast an eye over the affairs of the Venetians was Cassiodorus (AD 490–583). In the employ of Theodoric, he was for a while active at the highest levels of the imperial administration and based in Ravenna. It is from him that our earliest descriptions of the lagoon city come – to him the Venetians' houses seemed 'like seabirds' nests, half on sea and half on land'.

Middle Ages to the Renaissance In the Middle Ages, education was limited largely to private classes, among them philosophy sessions given in Rialto and financed by wealthy families.

Francesco Petrarca (Petrarch; 1304–74), one of the 'big three' behind the birth of literary Italian in Florence, came to live in Venice in the latter part of his life. He had already gained considerable fame for his sonnets in Italian, although he continued to write much in Latin as well. He encouraged instruction in Latin, but his humanistic ideals and belief in the need to spread and deepen education were not universally welcome in a still comparatively austere city. Only in the century following his death, as the city grew richer, did the noble classes begin to take a closer interest in learning.

One of the earliest Venetian writers of any importance was Leonardo Giustinian (1388–1446). A member of the Consiglio dei Dieci and author of various tracts in Latin, he is remembered for his *Canzonette* and *Strambotti*. They are a mix of popular verses wrought in an elegant Venetian-influenced Italian. Although he used Italian, Giustinian resisted the Tuscan hegemony established a generation before by the likes of Dante, Petrarch and Boccaccio.

By the time he died, humanist education had caught on. Professors of Greek were being invited to Venice to instruct students, more and more of whom were now able to study the seminal Greek philosophers in the original. This growing interest in what might be called a 'liberal education' encouraged another hobby among the well read – history.

Of the several figures who embarked on this kind of project, Marin Sanudo (1466–1536) left behind probably the most detailed account of early Renaissance Venice in his 58-volume *Diarii* (Diaries), written in Venetian dialect. Sanudo was not, to his lasting disappointment, appointed official historian of the Republic.

Era of the Printing Press That role fell to Pietro Bembo (1470–1547). His *Historia Veneta*, written in Latin and translated into Italian, was not, however, his most lasting work. In his *Rime* (Rhymes) and other works he defined the concept of platonic love and, above all, gave lasting form to Italian grammar.

Bembo also worked with Aldo Manuzio on a project that would help revolutionise the spread of learning and literature. Manuzio had arrived in Venice, where he would remain, in 1490 and set up his Aldine Press. During the following years he and his family became the most important publishing dynasty in all Europe. He produced the first printed editions of many Latin and Greek classics, along with a series of relatively cheap volumes of literature, including Bembo's *Cose Volgari* (Ordinary Things). In all, the Manuzio family are thought to have printed 1000 editions.

Domenico Venier (1517–82), virtually paralysed by illness and confined to his home, is viewed by many as a faithful follower of Bembo, although his poetic style was quite a deal more experimental. Although barely known now, he was considered one of the best poets of his time. The southern Italian Torquato Tasso, one of the great names of Italian poetry, humbly submitted his works to Venier for his appraisal before publishing.

In Paolo Sarpi (1552–1623) Venice found a powerful defender of the Republic and its only philosopher of note. A Servite friar, he had a distinguished career as a diplomat and theologian, travelling extensively throughout Italy before returning to Venice in 1588. He was one of the earliest proponents of the separation of Church and State, something that only came to pass in Italy in 1985. In 1606 he became the voice of Venice after Pope Paul V placed the city under an interdict (see the earlier History section) and Sarpi launched a campaign calling for numerous reforms of the Church. His ideas found their ultimate expression in the *Istoria del Concilio Tridentino* (History of the Council of Trent), considered a masterpiece of clear, unadorned Italian prose and translated into Latin, English, German and French in his lifetime.

A Ray of Gold Venice cannot be said to have enjoyed a golden age of literature, but a flash of glory came with the playwright Carlo Goldoni (1707–93). His stormy life saw him moving around from one city to another, at times practising law but dedicating most of his energies to theatre. From 1748 in particular, the prolific playwright produced dramas and comedies at an extraordinary rate.

He single-handedly changed the face of Italian theatre, abandoning the Commedia dell'Arte, with its use of masks, a certain rigidity in story-telling and concentration on standard characters. This form of theatre had dominated the stages and public squares of Italy, and to a large extent France, for the previous couple of centuries, but Goldoni would have none of it. Instead, he advocated more realistic characters and more complex plots. *Pamela* (1750) was the first play to dispense with masks altogether.

Some of his most enduring works came during the 1750s and 60s. Among the best known are *La Locandiera* (The Housekeeper), *I Rusteghi* (The Tyrants, written in Venetian dialect) and *I Malcontenti* (The Malcontent). Not everyone agreed with his ideas on theatre and, feeling the heat from some of his adversaries in Venice, he decided to shift to Paris in 1762. It was not an entirely happy move. With the exception of *Il Ventaglio* (The Fan), little of great note came out of his Paris years, which were mostly spent on writing memoirs. Overtaken by the French Revolution, he lost his pension and died in penury.

Goldoni by far overshadowed the competition. Giorgio Baffo (1694–1768) is known above all for his rather risqué dialect verse (he was a pal of Casanova and particularly enamoured of the female behind), while Francesco Gritti (1740–1811) satirised the decadent Venetian aristocracy. The bulk of the latter's work is brought together in *Poesie in Dialetto Veneziano* (Poetry in the Venetian Dialect).

From the 19th Century to Today A pale successor to Goldoni on the boards was Giacinto Gallina (1852–97), who wrote mostly in dialect. One of his last works, *La Famegia del Santolo*, was considered a masterpiece of realist theatre.

In 1963 a Venetian business association inaugurated the Campiello prize (won that year by Turin's Primo Levi for his *La Tregua*), which has become one of the country's most prestigious literary awards.

Among the city's several scribblers at work today, Paolo Barbaro (a self-confessed Venetian by adoption) has taken the Campiello prize three times. His books tend to have Venice as their theme or character and make interesting reading. In *Venezia – La Città Ritrovata* (Venice – the City Rediscovered) he struggles to come to terms with the wintry lagoon city again after several years' absence.

Music

A handful of Italy's great musicians hailed from Venice, which was also the first European city to throw opera open to a wide public by opening opera houses in the first half of the 17th century.

Renaissance, Baroque & Classical Born
in Cannaregio, Andrea Gabrieli (born 1510) was a student of the great Flemish composer Adriaan Willaert at the Basilica di San Marco. To Willaert is attributed by some the invention of the madrigal. On his return to Venice in 1564 after considerable travel abroad, Gabrieli became an organist at the basilica and dedicated himself to writing both gracious madrigals and large-scale choral and instrumental works for affairs of Church and State. The work for which he is principally remembered is his *Magnificat* for three choirs and orchestra.

Andrea's nephew Giovanni (1556–1612) joined him as an organist in 1584 and specialised in the composition of liturgical music, some of it choral and some instrumental. The bulk of his work was published in two books known as the *Sacrae Symphoniae*.

The greatest musical name to come out of Venice was Antonio Vivaldi (1678–1741). A gifted violinist from an early age, he completed his first important compositions in 1711. By the time he died, he had left a vast repertory behind him. Some 500 concertos have come down to us today. He was not simply prolific, but innovative, perfecting the three-movement concerto form and introducing other novelties that allowed

greater room for virtuoso displays. Surely his best-known concerto is *Le Quattro Stagioni* (The Four Seasons). Although instrumental works were his forte, he also wrote operas and, in his earlier days, sacred vocal music. For all the fame he enjoys today, Vivaldi struggled to make a decent living. Much of his music might have been lost to us if collections had not been maintained in Turin and Dresden (Germany).

A near contemporary much overshadowed by the genius of Vivaldi was Tomaso Albinoni (1671–1750). Albinoni was something of a dilettante who nevertheless produced a small body of exquisite music. Notable is the *Sinfonie e Concerti a 5*.

Marcello Benedetto (1686–1739) was a comparatively minor figure in the world of Venetian music. A member of the Quarantia and at one time governor of Pola in Istria (Croatia), he dabbled in music as a sideline. His only significant work was *Estro Poeticoarmonico*, a vocal and instrumental interpretation of the first 50 psalms.

Opera The combination of music and drama is as old as classical Greek theatre, but opera in the sense we understand it today was born in Italy in the latter half of the 16th century. Giulio Caccini (1550–1618) and Jacopo Peri (1561–1633) were among the first composers to try out and develop this form of entertainment in Florence. These composers, together with other intellectuals, frequented salons in Florence to discuss and perform their work. An occasional visitor was Claudio Monteverdi (1567–1643). Born in Cremona, he cut his teeth as a composer at the court of the Gonzaga family in Mantova. His opera *Orfeo* (Orpheus; 1607) has been commonly acclaimed as the first great opera ever presented. Monteverdi's relationship with the Gonzagas was not a happy one, so it is hardly surprising that he snapped up Venice's offer to make him music director at the Basilica di San Marco in 1613.

Here he sank himself into work on Church music, not only for the basilica, but elsewhere in the city. There was little interest in opera in Venice at this point, so he

Star of the Big Screen

Back in the 1980s a film archive in Venice found that the city had appeared, in one form or another, in 380,000 films (feature films, shorts, documentaries and so on). However, the city has starred in its own right in surprisingly few great flicks, tending rather to take bit parts.

From the early 1920s, Venetians Othello and Casanova got their fare share of runs on the silver screen. A good one was the 1927 *Casanova* by Alexandre Volkoff, with scenes actually shot in the city.

As the German film industry collapsed in the wake of Hitler's rise to power, mostly shifting to Hollywood, Venice began to get a bit of a run there too. Ernst Lubitsch's *Trouble in Paradise* (1932) probably has a lot more to answer for than the director could have imagined. In his studio re-creation of the lagoon city, he has a gondolier (dubbed with the voice of Enrico Caruso) singing that great Neapolitan song *O Sole Mio*. So that's where that modern tourist request came from!

Another Hollywood Venice was constructed for *Top Hat* (1935), one of the all-time great musicals starring Fred Astaire and Ginger Rogers.

Orson Welles had a go at *Othello* in 1952, a film he shot partly in Venice but mostly in Morocco and in which he plays the main man. The antithesis of this was standard Hollywood schmaltz, of which *Three Coins in the Fountain* (1954), directed by Jean Negulesco, is a fairly telling example. A year later, Katherine Hepburn fronted a somewhat more substantial production, David Lean's *Summertime*.

---

intermittently returned to Mantova to stage new operas, developing his musical theories. In opera, Monteverdi increasingly sought to portray real characters and reflect human emotion in the music he composed. As he grew older, his work acquired a poise and majesty missing in his more passionate earlier works.

Until 1637, opera and most chamber music had been the preserve of the noble classes, performed in private session for a privileged audience. This now changed in Venice. The city Monteverdi had adopted, and where he would die six years later, threw open the doors of the first public opera houses. As the only composer with any real experience in the genre, the elderly Monteverdi set himself to the task of producing material for the new houses. Perhaps his two greatest surviving works emerged at this time: *Il Ritorno di Ulisse al suo Paese* (The Return of Ulysses to his Country) and *L'Incoronazione di Poppea* (The Coronation of Poppea). Some have labelled these the first two works of modern opera. In each, Monteverdi created an astonishing range of plot and subplot, with strong characterisation and powerful music. Although he was not Venetian, the city liked to consider him one of its own – he was buried with honours in the Frari.

A singer at San Marco under Monteverdi's direction, Pier Francesco Cavalli (1602–76) went on to become the outstanding Italian composer of opera of the 17th century. He wrote 42 operas, which in his day were acclaimed as much for the splendour of the costumes and sets used as for the brilliance of his music and librettos.

Baldassare Galuppi (1706–84) opted for the light touch and in so doing gave birth to a new genre, the *opera buffa* – comic opera. Although he composed more serious material and instrumental works, it was for pieces like *Il Filosofo di Campagna* (The Country Philosopher) that he achieved widespread popularity.

Venice also likes to lay some claim to Domenico Cimarosa (1749–1801), despite the fact that he spent most of his life in Naples and travelled widely. Cimarosa continued the Italian tradition of opera buffa,

Star of the Big Screen

In 1961 Steve McQueen and a band of US sailors plan to rob the casino in *The Honeymoon Machine*. It's a fairly silly film but some of the shots of Venice are good. In 1968 the American director Mel Stuart took a gentle dig at tourists with *If It's Tuesday This Must Be Belgium*, in which Venice takes its rightful place on the list of destinations being ticked off.

Among the best known of films set in Venice is, perhaps, *Morte a Venezia* (Death in Venice), Luchino Visconti's 1971 rendition of the Thomas Mann novel, with a suitably ashen-looking Dirk Bogarde in the main role of Aschenbach. Perhaps less well known but a better film was Federico Fellini's *Casanova* (1977), starring Donald Sutherland. In this version of the life of the self-confessed lover and adventurer we are given a subtler look at the unhappy soul of a man seemingly almost condemned to his role.

Donald Sutherland was no stranger to Venice when he played Casanova. In 1973 he starred with Julie Christie in Nicolas Roeg's *Don't Look Now*. Based on a Daphne du Maurier novel, it shows Venice at its crumbling, melancholy best (or worst, depending on your point of view).

More recently, Venice has made appearances in *Indiana Jones and the Last Crusade* (1989) and Woody Allen's *Everyone Says I Love You* (1997), while films set in the city include the screen version of Ian McEwan's novel *The Comfort of Strangers* (1990), Oliver Parker's 1995 *Othello* and Henry James' story of love and betrayal *Wings of the Dove* (1997). *Dangerous Beauty* (1998) centres on the life of a courtesan in 16th-century Venice. 1999 saw the release of *The Venice Project*, starring Lauren Bacall and Dennis Hopper.

---

producing his masterpiece, *Il Matrimonio Segreto* (The Secret Marriage), in Vienna in 1792. He did some work in Venice, too, but the city's main boast on this score is that he died there (in a building on Campo Sant'Angelo, in the Sestiere di San Marco – you can read the plaque there).

SOCIETY & CONDUCT
Dos & Don'ts

In Venice, as elsewhere in Italy, the locals take a good deal more care about their dress and appearance than many outsiders consider absolutely necessary. In some cases, however, those outsiders seem to abandon any norms they might usually adhere to at home as soon as they hit the holiday trail. Leaving aside the sartorial spectacle of the loud-shirts-and-shorts brigade, there are those who seem to think walking around with precious little on is the only way to fly. In the streets, locals will hardly bat an eyelid (*ah, questi turisti* – ah, these tourists – you may hear them sigh), but you should try to pick up your act a little in restaurants or when going out.

Most churches (including the Basilica di San Marco) will not allow you entry if it is deemed you are inadequately clothed. No-one's suggesting you bring your Sunday best along, but a little common sense and sensitivity go a long way.

The standard form of greeting is the handshake. Kissing on both cheeks is generally reserved for people who already know one another. There will always be exceptions to these rules, so the best thing on being introduced to locals is probably not to launch your lips in anyone's general direction unless you are pretty sure they are expected. If this is the case, a light brushing of cheeks will do.

RELIGION

As elsewhere in Italy, Roman Catholicism is the dominant religion, but Venice and its people have traditionally viewed the Church with some disinterest. Venice clashed with the Vatican on several occasions during the life of the Republic, brushing aside Papal bans and interdicts with supreme indifference.

For a long time, La Serenissima was also a rare haven of religious tolerance. Although its Jews were squashed into what was known as the Ghetto (for more on this see the Things to See & Do chapter), they had a reasonable degree of autonomy in business and were free to practise their faith. After the fall of Constantinople, a wave of Greek Orthodox refugees arrived in Venice and were also accommodated (their parish church was San Giorgio dei Greci, in Castello). The Armenians, too, were made welcome here.

Only when the 1929 Lateran Treaty between the Vatican and the Italian state was modified in 1985 was Catholicism dropped as the state religion. Still, as many as 85% of Italians profess to be Catholic, and roughly the same figure can probably be applied to Venice.

LANGUAGE

There are 58 million speakers of Italian in Italy; half a million in Switzerland, where Italian is one of the official languages; and 1.5 million speakers in France, Slovenia and Croatia. As a result of migration, Italian is also spoken in the USA, Argentina, Brazil and Australia. In addition, Venice has its own dialect – Venessian (see the boxed text in the Language chapter).

Although many Italians speak some English because they study it in school, any effort to speak Italian is generally appreciated. Staff at most hotels, *pensioni* and restaurants in Venice usually speak a little English.

For more information on Italian, a list of useful words and phrases and a food glossary, see the Language chapter at the back of this book.

A fiery performance in Piazza San Marco ...

St Mark's lion on the Comune di Venezia flag

A Venetian bridge proves to be an inspiring spot.

... the most photographed square in the world.

You'll see more than gondolas on Venice's canals.

No, it's not washing day – it's art!

JM BRETTELL

The Grand Canal epitomises the timeless elegance of Venice.

OLIVIER CIRENDINI

Not quite lighting-up time yet

BETHUNE CARMICHAEL

View under the Bridge of Sighs to San Giorgio

Facts for the Visitor

WHEN TO GO

Venice, like any other of the great tourist centres in Italy, is at its worst in high summer. The whole world seems to think this a good time to be crawling around here, but it is cramped, hot and sticky. Mosquitoes can be a problem, too. Venetians mostly head for the hills at this time (which from Venice means quite a deal of running) and everything seems even more expensive than usual.

Other peak periods include Christmas, Easter, Carnevale time (around the end of February) and during the Mostra del Cinema (late August–September). Despite the difficulties of finding lodging and the usual problems associated with saturation tourism, the splendour of Carnevale (see Public Holidays & Special Events later in this chapter) warrants an effort.

The most pleasant time of year in Venice is from late March into May. The clear spring days are delightful and the hordes have yet to reach tsunami proportions (maybe Venice is sinking because of the combined weight of all its visitors), although May weekends tend to be busy with Italian tourists. Next choice is in the wake of summer. September is the best bet in terms of weather, but October is quieter.

Winter can be unpleasantly cold and this is when flooding is at its most regular (November and December are particularly bad, as rainfall is often heavy). That said, if you get lucky with the weather it can be an enchanting time to be here. When the sky is clear, that pale winter blue helps bring out the softest tones and colour in the city's buildings. And it doesn't happen often, but seeing Venice under snow is the stuff of fairy tales! Mid-January to early March is the window of opportunity. Most Europeans are exhausted and broke after Christmas-New Year silliness and unwilling to use up holiday time in a wintry city. Consequently, hotel and restaurant proprietors are on their best price behaviour and some extraordinary deals on air fares can be had.

ORIENTATION

What one might think of as the Greater Venice Area is an odd beast. As you approach from other points in Italy, you reach Mestre, the rather humdrum industrial town that spreads inland from Venice's protective lagoon, the Laguna Veneta. Its southern half is occupied by Porto Marghera, where all the heavy shipping docks are. Increasingly the 'life' of the city is here. The SS11 highway and the train line pass through Mestre and cross a 5km bridge, Ponte della Libertà (Liberty Bridge), south-east to Venice proper, which is known to the locals as the *centro storico* (historic centre).

Venice is built on 117 small islands and has some 150 canals and 409 bridges. Only three bridges cross the Grand Canal (Canal Grande): the Ponte di Rialto, the Ponte dell'Accademia and the Ponte degli Scalzi.

Stretching away to the north and south are the shallow waters of the Laguna Veneta, dotted by what seems a crumbling mosaic of islands, islets and rocks. Among them, Murano, Burano and Torcello are all of interest and lie to the north. Acting as a breakwater to the east, the long and slender Lido di Venezia stretches some 10km south, followed by another similarly narrow island, Pellestrina, which stretches down to the sleepy town of Chioggia. The latter marks where the mainland closes off the lagoon to the south.

The city is divided into six quarters (*sestieri*): Cannaregio, Castello, San Marco, Dorsoduro, San Polo and Santa Croce. These town divisions date back to 1171. In the east, the islands of San Pietro and Sant'Elena, largely ignored by visitors, are attached to Castello by two and three bridges respectively.

Main Transport Terminals

Marco Polo airport lies just east of Mestre, about 12km by road from Venice. Some flights land at a small airport just outside Treviso, about 50km north of Venice.

The Stazione di Santa Lucia train station is located in the north-west of town, virtually at the end of the Ponte della Libertà. The mainland Mestre station is a 10-minute ride west.

The bus station is on the opposite (south) side of the Grand Canal in Piazzale Roma. All local, regional and international buses leave from here. This is also one of the places where you have to leave your vehicle (the other is Tronchetto, just to the west) if you drive in.

You can get around the city by *vaporetto* (ferry) and *traghetto* (commuter gondola) or on foot. You'll find yourself doing a lot of the latter. For transport information see the Getting Around chapter.

A Street by Any Other Name

If you have travelled elsewhere in Italy and got to grips with common street terminology, abandon all hope ye who enter here. Why? Well, Venice always thought of itself as something quite apart from the rest of the peninsula and seemingly this applied even to street naming. The names for the types of street in use today go back to the 11th century.

Of course, the waterways are not streets at all. The main ones are called *canale*, while the bulk of them are called *rio*. Where a rio has been filled in it becomes a *rio terrà* or *rio terà*.

What anywhere else in Italy would be called a *via* (street) is, in Venice, a *calle*. A street beside a canal is called a *fondamenta*. A *ruga* or *rughetta* is a smaller street flanked by houses and shops, while those called *salizzada* (sometimes spelled with one 'z') were among the first streets to be paved. A *ramo* is a tiny side lane, often connecting two bigger streets. A *corte* is a small dead-end street or courtyard. A quay is a *riva* and where a street passes under a building (something like an extended archway) it is called a *sotoportego*. A *piscina* is not a swimming pool, but a one-time little lake of motionless water later filled in.

The only square in Venice called a *piazza* is San Marco – all the others are called *campo* (except for the bus station area, called Piazzale Roma). The small version is a *campiello*. Occasionally you come across a *campazzo*. On maps you may see the following abbreviations:

Calle – C, Cl
Campo – Cpo
Corte – Cte
Fondamenta – Fond, Fondam, F
Palazzo – Pal
Salizzada – Sal, Salizz

Street Numbering

Confused? You will be. Venice also has its own style of street numbering. Instead of a system based on individual streets, each sestiere has a long series of numbers. For instance, a hotel might give its address as San Marco 4687, which doesn't seem to help much. This system of numbering was actually introduced by the Austrians in 1841.

Because the sestieri are fairly small, wandering around and searching out the number is technically feasible and sometimes doesn't take that long. But there is precious little apparent logic to the run of numbers, so frustration is never far away. Most streets are named, so where possible we provide street names as well as the sestiere number throughout the guide. Even where this is not the case, using the maps at the back of this book in conjunction with the sestiere numbers should clear up any mysteries. See Maps on the next page for other suggestions on navigational aids.

To walk from the train station to Piazza San Marco along the main thoroughfare (the first part is called the Lista di Spagna) will take a good 30 minutes – follow the signs to San Marco. From San Marco, the routes to other main areas, such as the Rialto, Accademia and the train station, are signposted but can be confusing, particularly in the Dorsoduro and San Polo areas. The most entertaining signs are those pointing to the left and the right.

MAPS

You should be able to get by with the maps in the back of this book, but some of those on sale are also worthwhile investments. The free one handed out by the tourist office is next to useless.

Whichever map you buy, you will find inconsistencies. The *Venezianizzazione* (Venetianisation) of street names has created more problems than it could ever have solved. Pretty much all maps seem to take a haphazard approach to using Italian, Venetian or mongrel versions. Usually it's no great hassle to work out – but you need to use a little lateral thinking at times. We have tried to follow common usage, but you may notice differences between spellings on the maps in this book and on the ground or on other maps. Where such discrepancies (most of them minor) occur, it is usually easy to work out what's what.

One of the best maps is *Venezia*, produced by the Touring Club Italiano. It costs L10,000 and displays the city on a scale of 1:5000, but is not always available in local shops. Better still, but even rarer, is the TCI's ring-bound version of the same map, at a scale of 1:4500 (L15,000). Another reasonable one is the yellow FMB map, also simply entitled *Venezia* (L8000), which lists all street names with map references.

If you plan to stay for the long haul, *Calli, Campielli e Canali* (Edizioni Helvetica) is for you. This is the definitive street guide and will allow you to locate to within 100m any Venetian-style address you need – saves a *lot* of shoe leather. Posties must do a course in it before being sent out to deliver the mail!

TOURIST OFFICES
Local Tourist Offices

Azienda di Promozione Turistica (APT) offices have information on the town and the province. There is one central information line to call in Venice (☎ 041 529 87 11). The main APT office (Map 6) is at Piazza San Marco 71/f. The young staff will assist with information on hotels, transport and things to see and do in the city. The office is open daily from 9.40 am to 5.20 pm. Hours tend to change regularly, so if in doubt call ahead.

The smaller office at the train station (Map 3) is open daily from 8 am to 7 pm in summer, but again the times aren't guaranteed. There are also offices on the Lido (Map 14), at Gran Viale Santa Maria Elisabetta 6/a, and at the airport. In Mestre, there's an office (Map 15; ☎ 041 97 53 57) at Corso del Popolo 65.

In summer (ie from Easter until at least the end of September) information booths *(punti informativi)* are set up at Campo San Rocco (Map 5), Campo San Felice (Map 4), Campo Santo Stefano (Map 5), Campo SS Giovani e Paolo (Map 4) and Riva Ca' di Dio (Map 7). They open from 10 am to 5 pm (give or take).

The useful monthly booklet *Un Ospite di Venezia* (A Guest in Venice), published by a group of Venetian hoteliers, is sometimes available from tourist offices. If not, you can find it in most of the larger hotels. Similar, but a little less informative, is *Pocket Venice*, sometimes available from tourist offices.

Tourist Helpline The APT has set up a toll-free 24-hour tourist helpline in case you have a complaint to make about services poorly rendered (from hotels, restaurants, water taxis and the like). Call ☎ 800 355920 and follow the instructions.

Youth Information InformaGiovani can provide information ranging from assistance for the disabled to courses offered in the city. They have branch offices in the Assessorato alla Gioventù (see Rolling Venice Concession Pass in the Documents section later in this chapter) and in Mestre.

Tourist Offices Abroad

Information on Venice is available from the following branches of the Italian State Tourist Office (ENIT) abroad:

Australia
(☎ 02-9262 1666, fax 9262 5745)
c/o Italian Chamber of Commerce, Level 26, 44 Market St, Sydney, NSW 2000
Austria
(☎ 01-505 16 39)
Kärntnerring 4, 1010 Vienna
Canada
(☎ 514-866 7669)
Suite 1914, 1 Place Ville Marie, Montreal, Quebec H3B 2C3
France
(☎ 01 42 66 66 68)
23 rue de la Paix, 75002 Paris
Germany
(☎ 030-247 83 97)
Karl Liebknecht Strasse 34, 10178 Berlin
(☎ 069-25 93 32)
Kaiserstrasse 65, 60329 Frankfurt am Main
(☎ 089-53 13 17)
Goethestrasse 20, 80336 Munich
Netherlands
(☎ 020-616 82 44)
Stadhouderskade 2, 1054 ES Amsterdam
Switzerland
(☎ 01-211 79 17)
Uraniastrasse 32, 8001 Zürich
UK
(☎ 020-7408 1254, 0891 600280)
1 Princes St, London W1R 8AY
USA
(☎ 312-644 0996)
500 North Michigan Ave, Chicago, IL 60611
(☎ 310-820 2977)
Suite 550, 12400 Wilshire Blvd, Los Angeles, CA 90025
(☎ 212-245 4822)
Suite 1565, 630 Fifth Ave, New York, NY 10111

Sestante-CIT (Compagnia Italiana di Turismo), Italy's national travel agency, also has offices throughout the world (known as CIT or Citalia outside Italy). Staff can provide extensive information on travelling in Italy and will organise tours, as well as book individual hotels. CIT can also make train bookings. Offices include:

Australia
(☎ 03-9650 5510)
Level 4, 227 Collins St, Melbourne, Vic 3000

(☎ 02-9267 1255)
263 Clarence St, Sydney, NSW 2000
Canada
(☎ 514-845 4310, 800 361 7799)
Suite 750, 1450 City Councillors St, Montreal, Que H3A 2E6
(☎ 905-415 1060, 800 387 0711)
Suite 401, 80 Tiverton Court, Markham, Toronto, Ont L3R 0G4
France
(☎ 01 44 51 39 00)
5 blvd des Capucines, Paris 75002
Germany
(☎ 0211-69 00 30)
Geibelstrasse 39, 40235 Düsseldorf
UK
(☎ 020-8686 0677, 8686 5533)
Marco Polo House, 3–5 Lansdowne Rd, Croydon CR9 1LL
USA
(☎ 310-338 8615)
Suite 980, 6033 West Century Blvd, Los Angeles, CA 90045
(☎ 212-730 2121)
10th floor, 15 West 44th St, New York, NY10036

Branches of the Istituto Italiano di Cultura (IIC; Italian Cultural Institute) in major cities throughout the world have extensive information on study opportunities in Italy.

DOCUMENTS
Visas

Italy is one of 15 countries that have signed the Schengen Convention, an agreement whereby all European Union (EU) member countries (except the UK and Ireland) plus Iceland and Norway have agreed to abolish checks at common borders by the end of 2000. The other EU countries are Austria, Belgium, Denmark, Finland, France, Germany, Greece, Luxembourg, the Netherlands, Portugal, Spain and Sweden.

Legal residents of one Schengen country do not require a visa for another Schengen country. Citizens of the UK and Ireland are also exempt from visa requirements for Schengen countries.

In addition, nationals of a number of other countries, including Canada, Japan, New Zealand and Switzerland, do not require visas for tourist visits of up to 90 days to any Schengen country.

Various other nationals not covered by the Schengen exemption can also spend up to 90 days in Italy without a visa. These include Australian, Israeli and US citizens. However, all non-EU nationals entering Italy for any reason other than tourism (such as study or work) should contact an Italian consulate, as they may need a specific visa. They should also insist on having their passport stamped on entry as, without a stamp, they could encounter problems when trying to obtain a *permesso di soggiorno* (residence permit). If you are a citizen of a country not mentioned in this section, you should check with an Italian consulate whether you need a visa.

The standard tourist visa issued by Italian consulates is the Schengen visa, valid for up to 90 days. A Schengen visa issued by one Schengen country is generally valid for travel in all other Schengen countries. However, individual Schengen countries may impose additional restrictions on certain nationalities. It is, therefore, worth checking visa regulations with the consulate of each Schengen country you plan to visit.

Rules for obtaining Schengen visas have been tightened and it's now mandatory that you apply in your country of residence. You can apply for no more than two Schengen visas in any 12-month period and they are not renewable inside Italy. If you are going to visit more than one Schengen country, you are supposed to apply for the visa at a consulate of your main destination country or, if you have no main destination, the first country you intend to visit. It's worth applying early for your visa, especially in the busy summer months.

For information on visas required for working in Italy, see Work later in this chapter. For information on study visas, see Courses in the Things to See & Do chapter.

Travel Insurance
Medical costs might already be covered through reciprocal health-care agreements (see Health later in this chapter), but you'll still need cover for theft or loss and for unexpected changes in travel plans (such as ticket cancellation). You may also prefer a policy that pays doctors or hospitals directly rather than you having to pay on the spot and claim later. If you have to claim for anything later, make sure you keep all documentation. Some policies ask you to make a reverse-charge call to a centre in your home country where an immediate assessment of your problem is made.

Check that the policy covers ambulances or an emergency flight home.

Driving Licence & Permits
The pink-and-green driving licences issued in all EU member states (not the old-style UK green licence) are recognised throughout Europe, regardless of the length of your stay. Those with a non-EU licence are supposed to obtain an International Driving Permit (IDP) to accompany their national licence. These are available from national automobile associations.

For information on paperwork and insurance, see Car & Motorcycle in the Getting There & Away chapter.

Hostel Card
A valid Hostelling International (HI) card is required in all youth hostels run by the Associazione Italiana Alberghi per la Gioventù (AIG) in Italy. You can get this in your home country by joining your national Youth Hostel Association (YHA) or at youth hostels in Italy. In the latter case, you must collect six stamps in the card at L5000 each. You pay for a stamp on each of the first six nights you spend in a hostel, on top of the hostel fee. With six stamps you are considered a full international member. Membership also entitles the holder to various discounts and benefits in Italy, including reduced-price train travel, car hire with Hertz and entry to various attractions around the country. HI is on the Web at www.iyhf.org.

Student, Teacher & Youth Cards
The International Student Identity Card (ISIC), for full-time students, and the International Teacher Identity Card (ITIC), for full-time teachers and professors, are issued by more than 5000 organisations around the

world. The cards entitle you to a range of discounts, from reduced museum entry charges to cheap air fares. You also get use of an international helpline. Student travel organisations such as STA (Australia, the UK and the USA), Council Travel (the USA) and Travel CUTS/Voyages Campus (Canada) issue these cards. See under Air in the Getting There & Away chapter for some addresses, phone numbers and Web sites.

Anyone aged under 26 can get a Euro<26 card. This gives similar discounts to the ISIC and is issued by most of the same organisations. The Euro<26 has a variety of names, including the Under 26 Card in England and Wales and the CartaGiovani in Italy.

The Centro Turistico Studentesco e Giovanile (CTS; see Travel Agencies in the Getting There & Away chapter) can issue ISIC, ITIC and Euro<26 cards. You have to join the CTS first, however, which costs L45,000.

Seniors' Cards
If you are aged over 60 or 65 (depending on what you are seeking a discount for) you can get many discounts simply by presenting your passport or ID card as proof of age.

Rolling Venice Concession Pass
If you are aged between 14 and 29, take your passport and a colour photograph to the Assessorato alla Gioventù (Map 6; ☎ 041 274 76 37), Corte Contarina 1529, and pick up the Rolling Venice card. It costs L5000 and offers significant discounts on food, accommodation, entertainment, public transport, museums and galleries. The office is open from 9.30 am to 1 pm Monday to Friday and from 3 to 5 pm on Tuesday and Thursday. You can also pick up the pass at AIG (Map 5; ☎ 041 520 44 14), Calle del Castelforte 3101, San Polo, and Agenzia Arte e Storia (Map 3; ☎ 041 524 02 32), Corte Canal 659, Santa Croce. It is also available from tourist offices from July to September.

Copies
All important documents (passport data page and visa page, credit cards, travel insurance policy, air/bus/train tickets, driving licence etc) should be photocopied before

you leave home. Leave one copy with someone at home and keep another with you, separate from the originals.

There is another option for storing details of your vital travel documents before you leave – Lonely Planet's online Travel Vault. Storing details of your important documents in the vault is safer than carrying photocopies. It's the best option if you travel in a country with easy Internet access. Your password-protected travel vault is accessible online at any time. You can create your own travel vault for free at www.ekno.lonelyplanet.com.

EMBASSIES & CONSULATES
It's important to realise what your own embassy – the embassy of the country of which you are a citizen – can and can't do to help you if you get into trouble. Generally speaking, it won't be much help in emergencies if the trouble you're in is remotely your own fault. Remember that you are bound by the laws of the country you are in. Your embassy will not be sympathetic if you end up in jail after committing a crime locally, even if such actions are legal in your own country.

In genuine emergencies you might get some assistance, but only if other channels have been exhausted. For example, if you need to get home urgently, a free ticket home is exceedingly unlikely – the embassy would expect you to have insurance. If you have all your money and documents stolen, it might assist with getting a new passport, but a loan for onward travel is out of the question.

Italian Embassies & Consulates
The following is a selection of Italian diplomatic missions abroad. As a rule, you should approach the consulate rather than the embassy on visa matters. Bear in mind that in many of the countries listed below there are further consulates in other cities.

Australia
  Embassy:
  (☎ 02-6273 3333, fax 6273 4223, email ambital2@dynamite.com.au)
  12 Grey St, Deakin, Canberra, ACT 2600
  Consulates:
  (☎ 03-9867 5744, fax 9866 3932,

email itconmel@netlink.com.au)
509 St Kilda Rd, Melbourne, Vic 3004
(☎ 02-9392 7900, fax 9252 4830, email
itconsyd@armadillo.com.au)
Level 45, The Gateway, 1 Macquarie Place,
Sydney, NSW 2000
Austria
  Embassy:
  (☎ 01-712 51 21, fax 713 97 19, email
  ambitalviepress@via.at)
  Metternichgasse 13, Vienna 1030
  Consulate:
  (☎ 01-713 56 71, fax 715 40 30)
  Ungarngasse 43, Vienna 1030
Canada
  Embassy:
  (☎ 613-232 2401, fax 233 1484, email
  ambital@trytel.com)
  21st floor, 275 Slater St, Ottawa,
  Ont K1P 5H9
  Consulates:
  (☎ 514-849 8351, fax 499 9471, email
  consitmtl@cyberglobe.net)
  3489 Drummond St, Montreal, Que H3G 1X6
  (☎ 416-977 2569, fax 977 1119, email
  consolato.it@toronto.italconsulate.org)
  136 Beverley St, Toronto, Ont M5T 1Y5
France
  Embassy:
  (☎ 01 49 54 03 00, fax 01 45 49 35 81, email
  stampa@dial.oleane.com)
  47–51 rue de Varenne, Paris 75007
Germany
  Embassy:
  (☎ 0228-82 20, fax 82 22 10, email italia
  .ambasciata.bonn@t-online.de)
  Karl Finkelnburgstrasse 49-51,
  Bonn 53173
  Consulate:
  (☎ 030-25 44 00, fax 25 44 01 00, email
  italcons.berlino@t-online.de)
  Hiroshimastrasse 1–7, Berlin 10785
Ireland
  Embassy:
  (☎ 01-660 1744, fax 668 2759, email
  italianembassy@tinet.ie)
  63–65 Northumberland Rd, Dublin 4
Netherlands
  Embassy:
  (☎ 070-302 1030, fax 361 4932, email
  italemb@worldonline.nl)
  Alexanderstraat 12, 2514 JL The Hague
New Zealand
  Embassy:
  (☎ 04-473 5339, fax 472 7255, email
  ambwell@xtra.co.nz)
  34 Grant Rd, Thorndon, Wellington

Slovenia
  Embassy:
  (☎ 061-126 21 94, fax 125 33 02)
  Snezniska Ulica 8, Ljubljana 61000
Switzerland
  Embassy:
  (☎ 031-352 4151, fax 351 1026, email
  ambital.berna@spectraweb.ch)
  Elfenstrasse 14, Bern 3006
UK
  Embassy:
  (☎ 020-7312 2209, fax 7312 2230, email
  emblondon@embitaly.org.uk)
  14 Three Kings Yard, London W1Y 2EH
  Consulate:
  (☎ 020-7235 9371, fax 7823 1609)
  38 Eaton Place, London SW1X 8AN
USA
  Embassy:
  (☎ 202-328 5500, fax 328 5593, email
  itapress@ix.netcom.com)
  1601 Fuller St, NW, Washington,
  DC 20009
  Consulates:
  (☎ 213-820 0622, fax 820 0727, email
  cglos@aol.com)
  Suite 300, 12400 Wilshire Blvd, Los
  Angeles, CA 90025
  (☎ 212-737 9100, fax 249 4945, email
  italconsny@aol.com)
  690 Park Ave, New York, NY 10021-5044
  (☎ 415-931 4924, fax 931 7205)
  2590 Webster St, San Francisco,
  CA 94115

Consulates in Venice

A limited number of countries maintain
consulates in Venice. They include:

Austria
  (Map 5; ☎ 041 524 05 56)
  Santa Croce 251
France
  (Map 6; ☎ 041 522 43 19)
  Ramo del Pestrin, Castello 6140
Germany
  (Map 4; ☎ 041 523 76 75)
  Cannaregio 4201
Netherlands
  (Map 6; ☎ 041 528 34 16)
  San Marco 423
Switzerland
  (Map 5; ☎ 041 522 59 96)
  Dorsoduro 810
UK
  (Map 5; ☎ 041 522 72 07)
  Palazzo Querini, Dorsoduro 1051

The nearest Australian consulate (☎ 02 77 70 41) is in Milan, at Via Borgogna 2. The nearest US consulate (☎ 02 29 03 51) is also in Milan, at Via P Amadeo 2–10.

Embassies in Rome
Most countries have an embassy in Rome. Look them up under *ambasciate* in the *Pagine Gialle* (Yellow Pages). They include:

Australia
  (☎ 06 85 27 21)
  Via Alessandria 215
Austria
  (☎ 06 844 01 41)
  Via Pergolesi 3
Canada
  (☎ 06 44 59 81)
  Via GB de Rossi 27
France
  (☎ 06 68 60 11)
  Piazza Farnese 67
Germany
  (☎ 06 49 21 31)
  Via San Martino della Battaglia 4
Ireland
  (☎ 06 697 91 21)
  Piazza Campitelli 3
Netherlands
  (☎ 06 322 11 41)
  Via Michele Mercati 8
New Zealand
  (☎ 06 441 71 71)
  Via Zara 28
Slovenia
  (☎ 06 808 12 75)
  Via Leonardo Pisano 10
Switzerland
  (☎ 06 80 95 71)
  Via Barnarba Oriani 61
UK
  (☎ 06 482 54 41)
  Via XX Settembre 80/a
USA
  (☎ 06 4 67 41)
  Via Vittorio Veneto 119/a

CUSTOMS
Travellers entering Italy from outside the EU are allowed to bring in duty-free 1L of spirits, 2L of wine, 60 mL of perfume and 200 cigarettes.

On 1 July 1999 the sale of duty-free goods to people travelling within the EU was abolished. Under the rules of the single market, goods bought in and exported within the EU incur no additional taxes, provided duty has been paid somewhere within the EU and the goods are for personal consumption. 'Guidance levels' on quantities deemed appropriate for personal comsumption are set by the EU. These are: 10L of spirits, 90L of wine and 800 cigarettes.

MONEY
A combination of travellers cheques and credit or debit (cash) cards is the best way to take your money.

Currency
Until the euro notes and coins are in circulation (see the boxed text 'Introducing the Euro'), Italy's currency will remain the *lira* (plural *lire*). The smallest note is L1000. Other denominations in notes are L2000, L5000, L10,000, L50,000, L100,000 and L500,000. Coin denominations are L50, L100, L200, L500 and L1000.

Like other continental Europeans, Italians indicate decimals with commas and thousands with points.

country	unit		lira
Australia	A$1	=	L1183
Canada	C$1	=	L1221
euro	€1	=	L1936
France	1FF	=	L295
Germany	DM1	=	L989
Ireland	IR£1	=	L2458
Japan	¥100	=	L1608
New Zealand	NZ$1	=	L835
UK	UK£1	=	L2904
USA	US$1	=	L1824

Exchanging Money
If you need to change cash or travellers cheques, be prepared to queue. You can change money in banks, at post offices or in *bureaux de change* (currency exchange offices). Banks are generally the most reliable and tend to offer the best rates. However, you should look around and ask about commissions. These can fluctuate considerably and a lot depends on whether you are changing cash or cheques. The charge for a

Introducing the Euro

Since 1 January 1999, the lira and the euro – the new currency in 11 EU countries – have both been legal tender in Italy. Euro coins and banknotes have not been issued yet, but you can already get billed in euros and opt to pay in euros by credit card. Essentially, if there's no hard cash involved, you can deal in euros. Travellers should check bills carefully to make sure that any conversion has been calculated correctly.

The whole idea behind the current paperless currency is to give euro-fearing punters a chance to limber up arithmetically before euro coins and banknotes are issued on 1 January 2002. The same euro coins (one to 50 cents, €1 and €2) and banknotes (€5 to €500) will then be used in the 11 countries of what has been dubbed Euroland: Austria, Belgium, Finland, France, Germany, Ireland, Italy, Luxembourg, the Netherlands, Portugal and Spain. The lira will remain legal currency alongside the euro until 1 July 2002, when it will be hurled on the scrapheap of history.

Until that time, the 11 currencies have been fixed to the euro at the following rates: AS13.76, BF40.34, 5.95 mk, 6.56FF, DM1.96, IR£0.79, L1936, flux40.34, f2.2, 200$48 and 166.39 ptas. The Lonely Planet Web site at www.lonelyplanet.com has a link to a currency converter and up-to-date news on the integration process. Or have a look at europa.eu.int/euro/html/entry.html.

Euro exchange rates include:

Australia	A$1	=	€0.62
Canada	C$1	=	€0.66
Japan	¥100	=	€0.95
New Zealand	NZ$1	=	€0.50
UK	UK£1	=	€1.59
USA	US$1	=	€0.98

cash transaction starts at about L2500; travellers cheques attract even higher fees. Some banks charge L1000 per cheque with a L3000 minimum, others have a flat rate of L7500. In all cases you should compare the exchange rates too. The post office charges a flat rate of L5000 for all transactions, cash and cheque.

Bureaux de change often advertise 'no commission', but the rate of exchange can be inferior to that of banks. Watch out for bureaux de change that do charge commission. For example, Exact Change charges 9.8% on foreign currency travellers cheques. Another charges 5% on cash or travellers cheques, along with a set fee (L1000 for cash and L3000 for travellers cheques). Thomas Cook charges 4.5% (minimum L5500) for cash or cheques (except Thomas Cook travellers cheques, which are commission free). American Express (AmEx) offices do not charge commission to change travellers cheques – even other brands.

Where to Exchange You'll find most of the main banks in the area around the Ponte di Rialto and San Marco. Banks tend to open from 8.30 am to 1.30 pm and 3.30 to 4.30 pm Monday to Friday, although hours can vary. Most close at weekends, but you might get lucky and find one open on Saturday morning.

Endless queues indicate the position of the bank at the train station. An Exact Change booth in the platform area offers good rates (but watch the commission – see above) and opens daily from 8.20 am to 7.40 pm. You'll find other Exact Change booths on Campo San Bartolomeo (Map 6), near the Ponte di Rialto; at Rio Terrà Lista di Spagna 229 (Map 3), in Cannaregio; and at Merceria San Zulian 719 (Map 6).

The AmEx office (Map 6; ☎ 041 520 08 44) is on Salizzada San Moisè. The postal address is San Marco 1471. For AmEx cardholders, there's an express automated teller machine (ATM; *bancomat* in Italian). The office is open from 9 am to 5.30 pm Monday to Friday, and to 12.30 pm on Saturday. Thomas Cook has two offices, one at Piazza San Marco (Map 6; ☎ 041 522 47 51) and the other at Riva del Ferro 5126 (Map 6; ☎ 041 528 73 58), near Ponte di Rialto. They open from 9.10 am to 7.45 pm Monday to Saturday, and to 5 pm on Sunday.

When you first arrive, there are a couple of bureaux de change in the arrivals hall of the airport. A comparatively handy bank for both the train and bus stations is the Monte dei Paschi (Map 3) on Fondamenta di San Simeon Piccolo.

Cash Don't bring wads of cash from home (travellers cheques and plastic are much safer). It is, however, an idea to keep an emergency stash separate from other valuables in case you should lose your travellers cheques and credit cards.

You will often need cash for day-to-day transactions – many small *pensioni* (guesthouses), eateries and shops do not take credit cards.

Travellers Cheques These are a safe way to carry your money because they can be replaced if they are lost or stolen. They can be cashed at most banks and exchange offices. AmEx, Thomas Cook and Visa are widely accepted brands. If you lose your AmEx cheques, you can call a 24-hour toll-free number (☎ 800 872000).

It doesn't really matter whether your cheques are in lire or in the currency of the country you buy them in. Get most of your cheques in fairly large denominations (the equivalent of L100,000 or more) to save on any per-cheque commission charges. It's vital to keep your initial receipt, along with a record of your cheque numbers and the ones you have used, separate from the cheques themselves. Take along your passport when you go to cash travellers cheques.

Eurocheques Eurocheques (with guarantee card) were still fairly widely accepted at the time of writing, but the introduction of the euro means they are due to be phased out.

Credit & Debit Cards Carrying plastic (whether a credit or debit card) is the simplest way to organise your holiday funds. You don't have large amounts of cash or cheques to lose, you can get money after hours and at weekends and the exchange rate is generally good.

Major cards, such as Visa, MasterCard, Eurocard and Cirrus, are widely accepted in Venice and throughout Italy. They can be used for many purchases in shops and supermarkets, and in hotels and restaurants (although smaller places tend to accept cash only). Cards can also be used in ATMs displaying the appropriate sign, or (if you have no PIN) to obtain cash advances over the counter in many banks – Visa and MasterCard are among the most widely recognised for such transactions. Check charges with your bank but, as a rule, there is no charge for purchases on major cards and a 1.5% charge on cash advances and ATM transactions in foreign currencies.

It is not uncommon for ATMs in Italy to reject foreign cards. Don't despair or start wasting money on international calls to your bank. Try a few more ATMs displaying your card's logo before assuming the problem lies with your card rather than with the local system.

If your credit card is lost, stolen or swallowed by an ATM, you can telephone toll-free to have an immediate stop put on its use. For MasterCard the number in Italy is ☎ 800 870866, or make a reverse-charge call to St Louis in the USA on ☎ 314-275 6690; for Visa, phone ☎ 800 877232 in Italy. If, by chance, you have a credit card issued in Italy, call ☎ 800 822056 to have it blocked.

AmEx cards are also widely accepted (although they are not as common as Visa or MasterCard). There is an AmEx office in Venice (see the earlier Where to Exchange section). If you lose your AmEx card you can call ☎ 800 864046.

International Transfers It is inadvisable to send cheques by mail to Italy, due to the unreliability of the country's postal service. One reliable way to send money to Italy is by 'urgent telex' through the foreign office of a large Italian bank, or through major banks in your own country, to a nominated bank in Italy. Urgent-telex transfers should take only a few days, while other means, such as telegraphic transfer, or draft, can take weeks.

It is also possible to transfer money through AmEx and Thomas Cook. You will be required to produce identification, usually a passport, in order to collect the money. It is also a good idea to take along the details of the transaction.

Another option is to send money through Western Union. The fees charged for the virtually immediate transfer depend on the amount sent. For sums up to US$400, Western Union charges the sender US$20. The sender arranges the transfer in person at a Western Union outlet; both sender and receiver will need their passport or another form of ID. In Venice at present, the service is only available through the Exact Change exchange booths (see the earlier Where to Exchange section).

Security

Keep only a limited amount of your money as cash, with the bulk in more easily replaceable forms, such as travellers cheques or plastic. If your accommodation has a safe, use it. If you have to leave money in your room, divide it into several stashes and hide them in different places.

For carrying money on the street, the safest thing is a shoulder wallet or under-the-clothes money belt. External money belts tend to attract attention to your valuables rather than deflect it. Watch out for people who touch you or seem to be getting unnecessarily close, in any situation. See Theft & Loss under Dangers & Annoyances later in this chapter for more advice.

Italy has been rated by one London-based organisation, Card Protection Plan, as second only to Spain for credit-card theft from foreign travellers. More than half the cards that go missing in Venice are stolen, not lost.

Costs

As the cost of public transport (for tourists), accommodation, eating out, parking a car and doing just about anything else spirals ever upwards, the Venetians' long history of commercial canniness comes back to mind. Which is a nice way of saying that, in some cases at least, avarice seems to rule. The locals bank not only on the city's unique beauty, but on the fact that most visitors only hang about for a few days – long enough to be stunned at the expense, but not so long that said expense might deter them from staying at all.

Venetians point out, with some justification, that the city is expensive for everyone and that the prices reflect this. Whatever way you look at it, Venice is, with little doubt, the most expensive city in Italy.

Accommodation charges (especially in high season) and entrance fees for many sights keep daily expenditure high. A *very* prudent backpacker might scrape by on around L80,000 a day, but only by staying in the youth hostel, eating one simple meal a day (at the youth hostel), making sandwiches for lunch, walking (vaporetti fares alone can make quite a dent in a tight budget) and keeping the daily museum and gallery intake low.

One rung up, you can get by on L140,000 per day if you stay in the cheapest pensioni or small hotels, and keep sit-down meals and museums to one a day. Lone travellers may find even this budget hard to maintain, since single rooms tend to be pricey.

If money is no object, you'll find a plethora of ways to burn it in Venice. There's no shortage of luxury hotels, expensive restaurants and shops. Realistically, a traveller wanting to stay in a comfortable lower- to mid-range hotel, eat two square meals a day, not feel restricted to one museum a day and be able to enjoy the odd drink and other minor indulgences should reckon on a minimum daily average of L250,000 to L300,000.

A basic breakdown of costs per person during an average day for the budget to mid-range traveller could be: accommodation L20,000 (youth hostel) to L70,000 (single in a pensione or per person in a comfortable double), breakfast L4000 (coffee and brioche), lunch (sandwich and mineral water) L5000, bottle of mineral water L1500, public transport up to L18,000, entrance fee for one museum up to L12,000 and sit-down dinner L20,000 to L50,000.

Ways to Save Avoid, if you can, pensioni that insist on you paying for compulsory

FACTS FOR THE VISITOR

breakfast – a coffee and brioche in a cafe will cost less and be better. In reality this will be hard, as most automatically include breakfast in the price and don't countenance reductions for not taking breakfast.

In bars, prices can double (sometimes even triple) if you sit down and are served at the table. Stand at the bar to drink your coffee or eat a sandwich – or buy a sandwich or slice of pizza and head for the nearest *campo* (square).

Read the fine print on menus (usually posted outside eating establishments) to check the cover charge *(coperto)* and service fee *(servizio)*. These can make a big difference to the bill.

Aerograms (on sale only at the post office for L900) are the cheapest way to send international mail.

Tipping & Bargaining

You are not expected to tip on top of restaurant service charges, but it is common to leave a small amount. If there is no service charge, the customer might consider leaving a 10% tip, but this is by no means obligatory. In bars, Italians often leave any small change as a tip, often only L100 or L200. Tipping taxi drivers is not common practice, but you should tip the porter at higher-class hotels.

Bargaining is common in flea markets, but not in shops, although you might find that the proprietor is disposed to give a discount if you are spending a reasonable amount of money. It is quite acceptable to ask if there is a special price for a room in a *pensione* if you plan to stay for more than a few days.

Taxes & Refunds

A value-added tax of around 19%, known as Imposta di Valore Aggiunto (IVA), is slapped onto just about everything in Italy. If you are resident outside the EU and you spend in the same shop on the same day more than a certain amount (L300,000 in 1999), you may claim a refund on this tax when you leave the EU. The refund applies only to items purchased at retail outlets affiliated to the system – these shops display

a 'Tax-free for tourists' sign. If you don't see a sign, ask the shopkeeper. You must fill out a form at the point of purchase and have it stamped and checked by Italian customs when you leave the country (you will need to show the receipt and your purchases). At major airports and some border crossings you can then get an immediate cash refund at specially marked booths; alternatively, return the form by mail to the vendor, who will make the refund, either by cheque or to your credit card.

For information call ☎ 0332 87 07 70 or consult the rules brochure available in affiliated stores.

Receipts

Laws aimed at tightening controls on the payment of taxes in Italy mean that the onus is on the buyer to ask for and retain receipts for all goods and services. This applies to everything from a litre of milk to a haircut. Although it rarely happens, you could be asked by an officer of the Fiscal Police (Guardia di Finanza) to produce the receipt immediately after you leave a shop. If you don't have it, you may be obliged to pay a fine of up to L300,000.

POST & COMMUNICATIONS
Post

Italy's postal service is notoriously slow, unreliable and expensive. Don't expect to receive every letter sent to you, or that every letter you send will reach its destination.

Stamps *(francobolli)* are available from post offices and authorised tobacconists (look for the official *tabacchi* sign: a big 'T', often white on black). For letters that need to be weighed, what you get at the tobacconist's for international airmail will often be an approximation of the proper rate.

The main post office is on Salizzada del Fondaco dei Tedeschi, just near the Ponte di Rialto (Map 6). It's open from 8.15 am to 7 pm Monday to Saturday. Stamps are available at windows No 11 and 12 in the central courtyard. There is something quite special about doing your postal business in this former trading house. Stand by the well in the middle and try to imagine the bustle as

German traders and brokers shuffled their goods around on the ground floor or struck deals in their quarters on the upper levels back in the republic's trading heyday.

Postal Rates The cost of sending a letter airmail *(via aerea)* depends on its weight and where it is being sent. Letters up to 20g cost L800 to EU countries (L900 to the rest of Europe), L1300 to the USA and L1400 to Australia and New Zealand. Postcards cost the same. Aerograms cost only L900 to send anywhere and can be purchased at post offices.

A new service, *posta prioritaria* (priority post), began in 1999. For L1200, postcards and letters up to 20g posted to destinations within Italy, the EU, Switzerland and Norway are supposed to arrive the following day. There are no guarantees however.

Sending letters express *(espresso)* costs a standard extra L3600 and may help speed a letter on its way, but only within Italy, after which it will go by normal airmail. See Express Mail later in this section for more on sending urgent items.

If you want to post more important items by registered mail *(raccomandato)* or by insured mail *(assicurato)*, remember that they will take as long as normal mail. Raccomandato costs L4000 on top of the normal cost of the letter. The cost of assicurato depends on the weight of the object being sent (L6400 for letters up to 20g) and it is not available to the USA.

Sending Mail If you choose not to use posta prioritaria (see Postal Rates) an airmail letter can take up to two weeks to reach the UK or the USA, while a letter to Australia will take between two and three weeks. Postcards can take even longer because they are low-priority mail.

The service within Italy is not much better: local letters take at least three days and letters to another city up to a week.

Parcels *(pacchetti)* can be sent from any post office. You can buy posting boxes or padded envelopes from most post offices. Stationery shops *(cartolerie)* and some tobacconists also sell padded envelopes.

There are some strange regulations about how parcels should be sealed, and these appear to vary from one post office to another. Don't tape up or staple envelopes – they should be sealed with glue. Your best bet is not to close the envelope or box completely and ask at the counter how it should be done. Parcels usually take longer to be delivered than letters. A different set of postal rates applies.

Express Mail Urgent mail (maximum 20kg for international destinations) can be sent by an express mail service known as CAI Post, or *posta celere*, available at most main post offices. Letters up to 500g cost L30,000 to the UK, L46,000 to the USA and Canada, and L68,000 to Australia and New Zealand. A parcel weighing 1kg will cost L34,000 to the UK, L54,000 to the USA and Canada, and L80,000 to Australia and New Zealand. CAI Post is not necessarily as fast as private services. It will take two to three days for a parcel to reach European destinations, two to five days to the USA and four to eight days to Australia. You can follow your parcel on its journey overseas online at www.postacelere.com or by calling ☎ 800 009966 toll-free.

Couriers Several international couriers operate in Italy, but none have offices in Venice. DHL (☎ 800 345345), Federal Express (☎ 800 123800) and UPS (☎ 800 877877) all operate toll-free numbers. Note that if you are having articles sent to you by courier in Italy, you might be obliged to pay IVA of up to 20% to retrieve the goods.

Receiving Mail Poste restante is known as *fermo posta* in Italy. Letters marked thus will be held at the counter of the same name in the main post office in the relevant town. Poste restante mail should be addressed as follows:

> John SMITH,
> Fermo Posta,
> Posta Centrale,
> 30100 Venice
> Italy

euro currency converter L10,000 = €5.16

You will need to pick up your letters in person and present your passport as ID. Go to window 4.

AmEx card or travellers cheque holders can use the free client mail-holding service at the main Venice office (see Where to Exchange in the earlier Money section).

Telephone

The orange public pay phones liberally scattered about come in at least four types. The most common accept only telephone cards *(carte/schede telefoniche)*, although you will still find some that accept both cards and coins (L100, L200 and L500). Some card phones also accept special credit cards produced by Telecom – the formerly state-owned telecommunications company – and even commercial credit cards. A few send faxes. If you call from a bar or shop, you may still encounter old-style metered phones, which count *scatti*, the units used to measure the length of a call.

There is an unstaffed Telecom office next to the post office and a bank of telephones nearby on Calle Galeazza (Map 6). Other unstaffed offices can be found on Strada Nuova, on the corner of Corte dei Pali, in Cannaregio (Map 4); Ruga Vecchia San Giovanni 480, in San Polo (Map 4); and Calle San Luca 4585, in San Marco (Map 6). You will also find phones at the train station.

You can buy phonecards at post offices, tobacconists, newspaper stands and from vending machines in Telecom offices. To avoid the frustration of trying to find fast-disappearing coin telephones, always keep a phonecard on hand. They come in values of L5000, L10,000 and L15,000. Remember to snap off the perforated corner before using them.

Public phones operated by a new telecommunications company, Infostrada, can be found in airports and train stations. These phones accept Infostrada phonecards (available from post offices, tobacconists and newspaper stands), which come with a value of L3000, L5000 or L10,000. Infostrada's rates are slightly cheaper than Telecom's for long-distance and international calls, but you cannot make local calls from these phones.

Costs Rates, particularly for long-distance calls, are among the highest in Europe. Cheap rates apply from 6.30 pm to 8 am Monday to Friday, on Saturday afternoon and on Sunday and public holidays. For international calls, different times apply. Cheap rates to the UK apply from 10 pm to 8 am Monday to Saturday and all day Sunday, to the USA and Canada from 7 pm to 2 pm Monday to Friday and all day Saturday and Sunday, and to Australia from 11 pm to 8 am Monday to Saturday and all day Sunday.

A local call *(comunicazione urbana)* from a public phone will cost L200 for three to six minutes, depending on the time of day you call. Peak call times are 8 am to 6.30 pm Monday to Friday and 8 am to 1 pm Saturday.

Rates for long-distance calls within Italy *(comunicazione interurbana)* depend on the time of day and the distance involved. At the worst, one minute will cost about L340 in peak periods.

If you need to call overseas, beware of the cost – even a five-minute call to Australia after 10 pm will cost around L10,000 from a private phone (more from a public phone). Calls to most of the rest of Europe (except the UK, which is cheaper) cost L1245 for the first minute and L762 thereafter (closer to L1200 from a public phone).

In 1999 the competition started to heat up. A company called Tiscali put cards on the market to be used with public phones (and separate ones for private phones), with which they claim you pay 35% less on inter-city calls.

Domestic Calls Since July 1998, the one-time area codes have become an integral part of the telephone number. The codes all began with 0 and consisted of up to four digits. You must now dial this whole number, even if calling from next door. Thus any number you call in the Venice area will begin with 041.

Toll-free numbers *(numeri verdi)* that until February 1999 began with the digits 167 have been changed to 800 numbers, bringing Italy into line with an international trend (although you may still see such numbers advertised as 167 numbers).

For directory enquiries, dial ☎ 12.

Emergency Numbers

Military Police (Carabinieri)	☎ 112
Police (Polizia)	☎ 113
Fire Brigade (Vigili del Fuoco)	☎ 115
Highway Rescue	
(Soccorso Stradale)	☎ 116
Ambulance (Ambulanza)	☎ 118

Note Not only have area codes become part of the phone number, there are now plans to convert the initial 0 into a 4 by the end of 2000. Thus any number in the Venice area will start with 441.

International Calls Direct international calls can easily be made from public telephones by using a phonecard. Dial 00 to get out of Italy, then the relevant country and city codes, followed by the telephone number. Useful country codes are: Australia 61, Canada and the USA 1, New Zealand 64, and the UK 44. Codes for other countries in Europe include: France 33, Germany 49, Greece 30, Ireland 353 and Spain 34. Other codes are listed in Italian telephone books.

To make a reverse-charge international call from a public telephone, dial ☎ 170.

It is easier and often cheaper to use the Country Direct service. You dial the number and request a reverse-charge call through the operator in your country. Numbers for this service include:

Australia	– Telstra	☎ 172 10 61
	– Optus	☎ 172 11 61
Canada	– Teleglobe	☎ 172 10 01
	– AT&T	☎ 172 10 02
France		☎ 172 00 33
Germany		☎ 172 00 49
Ireland		☎ 172 03 53
Netherlands		☎ 172 00 31
New Zealand		☎ 172 10 64
UK	– BT	☎ 172 00 44
	– BT Chargecard	☎ 172 01 44
USA	– AT&T	☎ 172 10 11
	– IDB	☎ 172 17 77
	– MCI	☎ 172 10 22
	– Sprint	☎ 172 18 77

International directory inquiries is on ☎ 176.

International Phonecards The Lonely Planet eKno Communication Card (see the insert at the back of this book) is aimed specifically at travellers and provides cheap international calls, a range of messaging services and free email (though for local calls, you are usually better off with a local card). You can join online at www.ekno.lonelyplanet.com, or by phone from Italy by dialling ☎ 800 875691. Once you have joined, to use eKno from Italy dial ☎ 800 875683.

Several other private companies now distribute international phonecards, which are mostly linked to US phone companies such as Sprint and MCI. The cards come in a variety of unit sizes and are sold in some bars and tobacconists in the bigger cities.

Telecom has brought out its own Welcome Card, which costs L25,000 for 100 units. It's certainly cheaper than making international calls on a standard phonecard, but may not stand up to some of the competition.

Infostrada sells various cards, some of which are only good in the very limited number of Infostrada phones around. The best for international calls cost L20,000 and can be used from private or public phones (you dial a toll-free access number and then key in a provided code).

Calling Venice from Abroad Dial the international access code (00 in most countries), followed by the code for Italy (39) and the full number, including the initial 0. For mobile phones, however, drop the initial 0 of the prefix.

Telegram
These dinosaurs can be sent from post offices or dictated by phone (☎ 186) and are an expensive, but sure, way of having important messages delivered by the same or next day.

Fax
You can send faxes from post offices (such as the main one in the Fondaco dei Tedeschi) or fax offices, but the country's high telephone charges make them an expensive mode of communication. Some

FACTS FOR THE VISITOR

places charge per page and others charge per minute, and still others charge for both! In all cases, prices vary considerably from one office to another. However, in general, to send a fax within Italy you can expect to pay L4000 for the first page and L1500 for each page thereafter, or L3000 for the first minute and L1500 for subsequent minutes. International faxes can cost from L8000 for the first page and L5000 per page thereafter, depending on the destination. Per minute, a fax to an EU country can cost L7000 for the first minute and L3500 thereafter; to the USA it can cost L9000 for the first minute and L4500 thereafter. Faxes can also be sent from some Telecom public phones. It usually costs about L1000 per page to receive a fax.

The main post office operates a fax poste restante service. You can have faxes sent to you at Fax Fermo Posta. To retrieve the fax you will need a passport or some other photo ID. You pay L2000 for the first page received and L500 for each page thereafter. Ask at window 40. Faxes should be sent to 041 522 68 20.

Email & Internet Access

Travelling with a portable computer is a great way to stay in touch with life back home, but unless you know what you're doing it's fraught with potential problems.

If you plan to carry your notebook or palmtop computer with you, bear in mind that the power supply voltage in your hotel may vary from the voltage at home, risking damage to your equipment. The best solution is to invest in a universal AC adapter for your appliance, which will enable you to plug it in anywhere without frying the innards. You will also need a plug adapter for Italy (the standard European two round pin variety) – this is easier to buy before you leave home.

Also, your PC-card modem may or may not work once you leave your home country – and you won't know for sure until you try. The safest option is to buy a reputable 'global' modem before you leave home, or buy a local PC-card modem if you're spending an extended time in Italy.

Increasingly, Italian telephone sockets are being standardised to the US RJ-11 type. If you find yourself confronted with the old-style Italian three-prong socket, most electrical stores can sell you an adapter. For more information on travelling with a portable computer, see www.teleadapt.com or www.warrior.com.

Major Internet service providers (ISPs), such as CompuServe, at www.compuserve.com, and IBM Net, at www.ibm.net, have dial-in nodes throughout Italy; it's best to download a list of the dial-in numbers before you leave home. Some Italian servers can provide short-term accounts for Internet access. Flashnet (☎ 06 66 05 41) offers 20-hour renewable subscriptions for L30,000 (valid for one year); their Web site at www.flashnet.it has a list of authorised sales points in Italy. Agora (☎ 06 699 17 42) has subscriptions for two months for L84,000. Both of these providers have English-speaking staff.

If you intend to rely on cybercafes, you'll need to carry three pieces of information with you to enable you to access your Internet mail account: your incoming (POP or IMAP) mail server name, your account name and your password. Your ISP or network supervisor will be able to give you these. Armed with this information, you should be able to access your Internet mail account from any Net-connected machine in the world, provided it runs some kind of email software (remember that Netscape and Internet Explorer both have mail modules). It pays to become familiar with the process for doing this before you leave home. A final option to collect mail through cybercafes is to open a free eKno Web-based email account online at www.ekno.lonelyplanet.com. You can then access your mail from anywhere in the world from any Net-connected machine running a standard Web browser.

Cybercafes Expect to pay around L15,000 an hour at the following:

Café Noir
(Map 5; ☎ 041 71 09 25) Calle dei Preti Crosera 3805, Dorsoduro. This is the only true

Internet cafe in Venice. It was about to reopen after a stint closed for redecoration as writing was completed on this book. Check it out – the worst that can happen is that you have to go next door to Play the Game (see below).

Cartoleria Gianola
(Map 3; ☎/fax 041 524 06 74) Fondamenta di Cannaregio 1120, Sestiere di Cannaregio. This place is open from 8 am to 12.30 pm and 3.30 to 7.30 pm Monday to Friday, and 8 am to 12.30 pm on Saturday.

Internet Café
(Map 3; ☎ 041 524 12 00, fax 041 275 69 34) Ramo Chioverette 664/c, Santa Croce. Open from 8.30 am to 1 pm and 3 to 7 pm Monday to Friday, and 8.30 am to 1 pm on Saturday. In spite of the name, there is no coffee. An hour online costs L14,000.

Omniservice Internet Café
(Map 3; ☎ 041 71 04 70) Fondamenta dei Tolentini 220, Santa Croce. Open from 8.30 am to 1 pm and 3 to 6.30 pm Monday to Friday, and 9.30 am to 12.30 pm Saturday.

Play the Game
(Map 5; ☎ 041 275 01 70) Calle dei Preti Crosera 3804, Dorsoduro. Next door to Café Noir, Play the Game is a computer games store that doubles as an Internet navigation shop. It's open from 9.30 am to 12.30 pm and 3.30 to 7.30 pm Tuesday to Saturday, and 3.30 to 7.30 pm on Monday.

INTERNET RESOURCES

The World Wide Web is a rich resource for travellers. You can research your trip, hunt down bargain air fares, book hotels, check on weather conditions or chat with locals and other travellers about the best places to visit (or avoid!).

One of the best places to start your Web explorations is the Lonely Planet Web site (www.lonelyplanet.com). Here you'll find succinct summaries on travelling to most places on earth, postcards from other travellers and the Thorn Tree bulletin board, where you can ask questions before you go or dispense advice when you get back. You can also find travel news and updates to many of our most popular guidebooks, and the subWWWay section links you to the most useful travel resources elsewhere on the Web.

Scouring the Net for a few hours can lead you to some interesting tips about the city, including a lot of practical information like event listings and public transport details. Some good sites to visit include:

Associazione Veneziana Albergatori
www.doge.it
(hoteliers' information directory, with tips on hotels and eating options, upcoming events and links to other sites dealing with Venice)

Azienda Consorzio Trasporti Veneziana (ACTV)
www.actv.it
(all the transport details you are ever likely to want)

Consorzio dei Gondolieri
www.gondolaincoming.com
(for an idea of the wonderful world of gondolas and the wonderful sums you will need to have to get on board)

Excite
www.excite.com/travel/countries/italy/venice
(Excite's travel pages, with farefinder and bookings, and links to maps, restaurant tips and the like)

Internet Café Guide
www.netcafeguide.com
(for a list of Internet cafes in Venice and around Italy. It's not as up-to-date as you might expect such a site to be, but it is a start. See also Cybercafes in the previous section.)

Istituto Universitario di Architettura di Venezia
www.iuav.unive.it/~juli/vensave.htm
(links to sites dealing with some of Venice's problems, ranging from the La Fenice theatre disaster to news on restoration in the lagoon city)

Rialto: The Venice Marketplace
www.rialto.com
(Wanna shop in Venice without going there? This could be a site for you. Many of the city's prestige stores (and some perhaps not so prestigious) have contributed to this site. In many cases you can see catalogues and order online. Otherwise, you can just use this Web site as an extra shopping guide for when you are in the city.)

Veneto
www.veneto.org
(information about the region of which Venice is the capital, the Veneto, including history, language and local news)

Venice Incoming
www.elmoro.com
(private-sector guide to the city with some potentially useful tips on eating, drinking, shopping and other activities)

Virtual Venice
www.virtualvenice.com
(virtual tours of the city and listings guides)

BOOKS

Most books are published in different editions by different publishers in different countries. Your local bookshop or library is best placed to advise you on the availability of the following recommendations.

For bookshops in Venice, see the Shopping chapter.

Lonely Planet

If you are planning wider travels in the country, get hold of *Italy*. Hikers should take a look at *Walking in Italy*. Other companion titles include *Rome*, *Florence* and *Tuscany*. Also published by Lonely Planet, the *Italian phrasebook* lists all the words and phrases you're likely to need.

Lonely Planet's *World Food Italy* is a full-colour book with information on the whole range of Italian food and drink. It includes a useful language section, with the definitive culinary dictionary and a handy quick-reference glossary.

Guidebooks

If your Italian is good, the best guidebooks to the history, culture and monuments of Italy are the 23 exhaustive hardback volumes published by the Touring Club Italiano. The relevant ones in this instance are *Venezia e Dintorni* and *Veneto*.

About the closest you'll come to this in English is Alta Macadam's *Venice* in the Blue Guide series.

An attractively illustrated potted guide to Venetian art, monuments and history is *Venice for Pleasure* by JG Links.

For thematic guided strolls, try *Venice Walks* by Chas Corner and Alessandro Giannastasio.

Travel

For an idea of how an assortment of writers saw the city, have a meander through *Venice: the Most Triumphant City*, compiled by George Bull.

For some, the single most powerful evocation of the city is *Venice* by James (now Jan) Morris. Quirky, if a little irritatingly self-assured, is *Venice Observed* by Mary McCarthy.

Jan Morris revisited the subject with *The Venetian Empire – A Sea Voyage*, in which she set out by sea from La Serenissima to explore the widely scattered dominions of the one-time trading empire.

Literary companions are all the rage nowadays and *Venice – A Traveller's Companion*, compiled by John Julius Norwich, is full of anecdotes from characters ranging from King Theodoric's envoy to Venice in 523 to Mark Twain.

History & People

Italy Edward Gibbon's *History of the Decline and Fall of the Roman Empire* (available in six hardback volumes or an abridged single volume) remains the masterwork on that subject in English. Other, simpler offerings include *The Oxford History of the Roman World*, edited by John Boardman, Jasper Griffin & Oswyn Murray.

For a general look at Italy, you could do a lot worse than *History of the Italian People* by Giuliano Procacci. Other options to help you get started include *Italy: A Short History* by Harry Hearder and *The Horizon Concise History of Italy* by Vincent Cronin. *A History of Contemporary Italy: Society and Politics 1943–1988* by Paul Ginsborg is an absorbing analysis of the country's post-WWII travails.

Venice Two great works of scholarship stand out on the subject of Venetian history. John Julius Norwich's *A History of Venice* is the better read of the two, while the heavier in terms of sheer detail (and a fair share of anecdote) is *Venice – A Maritime Republic* by the American historian Frederic C Lane. The latter tends to concentrate on the seafaring side of Venetian life and is organised more thematically than chronologically. Less detailed but more approachable is Christopher Hibbert's *Venice: the Biography of a City*.

John Julius Norwich has also written a detailed account of the last days of the Republic, *Venice: The Greatness and the Fall*.

For a treatment of Venice's tangled relations with its imperial Eastern neighbour, traced until the fall of Byzantium to the

Turks in 1453, try *Byzantium & Venice* by Donald M Nicol.

Although the subject of Brian Pullan's *The Jews of Europe and the Inquisition of Venice, 1550–1670* covers wider ground beyond Venice, it sheds light on the lot of the city's Jewry. More specific to the history of Jews in the lagoon city is *Ghetto of Venice* by Riccardo Calimani and Katherine Silberblatt Wolfthal.

Anyone interested in Giacomo Casanova's version of his own life and loves might want to get a hold of his voluminous *Memoires of Jacques Casanova de Seingalt*, translated by Arthur Machen.

Art & Architecture

The number of books devoted to the subject of art in Italy is mind-numbing. Most people thinking of art and Italy have the Renaissance in mind. General references worth looking at include *The Penguin Book of the Renaissance* by JH Plumb and *Painters of the Renaissance* by Bernard Berenson. The 16th-century Florentine artist Giorgio Vasari wrote the definitive report on the art of the day in his *Lives of the Artists*.

For the narrower palette of Venice, you could try *Painting in Renaissance Venice* by Peter Humfrey and *Venetian Art from Bellini to Titian* by Johannes Wilde.

A couple of illustrated paperback studies are Michael Levey's *Painting in 18th Century Venice* and David Rosand's *Painting in Sixteenth Century Venice*. Levey also wrote the introduction to Venetian art that features in *The Glory of Venice: Art in the Eighteenth Century*, edited by Jane Martineau and Andrew Robinson. This is a weighty hardback tome packed with illustrations. *Treasures of Venetian Painting – The Gallerie dell'Accademia* is a marvellous illustrated work covering the best of this gallery's collection.

Patricia Fortini Brown tries to evoke a day in the life of Joe Venice four centuries ago through the prism of the city's art treasures in *Art and Life in Renaissance Venice*. It is one of several volumes she has dedicated to the study of Venetian art history.

The colour plates in *The Mosaic Decoration of San Marco, Venice* by Otto Demus are accompanied by knowledgeable discourse on the art form that to many observers defines the city.

People often forget that Germany's Albrecht Dürer, a prince among German Renaissance artists, spent some four years in Venice. His *Record of Journeys to Venice and the Low Countries*, a selection of the painter's letters edited by Roger Fry, gives us some insight into his time there.

The Stones of Venice, by John Ruskin, is still acclaimed by many as the greatest evocation of the city written in English. If you want more insight into Ruskin's thinking, try to track down *Ruskin's Letters from Venice, 1851–1852*. In *A History of Venetian Architecture*, Ennio Concina surveys the city from its origins to the present day.

A handy little volume you can pick up in the city (at Libreria Demetra, for example) is *Venice – an Architectural Guide* by Guido Zucconi, which offers quick glosses on about 250 landmark buildings. Editions in several different languages are available. More involved, and containing a little explanatory history on the evolution of Venetian building styles, is *A Guide to the Principal Buildings*, by Antonio Salvadori. It's published by Canal & Stamperia Editrice, which has a series of art- and architecture-related books on Venice and other cities.

Music

A close study of Venetian Renaissance music can be found in Denis Arnold's *Giovanni Gabrieli and the Music of the Venetian High Renaissance*.

Karl Heller's *Antonio Vivaldi: the Red Priest of Venice* is an insightful look into the life of the composer.

Fans of opera wanting to know about its early days might like to get a hold of Ellen Rosand's *Opera in Seventeenth Century Venice: The Creation of a Genre*.

Glass

Venetian Glass: Confections in Glass 1855–1914 by Sheldon Barr is like a visit to a museum of the most outstanding Murano creations at a time when mass tourism had not yet set the tone. The colour photography by John Bigelow Taylor is the main attraction of this book.

Fiction

If you were to buy just one piece of fiction concerning Venice, Thomas Mann's absorbing *Der Tod in Venedig (Death in Venice)* should be it. The city itself seems to be the main protagonist, reducing Gustav von Aschenbach, its feeble human 'hero', to a mere tragic shadow. In all its mysterious beauty, the cholera-struck city seems at the same time cloyingly infectious and coldly indifferent.

Food & Drink

The Food of Italy by Waverley Root is an acknowledged classic.

From fine food to the perfect Bellini, *The Harry's Bar Cookbook* by Arrigo Cipriani has more than 200 recipes unlocking at least a few of the secrets to the success of this Venetian institution. Cipriani, son of the bar's founder, also wrote *Harry's Bar: The Life and Times of the Legendary Venice Landmark*.

Pino Agostini and Alvise Zorzi's *A Tavola con I Dogi* is an exquisite and authoritative guide to Venetian cooking.

A jolly, anecdotal tome on the subject of eating in Venice is Sally Spector's *Venice and Food*, for which she wrote the text and drew the pictures. For a locals' guide to *osterie* and restaurants, Michela Scibilia's *Osterie & Dintorni* is a handy little pocket book.

See Lonely Planet earlier in this section for information on *World Food Italy*.

NEWSPAPERS & MAGAZINES

You can easily find a wide selection of national daily newspapers from around Europe (including the UK) at newsstands all over central Venice and at strategic locations like the train and bus stations. The *International Herald Tribune*, *Time*, the *Economist*, *Le Monde*, *Der Spiegel* and a host of other international magazines are also available.

Italian National Press

There is no 'national' paper as such, but rather several important dailies published out of major cities. These include Milan's *Corriere della Sera*, Turin's *La Stampa* and Rome's *La Repubblica*. This trio forms what could be considered the nucleus of a national press, publishing local editions up and down the country.

Reading Italian papers is a curious exercise. It is unlikely you will find such a dense and constant coverage of national politics in the press of any other European country. And yet the arcane shenanigans of Italy's political class are so convoluted that even most Italians confess to understanding precious little of what they are bombarded with in the press!

Most daily papers cost L1500, unless there is a weekly magazine *inserto* of one sort or another, in which case the cost can rise to L2200.

Local Press

Two papers dominate the local scene. *Il Gazzettino*, which has been in business since 1887, brings out separate editions in each province across the Triveneto area (the Veneto, Friuli-Venezia Giulia and Trentino), each with a local supplement. If you are in Venice and want decent coverage of national and foreign news but with solid local content, this is probably the paper you want. Its competition is the tabloid-size *La Nuova Venezia*, a more parochial rag.

Useful Publications

Venezia News is a monthly magazine (L4000) available at most newsstands. It has info on the latest events, cinema, music and the like, along with a hotchpotch of articles, some in English. It is not always as useful as one might like, but as a one-off monthly investment occasionally repays a close read.

RADIO

There are three state-owned stations: RAI-1 (1332kHz AM or 89.7MHz FM), RAI-2 (846kHz AM or 91.7MHz FM) and RAI-3 (93.7MHz FM). They offer a combination of classical and light music with news broadcasts and discussion programs. RAI-2 broadcasts news in English at three minutes past the hour from 1 to 5 am daily.

Radio Vaticano (1530kHz AM, 93.3MHz FM and 105MHz FM) broadcasts the news in English at 7 am, 8.30 am, 6.15 pm and 9.50 pm. The reports usually include a run-down on what the pope is up to on any particular day.

Local stations are not very inspiring. Radio Venezia (101.1MHz FM) is among the better ones, with news and, on balance, not a bad selection of music.

You can pick up the BBC World Service on medium wave at 648kHz, on short wave at 6.195MHz, 9.410MHz, 12.095MHz and 15.575MHz, and on long wave at 198kHz, depending on where you are and the time of day. Voice of America (VOA) can usually be found on short wave at 15.205MHz.

TV

The three state-run stations, RAI-1, RAI-2 and RAI-3, are run by Radio e Televisione Italiane. Historically, each has been in the hands of one of the main political groupings in the country, although in the past few years these affiliations have become less clear-cut.

Of the three, RAI-3 tends to have some of the more interesting programs. Generally, however, these stations and the private Canale 5, Italia 1 and Rete 4 tend to serve up a diet of indifferent news, tacky variety shows (with lots of near-naked tits and bums, appalling crooning and vaudeville humour) and talk shows.

Other stations are TMC (Telemontecarlo), on which you can see CNN if you stay up late enough (starting as late as 5 am), and regional channels. These include Telenuovo, Italia 7, Antenna 3 and TvSet. Quality is generally indifferent at best, but all carry more news and cultural items on Venice and the Veneto than the main stations.

VIDEO SYSTEMS

If you want to record or buy video tapes to play back home, you won't get a picture if the image registration systems are different.

TVs and nearly all pre-recorded videos on sale in Italy use the PAL (phase alternation line) system common to most of Western Europe and Australia but incompatible with France's SECAM system or the NTSC system used in North America and Japan. PAL videos can't be played back on a machine that lacks PAL capability.

PHOTOGRAPHY & VIDEO
Film & Equipment
A 36-exposure roll of 100 ASA Kodak film costs around L10,000. Developing costs around L18,000 for 36 exposures and L12,000 for 24 exposures. A roll of 36 slides costs around L15,000 plus L10,000 for developing.

Numerous outlets sell and process film, but beware of poor-quality processing. A roll of film is called a *pellicola*, but you will be understood if you ask for 'film'. Tapes for video cameras are often available at the same outlets or can be found at stores selling electrical goods.

Technical Tips
Bright middle-of-the-day sun tends to bleach out your shots. You get more colour and contrast earlier and later in the day. This goes both for still photographs and video, and is even more the case in summer, when glare can be a problem – the gentler winter light gives you greater flexibility.

Restrictions
Some museums and galleries ban photography, or at least flash, and the police can be touchy about it. Video is also often not allowed.

Photographing People
It's common courtesy to ask – at least by gesture – when you want to photograph people, except perhaps when they're in some kind of public event, like a procession.

Airport Security
The major Italian airports are all fully equipped with modern inspection systems that do not damage film or other photographic material carried in hand luggage.

TIME

Italy (and hence Venice) is one hour ahead of GMT/UTC during winter, two hours during the daylight-saving period from the last Sunday in March to the last Sunday in October. Most other Western European countries are on the same time as Italy year round, the major exceptions being the UK, Ireland and Portugal, which are one hour behind.

When it's noon in Venice, it's 3 am in San Francisco, 6 am in New York and Toronto, 11 am in London, 9 pm in Sydney and 11 pm in Auckland. Note that in North America and Australasia the changeover to/from daylight saving usually differs from the European date by a couple of weeks.

ELECTRICITY
Voltages & Cycles

The electric current in Venice is 220V, 50Hz, as in the rest of continental Europe. Several countries outside Europe (such as the USA and Canada) use 110V, 60Hz, which means that some appliances from those countries may perform poorly. It is always safest to use a transformer.

Plugs & Sockets

Plugs have two round pins, again as in the rest of continental Europe.

WEIGHTS & MEASURES

Italy uses the metric system. Like other continental Europeans, the Italians indicate decimals with commas and thousands with points. For a conversion chart, see the inside back cover of this book.

LAUNDRY

Self-service laundrettes are a comparative novelty in Italy and in Venice you have the grand choice of one. Bea Vita Lavanderia (Map 3) is in Santa Croce, at Calle Chioverette 665/b. You pay L6000 to wash 8kg and L1000 per minute to dry. It's open daily from 8 am to 10 pm. If it's shut or busy and you're desperate, Laundrette (Map 15), at Via Piave 41 in Mestre (about five minutes north of the train station), is an alternative.

The standard *lavanderie* (laundries), where you leave washing to be done, cost a small fortune.

TOILETS

Stopping in at a bar or cafe for a quick coffee and then a trip to the toilet is the common solution to those sudden urges at awkward times. Make sure your bar actually has a toilet before committing yourself! Otherwise, public toilets (visitors pay L1000, residents L500) are scattered about Venice – look out for the 'WC Toilette' signs.

LEFT LUGGAGE

There are left-luggage facilities at Santa Lucia and Mestre train stations, the Piazzale Roma bus station, the Stazione Marittima (ferry port) and Marco Polo airport. See the Getting There & Away and Getting Around chapters for more details. The cheapest service in the city itself is the one at the Piazzale Roma bus station (L5000 for 24 hours).

HEALTH

You should encounter no particular health problems in Venice. Mild gut problems are a possibility at first if you're not used to a lot of olive oil, but most travellers experience no problems.

Citizens of EU countries are covered for emergency medical treatment in Italy on presentation of an E111 form. Treatment in private hospitals is not covered and charges are also likely for medication, dental work and secondary examinations, including X-rays and laboratory tests. Ask about the E111 at your local health services department a few weeks before you travel (in the UK, the form is available at post offices).

Australia also has a reciprocal arrangement with Italy so that emergency treatment is covered – Medicare in Australia publishes a brochure with the details. Advise medical staff of any reciprocal arrangements *before* they begin treating you.

Travel insurance is still a good idea, however. You should really get it to cover you for theft, loss and unexpected travel cancellations anyway, and this way you will be covered for the cost of private health care as well.

Travellers who require a particular medication should take an adequate supply as well as the prescription, with the generic rather than the brand name, which will make getting replacements easier. Basic drugs are widely available and indeed many items requiring prescriptions in countries like the USA can be obtained over the counter in Italy. Tampons and condoms are available in pharmacies and supermarkets.

No vaccinations are required for entry into Italy unless you have been travelling through a part of the world where yellow fever or cholera is prevalent.

Medical Services & Emergency

For an ambulance, call ☎ 118. The Ospedale Civile (Maps 4 & 7; ☎ 041 529 45 17) is at Campo SS Giovanni e Paolo. For emergency treatment, go straight to the *pronto soccorso* (casualty) section, where you can also get emergency dental treatment.

On the mainland, Mestre's Ospedale Umberto I (Map 15; ☎ 041 260 71 11), Via Circonvallazione 50, is a modern hospital.

For night-time call-outs (locum doctors) between 8 pm and 8 am on weekdays and from 10 am the day before a holiday (including Sundays) until 8 am the day after, call ☎ 041 529 40 60 in Venice, ☎ 041 534 44 11 in Mestre and ☎ 041 526 77 43 on the Lido.

The Italian public health system is administered by local centres generally known as Unità Sanitaria Locale (USL) or Unità Socio Sanitaria Locale (USSL), usually listed under 'U' in the telephone book (sometimes under 'A' for Azienda USL). Just for fun, the Venetian version is ULSS. Under these headings you'll find long lists of offices – look for Poliambulatorio (polyclinic) and the telephone number for Accetazione Sanitaria. You need to call this number to make an appointment – there is no point in just rolling up. Clinic opening hours vary widely, with the minimum generally being about 8 am to 12.30 pm Monday to Friday. Some open for a couple of hours in the afternoon and on Saturday morning too.

For minor health problems, you can head to your local *farmacia* (pharmacy), where pharmaceuticals tend to be sold more freely without prescription than in places like the USA, Australia or the UK.

If your country has a consulate in Venice, staff there should be able to refer you to doctors who speak your language. However, if you have a specific health complaint, it would be wise to obtain the necessary information and referrals for treatment before leaving home.

In the USA, the non-profit International Association for Medical Assistance to Travelers (IAMAT; ☎ 716-754 4883, fax 519-836 3412), 417 Center St, Lewiston, NY 14092, can provide a list of English-speaking doctors in Venice trained in the USA, the UK or Canada.

Pharmacies

Pharmacies are usually open from 9 am to 12.30 pm and 3.30 to 7.30 pm. Most are closed on Saturday afternoon and Sunday. When closed, pharmacies are required to display a list of other pharmacies in the area that are open. Information on all-night pharmacies is listed in *Un Ospite di Venezia* (see Local Tourist Offices earlier in this chapter).

STDs & AIDS

It is possible to get tests for AIDS and other sexually transmitted diseases (STDs) done in Venice (normally you are tested for the lot in one go). Inquire at the Consultorio Familiare (Map 5; ☎ 041 529 40 04), Dorsoduro 1454. It's open from 9 am to 1 pm Tuesday and Friday and from 2.30 to 5.30 pm on Thursday. You need to book ahead for a consultation.

Women's Health

For gynaecological examinations, smear tests and the like on the public health service, go to the Consultorio Familiare (see STDs & AIDS above).

WOMEN TRAVELLERS

Of the main destinations in Italy, Venice has to be the safest for women. The kind of bravado that has more southerly Italians trying it on harder with foreign women seems largely absent here. If you do get unwanted attention, whatever methods you use at home to deal with it should work here.

Organisations

Centro Donna (☎ 041 534 29 91, fax 041 534 28 62), Viale Garibaldi 155/a, in Mestre, is a women's centre that offers various facilities, including a library, and cultural events aimed at women, whether Italian or foreign.

It also operates a service for women who have been assaulted. The Centro Anti-Violenza (☎ 041 534 92 05) offers legal advice, free counselling and support to women who have been attacked, regardless of nationality. The service is free.

GAY & LESBIAN TRAVELLERS

Homosexuality is legal in Italy and well tolerated in Venice and the north in general. The legal age of consent is 16. However, overt displays of affection by homosexual couples could attract a negative response.

Gay clubs, discos and the like are noticeable by their absence in Venice. In other parts of Italy, they can be tracked down through local gay organisations (see Organisations later in this section) or the national monthly gay magazine *Babilonia*, which, along with the annual *Guida Gay Italia*, is available at some newsstands. You can also read *Babilonia* on the Internet at www .babilonia.net.

International gay and lesbian guides worth tracking down are the *Spartacus Guide for Gay Men* (the Spartacus list also includes the comprehensive *Spartacus National Edition Italia*, in English and German), published by Bruno Gmünder Verlag GmbH, Mail Order, Leuschnerdamm 31, D-10999 Berlin, Germany, and *Places for Women*, published by Ferrari Publications, Phoenix, AZ, USA.

Organisations

The national organisations for gay men and lesbians are ArciGay and ArciLesbica (☎ 051 644 70 54, fax 051 644 67 22), Piazza di Porta Saragozza 2, 40123, Bologna.

You'll find any number of Italian gay sites on the Internet, but some are all but useless. However, ArciGay's Web site (www .gay.it/arcigay) has general information on the gay and lesbian scene in Italy and plenty of useful links. ArciLesbica's Web site can be found at www.women.it/~arciles/. Another interesting site that has plenty of links is La Comunità Gay/Lesbica/Trans Italiana. Go to www.webring.org and search on 'itgay'.

In Venice itself, you'll find ArciGay Nove (Map 3; ☎ 041 72 11 97) at San Giacomo dell'Orio 1507, in Santa Croce.

DISABLED TRAVELLERS

The Italian State Tourist Office in your country may be able to provide advice on Italian associations for the disabled and what help is available in the country. It may also carry a small brochure, *Services for Disabled People*, published by the Italian state rail company, Ferrovie dello Stato (FS), which details facilities at stations and on trains. Some of the better trains, such as the ETR460 and ETR500, have a carriage for passengers in wheelchairs and their companions.

The Italian travel agency CIT can advise on hotels with special facilities, such as ramps. It can also request that wheelchair ramps be provided on arrival of your train if you book travel through CIT. See Public Transport in the Getting Around chapter for information on getting around Venice in a wheelchair.

Organisations

The UK-based Royal Association for Disability & Rehabilitation (RADAR) publishes a useful guide entitled *Holidays & Travel Abroad: A Guide for Disabled People*, which provides a good overview of facilities available to disabled travellers throughout Europe. To get a copy, contact RADAR (☎ 020-7250 3222), Unit 12, City Forum, 250 City Rd, London EC1V 8AS.

Another UK organisation worth calling is Holiday Care Service (☎ 01293-774535). It produces an information pack on Italy for disabled people and others with special needs.

Mobility International (☎ 02-201 5608, fax 201 5763), 18 Blvd Baudouin, Brussels,

Belgium, organises all sorts of activities and events throughout Europe for the disabled.

In Italy itself you may also be able to get help. Co.In. (Cooperative Integrate) is a national voluntary group with links to the government and branches all over the country. It publishes a quarterly magazine for disabled tourists, *Turismo per Tutti* (Tourism for All), in Italian and English. It has information on accessible accommodation, transport and attractions. Co.In. (☎ 06 232 67 505) is at Via Enrico Giglioli 54/a, Rome. Its Web site is at andi.casaccia.enea .it/hometur.htm.

Promotur – Accessible Italy (☎ 011 309 6363, fax 011 309 1201), Piazza Pitagora 9, 10137 Turin, is a private company specialising in holiday services for the disabled, ranging from tours to hiring adapted transport. Check out its Web site at www .tour-web.com/accitaly.

SENIOR TRAVELLERS

Senior citizens are entitled to discounts on public transport and on admission fees at some museums. It's always worth asking. The minimum qualifying age is generally 60 years. You should also seek information in your own country on travel packages and discounts for senior travellers through senior citizens' organisations and travel agents.

VENICE FOR CHILDREN

Venice isn't for art-lovers and hopeless romantics alone. The city is varied enough to keep even the most recalcitrant juniors interested at least some of the time. Some of the stuff grown-ups like, such as gondola and vaporetto rides, exploring funny corners and watching the passing parade of boats along the canals, will appeal to quite a lot of kids.

If you are having a spot of bother, or have been unkind enough to drag the little mites around just a few too many monuments for their liking, you can try a couple of things to mollify them. The Giardini Pubblici (Map 8) and Parco Savorgnan (Map 3) both have swings and the like. In summer, a trip to the beach – the Lido, Sottomarina

(Chioggia) or Lido di Jesolo – should win you a few points. If you are using your own transport, remember to leave early to beat the horrible traffic jams. And forget it at weekends (except on the Lido) – whether you drive or catch buses you'll be stuck on the roads for an eternity either way.

Discounts are available for children (usually aged under 12) on public transport and for admission to museums, galleries and other sights.

Before You Go

There are no particular health precautions you need to take with your children in Venice. That said, kids tend to be more affected than adults by unaccustomed heat, changes in diet and sleeping patterns, and just being in a strange place. Nappies, creams, lotions, baby foods and so on are all easily available in Venice, but if there's some particular brand you swear by it's best to bring it with you.

Lonely Planet's *Travel with Children* has lots of practical advice on the subject, and first-hand stories from many Lonely Planet authors, and others, who have done it.

LIBRARIES

Access to the main libraries of the city generally requires a pass. You can find a list of the main libraries, with addresses, phone numbers and opening hours, in the monthly *Venezia News*.

UNIVERSITIES

The Università Ca' Foscari (Map 5; ☎ 041 257 81 11) is based in the *palazzo* (palace) of the same name at Dorsoduro 3246. Faculty buildings and subdivisions are scattered across the city. It began as Italy's first school of commerce in 1868 and was only made a university in 1968. There are four faculties: Economy, Foreign Languages and Literature, Literature and Philosophy, and Mathematics and Physical & Natural Sciences. The university has a Web site at www.unive.it.

The prestigious Istituto Universitario di Architettura di Venezia (IUAV; Map 5; ☎ 041 257 11 11), set up in 1963, is based

FACTS FOR THE VISITOR

in the former convent of San Nicolò da Tolentino, Santa Croce 191. Its various departments are spread across the city and some 11,000 students flock from all over the country to attend courses here. Its Web site is at www.iuav.unive.it.

A few foreign universities (such as Warwick University in the UK and New York University in the USA) run programs in Venice too.

CULTURAL CENTRES

There's a branch of the Alliance Française (Map 6; ☎ 041 522 70 79) at San Marco 4939. This French association offers classes in French, as well as organising cultural events, conferences, exhibitions and the like.

The local representative of the Goethe Institut, Deutsch-Italienische Kulturgesellschaft (Map 4; ☎ 041 523 25 44, fax 041 524 52 75), is at Palazzo Albrizzi, Fondamenta Sant'Andrea, Cannaregio 4118. It runs courses in German, as well as a full calendar of talks, exhibitions and other cultural events.

DANGERS & ANNOYANCES

All in all, the half-awake visitor to Venice should have no problems. Still, the presence of so many foreigners inevitably encourages pickpockets and like-minded small-time criminals.

Theft & Loss

Petty crime (pickpocketing, bag-snatching and the like) is the standard problem in Venice, as indeed in most major tourist destinations in Italy. Overall, though, Venice is a pretty safe place. The times to be on your guard are those moments when you will probably be most distracted. Arriving at the train station and getting oriented, squeezing onto crowded vaporetti (especially when you are burdened with all your bags) and pounding the packed tourist-trails (especially at certain points along the way from the train station to Piazza San Marco and around the Rialto) are moments when you may be vulnerable. A modicum of awareness and keeping anything valuable well hidden should be enough protection.

Prevention is better than cure. Only walk around with the amount of cash you intend to spend that day or evening. Hidden money belts or pouches are useful. The popular 'bum bags' and external belt pouches that people wear around their tummies are like a shining beacon to hawks looking for targets. You may as well wear a neon sign saying: 'Pick Me: I'm a Tourist'.

Never leave anything visible in your car and preferably leave nothing at all. Foreign and hire cars are especially vulnerable, and there have been occasional reports of trouble at some of the car parks – in Fusina in particular.

In hotels and hostels, use the safe if they have one. Try not to leave valuables in your room. If you must, then bury them deep in your luggage.

If anything does get lost or stolen, you must report it to the police and get a written statement from them if you intend to claim for them on your insurance. If your ID or passport disappears, contact your nearest consulate as early as possible to arrange for a replacement.

Rogue Taxis

A particular problem on Tronchetto island is false taxi drivers. These people may wear official-looking caps and badges and approach the freshly parked tourist with stories of having the only kind of vessel available to transfer people from Tronchetto to destinations elsewhere in Venice. This is rubbish, as vaporetti call here regularly. More often than not, the unwitting victims are transported somewhere (often not where

---

Lost & Found

Numbers for lost property are as follows:

Buses	☎ 041 272 28 38
Trains	☎ 041 78 52 38
Vaporetti	☎ 041 272 21 79

Otherwise, call the local police (vigili urbani) on ☎ 041 522 45 76.

Police Forces

If you run into trouble in Italy, you're likely to end up dealing with either the *polizia* (police) or the *carabinieri* (military police). The polizia are a civil force and take their orders from the Ministry of the Interior, while the carabinieri fall under the Ministry of Defence. There is a considerable duplication of roles, despite a 1981 reform intended to merge the two. Both are responsible for public order and security, which means you can call either in the event of a robbery or violent attack.

The carabinieri wear Gucci-designed black uniforms with a red stripe and drive equally black cars with a red stripe. They are well trained and tend to be helpful.

The polizia wear powder-blue trousers with a fuchsia stripe and a navy-blue jacket, and drive light-blue cars with a white stripe and Polizia written on the side. Tourists who want to report thefts and people wanting to get a residence permit will have to deal with them. They are based at the *questura* (police station; Map 7; ☎ 041 528 46 66) at Fondamenta di San Lorenzo 5053, in Castello.

Another type of police are the *vigili urbani*, who are basically traffic police. You will have to deal with them if you get a parking ticket or your car is towed away. In Venice they can be reached on ☎ 041 274 82 03.

Lastly, the *guardia di finanza* are responsible for fighting tax evasion and drug smuggling. It is highly unlikely, but you could be stopped by one of these grey-uniformed officers if you leave a shop without a receipt for your purchase.

they wanted to go) for outrageous sums of money. On occasion you will be whisked away to Murano to look at someone's cousin's glass shop.

Ignore all approaches from boat captains or illegal 'taxis'. The vaporetto lines 82 and 72 (summer only) will get you safely to most parts of Venice.

Bad Odours

In summer in particular, the smells emanating from the canals and sewers can be a little unpleasant. Put it down to local colour.

Tourists

The hordes of people meandering around the narrow *calli* (streets) of Venice and crowding onto the vaporetti can be a pain to one another and to locals. Try to be courteous. Don't amble three or more abreast down narrow calli, effectively blocking people coming up from behind who don't have all day to gawk at things, and cutting off oncoming traffic, too. Locals go into single file when they see oncoming pedestrians or hear someone behind trying to get past.

On the vaporetti, if you must hang around the embarkation barriers to look at things, be prepared to hop off at stops to let other passengers on and off before yourself getting back on to continue your trip.

LEGAL MATTERS

For some Italians, finding ways to get around the law (any law) is a way of life. They are likely to react with surprise, if not annoyance, if you point out that they might be breaking a law. Few people pay attention to speed limits, while most motorcyclists and many drivers don't stop at red lights – and certainly not at pedestrian crossings. No-one bats an eyelid about littering or dogs pooping in the middle of the footpath, even though many municipal councils have introduced laws against these things. But these are minor transgressions when measured against the country's organised crime, the extraordinary levels of tax evasion and the corruption in government and business.

The average tourist will probably have a brush with the law only if they are robbed by a bag-snatcher or pickpocket.

euro currency converter L10,000 = €5.16

Drugs

Italy's drug laws are lenient on users and heavy on pushers. If you're caught with drugs that the police determine are for your own personal use, you may be let off with a warning – and, of course, the drugs will be confiscated. If, instead, it is determined that you intend to sell the drugs in your possession, you could find yourself in prison. It's up to the police to determine whether or not you're a pusher, since the law is not specific about quantities.

BUSINESS HOURS

In general, shops are open from 9 am to 1 pm and 3.30 to 7.30 pm (or 4 to 8 pm) Monday to Saturday. They may remain closed on Monday morning or Saturday afternoon. Big department stores, such as Coin and Rinascente (in Mestre), and most supermarkets are open from 9 am to 7.30 pm Monday to Saturday. Some even open from 9 am to 1 pm on Sunday. Business hours have become more flexible since opening times were liberalised under new trading hours laws that came into effect in April 1999. At the time of writing it was difficult to determine what effect the new laws would actually have on opening hours.

Bars (in the Italian sense, ie coffee-and-sandwich places) and cafes generally open from 7.30 am to 8 pm, although some stay open after 8 pm and turn into pub-style drinking and meeting places.

For museum and gallery opening hours, see the Things to See & Do chapter. For bank opening hours see Where to Exchange under Money earlier in this chapter.

PUBLIC HOLIDAYS & SPECIAL EVENTS

The two main periods when *Veneziani* go on holiday are Settimana Santa (the week leading up to Easter Sunday) and, more noticeably, around the month of August.

Public Holidays

New Year's Day *(Anno Nuovo)*
    1 January
Epiphany *(Befana)*
    6 January
Good Friday *(Venerdì Santo)*
    March/April
Easter Monday *(Pasquetta/Giorno dopo Pasqua)*
    March/April
Liberation Day *(Giorno della Liberazione)*
    25 April
    (marks the Allied victory in Italy and the end of the German presence and Mussolini in 1945)
Labour Day *(Giorno del Lavoro)*
    1 May
Feast of the Assumption *(Ferragosto)*
    15 August
All Saints' Day *(Ognissanti)*
    1 November
Feast of the Immaculate Conception *(Concezione Immaculata)*
    8 December
Christmas Day *(Natale)*
    25 December
Boxing Day *(Festa di Santo Stefano)*
    26 December

Festivals

The APT publishes a list of annual events, including the many religious festivals staged by almost every church in the city.

January
Regatta delle Befane
    The first of more than 100 regattas on the lagoon throughout the year is held on the day of the Epiphany (6 January). Rowing Venetian-style *(la voga veneta)* involves boats somewhat resembling gondolas, whose crews row standing up.

February
Carnevale
    This is the major event of the year, when Venetians don spectacular masks and costumes for a week-long party in the run-up to Ash Wednesday (see the boxed text 'Carry on Carnevale' later in this section). The event was reinvented in 1979 and for some it is little more than a tacky tourist venture, albeit a popular one. Each year there is a different theme, so it is hard to pin down the program with any precision. The starting dates for Carnevale in the next few years are: 20 February 2001, 5 February 2002, 25 February 2003 and 17 February 2004.

April
Festa di San Marco
    The feast day of the city's patron saint, when menfolk are supposed to give their beloved a bunch of roses, is on 25 April.

May

Vogalonga

The 'long row' is a rowing regatta inspired by the Republic's glorious maritime history. This event began in November 1974, when a group of Venetians held their first race off the Isola di Burano in protest against pollution in the lagoon caused by the growing use of motorboats for business and pleasure. Since then it has developed into a friendly free-for-all, with 3000 or more participants and boats of all descriptions (powered by human muscle) participating in the 32km jaunt from the Bacino di San Marco up to Burano and back down to the Grand Canal via Cannaregio. A good spot to get a look at the latter end of the race is the Rialto area. Like quite a few events in Venice, it can't be pinned to a specific day, although it tends to be held fairly early in the month.

Festa della Sensa

This feast day falls on the second Sunday of May and marks the Feast of the Ascension. Already an important day in the Catholic calendar, it takes on a special significance in Venice. Every year since Ascension Day 998, when Venetian forces left to regain control of Dalmatia, the city has celebrated the Sposalizio del Mar (Wedding with the Sea; see the boxed text 'With This Ring I Thee Wet' in the History section of the Facts about Venice chapter). These days the mayor takes on the ducal role. The fun culminates with regattas off the Lido.

Late May–Early June

Palio delle Quattro Antiche Repubbliche Marinare

The former maritime republics of Amalfi, Genoa, Pisa and Venice take turns to host the colourful Historical Regatta of the Four Ancient Maritime Republics, in which four galleons, crewed by eight oarsmen and one at the tiller, compete for line honours. The challenge will be held in Venice again in 2003.

June

Marciliana

Since 1991, Chioggia has commemorated the siege of the city by Genoa in 1380 with a medieval pageant in late June involving parades and a competition between five *contrade*, or town quarters, that includes rowing and archery.

Sagra di San Pietro in Castello

A busy local festival in the last weekend of June with music, drinking and eating at the steps of the church that was once the city's cathedral.

July

Festa del Redentore

The feast of the Redeemer is marked by yet another regatta on the Grand Canal. The main celebrations, however, take place at the Chiesa del Redentore on Giudecca on the third weekend of the month. The Senato ordered the construction of this church in 1577 in thanksgiving for the end of a bout of the plague. Every year afterwards, the doge, members of the Senato, other VIPs and many of the city's people would cross the canal on a provisional pontoon to give thanks. Nowadays, the Canale della Giudecca fills with all sorts of boats to join in the festivities. The night before, people eat a traditional meal of roast duck and sit back to enjoy fireworks.

September

Regatta Storica

This historic gondola race along the Grand Canal is preceded by a parade of boats decorated in 15th-century style. Venetians first organised a rowing race in 1274, and have been doing it ever since. This regatta, one of the most important, is held on the first Sunday in the month. The mansions along the canal are draped in silks, flags and other festive decorations for the big day. Most of the competing boats are rowed by just two men, but in the past all sorts of vessels with crews of up to 50 competed. It may seem strange that in the past the involvement of women was far greater than today.

The race starts off at Castello and proceeds west up the canal to the former convent of Santa Chiara, where the boats turn around a *bricola* (pylon) to pound back down to the finishing line at Ca' Foscari.

November

Festa della Madonna della Salute

This procession over a bridge of boats across the Grand Canal to the Basilica di Santa Maria della Salute on 21 November is to give thanks for the city's deliverance from plague in 1630.

Arts & Music Festivals Venice hosts some major international arts festivals and a plethora of more minor but engaging events. They include:

June–October/November

Venezia Biennale

This major international exhibition of visual arts started in 1895 and was held every even-numbered year from the early 20th century.

Carry on Carnevale

History

Since pre-Christian days, people have been getting up to all sorts of shenanigans to celebrate the approaching end of winter – Ancient Rome's Saturnalia are a fine example. Earliest records of the word Carnevale date from the 12th century and scholars trace the Venetian festivities to the 15th-century Compagnie della Calza. These were private clubs whose members wore different coloured stockings (calze). They began organising competing masked balls on Martedì Grasso, during the run-up to Lent.

Over the centuries, all sorts of strange entertainments were conceived to heighten the revellers' enjoyment. The most bizarre of these was the firing of live dogs from cannons. A chosen few would also be selected to batter to death a fattened cat – with their heads. The town authorities even allowed the running of bulls through the streets (you have to wonder how many people and bulls ended up in the canals in this Venetian version of the Hemingway scene).

By the 18th century, the twilight years of La Serenissima, the ritual had evolved into a two-month party in which, if we are to believe the contemporary accounts, few holds were barred in the licentious activities of its participants. Seemingly immune to the political and economic decay of their once-proud city empire, the Venetians revelled in carnal pleasures.

After 1797 the locals sobered up a little under foreign occupation and Carnevale lost much of its mythical hedonistic verve. It disappeared altogether under Mussolini, who banned the wearing of masks in public.

In 1979 it took off again. 'Why?' is an interesting question. Some say it was a stunt to attract a little business in the slack winter month of February. If that is so, it worked. Carnevale is now firmly established as a must-see event, however hammed up it may seem.

However, the 1992 festival was postponed until 1993 so that there would be a festival on the Biennale's 100th anniversary in 1995. It is held in permanent pavilions in the Giardini Pubblici (Map 8), as well as at other locations throughout the city (including the Palazzo Grassi).

August/September
Mostra del Cinema di Venezia
The Venice International Film Festival, Italy's version of Cannes, is organised by the Biennale committee and held annually at the Palazzo del Cinema on the Lido (Map 13).

DOING BUSINESS

People wishing to make the first moves towards expanding their business into Italy should get in touch with their own country's trade department (such as the DTI in the UK). The commercial department of the Italian embassy in your own country should also have information – at least on red tape.

In Italy, the trade office of your embassy can provide tips and contacts.

Business Services

A GSM mobile phone and a good laptop computer will probably be all you need to do business in Venice. However, some of the better hotels have secretarial assistance for guests. Other companies that might be of help are listed in the *Pagine Gialle* (Yellow Pages) under 'Uffici Arredati e Servizi'. Translators/Interpreters are listed under 'Traduzioni Servizio'.

Exhibitions & Conferences

Venezia Congressi (☎ 041 522 84 00, fax 041 523 89 95), Dorsoduro 1056, and ENDAR (☎ 041 523 84 40, fax 041 528 68 46, email congress@endar.it), Castello 4966, can help with the organisation of business conventions in Venice. ENDAR's Web site is at www.enar.it.

Carry on Carnevale

Events

The festivities kick off on the Friday afternoon with La Festa delle Marie, a procession through the city. This is a precursor to the official opening on Saturday, when a traditional masked procession leaves Piazza San Marco around 4 pm and circulates through the calli. The following day there are jousts and other mock military tournaments.

The following Thursday is Giovedì Grasso, a festival that has always been a part of Venice's celebration of Carnevale. Friday afternoon's highlight is the Gran Ballo delle Maschere (Grand Masked Ball) in Piazza San Marco. Anyone with proper costume and mask who is able to dance the quadrilles and other steps of a few centuries ago may join in.

Saturday and Sunday are given over to musical and theatrical performances in Piazza San Marco. Also, on the Sunday, a beautiful procession of decorated boats and gondolas bearing masked passengers wends its way serenely down the Grand Canal.

The event winds up with a parade of the Re del Carnevale (Carnival King) and the one-time guilds of the city.

During the course of the festivities plenty goes on outside the main events – street performers fill the main thoroughfares and squares. Campo San Polo is often given over to children's theatre, jugglers and the like for the little ones. For a feel of how Carnevale was centuries ago, head for the Vecio Carnevale in Via Garibaldi.

The Grand Canal itself is the centre of the events. Throughout the Carnevale period it is kept lit by torchlight during the evenings.

For many, the biggest events are the *balli in maschera* (masked balls). You're looking at up to L400,000 for a ticket, plus the outlay for hiring a costume and mask. The tourist office can tell you exactly when and where the balls are taking place and how to make a booking.

WORK

It is illegal for non-EU citizens to work in Italy without a work permit *(permesso di lavoro)*, but trying to obtain one through your Italian consulate can be a pain. EU citizens are allowed to work in Italy, but they still need to obtain a residence permit *(permesso di soggiorno)* from a police station. New immigration laws require foreign workers to be 'legalised' through their employers, which can apply even to cleaners and babysitters. The employers then pay pension and health insurance contributions. This doesn't mean that illegal work can't still be found.

A useful guide is *Living, Studying, and Working in Italy* by Travis Neighbor and Monica Larner.

If you intend to look for work in Venice, you should bring along any paperwork that might help. English teachers, for instance, will need any certificates they have demon- strating qualifications and references from previous employers. Increasingly, there is cross-recognition of degrees and other tertiary qualifications, so it may be worthwhile bringing these as well. Translations validated by the Italian embassy in your country wouldn't hurt either.

Working Holidays

The best options are trying to find work in a bar, nightclub or restaurant during the tourist season. Another option is au pair work, organised before you come to Italy. A useful guide is *The Au Pair and Nanny's Guide to Working Abroad* by Susan Griffith & Sharon Legg. Susan Griffith's *Work Your Way Around the World* is also worth looking at.

Art students and graduates might consider one other possibility. The Peggy Guggenheim Collection takes on foreign students to staff the museum, cloakroom and so on for periods of up to three months. This is most easily pursued through your art school.

Language Teaching

The easiest source of work for foreigners is teaching English (or another foreign language), but even with full qualifications a non-EU citizen might find it difficult to secure a permanent position. Most of the larger, more reputable schools will hire only people with work and/or residence permits, but their attitude can become more flexible if demand for teachers is high and they come across someone with good qualifications.

The more professional schools will require teachers to have a Teaching English as a Foreign Language (TEFL) certificate. It is advisable to apply for work early in the year, in order to be considered for positions available in October (language-school years correspond roughly to the Italian school year: late September to the end of June).

Some schools hire people without work permits or qualifications, but the pay is usually low (around L15,000 an hour). It is more lucrative to advertise your services and pick up private students (rates vary wildly, from as low as L15,000 to up to L50,000 an hour), but of course this takes time to develop. The average rate is around L30,000. Although you may get away without qualifications or experience, bring along a few English grammar books (including exercises) to help you at least appear professional. Most people get started by placing advertisements in shop windows and on university notice boards.

To find language schools, look up 'Scuole di Lingue' in the *Pagine Gialle* (Yellow Pages).

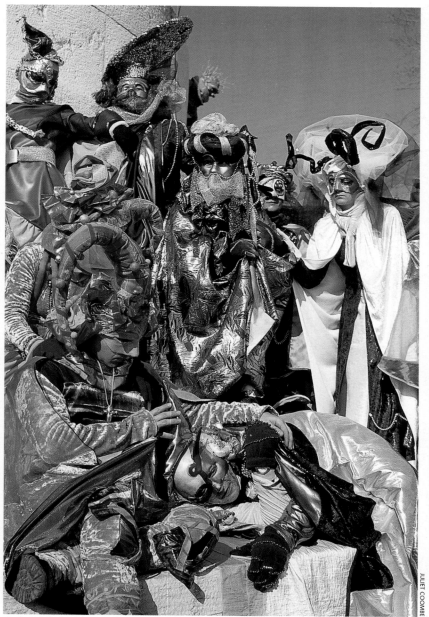

A silent riot of colour – a mime group performs at Venice's Carnevale.

Preparation for the Carnevale – first procure your costume and apply your make-up (top left and right), then hit the streets and let the serious business of revelry begin.

It's a cover up! The only way to be seen (or not) at Carnevale. Masks are *de rigueur* at many of the events, from balls to street processions.

JULIET COOMBE

JULIET COOMBE

OLIVIER CIRENDINI

JULIET COOMBE

SERVIZIO GONDOLE

Venice just wouldn't be the same without its gondolas, a most graceful and luxurious mode of transport. Here, gondoliers await business, while one boat awaits a lick of paint (top right).

Getting There & Away

There are direct flights to Venice from abroad and from within Italy. The city lies at the eastern end of major railway and road routes ranging across the north of the country from Milan, and it is also possible to arrive by sea – once the only way into the city.

For recommended travel agencies in Venice, see the Travel Agencies section at the end of this chapter.

AIR

Venice is one of Italy's smaller air traffic centres. Direct flights from major European centres and New York are available, alongside internal flights from the rest of Italy, but for intercontinental air travel you will generally have to consider flying to or from Milan or even Rome. Rome is the main international hub and visitors flying from distant locales such as Australasia will have little choice but to fly to Rome and connect from there by air or rail.

Although Venice is hardly a discount destination, occasional good deals turn up – see the following text for some examples.

Marco Polo airport is 12km from Venice, but some flights land at Treviso airport, about 30km north of the city. In the latter case, the airlines concerned sometimes provide a connecting bus to Venice. For more information on getting to and from the airports, and on facilities in the airports, see the Getting Around chapter.

Travellers with Special Needs

If you have a broken leg, are a vegetarian or require a special diet (such as kosher food), are travelling in a wheelchair or have some other special need, let the airline know so that they can make appropriate arrangements. You should call to remind them of your requirements at least 72 hours before departure and again when you check in at the airport. It may also be worth ringing round the airlines before you make your booking to find out how they can handle your particular needs. Some airlines publish

brochures on the subject. Ask your travel agency for details.

Guide dogs for the blind will often have to travel in a specially pressurised baggage compartment and are subject to quarantine laws when entering, or returning to, countries currently free of rabies, such as the UK or Australia. Quarantine laws in Britain were due to change at the time of writing; check the current situation with the Ministry of Agriculture, Fisheries and Food (☎ 0645 33 55 77).

Deaf travellers can ask for airport and inflight announcements to be written down for them.

Children aged under two travel for 10% of the standard fare (or free on some airlines), as long as they don't occupy a seat. They don't get a baggage allowance. Skycots, baby food and nappies (diapers) should be provided by the airline if requested in advance. Children aged between two and 12 can usually occupy a seat for half to two-thirds of the full fare and do get a baggage allowance. Pushchairs (strollers) can often be carried as hand luggage.

Departure Tax

Departure taxes are factored into your air tickets and vary according to destination and whether you are buying a one-way or a return ticket.

Other Parts of Italy

Travelling by plane is expensive within Italy – it makes better sense to use the efficient and considerably cheaper train and bus services. The domestic lines are Alitalia (☎ 800 050350) and Meridiana (☎ 0789 6 93 00). The main airports are in Rome, Milan, Naples, Pisa, Catania and Cagliari, but there are other, smaller airports throughout Italy. Domestic flights can be booked through travel agencies.

Alitalia offers a range of discounts for young people, families, seniors and weekend travellers, as well as occasional special

Air Travel Glossary

Baggage Allowance This will be written on your ticket and usually includes one 20kg item to go in the hold, plus one item of hand luggage.

Bucket Shops These are unbonded travel agencies specialising in discounted airline tickets.

Bumped Just because you have a confirmed seat doesn't mean you're going to get on the plane (see Overbooking).

Cancellation Penalties If you have to cancel or change a discounted ticket, there are often heavy penalties involved; insurance can sometimes be taken out against these penalties. Some airlines impose penalties on regular tickets as well, particularly against 'no-show' passengers.

Check-In Airlines ask you to check in a certain time ahead of the flight departure (usually one to two hours on international flights). If you fail to check in on time and the flight is overbooked, the airline can cancel your booking and give your seat to somebody else.

Confirmation Having a ticket written out with the flight and date you want doesn't mean you have a seat until the agent has checked with the airline that your status is 'OK' or confirmed. Meanwhile you could just be 'on request'.

Courier Fares Businesses often need to send urgent documents or freight securely and quickly. Courier companies hire people to accompany the package through customs and, in return, offer a discount ticket which is sometimes a phenomenal bargain. In effect, what the companies do is ship their freight as your luggage on regular commercial flights. This is a legitimate operation, but there are two shortcomings – the short turnaround time of the ticket (usually not longer than a month) and the limitation on your luggage allowance. You may have to surrender all your allowance and take only carry-on luggage.

Full Fares Airlines traditionally offer 1st class (coded F), business class (coded J) and economy class (coded Y) tickets. These days there are so many promotional and discounted fares available that few passengers pay full economy fare.

ITX An ITX, or 'independent inclusive tour excursion', is often available on tickets to popular holiday destinations. Officially it's a package deal combined with hotel accommodation, but many agents will sell you one of these for the flight only and give you phoney hotel vouchers in the unlikely event that you're challenged at the airport.

Lost Tickets If you lose your airline ticket an airline will usually treat it like a travellers cheque and, after inquiries, issue you with another one. Legally, however, an airline is entitled to treat it like cash and if you lose it then it's gone forever. Take good care of your tickets.

MCO An MCO, or 'miscellaneous charge order', is a voucher that looks like an airline ticket but carries no destination or date. It can be exchanged through any International Association of Travel Agents (IATA) airline for a ticket on a specific flight. It's a useful alternative to an onward ticket in those countries that demand one, and is more flexible than an ordinary ticket if you're unsure of your route.

No-Shows No-shows are passengers who fail to show up for their flight. Full-fare passengers who fail to turn up are sometimes entitled to travel on a later flight. The rest are penalised (see Cancellation Penalties).

Air Travel Glossary

On Request This is an unconfirmed booking for a flight.

Onward Tickets An entry requirement for many countries is that you have a ticket out of the country. If you're unsure of your next move, the easiest solution is to buy the cheapest onward ticket to a neighbouring country or a ticket from a reliable airline which can later be refunded if you do not use it.

Open Jaw Tickets These are return tickets where you fly out to one place but return from another. If available, this can save you backtracking to your arrival point.

Overbooking Airlines hate to fly empty seats and since every flight has some passengers who fail to show up, airlines often book more passengers than they have seats. Usually excess passengers make up for the no-shows, but occasionally somebody gets 'bumped' onto the next available flight. Guess who it is most likely to be? The passengers who check in late.

Point-to-Point Tickets These are discount tickets that can be bought on some routes in return for passengers waiving their rights to a stopover.

Promotional Fares These are officially discounted fares, available from travel agencies or direct from the airline.

Reconfirmation If you don't reconfirm your flight at least 72 hours prior to departure, the airline may delete your name from the passenger list. Ring to find out if your airline requires reconfirmation.

Restrictions Discounted tickets often have various restrictions on them – such as needing to be paid for in advance and incurring a penalty to be altered. Others are restrictions on the minimum and maximum period you must be away, such as a minimum of 14 days or a maximum of one year.

Round-the-World Tickets RTW tickets give you a limited period (usually a year) in which to circumnavigate the globe. You can go anywhere the carrying airlines go, as long as you don't backtrack. The number of stopovers or total number of separate flights is decided before you set off and they usually cost a bit more than a basic return flight.

Stand-by This is a discounted ticket where you only fly if there is a seat free at the last moment. Stand-by fares are usually available only on domestic routes.

Transferred Tickets Airline tickets cannot be transferred from one person to another. Travellers sometimes try to sell the return half of their ticket, but officials can ask you to prove that you are the person named on the ticket. This is less likely to happen on domestic flights, but on an international flight tickets are compared with passports.

Travel Agencies Travel agencies vary widely and you should choose one that suits your needs. Some simply handle tours, while full-service agencies handle everything from tours and tickets to car rental and hotel bookings. If all you want is a ticket at the lowest possible price, then go to an agency specialising in discounted fares.

Travel Periods Ticket prices vary with the time of year. There is a low (off-peak) season and a high (peak) season, and often a low-shoulder season and a high-shoulder season as well. Usually the fare depends on your outward flight – if you depart in the high season and return in the low season, you pay the high-season fare.

GETTING THERE & AWAY

promotional fares. One-way fares and standard returns (basically just two one-way tickets) are expensive. If you get a return, purchasing an Apex (or even better a Super Apex) fare will bring the price down considerably, in exchange for observing certain conditions (for example, staying over Saturday night or travelling midweek).

The following is a sample of one-way air fares to/from Venice:

destination	fare (L)	duration
Bari	300,000	1½ hours direct
Catania	370,000	2½ to four hours, via Rome
Milan	165,000	45 minutes
Naples	270,000	70 minutes
Palermo	370,000	three hours, via Rome, Naples or Milan
Rome	230,000	65 minutes

A return Apex fare to Rome, however, comes to L320,000. To Naples it would be L305,000.

Meridiana does not fly to Venice, but has connections from nearby Verona to Cagliari, Catania, Naples, Palermo and Rome. Fares are similarly high.

Other Countries

The UK Discount air travel is big business in London. Most British travel agencies are registered with ABTA (the Association of British Travel Agents). If you have paid for your flight with an ABTA-registered agent who then goes bust, ABTA will guarantee a refund or an alternative. Unregistered travel agencies are riskier, but sometimes cheaper. Advertisements for tickets appear in the travel pages of the weekend broadsheets, such as the *Independent* on Saturday and the *Sunday Times*.

One of the more reliable agencies is STA (☎ 020-7361 6161). It has offices throughout London, as well as branches on many university campuses and in cities such as Bristol, Cambridge, Leeds, Manchester and Oxford. Visit its Web site at www.statravel .co.uk. Another is usit Campus (☎ 020-7730 3402), which also has branches throughout

London and the UK. Its Web site is www .usitcampus.co.uk. Both these agencies sell tickets to all travellers, but cater especially for young people and students.

Trailfinders (☎ 020-7937 5400) is another recommended agency. Its short-haul booking centre is at 215 Kensington High St, London W8, and there are also Trailfinders offices in Bristol, Birmingham, Glasgow and Manchester.

The two principal airlines linking the UK and Italy are British Airways (BA; ☎ 0845 222111) and Alitalia (☎ 0870 5448259). Their Web sites are www.british-airways .com and www.alitalia.it respectively. Standard high-season fares on scheduled Alitalia flights to Venice are around UK£280 one way and UK£330 return. BA fares cost around the same.

However, unless you buy at the last minute and are unlucky, you shouldn't need to resort to standard fares. Both airlines offer occasional special deals and a couple of smaller companies also fly to Venice.

BA's low-cost airline, Go, flies to four Italian destinations, including Venice, from London Stansted Airport. Go offers two kinds of return fare: Standard and Flexible. The former is fixed and non-refundable, while the latter allows you to alter your plans. Standard returns start at around UK£100, while Flexible fares start at around UK£150. Often, however, you will pay more – prices rise as seats fill. You can book online (www.go-fly.com) or by phone (☎ 0845 60 54321 in the UK, ☎ 147 887766 in Italy).

The Irish low-cost airline Ryanair (☎ 0541 569569) also flies to Venice direct from Stansted at least once daily. This airline aims at a short-stay clientele and occasionally comes up with some extraordinary deals. By way of example, a five-day fare to Venice in February has cost as little as UK£50.70 (including taxes). Check out the Web site at www.ryanair.com. Ryanair lands at Treviso airport and provides a bus into Venice. You can contact Ryanair at Treviso airport on ☎ 0422 31 51 31.

Charter flights are another option worth considering. Italy Sky Shuttle (☎ 020-8748

1333), 227 Shepherd's Bush Rd, London W6 7AS, specialises in charter flights to 22 destinations in Italy from London, Birmingham, Manchester, Glasgow and Edinburgh. The best high-season return fare from London (Gatwick) to Venice is around UK£170. Sky Shuttle can also organise fly/drive deals.

The Charter Flight Centre (☎ 020-7565 6755), 15 Gillingham St, London SW1V 1HN, has return flights valid for up to four weeks from around UK£130 (including taxes) to around UK£170.

Another specialist in flights and holidays to Italy is Skybus Italia (☎ 020-7631 3444), 37 Harley St, London W1.

The Air Travel Advisory Bureau (☎ 020-7636 5000) can provide further details of discount travel agencies.

Youth Passes Alitalia offers people aged under 26 (and students aged under 31 with a valid ISIC) a Europa Pass from London and Dublin. The pass is valid for up to six months and allows unlimited one-way flights to all the airline's European and Mediterranean destinations for UK£62 per flight, with a minimum of four flights. The first flight has to be to Italy and the last flight back to the UK or Ireland from Italy. Internal flights in Italy with this pass cost UK£45 a pop.

Continental Europe Short hops can be expensive, but for longer journeys you can often find air fares that beat overland alternatives on cost.

France If time is at a premium, flying from Paris is not a bad option. Low-season deals with Alitalia or Air France cost 1674FF return at the time of writing – not too much more than the train. You needed to book 10 days in advance and stay at least one weekend.

AirDolomiti (☎ 08 02 02 00 30 in France, ☎ 800 01 33 66 in Italy), a regional airline in partnership with Lufthansa, operates two daily flights between Paris and Venice. You can visit its Web site at www.airdolomiti.it. Low-season return fares cost from around 1500FF.

STA Travel's outlet in France is Voyages Wasteels (☎ 08 03 88 70 04, in France only), at 11 rue Dupuytren, in Paris.

Germany Munich is a haven of budget travel outlets. Council Travel (☎ 089-39 50 22), Adalbertstrasse 32, is one of the best. STA Travel (☎ 089-39 90 96), Königstrasse 49, is also good.

In Berlin, Kilroy Travel-ARTU Reisen (☎ 030-310 00 40), at Hardenbergstrasse 9, is a good travel agency. In Frankfurt am Main, you could try STA Travel (☎ 069-70 30 35), Bockenheimer Landstrasse 133.

Typically, a return from Munich to Venice on a Lufthansa Airlines scheduled flight costs around DM450 (DM400 youth fare).

Netherlands The student travel agency NBBS Reiswinkels (☎ 020-620 50 71), Rokin 38, Amsterdam, offers reasonably low fares. Compare with the bucket shops along Rokin before deciding. NBBS has branches throughout the city.

From Amsterdam, KLM-Royal Dutch Airlines flies direct to Venice for f700 return. At the time of writing it was also possible to get return flights to Venice with Swissair via Zürich and with Air France via Paris for around f550.

Spain A good travel agency in Madrid is Viajes Zeppelin (☎ 91 542 5154), at Plaza de Santo Domingo 2. In Barcelona, you could try Halcón Viatges (☎ 93 412 4411), at Carrer de Pau Claris 108 (one of 25 branches in the city).

AirDolomiti (see the earlier France section) has a daily direct connection between Venice and Barcelona. Return fares start from around 30,000 ptas in the low season and 60,000 ptas in the high season.

The USA Council Travel (☎ 800 226 8624) and STA (☎ 800 777 0112) have offices in major cities across the USA. Their Web sites are www.counciltravel.com and www .statravel.com respectively. Discount travel agencies, known as consolidators, can be found in the weekly travel sections of the *New York Times*, the *Los Angeles Times*,

GETTING THERE & AWAY

the *Chicago Tribune* and the *San Francisco Examiner*.

At the time of writing, you could get a return fare from Los Angeles to Venice for around US$525 with Lufthansa via Frankfurt in the low season (roughly January to March). A more realistic average might be around US$650. From New York, you could fly with a variety of airlines (for example, Swissair via Zürich) for around US$520 return. After March, prices rise rapidly and availability declines. You will be lucky to find return flights from the east coast for under US$750, while from LA or San Francisco the average hovers around US$1300.

In June 1999, Air Europe (☎ 888 999 9090 toll free) began flying Venice–New York nonstop. Prices and schedules were still rather volatile at the time of writing.

Stand-by fares are often sold at 60% of the normal price for one-way tickets. Airhitch (☎ 800 326 2009 toll free), with a Web site at www.airhitch.org, specialises in this.

Another option is a courier flight, where you accompany freight or a parcel to its destination. A New York–Rome return on a courier flight can cost about US$300 (more from the west coast of the USA). Generally, courier flights require that you return within a specified period (sometimes within one or two weeks, but often up to one month). You will need to travel light, as luggage is usually restricted to what you can carry on to the plane (the parcel or freight you carry comes out of your luggage allowance). You may have to be a US resident and have an interview before they will take you on. Most flights depart from New York.

A good source of information on courier flights is Now Voyager (☎ 212-431 1616), Suite 307, 74 Varrick St, New York, NY 10013. Phone after 6 pm to listen to a recorded message detailing all available flights and prices or check the Web site at www.nowvoyagertravel.com. It is also possible to organise the flights directly through the courier companies. Look in the Yellow Pages under Courier Services.

If you can't find a good deal, it is always worth considering getting an inexpensive transatlantic hop to London and prowling around the discount agencies there (see the earlier UK section).

Canada There are no direct flights from Canada to Venice. Alitalia and Air Canada have direct flights to Rome and Milan from Toronto and Montreal. Whoever you fly with, you will have to make a connecting flight to reach Venice.

Travel CUTS (☎ 800 667 2887), called Voyages Campus in Quebec, has offices in all major cities in Canada; its Web site is www.travelcuts.com.

The *Toronto Globe & Mail*, the *Toronto Star* and the *Vancouver Province* carry travel agency advertisements and are good places to look for cheap fares. For courier flights, contact FB on Board Courier Services (☎ 514-631 7925), in Toronto.

Return fares to Rome in the low/high season with airlines such as Air Canada, Alitalia and Canadian Airlines International cost around C$1100/1500 from Montreal, C$1100/$1850 from Vancouver and C$700/1500 from Toronto.

Australia STA Travel (☎ 131 776) and Flight Centres International (☎ 131 600) are major dealers in cheap air fares. Their Web sites are www.statravel.com.au and www.flightcentre.com.au respectively. Heavily discounted fares can also be obtained through travel agencies. Some agencies, particularly smaller ones, advertise cheap air fares in the travel sections of weekend newspapers, such as the *Age* in Melbourne and the *Sydney Morning Herald*.

Discounted return air fares to Rome on mainstream airlines such as Alitalia and Qantas Airways through reputable agents can be surprisingly cheap. Low-season fares from Sydney or Melbourne to Rome average from around A$1600 to A$1800 return but can go as low as A$1300 with airlines like Gulf Air and EgyptAir. You might get an add-on to Venice pretty cheaply too.

On some flights between Australia and destinations like London, Paris and Frankfurt, a return ticket between that destination and another major European city is thrown in – you could use this to get to Venice, or at least as far as Rome or Milan.

For courier flights, try Jupiter (☎ 02-9317 2230), Unit 3, 55 Kent Rd, Mascot, Sydney 2020.

New Zealand STA Travel (☎ 09-309 0458, Auckland office) and Flight Centres International (☎ 09-309 6171, Auckland office) are popular agents, with branches throughout the country. Their Web sites are www.statravel.com.au and www.flight centre.com.au respectively. The *New Zealand Herald* has a travel section in which travel agencies advertise fares.

Return fares from New Zealand to Rome cost from around NZ$2000 to NZ$2250 in the low season with airlines such as Malaysia Airlines, Qantas and Thai Airways International. A Round-the-World (RTW) ticket may be cheaper than a normal return.

Asia Hong Kong, Bangkok and Singapore are all discount air-fare centres. Shop around. A one-way fare from Hong Kong to Europe can cost as little as US$660, while bucket shops in Bangkok can get you a one-way fare for about US$460.

STA has branches in Hong Kong (Sincerity Travel), Tokyo, Singapore, Bangkok and Kuala Lumpur.

Airline Offices
Airlines are listed under Linee Aeree in the *Pagine Gialle* (Yellow Pages). Generally, you won't find any offices in Venice itself. Most have reps at one or other of the airports and increasingly offer freephone numbers for you to call. The Clipper Viaggi travel agency in Mestre (Map 15) represents several airlines.

Alitalia
(☎ 147 865641, 041 258 12 22) Via Sansovino 7, Mestre
British Airways
(☎ 800 287287). The nearest office is in Padua (☎ 049 66 04 44), at Piazza Salvenini 5.
Canadian Airlines International
(☎ 041 98 77 44) Clipper Viaggi, Via Lazzari 1, Mestre

GO
(☎ 147 887766). The nearest office is at Malpensa airport, Milan.
Qantas Airways
(☎ 041 98 77 44) Clipper Viaggi, Via Lazzari 1, Mestre
Ryanair
(☎ 0422 31 51 31) Treviso airport
TWA
(☎ 041 98 77 44) Clipper Viaggi, Via Lazzari 1, Mestre

BUS
The bus is usually cheaper than the train, but less comfortable for long journeys. Where rail services are poor or absent in the Veneto, bus becomes the only option. Where you can get a train, it is generally preferable to do so.

The main bus station *(stazione autobus)* is at Piazzale Roma (Map 3). Buses leave here for destinations around the Veneto, the rest of Italy and abroad. Along with ticket offices, you'll find a Telecom phone booth, hotel booking booth, bureau de change, car hire agencies and a left-luggage office *(deposito bagagli)*. The left-luggage office is open daily from 8 am to 9 pm and charges L5000 per item per 24 hours.

Other Parts of Italy
ACTV buses (☎ 041 528 78 86) serve the area immediately surrounding Venice, including Mestre and Chioggia.

ATVO (Azienda Trasporti Veneto Orientale; ☎ 041 520 55 30) operates buses to destinations all over the eastern part of the Veneto. A slew of other companies go farther west in the Veneto, across into Friuli-Venezia Giulia (Italy's easternmost region) and elsewhere throughout the country. Tickets and information are available at the ticket office in Piazzale Roma (Map 3).

Note, however, that for principal destinations (Padua, Vicenza, Verona and Treviso in the Veneto; Bologna, Florence, Milan, Rome and Trieste beyond) it is much easier to get the train. In the case of Vicenza and Verona, for example, you would first have to get a bus to Padua (departures every half-hour or so) and then make an onward connection. The train is incomparably simpler.

GETTING THERE & AWAY

Throughout the Excursions chapter you will find information on how to get to your destination. If a bus is suggested, board it in Piazzale Roma.

Other Countries

Eurolines, in conjunction with local bus companies across Europe, is the main international carrier. The Busabout network also covers Venice, but is of interest only to those who intend to travel a lot beyond Italy as well. Based in London, Busabout (☎ 020-7950 1661, fax 7950 1662, email info@busabout.co.uk) has a Web site at www.busabout.com.

Eurolines From London, Eurolines (☎ 0870 5143219), 52 Grosvenor Gardens, Victoria, London SW1W 0AU, runs buses to Venice via Milan (where you must change) on Wednesday and Saturday (an extra bus leaves on Friday in summer). The trip takes 30½ hours. The one-way and return fares are, respectively, around UK£90 and UK£125 (UK£80 and UK£115 for those aged under 26 and seniors). The standard one-way adult fare going the other way is around L220,000. Fares rise in the peak summer season (July and August) and in the week before Christmas. Buses depart from Victoria Coach Station, a couple of blocks from the Eurolines office.

Eurolines has offices in several French cities, including in the Paris bus station (☎ 01 49 72 51 51), 28 ave du Générale de Gaulle, and on the left bank at 55 rue St Jacques (☎ 01 43 54 11 99), off blvd St Germain. Passengers going to or coming from the UK often have to change buses here. The standard one-way/return fare to Venice is around 570/940FF (L165,000/270,000 from Venice).

Eurolines also runs services direct from Venice to Amsterdam, Barcelona (with connections to Alicante and Madrid), Brussels, Budapest, Marrakesh, Montpellier, Nice and Perpignan. For buses to other European cities, you often need to change in Milan and, depending on your destination, en route.

In Venice, Eurolines tickets can be bought from Agenzia Brusutti (Map 3; ☎ 041 522 97 73), Piazzale Roma 497/e.

Eurolines' Web site at www.eurolines .com provides links to the sites of all the national operators.

TRAIN

From Stazione di Santa Lucia, known in Venice simply as the *ferrovia*, you can get direct trains west to Padua, Verona, Milan and Bologna, and on into France and Switzerland. Heading east, you can travel to Trieste and on to Slovenia, Croatia, Hungary and beyond. Connections to Florence, Rome and farther south can easily be made too.

Eurail, InterRail and Europass rail passes are valid on the national rail network, the Ferrovie dello Stato (FS).

There's another station in Mestre.

Information

Stazione di Santa Lucia There's a rail travel information office inside the station opposite the APT office. It's open daily from 7.30 am to 9 pm and usually has quite a queue outside. Just outside the train station doors, to the right as you exit, is a Transalpino office (see Travel Agencies later in this chapter).

For fare and timetable information, you can call ☎ 147 888088. It's an automated service in Italian only. Train timetables are posted at Stazione di Santa Lucia. The main timetable *(orario)* displays arrivals *(arrivi)* on a white background and departures *(partenze)* on a yellow one. Impending arrivals and departures also appear on electronic boards. You will notice a plethora of symbols and acronyms on the main timetables, some of which are useful for identifying the type of train concerned (see Types of Train in the following Other Parts of Italy section).

It is possible to get a paperback-sized timetable, with details of all the main services, from selected outlets outside Italy. In the UK, for instance, you can find it at Italwings (☎ 020-7287 2117), 162–168 Regent St, London W1R 5TB. The timetable is available at many newsstands in Italy. You may be able to get a free booklet covering the main lines from Venice at the rail information office. It is called *In Treno Triveneto* and covers main national routes as well as all lines operating within the Triveneto area (ie the Veneto, Friuli-Venezia Giulia and Trentino).

Next door to the APT office in the station is an Associazione Veneziana Albergatori hotel booking service.

The deposito bagagli is opposite platform 7 and open from 3.45 am to 12.30 am. You pay L5000 per piece for 12 hours.

Opposite platform 11 there's an Exact Change booth, open daily from 8.20 am to 7.40 pm. There's also an automatic exchange machine if you are desperate for lire outside working hours. Just outside the booth is a credit card pay phone, and standard Telecom phones are scattered about the station.

Mestre You will find similar services at Mestre station (Map 15), including rail information, a hotel booking office (see Seasons & Reservations in the Places to Stay chapter), phones (including a credit card phone) and a bureau de change (open daily from 8 am to 8 pm). The deposito bagagli is open daily from 4 am to 1 am. Charges are the same as at Stazione di Santa Lucia.

Other Parts of Italy
Types of Train A wide variety of trains can be found on the Italian rail network. They start with slow all-stops *locali*, which generally don't travel much beyond their main city of origin or province. Next come the *regionali*, which also tend to be slow, but cover greater distances, sometimes going beyond their region of origin. *Interregionali* cover greater distances still and don't necessarily stop at every station.

From this level, there is a qualitative leap upwards to InterCity (IC) trains, faster, long-distance trains operating between major cities, for which you generally have to pay a *supplemento* on top of the normal cost of a ticket. EuroCity (EC) trains are the international version. They can reach a top speed of 200km/h (but rarely get the chance!).

Comfort and speed on the most important lines are provided by the *pendolino* trains, so-called because they 'lean' up to 8° into

curves to increase standard InterCity speeds by up to 35%.

Pendolini and other top-of-the-range services, which on high-speed track can zip along at more than 300km/h, are now collectively known as Eurostar Italia (ES). The Eurostar Italia runs once daily between Venice and Milan and takes just 2 hours 50 minutes. There are five services to Rome via Florence from Venice. The other main routes for these top-level trains are Milan–Rome (4½ hours) via Florence (and in some cases south to Naples), and south-east from Milan to Ancona via Bologna.

Other train types you may encounter are the *diretto* (D) and *espresso* (E). They are slow and are gradually disappearing.

Night trains *(notturne)* are either old espressi or, increasingly, InterCity Notte (ICN) services. You generally have the option of *cuccette* (couchettes) – four or six fold-down bunk beds in a compartment – or a proper bed in a *vagone letto* (sleeping car). A place in the latter is much more expensive than a simple *cuccetta*. The international version is the EuroNight (EN).

Tickets The cost of train travel is lower in Italy than in most of Western Europe. Fares are generally calculated according to distance travelled. All this may change, as the national government has announced sweeping changes in fare calculation and hefty price rises, possibly by the end of 1999.

There are many ticket possibilities. Apart from the standard division between 1st and 2nd class *(prima classe* and *seconda classe)* on the faster trains (generally you can only get 2nd-class seats on locali and regionali), you usually have to pay a supplement for being on a fast train. As with tickets, the price of the supplement is calculated according to the length of the journey. You can pay the supplement separately from the ticket. Thus, if you have a 2nd-class return ticket from Venice to Milan, you might decide to avoid the supplement one way and take a slower train, but pay it on the way back to speed things up a little. Whatever you decide, you need to pay the supplement before boarding the train.

GETTING THERE & AWAY

It is advisable, and in some cases obligatory, to book long-distance tickets in advance, whether international or domestic. In 1st class, booking is often mandatory (and free). Where it is optional (which is more often, but not always, the case in 2nd class), you may pay a L5000 booking fee. Tickets can be booked at the windows in the station or at most travel agencies.

The following prices are approximate standard 2nd-class one-way fares (plus supplement) on InterCity trains. Pendolino and Eurostar Italia fares are higher.

destination	fare (L)	duration
Bologna	14,000 (+8500)	Two hours
Florence	22,000 (+12,000)	Three hours
Milan	22,000 (+12,000)	2¾ hours
Naples	60,000 (+21,500)	Nine hours
Rome	45,500 (+18,500)	5½ hours

Validate your ticket by stamping it in one of the yellow machines scattered about all stations (usually with a *convalida* sign on them). Failure to do so will be rewarded with an on-the-spot L40,000 fine if you're caught by the conductor. If you buy a return ticket, you must stamp it each way (each end of the ticket).

The ticket you buy is valid for two months until stamped. Once stamped it is valid for 24 hours if the distance of the journey (one-way) is greater than 200km, six hours if it is less. The time calculated is for each one-way journey (so on a short return trip, you get six hours from the time of stamping on the way out and the same on the way back).

The Veneto Almost all services, from the humble locali to the high-speed Eurostar Italia trains, stop at the main centres of Mestre, Padua, Vicenza and Verona on the westward journey across the Veneto. Remember that getting an InterCity or Eurostar Italia train on short journeys such as these means paying a supplement, which in these cases will often be as much as double the cost of the fare – it is up to you to decide to what extent time is money.

To other destinations in the Veneto, rail services are comparatively limited – you can head north to Treviso and north-west to Bassano del Grappa easily, but beyond those places it becomes more sensible to work out alternatives by bus.

See the individual sections in the Excursions chapter for information on how to get about the Veneto.

Other Countries
The UK The Channel Tunnel allows for land transport links between Britain and Continental Europe. The Eurostar passenger train service (☎ 0990 186186) travels between London and Paris and London and Brussels. Visit its Web site at www.eurostar .com. The Eurotunnel vehicle-carrying service (☎ 0990 353535) travels between terminals in Folkestone and Calais. Its Web address is www.eurotunnel.com.

Alternatively, you can get a train ticket that includes the Channel crossing by ferry, SeaCat or hovercraft. After that, you can travel via Paris and southern France or by swinging from Belgium down through Germany and Switzerland. As a rule, however, it is quicker to travel via Paris.

The cheapest standard fares to Venice via Paris by train and ferry on offer at the time of writing were around UK£75/145 one-way/return for students and those aged under 26, while the full adult fares were around UK£95/160.

Always ask about discounts. As a rule, toddlers aged under four go for free. Kids aged four to 11 travel for half the adult fare. Seniors can get a Rail Europe Senior card (valid for one year only for trips that cross at least one border). You pay UK£5 for the card, but you must already have a Senior Citizens Rail Card (UK£18), available to anyone who can prove they are aged over 60 (you are not required to be a UK resident). The pass entitles you to roughly 30% off standard fares. The card is known in Italy as Carta Rail Europe Senior and costs L33,000. Groups often qualify for discounts too.

For information on international train travel using the Eurostar, contact the Rail

Europe Travel Centre (☎ 0870 5848848), 179 Piccadilly, London W1V 0BA. For rail travel to Italy using cheaper train-ferry combinations, go to Wasteels (☎ 020-7834 7066), opposite platform 2 at Victoria train station in London.

Orient Express The Venice Simplon Orient Express runs between Venice and London via Verona, Zürich and Paris twice weekly from March to November. It departs from London at 12.15 pm on Thursday and Sunday, arriving in Venice at 5.35 pm the following day. Going the other way, departures are at 10.42 am on Wednesday and Saturday. The fare one way costs a rather staggering UK£1165 so enjoy the luxury while it lasts.

The company that runs these trains has developed a wider range of variations on this old-world luxury theme. For instance, you can extend the London–Venice trip to Florence or Rome (this service only operates once a week), in which case you arrive in Rome at 9.27 am the day after reaching Venice. The one-way ticket costs UK£1465.

From Venice, you also have the choice of travelling to London via Vienna, Prague and Paris (the service doesn't operate from London). The one-way fare is a mere UK£1420.

As a rule, passengers travel one way on the Orient Express and make the outgoing or return journey by more prosaic means. The company offers packages involving a couple of nights in the destination city, the train trip and an air fare. For instance, an eight-day package could involve two nights in Rome, travel to Venice by Orient Express, three nights in Venice and travel to London on the Orient Express. You would be looking at over UK£2000 for this. (For those itching to know if it is possible to catch the Orient Express to its one-time final destination, Istanbul, the answer is yes – but not via Venice.)

Any travel agent in Venice can assist with booking tickets. Otherwise, you can get in touch with the headquarters in London (☎ 020-7928 6000). The Web site at www .orient-expresstrains.com often has details of special offers.

France From France, about the quickest you can hope to get to Venice is in 9½ hours. This involves getting the TGV to Milan Centrale from Paris Gare de Lyon and changing there to a Eurostar Italia train for Venice.

A standard one-way 2nd-class ticket costs from around 665FF to 725FF, depending on the type of train connection you make in Milan. Booking is necessary. The cheapest one-way ticket for those aged under 26 is around 425FF. This is on the (comparatively slow) overnight sleeper, so you would need to add the price of a couchette.

Alternatively, but adding from two to three hours to your journey, you can travel via Lausanne and/or Geneva in Switzerland.

Switzerland & Germany The most comfortable way into Switzerland by rail is the modern Cisalpino (CIS) service. Most of these trains start in Milan, from where you can reach Basle, Bern, Geneva and Zürich. One service connects Venice directly with Geneva, via Milan. That trip costs around L145,000 (Sfr103) one way and takes about seven hours.

From Switzerland it is then possible to connect with fast services into Germany, to get to destinations such as Stuttgart, Frankfurt am Main and Cologne.

Austria & the Czech Republic A couple of trains a day connect Venice (via Tarvisio in the north-east of Italy) with Vienna (Südbahnhof), and another service goes to Prague.

Slovenia There are four trains a day from Venice (Santa Lucia) to Ljubljana. A fifth leaves from Mestre only. Of these, two go on to Zagreb (Croatia) and Budapest, and one to Moscow.

Spain Direct overnight trains run from Milan to Barcelona's Estació de França (12¾ hours), from three to seven days a week depending on the season. Prices range from around L170,000 for a seat and L210,000 for a couchette to L510,000 for a first-class single sleeper. From there you can connect with trains to other points in Spain (this means getting across to Barcelona's other main train station, the Estació Sants). Total travel time from Venice (taking into account the connection in Milan) would be around 17 hours.

CAR & MOTORCYCLE

To give you an idea of how many clicks you'll put behind you if travelling with your own wheels, Venice is 279km from Milan, 529km from Rome, 579km from Geneva, 1112km from Paris, 1135km from Berlin, 1515km from London and 1820km from Madrid.

Coming from the UK, you can take your car across to France by ferry or the Channel Tunnel car train, Eurotunnel (☎ 0870 5353535). The latter runs around the clock, with up to four crossings (35 minutes) an hour between Folkestone and Calais in the high season. You pay for the vehicle only and fares vary according to time of day and season. The cheapest economy fare (January to May) is around UK£200 return (valid for a year) and the most expensive (May to late September) around UK£290, if you depart during the day Friday to Sunday.

The main points of entry to Italy are: the Mont Blanc tunnel from France at Chamonix (closed at the time of writing following a fire in March 1999 and not due to reopen until autumn 2000 at the earliest), which connects with the A5 for Turin and Milan; the Grand St Bernard tunnel from Switzerland (Sfr27), which also connects with the A5; and the Brenner pass from Austria (AS130), which connects with the A22 to Bologna. Mountain passes in the Alps are often closed in winter and sometimes in autumn and spring, making the tunnels a less scenic but more reliable way to arrive in Italy. Make sure you have snow chains in winter.

Europe is made for motorcycle touring and Italy is no exception. Motorcyclists literally swarm into the country in summer to tour the winding, scenic roads. Motorcyclists rarely have to book ahead for ferries.

An interesting Web site loaded with advice for people planning to drive in Europe is www.ideamerge.com/motoeuropa. If you want help with route planning, try out www.shell.com/euroshell/routeplanner.

Once in Italy, the A4 is the quickest way to reach Venice from east or west. It connects Turin with Trieste, passing through Milan and Mestre. Take the Venice exit and follow the signs for the city. The A4 is a toll road (Venice–Milan costs L21,500). Coming from the Brenner Pass, the A22 connects with the A4 near Verona. From the south, take the A13 from Bologna, which connects with the A4 at Padua. A more interesting route is to take the SS11 from Padua to Venice.

Paperwork & Preparations

Vehicles must be roadworthy, registered and insured (third party at least). The Green Card, an internationally recognised proof of insurance obtainable from your insurer, is mandatory. Also ask your insurer for a European Accident Statement form, which can simplify matters in the event of an accident.

A European breakdown assistance policy, such as the AA Five Star Service or the RAC Eurocover Motoring Assistance in the UK, is a good investment. For information on driving licences, see Documents in the Facts for the Visitor chapter.

Of course, you will not be doing any driving at all in Venice itself. For details of driving in the immediate area, as well as the hire or purchase of vehicles, see Car & Motorcycle in the Getting Around chapter.

Driving in Italy

Road Rules In general, standard European road rules apply. In built-up areas, the speed limit is usually 50km/h, rising to 90km/h on secondary roads, 110km/h on main roads (caravans 80km/h) and up to 130km/h (caravans 100km/h) on *autostrade* (toll and toll-free motorways). Motorcyclists must use headlights at all times. Crash helmets are obligatory on bikes of 125cc or more.

Vehicles already on roundabouts often have right of way. However, this is not always the case and working out which type you are confronted with is best done by paying careful attention to local example.

The blood-alcohol limit is 0.08%. Random breath tests are conducted – penalties range from on-the-spot fines to confiscation of your driving licence.

Petrol Petrol *(benzina)* in Italy is some of the most expensive in Western Europe. Super costs L2050 a litre, unleaded *(senza piombo)* L1965 a litre and diesel *(gasolio)* L1610 a litre. Prices can be up to L50 less in some service stations, especially those with *fai da te* offers, where you serve yourself rather than wait for an attendant. Stations on motorways charge about L20 more per litre.

If you are driving a car that uses LPG (liquid petroleum gas), you will need to buy a special guide to service stations that have *gasauto* (GPL in Italy). By law, these must be located in nonresidential areas and are usually in the country or on city outskirts, although you'll find plenty on the autostrade. GPL costs around L960 a litre (although it can be as low as L850).

You can pay with most credit cards at the great majority of service stations. Those on the autostrade are open round the clock. Otherwise, opening hours are generally from around 7 am to 12.30 pm and 3.30 to

7.30 pm (7 pm in winter). Up to 75% are closed on Sunday and public holidays; others close on Monday. Don't assume you can't get petrol if you pass a station that is closed. Quite a few have self-service pumps that accept banknotes. It is illegal to carry spare fuel in your vehicle.

Toll Roads & Highways Many of Italy's autostrade (four- to six-lane motorways) are toll roads and the tolls tend to be expensive. Some reasonable highways known as *superstrade* are toll-free. More often than not you will have the choice between a toll road and a busy *strada statale*. These tend to pass right through towns and can as much as double your travel time. The SS11 from Padua to Venice is an example. Smaller roads are known as *strade provinciali* (P).

You can pay tolls by credit card (including Visa, MasterCard, AmEx and Diners Club) on most autostrade in northern Italy. Another way to pay is to buy a Viacard, available from toll booths and some service stations and tourist offices. You present it to the attendant or insert it into the appropriate Viacard machine as you exit an autostrada. Leftover credit is not refundable on leaving Italy.

Sign Language

You won't be doing any driving in Venice itself, but if you plan to drive in Italy at all, you'll save yourself some grief by learning what a few of the many road signs mean:

ENTRATA	ENTRANCE (eg to autostrada)
INCROCIO	INTERSECTION/CROSSROADS
LAVORI IN CORSO	ROADWORKS AHEAD
PARCHEGGIO	CAR PARK
PASSAGGIO A LIVELLO	LEVEL CROSSING
RALLENTARE	SLOW DOWN
SENSO UNICO	ONE-WAY STREET
SENSO VIETATO	NO ENTRY
SOSTA VIETATA	NO STOPPING/PARKING
SOSTA AUTORIZZATA	PARKING PERMITTED (during times displayed)
SVOLTA	BEND
TUTTE LE DIREZIONI	ALL DIRECTIONS (useful when looking for town exit)
USCITA	EXIT (eg from autostrada)

Road Assistance As a rule, members of foreign motoring organisations, such as the RAC, AA (both UK) and AAA (USA), and people who arrange car insurance through them will be provided with an emergency assistance number to use while travelling in Italy.

You can also get roadside assistance from the Automobile Club Italia by calling ☎ 116. Your insurance may cover this. Otherwise, you'll pay a minimum fee of L150,000. In any case, it is likely that, whichever number you use, an ACI truck will arrive.

Spot Checks Theft of foreign cars is a problem in Italy, so you may well find yourself being pulled over, usually by the Carabinieri (military police), to have your papers checked. If the car is not yours, you need a letter from the owner granting you permission to drive it (unless they are with you), otherwise you risk having the car impounded.

BICYCLE

If you plan to bring your own bike, check with the airline about additional costs. The bike will have to be disassembled and packed for the journey.

Once in Italy, you can take your bicycle on certain trains. Those marked with a bicycle symbol on timetables have a carriage set aside for the transport of bicycles. Otherwise you need to dismantle and pack your bike, or send it as registered luggage. You cannot take your bike on Eurostar Italia services requiring a booking. In all cases where you can take the bike, you must pay a supplement of L5000 to L10,000.

The country around Venice is pretty flat until you start heading towards the Alps, so potentially ideal (if not always riveting) for getting about on your bike.

UK-based cyclists planning to cycle about beyond Venice might want to contact the Cyclists' Touring Club (☎ 01483-417217), Cotterell House, 69 Meadrow, Godalming, Surrey GU7 3HS. It has a Web site at www .ctc.org.uk and can supply information to members on cycling conditions, itineraries and cheap insurance. Membership costs UK£25 per annum.

HITCHING

Hitching is never entirely safe and we don't recommend it. Travellers who decide to hitch should understand that they are taking a small but potentially serious risk. People who do choose to hitch will be safer if they travel in pairs and let someone know where they are planning to go.

To get out of Venice, you need to start at one of the highway exits from Mestre. The chances of anyone stopping for you on autostrade are low (the practice is illegal) – try the more congested toll-free highways, such as the SS11 to Padua.

BOAT

Ferries connect Venice to Greece. The one-time luxury liner service to Alexandria, in Egypt, has been out of service for some years now. Other services from Venice to Croatia and Albania may be resuscitated one day, but don't hold your breath.

Of course, you can reach many other parts of Italy by sea, with car ferries linking ports up and down the peninsula with Albania, Corsica (France), Croatia, Greece, Malta, Spain and Tunisia.

Detailed below are services from Venice. Tickets can be bought direct or arranged through travel agencies.

Albania & Croatia

Kompas Italia (☎ 041 528 65 45), San Marco 1497, used to operate some ferry and hydrofoil services to Croatia in summer - whether it does now depends on the situation in the former Yugoslavia.

You can get to Albania and Croatia by sea, depending on the political situation from Trieste (about 150km east of Venice). In Trieste, Agemar (☎ 040 36 40 64), Via Rossini 2, is a good place to inquire about this. Alternatively, Adriatica normally has twice-weekly runs to Durrés, Albania (deck class L140,000 one way in the low season). In summer, the same company usually has a couple of services to the Croatian coast.

Greece

Minoan Lines (☎ 041 271 23 45), Porto Venezia, Zona Santa Marta, runs ferries to

Greece (Corfu, Igoumenitsa and Patras) from Venice daily in summer (three times a week in winter). Passengers pay up to L124,000 one way for an airline-style seat, depending on the season.

Strintzis Lines (☎ 041 277 05 59), Stazione Marittima 103, operates up to four ferries a week in summer to the same destinations in Greece. A simple spot on the deck costs from L60,000 in the lowest season up to L98,000. Airline-style seats cost about the same as with Minoan Lines.

These services all depart from the Stazione Marittima (passenger port) in Dorsoduro (Map 5). There's a left-luggage office at the back of the building.

ORGANISED TOURS

Options for organised travel to Italy abound. The Italian State Tourist Office (see Tourist Offices Abroad in the Facts for the Visitor chapter) can provide a list of tour operators, noting what each specialises in. Tours can save you hassles, but they rob you of independence and generally do not come cheap.

In the UK, a couple of big specialists may be worth investigating initially, if only for the variety of tours they present: Magic of Italy (☎ 020-8748 7575), 227 Shepherd's Bush Rd, London W6 7AS, and Alitalia's subsidiary, Italiatour (☎ 01883-621900).

Sestante-CIT (aka CIT or Citalia), with offices worldwide (see Tourist Offices Abroad in the Facts for the Visitor chapter), also organises many types of tour, including city breaks.

Voyages Jules Verne (☎ 020-7616 1000), 1 Dorset Square, London NW1 6QG, offers a tour that takes in Venice, Florence and Rome in seven days, including three nights spent cruising the Venetian lagoon. It costs UK£595.

Kirker Travel Ltd (☎ 020-7231 3333), 3 New Concordia Wharf, Mill St, London SE1 2BB, specialises in short breaks from London. Such trips start at about UK£390 per person for three nights in twin accommodation with air fare, transfers and breakfast included. Depending on the hotel you choose, the price can rise considerably. Prices also rise in summer.

Shopping around before making your final choice usually pays off. It is not unheard of for different operators to offer the same thing for considerably different prices. Hotel packages are the easiest to compare, and there's nothing worse than finding out you got the same holiday as someone else but paid much more for the pleasure.

TRAVEL AGENCIES

Venice is not a major centre for discount air tickets. You could start with the following agencies, but there is no substitute for shopping around.

For budget student travel, contact the Centro Turistico Studentesco e Giovanile, CTS (Map 5; ☎ 041 520 56 60), Calle Foscari 3252, Dorsoduro, the main Italian student and youth travel organisation. There are other branches in Mestre (Map 15; ☎ 041 96 11 25), at Via Ca' Savorgnan 8, and in Chioggia (☎ 041 550 02 80), at Via San Domenico 1124.

For student and under-26 rail travel, Transalpino (Map 3) is to the right as you exit the train station. It's open from 8.30 am to 12.30 pm and 3 to 7 pm Monday to Friday and from 8.30 am to 12.30 pm on Saturday.

WARNING

The information in this chapter is particularly vulnerable to change: prices for international travel are volatile, special deals come and go, and routes, schedules and visa requirements change. Airlines and governments seem to take a perverse pleasure in making price structures and regulations as complicated as possible. You should check with the airline or a travel agent to make sure you understand how a fare (and any ticket you may buy) works. The travel industry is highly competitive and there are many lurks and perks.

Get quotes and advice from as many airlines and travel agents as possible before you part with your hard-earned cash. The pointers in this chapter are no substitute for your own careful research.

Getting Around

THE AIRPORTS

Most people flying into Venice will arrive at Marco Polo airport, at Tessera, just outside Mestre and about 12km from Venice. Ryanair and a few charter flights from London and a couple of other European cities land at Treviso's tiny airport, about 35km north of Venice.

Marco Polo Airport

The airport (☎ 041 260 92 60 for flight information) is just east of Mestre. The terminal building is divided into two parts. As you drive in, the first section you come to is Arrivi (Arrivals). Immediately beyond, in the same low building, is Partenze (Departures).

In the arrivals hall, there's a tourist office (for details see Local Tourist Offices in the Facts for the Visitor chapter), along with hotel booking counters, a couple of bureaux de change and a row of car hire outlets.

More bureaux de change, banks and ATMs (all of which accept most main credit/debit cards) can be found in the departures lounge, where there are also a post office, first aid station, shops and bars.

The Deposito (left luggage office) is in the arrivals hall. It's open from 6 am to 9 pm and charges L3500 per item per day. Next door is the Bagagli Smarriti (lost luggage) office, open daily from 9 am to 8 pm.

To/From the Airport There are several options for getting to Venice from the airport, from the super-expensive water taxi to the cheap and relatively straightforward bus. The main problem is with night flights that arrive late. Some people have found themselves at the airport faced with a long wait for public transport and no taxis.

Bus ATVO buses (☎ 041 520 55 30) run to the airport from Piazzale Roma via Mestre train station. The trip takes 20 minutes and costs L5000. Some of these are nominated Go-Fly Buses and connect with Go flights to/from London.

Regular ACTV city bus No 5 also serves the airport from Piazzale Roma (L1500). It makes more stops and takes closer to 30 minutes. Departures are roughly every 30 minutes from 4.40 am to 12.40 am. The first departure from the airport is at 4.05 am.

Boat The Alilaguna hydrofoil to the airport costs L17,000 from Venice or the Lido and L8500 from Murano. You can pick it up at the Zattere (Map 5) or near Piazza San Marco, in front of the Giardini ex Reali (Map 6).

Water Taxi The official rate for the ride between Piazzetta di San Marco and the airport is L87,000. To/from the Lido costs L107,000.

Taxi Just as efficient as the waterborne version, if more prosaic, are taxis with wheels. You generally pay L50,000 to get to Piazzale Roma from the airport – a trip of around 15 minutes.

Parking Marco Polo Park (☎ 041 541 59 13) allows short- and long-term parking. For the latter you pay around L87,000 a week (up front). Short-term rates range up to L22,000 for 24 hours. Otherwise, Brusutti car park, about 1km from the airport, charges L10,000 a day or L40,000/60,000 a week (open air/under cover). The hitch here is that you then have to get a shuttle bus to the airport.

Short-term parking opposite the terminal costs L2000 an hour (maximum two hours). Feed the machine, extract the ticket and leave it on display.

Treviso Airport

You are less likely to land at the minuscule Treviso airport (which according to some sources is called San Giuseppe airport, and Sant'Angelo according to others), but if you do, don't panic! It is only about 5km southwest of Treviso.

The arrivals hall boasts a small, thinly stocked regional tourist information booth, a lost luggage booth next to it, a bureau de change and three car hire outlets (Hertz, Avis and Europcar). Next door in departures you'll find an ATM and a couple of tour and airline offices (including Ryanair). There is no left-luggage service.

To/From the Airport Those travelling from the UK may well come on Ryanair, the low-cost Irish airline. ATVO's Eurobus service connects with Ryanair's flights. The trip to/from Piazzale Roma takes 65 minutes and costs L8000 (L14,000 return – but the ticket is valid for one week only). If you arrive by charter, check with the charter company whether there is a special service. If all else fails, local bus No 6 into Treviso stops right outside the terminal gates and goes to the main train station in Treviso. From there you can proceed to Venice by rail.

If you need to get a taxi, be prepared to pay L110,000 to reach Piazzale Roma. The trip can take up to one hour.

Parking Parking is provided about 300m south of the airport – follow the signs. If you just need to drop someone off or pick up, you can park beside the terminal.

PUBLIC TRANSPORT
The Azienda Consorzio Trasporti Veneziano (ACTV) runs public transport in the Comune di Venezia (the municipality). For information, call ☎ 041 272 21 11 or fax 041 520 71 35. Alternatively, check their Web site at www.actv.it.

Public transport comprises the *vaporetti* ferry service in the city and around the lagoon, as well as buses connecting Venice with mainland areas of the municipality, and beyond (Mestre, Marghera and Chioggia).

You can pick up timetables and route maps for vaporetti and buses from the ACTV information office on Piazzale Roma.

Facilities for the Disabled
Disabled people have not been completely left out of what is, after all, a fairly unfriendly environment for wheelchair-users or those with other mobility problems.

The map available from APT (tourist) offices has areas of the city shaded in yellow

to indicate that they can be negotiated without running into one of Venice's many bridges. The office can also provide more detailed advice on how to get between and beyond these areas using vaporetti.

Most of the important *vaporetto* lines allow wheelchair access. Those that don't are Nos 10, 13, 20 and 52. Only the last of these is generally of any great interest to visitors anyway.

Six bus lines have also been adapted for wheelchair-users: No 2 (Piazzale Roma to Mestre train station), No 4 (Piazzale Roma to Corso del Popolo in Mestre), No 5 (Piazzale Roma to Marco Polo airport), No 4/ (Piazzale Roma to Corso del Popolo), No 6/ (Tronchetto and Piazzale Roma to the mainland) and No 15 (a mainland service).

Vaporetto
The most common form of transport around Venice after your own two feet are the vaporetti, the town's ferries. Actually, there are at least three kinds of ferry: the standard, ponderous vaporetto (as in line No 1 down the Grand Canal), the sleeker *motoscafo*, which also runs local routes, and the *motonave* – big, inter-island boats that head for Torcello and other more distant destinations.

It's hard not to see the difference in fares for local residents and out-of-towners as a blatant rip-off, but if you want to get around this way, there's not a lot you can do about it. If you're thinking about risking it and not bothering with tickets, spot checks do happen, though not too regularly. On longer routes, such as out to the islands, the risk of getting caught is greater. It's up to you – if you are caught there are no excuses, as signs are up all over the place in several languages (including English) laying down the rules. If you are caught on a vaporetto without a ticket, you will charged for the ticket plus an on-the-spot fine of L26,000.

Something to remember: the vaporetti get very crowded and visitors have a habit of gathering by exits. If you are standing near one, it is common practice on reaching a stop to get off and let passengers behind you disembark before then getting back on.

GETTING AROUND

Routes From Piazzale Roma, vaporetto No 1 zigzags up the Grand Canal to San Marco and then on to the Lido. If you aren't in a hurry, it is a great introduction to Venice.

Ferry No 17 transports vehicles from Tronchetto, near Piazzale Roma, to the Lido.

Routes and route numbers change regularly, so the following list should be taken as a guide only. Not all routes go both ways.

No 1
   Piazzale Roma–Ferrovia–Canal Grande–Lido (and back)
No 6
   San Zaccaria–Lido (and back)
No 10
   San Zaccaria–San Servolo–San Lazzaro (and back)
No 12
   Fondamenta Nuove–Murano–Burano–Torcello–Punta Sabbioni (and back)
No 13
   Fondamenta Nuove–Murano–Vignole–Sant'Erasmo–Treporti (and back)
No 14
   San Zaccaria–Lido–Litorale del Cavallino (Punta Sabbioni & Treporti). The one-way trip beyond the Lido costs an extra L5000.
No 17
   Car ferry: Tronchetto–Lido (and back)
No 20
   San Zaccaria–Grazia–San Clemente (and back)
No 41
   Circular line: Piazzale Roma–Sacca Fisola–Giudecca–San Zaccaria–San Pietro–Fondamenta Nuove–Ferrovia
No 42
   Circular line in reverse direction to No 41
No 51
   Circular line: Piazzale Roma–Zattere–San Zaccaria–Lido–Ferrovia
No 52
   Circular line in reverse direction to No 51
No 61
   Limited-stops circular line: Ferrovia–Piazzale Roma–San Zaccaria–Lido (extends to the Casinò in summer)
No 62
   Circular line in reverse direction to No 61
No 71
   Limited-stops line (summer only): San Zaccaria–Murano–Ferrovia–Piazzale Roma–Tronchetto
No 72
   Limited-stops line in reverse direction to No 71

No 82
   San Zaccaria–San Marco–Canal Grande–Ferrovia–Piazzale Roma–Zattere–Giudecca–San Giorgio–Lido (in summer only). A Limitato San Marco or Limitato Piazzale Roma sign means it will not go beyond those stops
N
   All-stops night circuit: Piazzale Roma–Tronchetto–Giudecca–San Giorgio–Canal Grande–Lido

Tickets Tickets can be purchased from the ticket booths at most landing stations and should be validated in the machines at each landing station before you get on the boat – unless they are sold to you already validated (check this if you want to buy several single tickets for later use). Otherwise, you can buy them on the boat (at a slightly higher price).

You could be forgiven for feeling vexed by the sky-high cost of water transport (for non-residents) in Venice. The vaporetti are frequently overloaded, largely with visitors, so it is just conceivable that the high cost is partly intended to encourage people to walk where possible. On the other hand, it may well be just plain old avarice.

For those who intend to stay for any length of time, there is a way around these prices – see Period Passes later in this section.

Single Tickets Unless you plan to use the vaporetti very little, a *corsa semplice* (single ticket) is poor value indeed at L6000.

Note that if you make an extra-short trip, such as crossing from one side of the Grand Canal to the other on the No 1 (one stop), the fare is L3000. Another example is the ferry between Zattere and Giudecca. On the other hand, you may find yourself expected to pay double the fare if you have lots of luggage.

You can get a *carnet* of 10 single tickets for L50,000. But even this is not good value unless you plan to use the vaporetti very sparingly. Should you decide to buy a one-off single, groups of three/four/five people save L1000 each if they buy a *biglietto family* instead. These cost L15,000/20,000/25,000 respectively.

Even less likely to be of use than the above is a round-trip ticket (*biglietto di andata e ritorno*), which costs L10,000.

Passes Those planning to use the vaporetti even moderately are advised to invest in a *biglietto a tempo*, a ticket valid on all transport (except the Alilaguna, Clodia and LineaBlù services; see Other Services). They are valid for 24 hours from the first *convalida* (validation). Generally nowadays the ticket is stamped by the vendor (watch this if you are buying a ticket but don't want to start using it immediately).

The ticket costs L18,000. There are family versions costing L45,000/60,000/75,000 for three/four/five people.

Better value still is the *biglietto tre giorni*, a three-day version which costs L35,000 (L25,000 if you have a Rolling Venice Concession Pass; see Documents in the Facts for the Visitor chapter). Finally, a weekly pass, or *biglietto sette giorni*, costs L60,000.

The 24-hour tickets cost L10,000 each for school children or seniors in groups of at least 20.

Other Services Several services operate a different fare structure, including the Alilaguna boat to/from Marco Polo airport (see The Airports earlier in this chapter). This service also runs between Murano and the Lido or Piazzale Roma (both L8500).

Tickets for the fast LineaBlù boats to the Casinò (on the Lido) from Tronchetto cost L12,000 one way and L18,000 return.

The Linea Clodia boat service to Chioggia costs L18,000 (L9000 for kids under 12) for a same-day return from Venice. Cheaper is the combined boat and bus service (the No 11 line) to Chioggia, which costs L8000 one way.

The 20-minute LineaFusina service between Zattere and Fusina, on the mainland (where there is a camp site), costs L8000 one way and L15,000 return. The biglietto tre giorni is also valid on this route. The same company also runs a summertime service four times a day direct from Fusina to the Alberoni beach on the Lido for the same price.

Biglietti turistici, valid for 12 hours, are available on three routes: the No 11 bus and boat route to Chioggia, No 1 (the Grand Canal) and the Laguna Nord line (Murano, Burano and Torcello). They cost L15,000.

Special tickets are available for particular events, such as soccer matches at the Stadio Penzo or congresses. Ask at ticket offices.

Transporting Cars, Motorcycles & Bicycles Passenger tickets on the *nave traghetto* style of ferry that also takes vehicles cost the same as for vaporetti. To take a car from, for example, Tronchetto to the Lido, you pay an extra L17,000 (one way) for a car under 4m or a motorcycle. From Tronchetto to Punta Sabbioni it costs L20,000 and from Alberoni (the Lido) to Santa Maria del Mar costs L10,000.

On these and line Nos 6, 12, 13 and 14, a single ticket for you and your bicycle will cost L7000.

Residents Permanent residents in the Comune di Venezia are entitled to massive discounts on fares. By way of example, a single ticket costs L1500 and is valid (with as many changes as you like) for an hour. A book of 10 tickets costs L14,000. A short hop (as described under Single Tickets) costs residents L800.

In other words, public transport prices for locals are the same as they are for people in any other Italian city. Residents have to apply for a CartaVenezia to qualify for these fares.

Period Passes Non-residents can't get the CartaVenezia, but if you intend to stay for a serious length of time, try to get an *abbonamento* – a pass valid for one month. These are available from the ACTV offices in Venice – Piazzale Roma (Map 3), Calle dei Fuseri, San Marco (Map 6) and Mestre (Map 15). You pay a one-off fee of L10,000 plus the cost of the pass, which is L45,000 (L30,000 for students). The L10,000 gets you a three-year ID card with which you can renew your abbonamento. You don't need a Carta Venezia but are supposed to produce some kind of document proving you work or study here. A bit of blagging often does the trick. You will need a photo. It can take a week or two for the pass to be prepared, but in the meantime you will be given a receipt valid for immediate use.

GETTING AROUND

Gondola

There was a time when the only way to get about effectively in Venice was by boat. But things have gradually changed over the past few centuries as more and more canals and other waterways have been filled in and bridges have been added. Today Venice is really a pedestrian city and not, as romantically imagined, a boat town. Of course, the canals are the only way to move goods around, but your average Venetian will walk to get from A to B. Only when they have to get from one end of town to the other will they bother with a vaporetto, while the traghetti come in handy for crossing the Grand Canal at strategic points and cutting down walking detours to bridges.

This means that virtually no-one uses gondolas as a form of transport any more. Sad but true, the gondola (apart from those in service as traghetti) is pretty much a tourist activity.

Gondolas Ago-Go

Back in the 16th century, someone counted up the total number of gondolas in use in Venice and came up with the figure of 10,000. It would be interesting to know how they worked this out. At any rate, considerably fewer ply the canals nowadays. In those distant days their owners painted them every colour of the rainbow, and those with money to spare went to enormous lengths to bedeck them with every imaginable form of decoration. Finally, the Senato decided in 1630 that this was getting out of hand and ordered that gondoliers could paint their vessels any colour they wanted so long as it was black. Nothing has changed since.

No-one knows for sure the origin of the term gondola, but it seems probable that it came from the Near East. These people-movers don't just come in the standard size you see every day on the canals. Special ones come out to play for events such as the Vogalonga in May–June. These include the *dodesona* (with 12 oarsmen), the *quatordesona* (14 oarsmen) and the *disdotona* (18 oarsmen). The *gondolino da regata*, or racing gondola, is longer and flatter than the standard model.

More observant visitors will soon start to make out other types of vessel. Perhaps the most common is the *sandalo* (sandal) and its little brother, the *sandaletto*, with squared-off prow and stern. Two standing oarsmen power them along, although a skilled oarsman can row them alone. The *vipera* is similar to the sandalo but pointed at each end – having no stern, it can be rowed in either direction. It was introduced by Austrian customs officials. If they suddenly found bandits scooting away behind them, it was not necessary to turn around to chase them!

Plying the canals is a series of heavy, sluggish-looking transport vessels powered with outboard motors. Known as *peate*, they are the city's workhorses and used for everything from vegetable deliveries to house removals. The *bragozzo* is similar, but sometimes sports sails on two masts. Typical of light lagoon-going transport vessels is the *caorlina*. It usually sports a single big sail on a long slanted yardarm.

The construction and maintenance of all these vessels required the expertise of the *squerarioli*, master carpenters and shipbuilders. *Squeri*, the small-scale shipyards where they carried on their trade, once dotted the city. By 1612 the one near the Chiesa di San Trovaso employed 60 masters and scores of apprentices. It still operates today along wholly traditional lines, as does another, farther west on Rio della Avogaria. Another, on Giudecca, produces gondolas by more 'production-line' methods, but their detractors claim the quality is not the same. Like most other artisans in Venice, the squerarioli had a guild and belonged to a religious confraternity.

Still, a gondola ride is the quintessence of romantic Venice, although at L120,000 for 50 minutes (L150,000 after 8 pm) the official price brings you back to reality with a bump. The rates are for a maximum of six people – less romantic but more affordable. After the first 50 minutes you pay in 25-minute increments (L60,000, or L75,000 after 8 pm).

Some say there are few things more fake than being trundled about in a gondola, but it can be quite a pleasing experience if you do it right. The tackiest thing you can do is sign up for a *carovana*, where whole groups are loaded up onto a small fleet of gondolas and rowed about the place. You can also go the whole hog and be 'serenaded' by someone (at an extra negotiable rate).

A couple of other things are worth noting. When the tide is low, a gondola ride can be a stinky experience. If the tide is too high, it can become difficult for the gondolier to pass under certain bridges.

Gondolas Ago-Go

Making a good gondola is no easy task – seven different types of wood are employed to make 280 pieces for the hull alone. Also, it has to be asymmetrical. The left side has a greater curve to make up for the lateral action of the oar, and the cross section is skewed to the right to counterbalance the weight of the gondolier.

Nowadays, a master craftsman can build a gondola in about a month. Your standard model costs from L35,000,000. If you want more wood-carved decoration, gold leaf and other ornament, the price starts to rise. A really 'pretty' gondola can cost L100,000,000. Only senior and experienced gondoliers tend to go for such luxury. They do so in part as a sign of their standing within the profession, in part also in the hope of attracting more or better-off customers. A newly arrived gondolier, however, would satisfy himself with a simple, second-hand vessel to get started in the business.

NICKY CAVEN

Going nowhere fast? Maybe your gondola is just too straight.

A well-made gondola will last at least 30 years and often longer. One way to tell whether a gondola is old or new is to inspect the paint work. Most gondolas get a fresh coat once a year. As coat is added to coat, the paint's thickness increases and the carvings lose their clarity.

Making a good gondolier is no easier than making a good vessel. At the last count there were 406 gondoliers (all men). Every year a *selezione* (selection) is held and, as a rule, many more candidates apply than places can be found. The trade was by tradition passed down from father to son, but the selezione is now open to all comers. Accusations of racism and sexism were made at the 1999 trials, when a German woman was failed after training for three years. The incentive to pass is great, as a gondolier can make a fortune in the months from Easter to September – enough to take it easy for the rest of the year.

What about those who ferry the traghetti back and forth across the Grand Canal? They are contracted by the Comune (municipality) to provide this service. As members of a co-operative, they also have an arrangement by which they run the traghetti part of the time and are otherwise free to chase their own business as independent gondoliers.

GETTING AROUND

Gondolas are available near main canals all over the city, or can be booked by telephone in the following areas: San Marco (☎ 041 520 06 85), Rialto (☎ 041 522 49 04), Piazzale Roma (☎ 041 522 11 51) and the train station (☎ 041 71 85 43). If money is no object and you don't want to rub shoulders with the hoi polloi, the latter might be useful to ferry yourself and luggage to the station.

Traghetto

The poor man's gondola, *traghetti* are used by locals to cross the Grand Canal where there is no nearby bridge. There is no particular limit (except common sense) on the number of passengers, who stand.

Traghetti operate between Campo del Traghetto (near Santa Maria del Giglio) and Calle de Lanza (Map 5); Campo San Samuele, north of the Ponte dell'Accademia, and Calle Traghetto (Map 5); Calle Mocenigo, farther north, and Calle Traghetto (Map 5); Fondamenta del Vin and Riva del Carbon, near the Ponte di Rialto (Map 6); and Campo Santa Sofia and Campo della Pescaria (Map 4), near the produce market.

Several other traghetto routes exist (you can see the signs) but they are out of action. The ride costs L700 (although some locals round it up to L1000).

Water Taxi

Water taxis (motorboats) are prohibitively expensive, with a set L27,000 charge for the first seven minutes. Every additional 15 seconds, another L500 clicks on. On top of this there are all sorts of surcharges. You pay L8000 if you order one by telephone and a night surcharge of L8500 between 10 pm and 7 am. Each piece of luggage costs L2200. If more than four people are travelling there is a L3100 extra charge per head. On holidays you pay L9000 extra (but in this case you don't pay the night surcharge).

The high prices are explained in part by the cost of the taxis themselves. The better quality mahogany jobs cost up to L200 million to build.

There are water taxi stands at regular intervals along the Grand Canal. Otherwise,

call one of the operating companies. Numbers include ☎ 041 523 24 73, ☎ 041 522 87 77 and ☎ 041 522 23 03.

Bus

You can't take buses anywhere around Venice itself, but there are regular runs across the bridge to Mestre. You can also use them to get up and down along the Lido. Tickets (valid for one hour from the time you validate them in the machine on the bus) cost L1500. A book *(carnet)* of tickets costs L14,000. Don't rip each ticket off as you use it (they are double sided), as the whole carnet has to be shown if an inspector comes along.

You can buy tickets at the main bus station in Piazzale Roma, as well as many newsstands and *tabacchi* (tobacconists).

Train

Pretty near all trains leaving Santa Lucia station stop in Mestre. Trains run between the two stations from 3.50 am to 11.57 pm. The ride takes about 10 minutes and tickets (available from ticket windows and station tabacchi) cost L1500 a pop.

For more information and details of the facilities available in stations, see Train in the Getting There & Away chapter.

Porters

Getting from the vaporetto stop to your hotel can be difficult if you are heavily laden with luggage. There are several stands around the city where porters *(portabagagli)* can be engaged to escort you to your hotel. They charge L20,000 for one item and roughly L10,000 for each extra one. Prices virtually double to transport bags to any of the other islands, including Giudecca.

Points where porters can be found include the Ponte dell'Accademia (☎ 041 522 48 91), the train station (☎ 041 71 52 72), Piazzale Roma (☎ 041 520 30 70), the Ponte di Rialto (☎ 041 520 53 08) and San Marco (☎ 041 523 23 85).

CAR & MOTORCYCLE

Those who insist on driving their cars right into Venice pay a hefty price for the pleasure, and not necessarily just in parking fees. On busy days (especially holiday week-ends) day-trippers driving in frequently find themselves stuck on the Ponte della Libertà making little forward progress and unable to go back. It is not unknown for traffic to get so jammed that the police shut the city off from the mainland. Why risk it?

Parking

Venice Driving in Venice is, of course, im-possible. Once over the Ponte della Libertà from Mestre, cars must be left at one of the huge car parks in Piazzale Roma or on the island of Tronchetto.

It costs to tie up your beastie in Venice. The best value, given its proximity, is the Garage Comunale (Map 3), at Piazzale Roma, which is open 24 hours. It costs L30,000 a day. The nearby private Parking San Marco is also open all day and charges an incredible L8000 for every two hours or fraction thereof. At Tronchetto, farther out, you pay L25,000 for 24 hours, but of course it is not quite so handy.

There is a small area in Piazzale Roma where you can drop a car for 30 minutes (in practice, people tend to leave their cars longer). Queuing to get into one of these few spaces can be supremely frustrating, but locals generally observe the first come, first served rule.

Lido Garage Lido (Map 13), at Via Emo, is open from 7 am to midnight and charges L35,000 for 24 hours.

Fusina You could also leave your car at Fusina, south of Mestre and Marghera, and catch the LineaFusina vaporetto (No 16) to the Zattere. You pay L15,000 for 10 hours in the guarded car park, or you can take a risk and park near the vaporetto landing for free. There have been reports of break-ins in the free parking area.

Mestre There are several car parks near the train station in Mestre. At Serenissima Park-ing, for example, you pay L8000 a day. It's at Viale Stazione 10 and is open 24 hours.

Most of the street parking is metered in Mestre, although a determined hunt around

the small streets around the train station may turn up a free parking space. If you choose this option, be aware that parking regulations can be pretty confusing and the local police take some pleasure in removing incorrectly parked vehicles.

Illegal Parking If you return to your car to find that it's no longer there, you can call any of the police forces, as they are all en-titled to have cars towed away if they see fit. In reality, the Vigili Urbani are respon-sible for about 90% of cars towed. They use the national motoring association (ACI) to remove the vehicles, which are then dumped in one of three depots. The best number to call if you think your car has met this fate is ☎ 041 274 70 70. The Vigili Urbani staff it daily from 7 am to midnight.

The cost of freeing your vehicle is L160,000 for the tow plus L10,000 per day storage. To this is added the fine for which it was towed in the first place, which can range from L60,000 to L200,000.

Warning More worrisome than the confu-sion of parking legally are the thieves that tend to haunt some of the car parks, particu-larly those in Mestre. With so many foreign and hired cars among the prey, the tempta-tion is often hard to resist. Do not leave any-thing, of even remote value, in a parked car.

Rental

Avis has an office in Piazzale Roma (☎ 041 522 58 25), as do Europcar (☎ 041 528 95 51), Hertz (☎ 041 528 35 24) and Auto-noleggio Venezia (☎ 041 520 00 00). They all have reps at Marco Polo airport too.

Purchase

Only people legally resident in Italy can buy vehicles there. The only way around this might be to get an Italian friend to buy one and put it in their name.

TAXI

If you need a land taxi to the airport or any-where between Venice and Mestre, you can pick one up from the rank in Piazzale Roma or call ☎ 041 523 77 74.

GETTING AROUND

BICYCLE & MOPED

For obvious reasons, you won't have much need of a bicycle or moped for getting around Venice. Indeed, bicycle riding is officially banned in the lagoon city, although bamboozled out-of-towners can be seen sighing as they drag their two-wheelers up and down the seemingly innumerable bridges.

Cycling is a nice way to get around the Lido. See the Lido di Venezia section in the Things to See & Do chapter for details of where you can hire bicycles.

WALKING

Except for when you hop onto waterborne craft, you don't really have much choice but to walk if you want to get anywhere. As

---

From Soap St to Tits Bridge

The Venetians have always had a reputation for being relatively hard-headed and practical. So it should come as little surprise that a good number of street names, many of which have remained unchanged since a more-or-less organised effort to name streets began in 1100, have their origins in one-time everyday life.

A good number of these street names repeat themselves from one quarter of the city to another and give you a clue as to where local trade was once carried out. Around the Rialto area, for instance, we find the Fondamenta del Vin (Wine Quay) on the west bank and, opposite, the Riva del Ferro (Iron Quay) and Riva del Carbon (Coal Quay). These canal-side walkways are among the few that exist along the Grand Canal and their existence serves to underline the Rialto area's historic role as the centre of Venetian commerce. The lanes around the San Polo side of the Ponte di Rialto were reserved for other particular goods and trades: Ruga dei Speziali (Spice Lane), Ruga degli Orefici (Goldsmiths' Lane), Pescaria (Fish Market), Fondamenta dell'Olio (Oil Quay), Calle del Storione (Sturgeon Street) and so on.

All over the city you will stumble across streets with standard names like Forno (bakery), Spezier (spice shop), Magazen (warehouse), Pistor (another word for baker) and Cafetier (coffee shop). Malvasia was a sweet wine imported from Venice's Greek possessions (what Shakespeare dubbed Malmsey) – streets with this name abound and you can be sure that wherever they are there was also once a discreet little *malvasia*, or tavern where you could quaff the stuff. Nearby you will almost always find a Calle del Forno. Sensible tipplers would pop in to pick up some bread or pastries to take down to the tavern for a bite with a soothing jar (or six) of malvasia.

Calle del Traghetto will sometimes still lead you down to one of the stops for gondolas serving as cross-Canal shuttles. Wandering down any Calle del Squero used to take you to the local gondola boatyards, most of which have now disappeared. That soap was a fairly rare product is indicated by the fact that about the only streets dedicated to its production and sale (Saoneri) are clustered together in San Polo (with a few up in Cannaregio).

Perhaps one of the most colourful place names in Venice is Ponte delle Tette (Tits Bridge), at the heart of what was, from the 16th century, long the red-light district, on the dividing line between San Polo and Santa Croce.

Other place names indicate the presence of an important family's residence (Venier, Correr, Morosini etc). Others again designated concentrations of particular groups of people, such as Albanians (Albanesi) or traders from Hormuz (Ormesini). Still others refer to nearby churches, religious schools and the like.

If you really want to get behind the secrets of the Venetian street names, the best source is, without doubt, Giuseppe Tassini's *Curiosità Veneziane*.

you will soon notice, the streets are generally pretty narrow. Most Venetians will stick to the right when someone is coming the other way. If they are in a group, they generally move into single file so as not block human 'traffic'. What infuriates them is that most non-Venetians don't stick to the same rules, wandering around five abreast at a snail's pace, gawping around them and completely indifferent to other peoples' attempts to get somewhere.

ORGANISED TOURS

You can join free tours for a biblical explanation of the mosaics in the Basilica di San Marco. They are arranged by the Patriarcato (the church body in Venice) and take place in Italian daily except Sunday at 11 am (except on Wednesday, when it is at 3 pm). In English, the tours are at 11 am on Monday, Thursday and Friday, and at the same time on Thursday in French. This timetable seems to be subject to regular change, so inquire.

Enjoy Venice (☎ 800 274819, Castello 5144) organises small group walks of three hours with English-speaking guides. Themes include Casanova, How to Build a Gondola, and Casinos and Cut-throats. They leave from the Thomas Cook office at the Rialto at 10 am Monday to Saturday and cost L30,000 (L25,000 for those aged under 26).

Consult *Un Ospite di Venezia* for details of other visits to churches and sights in the city. The APT has an updated list of authorised guides, who will take you on a walking tour of the city. The going rate is L172,000 for a three-hour tour for up to 30 people. With tourism projected to just keep on growing, the Veneto regional government is trying to train up new guides in various languages just as quickly as it can.

Travel agencies all over central Venice can put you onto all kinds of city tours, ranging from guided walks for L30,000 to gondola rides with serenade for L50,000 a person.

Tours Outside Venice

Avventure Bellissime (☎ 0434 57 32 75) organises daily tours of the Veneto from Venice. They start at 8.40 am and return at 6.20 pm. The tours take in places such as Marostica, Bassano del Grappa and some of the Palladian villas. They also include a little wine tasting. The cost is L120,000 (plus L25,000 for lunch, if you want it). Generally, you can book through your hotel.

Things to See & Do

Highlights

- Take the No 1 *vaporetto* down the length of the Grand Canal

- Tour the Gothic seat of Venetian power, the Palazzo Ducale

- Admire the Byzantine mosaics in the Chiesa di Santa Maria Assunta on Torcello

- Sip a Bellini at Harry's Bar

- Get lost in the back lanes of the city, far from the madd(en)ing crowds of tourists

- Feast your eyes on art in the Galleria dell'Accademia, the Peggy Guggenheim Collection and various churches in the city

- Wander among the gaily painted houses on Burano

- Allow yourself to be amazed by the wonders of the Basilica di San Marco – everyone else does it too, but you really can't come to Venice and say no

The grandest surprise for the casual stroller in Venice is that the city is not completely teeming with outsiders in the manner of a wheat field swarming with locusts. Certainly, the main trails linking the train station to Piazza San Marco and the *vaporetti* of the Grand Canal are a year-round stage for the incessant and sometimes awkward pageant of international tourism. But most of Venice's visitors get little farther – many are in town too briefly to venture into the unknown; others are simply too bemused by the tangle of lanes and canals that twist and bend around the cityscape like an Escher drawing. However, it is an uncommon pleasure to lose yourself in the backstreets and marvel in comparative calm at the many faces of this unique creation.

Of course, most people want to poke around the great monuments and art centres as well, and these are explored in this chapter. Make some time to visit the outlying islands too – each is possessed of its own peculiar charm.

If you begin to feel like you've landed in a theme village (Venice Town), you may be able to gain a truer sense of the singularity of La Serenissima and, hopefully, dispel any disagreeable sentiments by exploring the mainland a little (see the Excursions chapter).

This chapter is divided into sections covering Venice's six *sestieri*, or old municipal boundaries, followed by a section on the surrounding islands. The Grand Canal is covered in a separate colour section.

In each section covering central Venice (San Marco, Dorsoduro, San Polo & Santa Croce, Cannaregio and Castello) we follow a loose walking route to take in the 'must sees', along with various curiosities. The suggested routes provide possible links from one section (and hence sestiere) to the next. If you kept to the order in this chapter (and no-one is suggesting you should!), you would at the end of several days' hard slog find yourself meandering west along the Riva degli Schiavoni in Castello towards the starting point – Piazzetta San Marco. The routes should be viewed as suggestions for orientation. Let your imagination do the work and wander off wherever your nose leads you.

Museum Opening Hours

Check with the APT (see Local Tourist Offices in the Facts for the Visitor chapter) for the latest opening days and hours, as they can vary. Times given here are based on summer (Easter to the end of September) timetables and were correct at the time of writing. Opening hours tend to be shorter during the rest of the year (with places often closing for a couple of hours in the middle of the day). Tourist offices can provide you with a list of all monuments and their opening times.

THINGS TO SEE & DO

Special Tickets

There's a *biglietto cumulativo* (combined ticket) that covers entry to the Palazzo Ducale (Doge's Palace), Museo Correr, Museo Archeologico, Libreria Nazionale Marciana, Museo Vetrario on Murano, Museo del Merletto on Burano and the rather minor Palazzo Mocenigo, which houses a museum dedicated to textiles and period furniture. The ticket costs L18,000, is valid for several months and can be purchased from any of these museums.

For L18,000 you can also get a special ticket to the Gallerie dell'Accademia, the Galleria Franchetti in the Ca' d'Oro and the Museo d'Arte Orientale in Ca' Pesaro (L8000 will get you a discounted ticket to the latter two only).

Rolling Venice Concession Pass

See Documents in the Facts for the Visitor chapter for details about this discount card.

GRAND CANAL

Nowhere can it be said more truly of a city's main thoroughfare than of Venice's Grand Canal (Canal Grande) that it is the artery along which courses the city's lifeblood. To sail its length time and again, on each occasion making new observations and 'discoveries', is a pleasure only the most insensitive souls could tire of. For the newcomer it is difficult to recommend a more appropriate introduction to the city. For a blow-by-blow itinerary, see the special colour section 'Along the Grand Canal'.

SESTIERE DI SAN MARCO
Piazzetta San Marco (Map 6)

Ever since the rail link with the mainland opened in the 19th century, the magical symbolism of Piazzetta San Marco has to a great extent been lost to the city's visitors.

Stand between the two columns bearing the emblems of Venice's patron saints – the winged lion of St Mark and the figure of the demoted St Theodore, whom St Mark replaced. The lion faces east, perhaps to signify Venice's domination of the sea, while St Theodore stands calmly atop a crocodile-like dragon. The tip of his spear is pointed skywards, so perhaps he has killed his prey (some say the statue represents St George). He also holds a shield, as if to say Venice defends itself but does not seek to attack.

Try to imagine yourself on a galley after months at sea on a trading voyage or battle and now making your way to La Serenissima. To some observers, the lion's and dragon's tails face each other to form the crossbeam of a perennially open gate – as if to say that Venice is open to whoever visits. It must, at any rate, have been a welcome sight to Venetians returning home, and a heartening one to others arriving for the first time.

A Chorus Line

An organisation called Chorus, which is involved in the upkeep of Venice's most artistically significant churches, offers visitors a special three-day ticket providing entry to six churches for L15,000.

The churches from which you can choose are, in no particular order: Santa Maria Gloriosa dei Frari, Santa Maria del Giglio, Santo Stefano, Santa Maria Formosa, Santa Maria dei Miracoli, San Polo, San Giacomo dell'Orio, San Stae, Sant'Alvise (closed at the time of writing), La Madonna dell'Orto, San Pietro di Castello, Redentore (closed at the time of writing) and San Sebastiano. The ticket, which is available from any of these churches, also includes the option of visiting the Tesoro of the Basilica di San Marco.

You may want to be choosy about which churches you include on your list of six (remembering that admiring the outside costs nothing). For this writer, the best options are San Marco (Tesoro), Santa Maria Gloriosa dei Frari, San Giacomo dell'Orio, Santo Stefano, San Polo and San Sebastiano.

The savings are not remarkable, but it's a nice gesture. As Chorus points out, what you are being asked to pay is a small contribution to the upkeep of the art you are (presumably) enjoying.

Saving Venice

Floods, neglect, pollution and other factors have contributed to the degeneration of Venice's monuments and art treasures. Since 1969, however, a group of private international organisations, under the aegis of UNESCO, has been working to repair the damage.

The Joint UNESCO-Private Committees Programme for the Safeguarding of Venice has raised millions of dollars for restoration work in the city; between 1969 and 1996 nearly 100 monuments and more than 900 works of art were restored.

Major restoration projects completed include the Chiesa di Madonna dell'Orto, the facade of the Chiesa di San Zulian, the Chiesa di San Francesco della Vigna, the Chiesa di Santa Maria Formosa and the Chiesa di San Nicolò dei Mendicoli. The Basilica di Santa Maria Assunta on Torcello was also the object of extensive work between 1978 and 1994.

Funding for the program comes from 24 private and charitable organisations from Italy and a dozen other countries. Apart from restoration work, the program also finances specialist courses for trainee restorers in Venice. Among the higher-profile groups involved in the effort are the UK's Venice in Peril Fund, chaired by Lord Norwich, perhaps the greatest historian of Venice writing in English. The sources of their funding are numerous – the UK restaurant chain Pizza Express, for example, has raised hundreds of thousands of pounds by adding a discretionary 25p charge to its Veneziana pizzas. The fund is presently helping to restore the 14th-century Jewish cemetery on the Lido and plans to restore the Emiliana chapel on San Michele. For UK£50 a year you can join the Venice in Peril fund (☎ 020-7636 6138).

Important though the work of these organisations is in keeping Venice's difficulties in the public eye, more than 90% of the finance for restoration and related projects in Venice since 1966 has come from the Italian government.

The columns were erected in 1172. In succeeding centuries the area around them was a hive of activity with stores selling all manner of goods and food. On a more sinister note, public executions took place between the two columns.

The square is one of the lowest parts of the city – it is always the first to be covered in water when the *acqua alta* (see the boxed text 'Acque Alte' under Ecology & Environment in the Facts about Venice chapter) arrives. In fact, until the 12th century there was nothing but water here. Like so much of Venice, this area is the result of landfill.

Palazzo Ducale (Map 6)

Looking onto the Piazzetta San Marco, this unique example of Venetian Gothic fantasy and its simpler predecessors were La Serenissima's political heart for almost the entire duration of the Republic's existence. As the palace's name suggests, the doge (or 'duke') called it home, but in its halls and

dependencies were also housed all the arms of government, not to mention prisons.

Established in the 9th century, the building began to assume its present form 500 years later, with the decision to build the massive Sala del Maggior Consiglio to house the members of the Great Council, who ranged in number from 1200 to 1700. The hall was inaugurated in 1419.

The palace's two magnificent Gothic facades in white Istrian stone and pink Veronese marble face the water and Piazzetta San Marco. Much of the building was damaged by fire in 1577, but it was successfully restored by Antonio da Ponte (who also designed the Ponte di Rialto). Thankfully, Palladio's pleas to have the burnt-out hulk demolished and replaced by another of his creations fell on deaf ears. Venice's city fathers wanted their *palazzo* back just as it had been.

You enter the palace through the entrance facing the waterfront. Beyond the ticket office and to the left is the entrance to the **Museo dell'Opera**. It contains a total of 42 capitals that once adorned the porticoes of the palace and have at one time or another been replaced by copies to protect the originals from further deterioration. At the moment, only six of them, restored, are on public view. Careful observation reveals a wealth of sculptural whimsy.

When you leave the museum you have no choice but to emerge into the main courtyard. The north and west flanks are closed to visitors, as is access to Antonio Rizzi's magnificent marble **Scala dei Giganti** (Giants' Staircase), at the north-eastern end of the courtyard. It is topped by statues of Mars and Neptune by Sansovino. Behind the statues, the swearing-in ceremony of the doge traditionally took place. Here he would be presented with his ducal *zoia* (hat) and swear fidelity to the laws of the Republic. The two 16th-century wells in the middle of the courtyard are the most exquisite in the city.

To continue, climb the **Scala dei Censori** up to the **Piano delle Logge** and follow the arrows to Sansovino's grand **Scala d'Oro**. The floor of the loggia is a classic *terrazzo alla Veneziana* (see the boxed text 'Of Floors & Walls' under Sestiere di Castello later in this chapter), of which you will see more inside of the building.

After climbing the Scala d'Oro, you enter a series of rooms that comprised the ducal apartments. Among these, the **Sala delle Mappe** is interesting. It contains maps depicting the Republic's territories and the voyages of Marco Polo dating from 1762. Also here is the standard of the last of the doges, Manin. It is therefore also known as the Sala dello Scudo (Coat-of-Arms Room). You pass through several smaller rooms before reaching the long hall known as the **Sala dei Filosofi**, so called because portraits of great philosophers once hung here. Of particular interest is Titian's *San Cristoforo* (St Christopher), a fresco above a side stairwell (signposted) and one of the few works to survive the 1577 fire. They say he finished this fresco in just three days.

The highest organs of the government met in rooms up on the next floor. Follow the arrows up the Scala d'Oro and turn right into the **Sala delle Quattro Porte**, where ambassadors would be requested to await their ducal audience. Palladio designed the ceiling and Tintoretto added the frescoes. Titian's memorable *Il Doge Antonio Grimaldi in Ginocchio davanti alla Fede, Presente San Marco* (Doge Antonio Grimaldi Kneels Before the Faith in the Presence of St Mark) dominates the wall by the entrance.

Off this room is the **Anticollegio**, which features four Tintorettos and the *Ratto d' Europa* (Rape of Europa) by Veronese. Through here is the splendid **Sala del Collegio**, the ceiling of which features a series of works by Veronese and a few by Tintoretto. Next is the **Sala del Senato**, graced by yet more Tintorettos. Senators met here in the presence of the doge and the Signoria (a council of 10 men that advised the doge on policy), who sat on the high tribune.

Veronese was again at work in the **Sala del Consiglio dei Dieci**. This council came to wield considerable power, acting as the Republic's main intelligence-gathering agency. The next room is known as the **Sala della Bussola**. Note the small box in the wall. Members of the Consiglio dei Dieci picked up denunciations left here – they were poked though a hole on the other side of the wall rather like the way you post a letter.

From here, stairs (the Scala dei Censori, by which you first entered the building from the courtyard) take you up to the **Armeria**, what is left of the palace's once considerable collection of arms of all types. After this, follow the arrows back down a couple of floors to the **Andito del Maggior Consiglio**, a corridor off which is the **Sala della Quarantia Vecchia**. This body oversaw administrative matters regarding the city. In the small **Sala dell'Armamento** next door you can see the remains of Guariento's 14th-century fresco *Paradiso* (Heaven), badly damaged in the 1577 fire.

The indicated route (you have no choice in the matter) then takes you to the immense **Sala del Maggiore Consiglio**. This is dominated at one end by Tintoretto's replacement *Paradiso*, one of the world's largest oil paintings, measuring 22m by 7m. Among the many other paintings in the hall is a masterpiece, the *Apoteosi di Venezia* (Apotheosis of Venice) by Veronese, in one of the central ceiling panels. Note the black space in the frieze on the wall depicting the first 76 doges of Venice. Doge Marin Falier would have appeared had he not been beheaded for treason in 1355.

The room off the north-western corner of the Sala del Maggiore Consiglio was home to the **Quarantia Civil Nuova**, a kind of appeal court, while beyond lies the **Sala dello Scrutinio**, where elections to the Maggior Consiglio were held. It was closed to the public at the time of writing.

From the north-eastern end a trail of corridors leads you to the small, enclosed **Ponte dei Sospiri** (Bridge of Sighs). The bridge is split into two levels, for traffic heading into and out of the **Prigioni Nuovi** (New Prisons), built on the eastern side of the Rio di Palazzo della Paglia in the 16th century to cater for the overflow from the Prigioni Vecchie (Old Prisons) within the Palazzo Ducale itself. The bridge is presumably named after the sighs that prisoners heaved as they crossed it on their way into the dungeons. You get to wind your way all over the cells of the Prigioni Nuovi. They are small and dank, but not too bad by the standards of the times.

Re-emerging from the prison, you recross the Bridge of Sighs to wind up in the offices of the Avogaria Comun and the **Sala dello Scrigno** (Room of the Coffer). Here the Libro d'Oro was administered. The Libro identified those noble families of impeccable Venetian descent who had the right to join the Maggior Consiglio. Inter-class weddings were forbidden and a vigilant watch was maintained for fraudulent attempts to pass off unsuitable persons as nobles.

The last office you pass through before arriving back in the courtyard is the **Milizia da Mar**. An office of 20 senators was set up in 1545 to organise the rapid equipping and manning of emergency war fleets whenever the need arose. The organisation began here.

You exit the courtyard by what was traditionally the main entrance, Giovanni and Bartolomeo Bon's 15th-century **Porta della Carta** (Paper Door), to which government decrees were fixed (hence the name).

The palace is open daily from 8.30 am to dusk (7 pm in summer and as early as 4 pm in winter) and admission costs L18,000 (on a ticket that includes entrance to the Museo Correr and a number of other museums; see Special Tickets at the start of this chapter). Note that last tickets are sold at 5.30 pm in summer. Infra-red radio receivers (which pick up an audio-loop commentary in each room) can be hired near the ticket desk for L7000.

Itinerari Segreti The 'secret itineraries' is a guided tour of lesser-known areas of the palace, including the original Prigioni Vecchie.

The 1½-hour tour, even if you end up on the Italian one and understand little, is an intriguing look at the underside of the palace and the workings of government in the days of La Serenissima. You are taken first through administrative offices, small rooms in which the Republic's civil service beavered away. You then get to pass through a torture chamber, the Sala dei Tre Capi del Consiglio dei Dieci (Room of the Three Heads of the Council of Ten) and the Inquisitors' office.

After all this the route winds upstairs to the **Piombi** (Leads), prison cells beneath of the roof of the building. Here prisoners froze in winter and sweltered in summer. Giacomo Casanova got five years here for his apparently wayward and reckless lifestyle. The guide will show you how he made his escape. You also get an explanation of the engineering behind the ceiling of the immense Sala del Maggior Consiglio below.

The toughest prisoners of all ended up not in the Piombi, nor in the Prigioni Nuovi (see earlier), but rather in the **Pozzi** (Wells), two bottom storeys of dank cells at water level. They are closed to the public but from all accounts, by the rather dismal standards of the Middle Ages, were far from being the worst residence for criminals.

The English-language tour starts at 10.30 am and tickets cost L24,000. Tours in Italian start at 10 am and 12.30 pm. You need to book ahead – call ☎ 041 522 49 51. The ticket for this tour is quite separate from the normal L18,000 ticket. Both admit you to the Palazzo Ducale, but if you want to visit the Museo Correr and other museums on the standard ticket *and* do the Itinerari Segreti, you'll have to pay for both.

Libreria Nazionale Marciana (Map 6)

Across the Piazzetta San Marco lies the gracious form of what Palladio once described as the most sumptuous palace ever built. Jacopo Sansovino designed it in the 16th century.

The building occupies the entire west side of the Piazzetta San Marco and houses the **Libreria Nazionale Marciana**, or National Library of St Mark (aka the Libreria Vecchia, or Old Library, and Libreria Sansoviniana, after its architect) and the **Museo Archeologico**. The library extends around the corner on the waterfront into what was once the Zecca, the Republic's mint.

For more on the Libreria Nazionale Marciana and the Museo Archeologico, see Museo Correr later in this section. Admission to both is through that museum and included in the combined ticket described under Special Tickets at the start of this chapter.

Piazza San Marco (Map 6)

Napoleon thought of Piazza San Marco as the 'finest drawing room in Europe'. Enclosed by the basilica and the arcaded Procuratie Vecchie and Nuove, the square plays host to competing flocks of pigeons and tourists. Stand and wait for the bronze Mori (Moors) to strike the bell of the 15th-century Torre dell'Orologio, which rises above the entrance to the Mercerie, the series of streets that forms the main thoroughfare from San Marco to the Rialto. Or sit and savour a coffee at Florian, Quadri or Lavena, the 18th-century cafes facing each other on the piazza – but expect to pay L10,000 for a cappuccino (more if there is music). On occasion you may witness a minor military ceremony to hoist or haul in the three flags (Venice, Italy and the EU). The flagpoles have been around a lot longer than the EU, so one wonders what the third flag used to be?

Stop the Pigeons!

If you get the impression there are more pigeons in Piazza San Marco than inhabitants in the whole of Venice, you're right. Officials estimate the pesky pigeon population at around 100,000 (but how do you count them?). Anyone who has been dive-bombed by squadrons of these parasitic marauders on this most beautiful of squares will probably not be overly unhappy to hear that La Serenissima is striking back. Tests have shown that around 15% of the flock have salmonella and can pass it on to their hapless human victims, and so the city fathers have ordained a culling program. In the past there was an attempt to sterilise them with chemically treated birdseed, but they didn't swallow it. Equally unsuccessful is the supposed ban on feeding the little beggars. There is purportedly a L100,000 fine for this activity, but to judge by the birdseed vendors and the throngs of delighted tourists allowing birdies to

What not to do in Piazza San Marco

poop on their shoulders for that memorable Piazza San Marco photo, that rule died at birth.

Worse than the poop on the people is that on the monuments – the acid in bird droppings eats away at the stone. People involved in restoration pull their hair out at the thought of the vast sums spent to restore monuments, only for the work imperilled by the toilet habits of these birds. Please don't feed them!

Basilica di San Marco (Map 6)

No doubt some of you have skipped all the above prattling and turned straight to what for most is the number one attraction in Venice. Let's hope you have time to do it more justice than space here allows us to! It is at once a remarkable place of worship and a singular declaration of commercial-imperial might.

St Mark's Basilica embodies a magnificent blend of architectural and decorative styles, dominated by the Byzantine and ranging through Romanesque to Renaissance. Building work on the first chapel to honour the freshly arrived corpse of the evangelist St Mark (see the boxed text 'Making His Mark' in this section) began in AD 828, but the result disappeared in a fire in 932. The next version didn't have a much happier run, for in 1063 Doge Domenico Contarini decided it was poor in comparison to the grander Romanesque churches being raised in mainland cities and had it demolished.

The new basilica, built on the plan of a Greek cross, with five bulbous domes, was modelled on Constantinople's Church of the Twelve Apostles (later destroyed) and consecrated in 1094. It was actually built as the doges' private chapel and remained so until it finally became Venice's cathedral in 1807. But no-one was in any doubt that this was the city's principal church.

For more than 500 years, the doges enlarged and embellished the church, adorning it with an incredible array of treasures plundered from the East, in particular Constantinople, during the Crusades.

The arches above the doorways in the **facade** boast fine mosaics. The one at the left end, depicting the arrival of St Mark's body in Venice, was completed in 1270. Above the doorway next to it is an 18th-century mosaic depicting the doge venerating St Mark's body. The mosaics on the other side of the main doorway both date from the 17th century. The one at the right

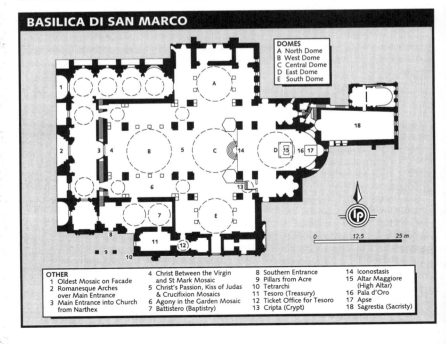

BASILICA DI SAN MARCO

DOMES
A North Dome
B West Dome
C Central Dome
D East Dome
E South Dome

OTHER			
1 Oldest Mosaic on Facade	4 Christ Between the Virgin and St Mark Mosaic	8 Southern Entrance	14 Iconostasis
2 Romanesque Arches over Main Entrance	5 Christ's Passion, Kiss of Judas & Crucifixion Mosaics	9 Pillars from Acre	15 Altar Maggiore (High Altar)
3 Main Entrance into Church from Narthex	6 Agony in the Garden Mosaic	10 Tetrarchi	16 Pala d'Oro
	7 Battistero (Baptistry)	11 Tesoro (Treasury)	17 Apse
		12 Ticket Office for Tesoro	18 Sagrestia (Sacristy)
		13 Cripta (Crypt)	

A seat with a view in Piazza San Marco

Piazza San Marco at full stretch

The baroque Chiesa di Santa Maria della Salute

Full of Eastern promise – Basilica di San Marco

Venice from 99m – the vista from the Campanile

The glittering facade of the 11th-century basilica

Carnevale revellers in Piazza San Marco

Ascension scene on the basilica's facade

Detail of the richly adorned Basilica di San Marco

St Mark's body arrives at the basilica.

Mosaic depicting the theft of St Mark's body

Trinket shops line the 1592 Ponte di Rialto.

end depicts the stealing of St Mark's body, while next to it the Venetians receive the body of the saint. The three arches of the main doorway are decorated with Romanesque carvings dating from around 1240.

The only original entrance to the church is the one on the south side that leads to the Battistero (Baptistry). It is fronted by two pillars brought to Venice from Acre in the Holy Land in the 13th century. The Syriac sculpture, the *Tetrarchi* (Tetrarchs), next to the Porta della Carta of the Palazzo Ducale, dates from the 4th century and is believed to represent Diocletian and his three co-emperors, who together ruled the Roman Empire in the 3rd century AD.

On the Loggia dei Cavalli above the main door are copies of four gilded bronze horses: the originals, on display inside, were stolen when Constantinople was sacked in 1204, during the Fourth Crusade. Napoleon removed them to Paris in 1797, but they were returned after the fall of the French Empire.

Through the doors is the **narthex**, or vestibule, its domes and arches decorated with mosaics, mainly dating from the 13th century. The oldest mosaics in the basilica, dating from around 1063, are in the niches of the bay in front of the main door from the narthex into the church proper. They feature the Madonna with the Apostles. Look for the red marble spot in the floor. This marks where Pope Alexander III and Barbarossa kissed and made up in 1177.

The **interior** of the basilica is dazzling: if you can take your eyes off the glitter of the mosaics, take time to admire the 12th-century marble pavement, an infinite variety of geometrical whimsy interspersed with floral motifs and depictions of animals. (It has subsided in places, making the floor uneven.) The lower level of the walls is lined with precious Eastern marbles, and above this decoration the extraordinary feast of gilded **mosaics** begins. Work started on the mosaics in the 11th century and continued until well into the 13th century and beyond. Mosaics in the baptistry and side chapels date from the 14th and 15th centuries, and as late as the 18th century mosaics were still being added or restored.

Notable mosaics include: the 12th-century Ascension in the central dome; those on the arch between the central and west domes, dating from the same period and including Christ's Passion, the Kiss of Judas and the Crucifixion; the early-12th-century mosaics of the Pentecost in the west dome; the lunette over the west door depicting Christ between the Virgin and St Mark (13th century); the 13th-century Agony in the Garden on the wall of the right aisle; the early-12th-century mosaics in the left-transept (north) dome portraying the life of St John the Evangelist; those in the east dome depicting the Religion of Christ as foretold by the Prophets (12th century); 12th-century mosaics in the right-transept (south) dome depicting a series of saints; and those between the windows of the apse depicting St Mark and three other patron saints of Venice, which are among the earliest mosaics in the basilica.

Separating the main body of the church from the area before the high altar is a magnificent multicoloured marble **iconostasis**. Dividing the iconostasis in two is a huge cross of bronze and silver. To each side line up the Virgin Mary and the Apostles. Beneath the majestic marble **altar maggiore** (high altar) lie the remains of St Mark.

Behind the altar is one of the basilica's greatest treasures, the exquisite **Pala d'Oro**, a gold, enamel and jewel-encrusted altarpiece made in Constantinople for Doge Pietro Orseolo I in 976. It was enriched and reworked in Constantinople in 1105, enlarged by Venetian goldsmiths in 1209 and

Stepping out proudly high above Piazza San Marco – the horses known as the Quadriga

DAMIEN SIMONIS

again reset in the 14th century. Among the almost 2000 precious stones that adorn it are emeralds, rubies, amethysts, sapphires and pearls. Admission costs L3000.

The **Tesoro** (Treasury), accessible from the right transept, contains most of the booty from the 1204 raid on Constantinople, including a thorn said to be from the crown worn by Christ. Admission costs L4000.

Through a door at the far right end of the narthex is a stairway leading up to the **Galleria** (also called the Museo di San Marco), which contains the original gilded bronze horses and the **Loggia dei Cavalli**. The Galleria affords wonderful views of the church's interior, while the loggia offers equally splendid vistas of the square. Admission costs L3000. Access to the crypt and baptistry is only possible if you have specific permission from the church administrators.

Although the church is open for longer hours, visiting hours for the Pala d'Oro, Tesoro, Galleria and Loggia are from 9.30 am to 4.30 pm Monday to Saturday and from 2 to 4.30 pm on Sunday and holidays.

The mosaics are best seen when illuminated. This means weekdays from 11.30 am to 12.30 pm and 'all day' at weekends. This 'all day' really means when Masses are being held. On Saturday, in particular, there is nothing to say the lights won't go out for a good part of the day when no service is on.

Making His Mark

The story goes that an angel appeared to the Evangelist Mark when his boat put in at Rialto while on his way to Rome from Aquileia. The winged fellow informed the future saint that his body would rest in Venice. When he did die some years later, it was in Alexandria, Egypt. In 828, two Venetian merchants persuaded the guardians of his Alexandrian tomb to let them have the corpse, which they then smuggled down to their ship in port.

You've got to ask yourself why they would bother with such a strange cargo. Well, in those days, any city worthy of the name had a patron saint of stature. Venice had St Theodore (San Teodoro), but poor old Theodore didn't really cut the mustard in the Christian hierarchy. An Evangelist, though, would be something quite different. Did Doge Giustinian Partecipazio order this little body-snatching mission? We will never know. Whatever the truth of this tale, it seems that *someone's* putrid corpse was transported to Venice, and that everyone rather liked to think St Mark was now in their midst. St Theodore was unceremoniously demoted and the doge ordered the construction of a chapel to house the newcomer. That church would later become the magnificent Basilica di San Marco. St Mark was symbolised in the Book of Revelation (the Apocalypse) as a winged lion and this image came to be synonymous with La Serenissima.

NICKY CAVEN

The winged lion of St Mark – a rather scholarly feline

Legend also has it that, during the rebuilding of the basilica in 1063, the body of St Mark was hidden and then 'lost' when its hiding place was forgotten. In 1094, when the church was consecrated, the corpse (which must have been a picture of frailty by this time) broke through the column in which it had been enclosed. 'It's a miracle!' the Venetians cried. Or was it just incredibly dodgy plasterwork? St Mark had been lost and now was found. A grateful populace buried the remains in the church crypt where they now lie beneath the basilica's high altar.

Campanile (Map 6)

The basilica's 99m-tall bell tower was raised in the 10th century but suddenly collapsed on 14 July 1902 and was rebuilt brick by brick (*dov'era, com'era*; 'where it was and as it was'). Alterations had already been made in the 12th and 16th centuries. On the second occasion a statuette of the Archangel Gabriel was positioned at the tip of the tower to serve as an elaborate weather vane. After the collapse in 1902, the tower took 10 years to rebuild. Oddly, it contains just one bell, the *marangona*, which survived the fall.

You can pay L8000 to take a lift to the top, from where there are views across the entire city. The campanile is open daily from 9 am to 7 pm (9.30 am to 5.30 pm in winter).

Procuratie (Map 6)

Formerly the residence and offices of the Procurators of St Mark, who were responsible for the upkeep of the basilica, the **Procuratie Vecchie** were designed by Mauro Codussi and occupy the entire north side of the Piazza San Marco. On the south side of the piazza are the **Procuratie Nuove**, designed by Jacopo Sansovino and completed by Vincenzo Scamozzi and Baldassare Longhena.

Ala Napoleonica (Map 6)

When Napoleon decided to make the Procuratie Nuove his official residence in Venice (not that he was ever around to enjoy it), he also decided that he needed to leave his architectural mark on the city. So he had the church of San Geminiano, at the western end of the piazza, demolished to make way for a new wing that would connect the Procuratie Nuove and Vecchie and house his ballroom.

At first glance, it seems to blend in perfectly with the Procuratie, but a slightly more attentive look soon reveals differences. The row of statues at the top is not matched anywhere else around the piazza. Just in case anyone had doubts about how Napoleon thought of himself, the statues are of Roman emperors.

Museo Correr (Map 6)

The Ala Napoleonica is now home to the **Museo Correr**, dedicated to the art and history of Venice.

Once inside, you turn right into a hall lined with statuary and bas-reliefs by Canova. More of his creations adorn the following couple of rooms, collectively known as the Sale Neoclassiche (Neoclassical Rooms). Keeping the statues company is an assortment of 19th-century paintings (including some by Hayez and others by Canova), books, documents, medallions, musical instruments and other bits and bobs.

From here you slide on into the rooms dedicated to Civiltà Veneziana (Venetian Civilisation), where you can inspect coins and standards of the Republic, model galleys, maps, navigation instruments and a display of weaponry from bygone days.

You are then encouraged to continue straight on to the **Museo Archeologico**, crammed mostly with statues, Greek and Roman, along with a vast collection of ancient coins and ceramics. Some, but by no means all, of the material was collected in the Veneto. You will be asked to show your ticket here, as you will again in the adjoining **Libreria Nazionale Marciana**.

You enter the library, in a sense, through the back door. The Sala della Libreria is the main reading hall, built in the 16th century to house the collection of some 1000 codexes left to the Republic by Cardinal Bessarione in 1468. The ceiling was decorated by a battalion of artists chosen by Titian and Sansovino, the architect. Of them, Veronese was considered the best; his three contributions form the second line of medallions after you enter.

You then pass into the Vestibolo (Vestibule). The centrepiece of the ceiling ornamentation is *Sapienza* (Wisdom) by Titian. The ancient statues cluttering the floor were part of a wider collection placed here late in the 16th century. Most were later shunted over to what would become the Museo Archeologico. Finally you arrive at the top end of the fine entrance stairway – a sort of twin to the Scala d'Oro in the Palazzo Ducale across the square.

You now have to backtrack all the way to the armoury in the Museo Correr. The western corridor of the Ala Napoleonica contains further baubles relating to Civiltà Veneziana. About halfway along, a stairway leads up to two other collections belonging to the Museo Correr. The modest **Museo del Risorgimento**, on the 2nd floor, traces the fall of the Venetian Republic and Italian unification. It was closed at the time of writing. The **Arte Antica** collection is a kind of Noah's Ark of largely second-rate art, starting with 14th-century Byzantine painters and proceeding to Gothic art, with a series of rooms given over to Flemish and German paintings, and a room with eight works that came out of the Bellini workshop. A few items of interest by Carpaccio and Lorenzo Lotto dot the remaining rooms. The last of them contain porcelain and a library.

After going back downstairs, you turn left to walk through the remainder of the Civiltà Veneziana collection and so return to the ticket counter.

Admission to the Museo Correr is included in the combined ticket described under Special Tickets at the start of this chapter. The museum is open daily from 9 am to 7 pm.

West of Piazza San Marco

Heading west from the Ala Napoleonica, you will soon find yourself on Salizzada di San Moisè. Down the first street to your left, Calle Vallaresso, is a gaggle of fashion stores and Harry's Bar. Also, at No 1332, there's the closed **Teatro al Ridotto** (Map 6).

Back in the 17th century, the Ridotto gained quite a name for itself as the city's premier gaming house. During the twilight years of La Serenissima, Venetian nobles were wiping out their entire fortunes at the gaming tables. Even if the state was getting a share, it was hardly sufficient compensation for the ruin being brought to an already shaky local economy. Finally, in November 1774 the Ridotto was shut by the authorities *per tutti i tempi ed anni avvenire...* ('for all time and years to come...'). All time was a relative term and less than 20 years later it was back in operation. It remained so until

the Austrians shut it for good in the early 19th century.

As you approach Campo San Moisè, you pass a busy shopping street on your right, **Frezzeria** (Map 6). In medieval days no-one had dreamt of opening fashion stores here: the product on sale was *frecce* (arrows). In those days, all males above a certain age had to do regular archery practice and so be ready to sail off to war – or at least on military escort duty for merchant convoys – when necessary.

Campo San Moisè (Map 6) is dominated by the church of the same name. Legend has it that the first church was founded in the 8th century, but the rather unrestrained baroque facade you see today is a product of the 1660s.

From here, the street widens into Calle Larga XXII Marzo, which was opened in 1881 and commemorates the surrender of the Austrians to Venetian rebels on 22 March 1848. The victory was short-lived, however, and it would be another 18 years before the Austrians were given their definitive marching orders. One Italian guide rather hopefully describes this as 'the City of Venice', given the presence of the Borsa (stock exchange) and several banks. Down Calle del Pestrin, which runs south off Calle Larga XXII Marzo, is the landward entrance to the **Palazzo Contarini-Fasan** (Map 6). It is nothing much to look at, but legend has it that Desdemona, the wife of Othello and victim of his jealousy in Shakespeare's play, lived here.

Calle Larga XXII Marzo then contracts into Calle delle Ostreghe (Oysters St) and brings you to Campo Santa Maria del Giglio.

Chiesa di Santa Maria del Giglio (Map 5)

This church is also known as Santa Maria Zobenigo. Its baroque facade features maps of European cities as they were in 1678. The facade also hides the fact that a church has stood here since the 10th century.

The church itself is a rather small affair, but quite jammed with an assortment of paintings. Of interest is Peter Paul Rubens' *Madonna col Bambino e San Giovanni*

(Madonna with Child and St John), the only work of his in Venice. Behind the altar lurk Tintoretto's typically moody depictions of the four evangelists, and the church is fully stuffed with other works by lower-ranking Venetian painters.

Outside, the oddly out-of-place square brick building in the middle of the *campo* was the base of the church's bell tower, knocked down in 1775 because it was in danger of falling over of its own accord.

The church is part of the Chorus scheme (see the boxed text 'A Chorus Line' earlier in this chapter). It's open from 10 am to 5 pm Monday to Saturday and 1 to 5 pm on Sunday. Admission costs L3000.

Palazzo Corner/Ca' Grande (Map 5)

After crossing two bridges in quick succession, you could wander south towards the Grand Canal and sidle up next to this, Sansovino's 16th-century masterpiece of residential building. He built it for Jacopo Corner, a nephew of the ill-fated Caterina, the queen of Cyprus (see the boxed text 'A Queen Cornered' in the Excursions chapter). Now the seat of the Prefettura and other government offices, the mansion has apparently lost much of its lustre inside, not that you'll be able to get in and find out. From the Canal you can tell which building it is by the two Carabinieri standing guard outside – are they awaiting a waterborne assault?

Campo San Maurizio (Map 5)

Occasionally the scene of an antiques market, the square is surrounded by elegant 14th- and 15th-century mansions, along with the church of the same name. Just off this square to the north you can sneak around to Campiello Drio la Chiesa and get a close-up look at just how much the bell tower of the Chiesa di Santo Stefano (see the next entry) is leaning. Pause, too, when you cross the bridge leading from Campo San Maurizio to Campo Santo Stefano. Looking north, you can see how the same church is in part actually built over the Rio del Santissimo.

More than Wishing Wells

Sooner or later you will probably ask yourself, as you enter one *campo* (square) or another: what are those squat stone cylinders with the metal lids firmly clamped on top? The answer is obvious enough once you think about it: wells.

That there are so many (some of them have been marked on the maps, in case you are wondering what we are talking about) reflects every neighbourhood's need to have its own source of drinking water in the good old days. With bridges few and far between throughout much of the history of the city, it was easier to provide each of the many *insulae* that make up the fabric of Venice with its own well than attempt to transport water.

There's a whole lot more to this system than meets the eye. In general, the well is surrounded by up to four depressions around 4m from it. Rainwater drained to these depressions and seeped into a cistern below. Sand and/or gravel inside the cistern acted as a filter for the water. In the middle of the cistern, a brick cylinder (the well) extends to the bottom. The cistern itself was sealed off with impenetrable clay to keep salty water out. Engineers also sought out relatively high spots for wells to shield them from the *acque alte*.

With the introduction of running water direct to all Venice's buildings, the wells have been closed up and are no longer in use. But it is intriguing to think of how much the city's survival depended on these ingenious structures.

DAMIEN SIMONIS

Wells are a common sight

Chiesa di Santo Stefano (Map 5)

When you walk in here (entry on the western side) look up at possibly the finest wooden ceiling (*a carena di nave* – like an upturned ship's hull) of any church in Venice. The church was one of the three attached to a convent in Venice (the others were Santa Maria Gloriosa dei Frari and SS Giovanni e Paolo).

The church is part of the Chorus scheme (see the boxed text 'A Chorus Line' earlier in this chapter). You only pay here to go into the small museum off to the right of the altar, where a collection of Tintoretto's paintings has been crammed. Among the most notable are the *Ultima Cena* (Last Supper), *Lavanda dei Piedi* (Washing of the Feet) and *Orazione nell'Orto* (Agony in the Garden). It's open from 10 am to 5 pm Monday to Saturday and 1 to 5 pm on Sunday. Admission costs L3000.

Unfortunately visitors cannot get into the cloisters, which are no longer church property.

From the church, it is a brief stroll south across the grand expanse (a rare thing in Venice) that is the Campo Santo Stefano (also known as Campo Francesco Morosini after the 17th-century doge) to the Grand Canal and the Ponte dell'Accademia that spans it.

Ponte dell'Accademia (Map 5)

Built in 1930 to replace a 19th-century metal structure, the third and last of the Grand Canal bridges was supposed to be a temporary arrangement until a satisfactory design for a more permanent structure was produced. All that seems to have been forgotten, which is fine, because it is really quite attractive as it is. From the middle the views both ways up the Grand Canal are spellbinding.

At this point you may decide to skip the rest of the Sestiere di San Marco itinerary and cross the bridge to the Sestiere di Dorsoduro. If so, brace yourself for an intense blast of high culture. Your eyes are going to have to work overtime in two of the city's most important art galleries. Proceed to the Sestiere di Dorsoduro section.

Santa Stefano to Ponte di Rialto (Maps 5 & 6)

If you decide to hang about in the San Marco area for a while, head for the south-western end of Campo Santo Stefano, where Calle Fruttarol swings off to the north-west on a twisting and winding route towards the Ponte di Rialto.

You immediately cross a narrow canal and then another, the Rio del Duca. The building on the west bank of this *rio*, with a fine facade on the Grand Canal, is the **Ca' del Duca** (Map 5), so called because the duke of Milan, Francesco Sforza, bought it from the Corner family in 1461. Above the 14th-century ground floor, the rest of the mansion was rebuilt in the 19th century. At the next street, Calle del Teatro, turn left. The street name is all that remains of the Teatro San Samuele, where Carlo Goldoni (see Literature in the Facts about Venice chapter) first hit the limelight.

Turn right and follow the rear side of the **Palazzo Malipiero** (Map 5), in the wall of which you may notice a plaque just before you enter Salizzada Malipiero. It reminds us that in a house along this lane Giacomo Casanova was born in 1725.

NICKY CAVEN

Not quite Romeo – that other famous lover, Casanova, was born in Venice.

Palazzo Malipiero forms the southern limit of the quiet little Campo San Samuele on the Grand Canal. On the eastern side is the unobtrusive outline of the former Chiesa di San Samuele and to the north the stately **Palazzo Grassi** (Map 5), frequent host to temporary art exhibitions and owned by Fiat. Massari's 1749 design clearly shows a tendency towards neoclassicism.

Wheeling around the church, we head more or less east along Calle delle Carrozze and on into Salizzada San Samuele. A number of shops, flogging everything from expensive glass to wooden sculptures of un-ironed shirts, line these streets. You can only wonder what **Paolo Veronese**, who lived at No 3337, would have thought of it all.

Although this itinerary barrels along towards Calle dell'Albero, unhurried strollers might like to wander down any of the several lanes around here that end at the Grand Canal. Just off Calle dell'Albero is a neat little square, the Corte dell'Albero, walled on two sides by the interesting **Casa Nardi** (Map 5) at Nos 3884–3887, built in 1913 and incorporating Veneto-Byzantine architectural themes. It has a hint of the Barcelona Modernista style to it (and especially calls to mind the architect Lluís Domènech y Montaner) in its use of brick and the attempt to recycle a proud and distant design tradition.

Facing the Grand Canal at No 3877 is Codussi's **Palazzo Corner-Spinelli** (Map 5), later reworked by Sanmicheli.

Campo Sant'Angelo (Map 5) From Calle dell'Albero, you cross a tiny canal and then head south down Calle degli Avvocati, which leads directly into Campo Sant'Angelo. You may notice that a good deal of the square is raised. The two wells clue you in that directly below is a large cistern.

The Chiesa di Sant'Angelo Michele has long since disappeared, but in the distance you can see the leaning tower of Venice – the bell tower of the Chiesa di Santo Stefano (see the previous page).

In 1801 the Italian musician Domenico Cimarosa died in the 15th-century **Palazzo Duodo** (No 3584), which in those days was the Albergo Tre Stelle. **Palazzo Gritti**, across

the square, was built around the same period. All sorts of unpleasant things occurred in this square, according to city chronicles. In 1476 a launderer by the name of Giacomo was jailed after having taken a certain Bernardino degli Orsi under the portico of the Chiesa di Sant'Angelo Michele and raped him. In 1716 the body of a violently murdered woman was discovered in one of the wells. A Florentine was accused of assaulting, robbing and murdering the poor wretch.

There's more where that came from, but enough. It's time to get a move on.

La Fenice & Campo San Fantin (Maps 5 & 6) Take Calle Caotorta and cross the first bridge you see. After the bridge, if you turn immediately left and then right you'll end up in Calle della Fenice, a tunnel of scaffolding along the northern wall of the star-crossed opera house. A few steps along this street turn left again. The hotel on the tiny square (Campiello della Fenice; Map 5) is covered in cannon balls used by the Austrians in their campaign to retake control of the city in 1849. Follow this little arc around and you are again in Calle della Fenice. The posters for the 1995–6 season are still up – a rather poignant reminder that this unhappy hulk was one of the world's favourite opera houses. For more on its fate since flames destroyed it in 1996, see the boxed text 'Faltering Phoenix' in the Entertainment chapter.

You now emerge into Campo San Fantin. Opposite the theatre is the **Chiesa di San Fantin** (Map 6), whose final incarnation was wrought either by Sansovino or Pietro Lombardo.

The other main building on this square is the **Ateneo Veneto** (Map 6), a learned society founded in Napoleon's time. Previously it had been the headquarters of the confraternity of San Girolamo and Santa Maria della Giustizia. The main charitable work of confraternity members was to accompany criminals on death row in their last moments before being executed.

To proceed, take Calle della Verona north out of the square. Just before you hit the T-junction with Calle della Mandola, you cross Rio Terrà degli Assassini. Apparently, in medieval times this was a good place to avoid, because murder was among the more common nocturnal activities. Street crime got so bad that in 1128 the government banned the wearing of certain 'Greek style' beards that, it was said, were in vogue among wrongdoers to prevent them being identified. It was at that time too that the first all-night lamps were set burning in the dodgier parts of town – the devotional niches you still see around were created specifically for this purpose – and the Signori di Notte (Night Masters), whose task was to deal with flourishing crime of all sorts in the dark hours, started patrolling the lanes.

Campo San Beneto (Map 5) At Calle della Mandola we turn left then right into Rio Terrà della Mandola. This street bumps right into the side of the splendid, but rather neglected, **Palazzo Fortuny**. The building sports two rows of *hectafores*, each a series of eight connected Venetian-style windows. Mariano Fortuny y Madrazo, an eccentric Spanish painter and collector, bought the building at the beginning of the 20th century. He left his works here and, together with another 80 by the Roman artist Virgilio Guidi, they make up the bulk of the Museo Fortuny. It has been closed for some time for restoration.

The **Chiesa di San Beneto**, in the same square, was rebuilt in the early 17th century and is also closed.

Campo Manin (Map 6) From Campo San Beneto, drop south along Calle del Teatro Goldoni, passing the supremely ugly Cinema Rossini, and turn left at the junction into Calle de la Cortesia, which leads over a bridge and into Campo Manin. At the square's centre stands the proud statue of Daniele Manin, a lion at his feet. He led the anti-Austrian revolt of 1848–9. The square also boasts a remarkably thoughtless 20th-century contribution at its eastern end, the Cassa di Risparmio di Venezia bank.

More interesting than the square itself is what lies off it. Take Calle della Vida south of the square and follow the signs to the

Renaissance **Palazzo Contarini del Bovolo**, so named because of the dizzying external spiral (*bovolo* in the Venetian dialect) staircase. Built in the late 15th century, the palace still maintains a hint of the Gothic in its arches and capitals. You can enter the grounds (L3000) daily from 10 am to 6 pm, but you can see the staircase quite well from outside.

NICKY CAVEN

It's enough to make your head spin – the staircase of the Palazzo Contarini del Bovolo.

Along the Grand Canal (Map 6) From the dead-end at the Palazzo Contarini del Bovolo our route proceeds east along Calle delle Locande to Calle dei Fuseri, which, heading north across Campo San Luca, brings us to the Grand Canal along Calle del Carbon (Coal St). Not surprisingly, Coal St leads to Coal Quay (Riva del Carbon), which until well into the 19th century was the main unloading point for the city's coal supply. Calle del Carbon, it is said, was also something of a red-light district.

To the left of Calle del Carbon are the **Palazzo Loredan** and **Ca' Farsetti**. Both started life in the 12th century as *fondachi*. These were family houses where the ground floor, with a grand entrance on the canal, was used for the loading, unloading and storage of the merchandise upon which the wealth and standing of most of the great patrician families of Venice long depended. In some cases (as in the nearby Fondaco dei Tedeschi), a *fondaco* was more a trading house and hotel for foreign communities.

In 1826 the town hall moved its offices to the Ca' Farsetti from the Palazzo Ducale. Forty-two years later it also acquired Palazzo Loredan. You can wander into the foyer of the latter, but generally that's as far as you'll get. On the corner of Calle del Carbon is a plaque announcing that Eleonora Lucrezia Corner Piscopia (of the family that once owned Palazzo Corner) was the first woman to receive a degree – whether the first woman *ever* or just in Venice isn't clear. Anyway, she got her piece of parchment with all the appropriate seals in 1678.

Just west of Ca' Farsetti, the Renaissance **Palazzo Grimani** (Map 5) was completed by Sanmicheli, although the second floor was done later. It houses law courts.

Walking east towards the Ponte di Rialto from Calle del Carbon, you may notice the narrow, Gothic, 14th-century **Palazzo Dandolo**. It's just left of Bar Omnibus, a touristy restaurant that started life as a cafe in the 19th century. The house belonged to blind doge Enrico Dandolo, who led the Fourth Crusade to a famous victory over Constantinople in 1204. Never mind that the Crusaders were actually supposed to be toughing it out against the infidels in the sands of the Middle East rather than bludgeoning their fellow (albeit Orthodox) Christians in Byzantium (see History in the Facts about Venice chapter)!

Wedged in between Calle Bembo and Rio di San Salvador is the magnificent red facade of **Palazzo Bembo**. What you see is the result of 17th-century restoration of a 15th-century late-Venetian-Gothic structure. It is thought almost certain that Pietro Bembo, cardinal, poet, historian and founding father of the grammar of standard Italian, was born here. On the other side of Rio di San Salvador, the **Palazzo Dolfin-Manin**, easily identified by its portico, was designed by Sansovino and completed in 1573. At this point we turn away from the Grand Canal and proceed inland a block along Calle Larga Mazzini.

Chiesa di San Salvador & Around
(Map 6) In front of you is the main entrance to the **Chiesa di San Salvador**, built on a plan of three Greek crosses laid end to end. The church is among the city's oldest, although the bulk of what you see dates from later periods. The present facade was erected in 1663. Among the noteworthy works inside are Titian's *Annunciazione* (Annunciation), at the third altar on the right as you approach the main altar. Behind the main altar itself is another of his contributions, the *Trasfigurazione* (Transfiguration). The church is open daily from 9 am to noon and 4 to 7 pm. To its right is the former monastery of the same name, now owned by Telecom. You can get just a glimpse of one of the cloisters by peering through the window nearest the church.

Diagonally opposite is the **Scuola Grande di San Teodoro**, one of the many confraternity headquarters in Venice (see the boxed text 'When School Was Cool' later in this chapter), now used frequently for music recitals and exhibitions.

Heading north-east from here, we pass the small and much interfered with **Chiesa di San Bartolomeo**, which at one time served as the parish church for the local German-merchant community based at the Fondaco dei Tedeschi. When the Republic meekly surrendered to Napoleon in 1797, an angry mob set about looting the houses of those they held responsible for such ignominy in the area around **Campo San Bartolomeo**. The Venetian militia set up cannons on the Ponte di Rialto to control the unrest – the last time the guns of San Marco were fired in anger they spilled the blood of their own people. The statue in the middle of the square is of Carlo Goldoni, Venice's great playwright.

Fondaco dei Tedeschi (Map 6) From the 13th century onwards, the German trading community (who enjoyed something of favoured status in Venice) occupied a fondaco (or *fontego*) on this privileged site. After a fire in 1505 the present building was erected in a little under three years (1508), not bad going for the time.

It may look a little sombre now, but you have to try to imagine the exterior adorned with frescoes by Giorgione and Titian. To help in this task, you can see some fragments in the Ca' d'Oro (see the later Sestiere di Cannaregio section).

The two artists, when they turned up at the Palazzo Ducale to pick up their payment of 150 ducats, were told their work was only worth 130 ducats. Incensed, they insisted on an independent appraisal, which confirmed the figure of 150 ducats. The artists were then told that more than 130 ducats couldn't be arranged that day, so they could take it or leave it. Perhaps such penny-pinching lay partly behind Titian's increasing tendency to accept commissions from abroad!

Inside, the building is simple but dignified. The Germans used the porticoed floors above the courtyard as lodging and offices, storing their merchandise below. They even had their own well (which remains). The courtyard was covered over in 1937 and the building now serves as the central post office.

Back to Piazza San Marco (Map 6)

At this point, you are spoilt for choice of options. You could proceed north into Cannaregio (see later in this chapter) or duck around and cross the Ponte di Rialto to explore San Polo and Santa Croce (see later in this chapter). Or you could close the circle and finish up the itinerary within the Sestiere di San Marco.

To do the latter, retrace your steps to the Chiesa di San Salvador and follow the narrow shopping street around its northern flank, the Mercerie San Salvador. Where the street runs into a canal, you can see the late Gothic **Palazzo Giustinian-Faccanon**, which for a long time housed the city's main newspaper, *Il Gazzettino*.

Knocking Rebellion on the Head

By 1310, Venice was having some serious difficulties. Doge Pietro Gradenigo's pursuit of mainland conquest had brought upon the city a papal interdict. The pope was in no way amused by Venice's attempts to seize control of the city of Ferrara, to which the Holy See had a long-standing claim. The Venetians had been defeated in the field and many Venetian merchants abroad had been arrested and all their goods confiscated.

Gradenigo was not without his opponents, foremost among them the Querini family. Marco Querini, who had been in command of Ferrara and been defeated, claimed Venice had not given him the support he needed. Marco convinced General Baiamonte Tiepolo to lead a revolt against Gradenigo. They both lived in the San Polo area, near Rialto, and so planned to send two armed columns over the bridge. Querini's would proceed down Calle dei Fabbri to Piazza San Marco and Tiepolo's down the Mercerie. They would join in the piazza and combine to attack the Palazzo Ducale, at which point a third force would arrive across the lagoon from the mainland.

It might have worked, but word of the plan got out. Gradenigo and his allies gathered forces in Piazza San Marco, put the workers of the Arsenale (who traditionally served as a kind of ducal militia in times of uncertainty) on alert and ordered the *podestà* (mayor) of Chioggia to intercept the invasion fleet.

Things went wrong from the start. A storm delayed the fleet and while Marco Querini marched on Piazza San Marco, Tiepolo's troops hung about looting the public treasury at

The lanes that lead from San Salvador to the Torre dell'Orologio and into Piazza San Marco are all called *merceria* (*marzaria* in Venetian dialect), referring to the merchants who traditionally lined this route. For centuries this was one of the busiest thoroughfares in the city, directly linking Piazza San Marco with Rialto (in other words, the political with the financial lungs of La Serenissima).

The arrival of the railway in the 19th century and a new axis through Cannaregio did nothing to change this. The flux of *foresti* (foreigners – ie non-Venetians) along this narrow commercial trail remains a constant. Whether you're coming from the train station or from Rialto, the Mercerie are to this day one of the most direct routes to Piazza San Marco.

It was also thus for the conspirators in the 1310 plot to overthrow Doge Pietro Gradenigo (see the boxed text on this page), who came a cropper in the Mercerie dell'Orologio just before the Torre dell'Orologio.

Where Merceria dell'Orologio begins, you can see off to the left (east) the **Chiesa di San Zulian**, supposedly founded in 829, though its actual form, covered in a layer of Istrian stone, was designed by Sansovino. Inside are a few works by Palma il Giovane.

Heading right (west) from the top of Merceria dell'Orologio over the bridge, duck right into the first little lane. In the *sotoportego* just before the T-junction you will see on your right, at No 956/b, the entrance to the **Chiesa della Santa Croce degli Armeni**. On Sundays only, Armenian priests from the Isola di San Lazzaro celebrate a service here. The church has been active at least since the 14th century.

Return to Merceria dell'Orologio and proceed down (south) towards the Torre dell'Orologio and pass below it. You are now back in Piazza San Marco.

SESTIERE DI DORSODURO

Let's assume you are on the Ponte dell'Accademia having come through Campo Santo Stefano in the Sestiere di San Marco. Once you step down the other side of the bridge you are in Campo della Carità. Now it's time for some serious art appreciation.

Knocking Rebellion on the Head

Rialto. By the time they went clattering down the Mercerie, Querini was already battling it out with ducal troopers in Piazza San Marco.

Tiepolo's boys were engaged while still in the Mercerie. The decisive moment came when a local housewife, who was leaning out of her window and bombing the rebels with anything that came to hand, pelted Tiepolo's standard-bearer on the head with a mortar. The standard fell and the fight was over. Querini had already died in the fight in Piazza San Marco. The leader of the fleet was captured and summarily executed on a charge of armed rebellion. Tiepolo managed to beat a hasty retreat to his home, from where he negotiated to keep his life but agreed to go into exile.

The woman who had struck the winning blow requested the right to hang the flag of the Republic from her balcony on holidays. This she received, but she was no sentimental dummy – she also asked that the rent on her house never be raised by the Procurators of St Mark, who owned the building. In 1436 the procurators actually did raise it while one of the long-deceased woman's descendants was away on military service. Thirty-two years later he demanded, and obtained, a return to the original rent.

Today a bas-relief of the woman leaning out of her window marks the spot on Merceria dell'Orologio (just above the Sotoportego e Calle del Cappello). A simple stone with the date of the incident in Roman numerals (XV.VI.CCCX) marks the place on the ground where the standard-bearer fell.

Gallerie dell'Accademia (Map 5)

The first buildings you virtually bump into on crossing the Ponte dell'Accademia constitute the Gallerie dell'Accademia, Venice's single most important art collection. The former church and convent of Santa Maria della Carità, with additions by Palladio, houses a swathe of works that follows the progression of Venetian art from the 14th to the 18th centuries.

The rococo painter Gian Battista Piazzetta founded the art school in 1750 that later became the Accademia, Venice's official arbiter of artistic taste. The collection of paintings was assembled in 1807 and opened to the public 10 years later. The first works came from churches and other religious institutions suppressed during the brief years of Napoleonic rule. Later additions came from private collections. In 1878 the galleries were hived off from the art school and passed into state control. Acquisitions have continued ever since.

From the ticket office, you pass upstairs to Room (Sala) 1, where the gallery's more or less chronological display begins. You are in what was the main meeting hall of the Scuola Grande di Santa Maria della Carità, the oldest of the Scuole Grandi (see the boxed text 'When School Was Cool' later in this chapter). The magnificent timber ceiling is divided into squares, at the centre of each of which is a sculpted face – every one different – of an angel. The room is given over to the religious art, triptychs and the like, of the 14th century, including Paolo Veneziano's *Incoronazione di Maria* (Coronation of Mary).

Room 2, designed by Carlo Scarpa and with a *terrazzo alla Veneziana* (see the boxed text 'Of Floors & Walls' in the Sestiere di Castello section of this chapter), contains nine paintings, including a couple each by Giovanni Bellini, Vittore Carpaccio and Cima da Conegliano. Note the commonality in themes adopted by all three in their depictions of the Madonna and child, for instance the musicians at the Madonna's feet.

The most enthralling of the works is, however, Carpaccio's altarpiece *Crocifissione e Apoteosi dei 10,000 Martiri del Monte Ararat* (Crucifixion and Apotheosis of the 10,000 Martyrs of Mt Ararat). The story goes that some 10,000 Roman soldiers sent to quell rebellion in Armenia instead converted to Christianity. The Emperor was unimpressed and sent more troops. They were ordered to subject the 10,000 to the same trials that Christ had suffered if they didn't change their minds. The result was a massacre. The painting, representing a kind of collective sainthood, was a departure from the standard depiction of one or two saints in religious painting. The soldiers all have the appearance of Christ, while their executioners appear in the garb of nasty Turks – no doubt reflecting Venetian and European feelings towards the infidels of their own time.

In Rooms 4 and 5 you can enjoy a mixed bag, including some non-Venetians. They include Andrea Mantegna's *San Giorgio* (St George) and works by Cosmè Tura, Piero della Francesca and Jacopo Bellini. In the latter's pieces, observe the comparative stiffness of his characters, a faithful reflection of a painting style still crossing over from earlier Gothic tenets.

His son Giovanni has 11 paintings here and the greater suppleness and reality of expression is clear – take for instance the remarkable *Madonna col Bambino tra le Sante Caterina e Maddalena* (Madonna with Child Between Saints Catherine and Mary Magdalen).

The most striking paintings in these rooms are the two rare contributions by Giorgione, *La Tempesta* (The Storm) and *La Vecchia* (The Old Woman). Look at the latter closely. The lines and brush strokes, the look in the eyes, indeed the very subject matter, belong to another century. Its complete lack of stylisation makes it readily identifiable with 19th-century portraiture.

In Room 6 are six works by Tintoretto, five by Veronese and a modest contribution from Titian. In Tintoretto's *La Creazione degli Animali* (The Creation of the Animals) we can see the thick splashy paint strokes that characterised much of this Mannerist painter's work. His use of muted crimsons and blues in *Assunzione della*

Vergine (Assumption) reminds one of El Greco. Or rather, in Tintoretto's work we can see support for the claim that El Greco took with him to Spain a good deal of what he had learned in Venice.

The main interest in Rooms 7 and 8 is Lorenzo Lotto's *Ritratto del Giovane Gentiluomo nel Suo Studio* (Portrait of a Young Gentleman in His Studio). What's the lizard doing on his desk? Others represented here are Titian, Palma il Vecchio and even Giorgio Vasari.

In Room 10 we are confronted by some major works, one of the highlights of which is Paolo Veronese's *Convito in Casa di Levi* (Feast in the House of Levi). Originally called *Ultima Cena* (Last Supper), the painting's name was changed at the behest of the Inquisition (see Painting in the Facts about Venice chapter). The room also contains one of Titian's last works, *Pietà*. The almost nightmarish quality of the faces has a Goya-esque touch and reflects, perhaps, the fact that Titian was working on it during an epidemic of the plague. Finally, there are some remarkable Tintorettos dedicated to the theme of St Mark. The *Trafugamento del Corpo di San Marco* (Stealing of St Mark's Body) is a mighty example of this artist's daring with a brush.

Another fine Tintoretto is his *Crocifissione* (Crucifixion) in Room 11, where you can also admire decoration by Tiepolo saved from Chiesa dei Scalzi after an Austrian bomb missed its target (the nearby train station) in 1915 and hit the church. His long frieze *Castigo dei Serpenti* (Punishment of the Snakes) was for many years rolled up and stashed away, which explains the damage evident today.

Room 12 contains minor 18th-century landscape painting, while Room 13 has works by Jacopo Bassano, Palma il Giovane, Tintoretto and Titian. Rooms 14, 15, 16 and 16a are of less interest, although a few minor Tiepolos appear. Room 17 is crammed with small works, including a rare (in Venice) couple by Canaletto. Francesco Guardi, Pietro Longhi, Marco Ricco and Rossalba Carriera also figure here, as do some studies by Tiepolo.

Minor Veneto landscape artists *(vedutisti)* line the walls of Room 18, while Room 19 is given over to 15th- and 16th-century artists – thus breaking the chronological order established so far.

Just as you might have thought the exhibition was losing steam and interest, you enter Room 20. The crowd scenes, splashes of red and activity pouring from the canvases in this cycle dedicated to the *Miracoli della Vera Croce* (Miracles of the True Cross) come as quite a shock. They were carried out by Vittore Carpaccio and Gentile Bellini for the Scuola di San Giovanni Evangelista, which is home to a relic of the True Cross. Today, much of their fascination lies in the depiction of a Venice of centuries ago, with gondolas pootling about, classic Venetian chimneys in evidence everywhere and a faithful depiction of the timber Rialto bridge that preceded the present one.

Carpaccio's extraordinary series of nine paintings recounting the life of Santa Orseola follows in Room 21.

Room 22 hosts a few neoclassical sculptures, while Room 23 is actually the former Chiesa di Santa Maria della Carità. The main point of interest here are the triptyches in the apse, carried out by the Bellini family and workshop. The last room was the Sala dell'Albergo of the Scuola Grande di Santa Maria della Carità, and is dominated by an exquisite timber ceiling and Tiepolo's *Presentazione di Maria al Tempio* (Presentation of Mary at the Temple).

The gallery's opening times are complex. At last check they were: Monday from 9 am to 2 pm, Tuesday to Saturday from 9 am to 6.30 pm, and Sunday from 9 am to 1 pm. In 1999 an experimental late-night opening system was in place during the summer (May to October). Under this scheme, the gallery remained open until 9 pm on weekdays except Monday, until midnight on Saturday and until 8 pm on Sunday and holidays. These times are subject to change at any time. Admission costs L15,000. For L8000 more you can be taken on a guided tour. In each of the rooms there are detailed description sheets in English and Italian – remember to put them back before proceeding to the next room!

When the galleries are crowded, the queues outside can be a pain – a ceiling of 300 visitors at any one time is imposed.

Galleria di Palazzo Cini & Palazzo Barbarigo (Map 5)

If you follow the signs for the Peggy Guggenheim Collection eastward from the Gallerie dell'Accademia, you soon arrive at the relatively minor collection of the Fondazione Cini. Oddly enough, the main facade of this 16th-century building looks over the Rio di San Vio rather than the Grand Canal.

Spread out over two floors you will find around 30 works of Tuscan art, mostly from the 14th and 15th centuries. Among others, you will see a handful of works by Lippi, Piero della Francesca (*Madonna col Bimbo*; Madonna and Child), Botticelli (*Il Giudizio di Paride*; The Judgement of Paris) and Beato Angelico. Mixed in are some fine pieces of 15th-century Venetian furniture, porcelain collections and other odds and ends. The entry price of L8000 is a little steep, unless there's an interesting temporary exhibition on. Opening hours are from 9 am to 1 pm and 2 to 6 pm Tuesday to Sunday.

Cross the bridge into the rather cute little Campo San Vio, one of the handful of small squares that back right on to the Grand Canal. Its eastern flank is occupied by the **Palazzo Barbarigo**, whose facade is rather strikingly decorated with mosaics on a base of gold. They were carried out at the behest of the Compagnia Venezia e Murano, a glass and mosaics manufacturer that moved in here towards the end of the 19th century. You can't really see it from the square, but keep an eye out for it when you chug up or down the Grand Canal on the vaporetto.

Peggy Guggenheim Collection (Map 5)

Calle della Chiesa and then Fondamenta Venier lead you to Venice's premier excursion into the world of contemporary art.

Peggy Guggenheim called the unfinished Palazzo Venier dei Leoni home for 30 years, until she died in 1979. She left behind a collection of works by her favourite modern artists, representing most of the major movements of the 20th century.

Miss Guggenheim came into her fortune in 1921 and set off for Europe with no particular aim in mind. During the 1930s she became increasingly interested in contemporary art and the avant-garde. In 1938 she opened an art gallery in London, the Guggenheim Jeune, and embarked on a program of collection that continued well into 1940. Seemingly oblivious to the war raging around her, she only decided to return to New York from Paris when the Nazis were at the gates of the city. In New York she opened the Art of this Century gallery in 1942, but five years later decided to return to Europe. By 1949 her home and museum in Venice was open to the public. The Palazzo Venier dei Leoni was so called because, it is said, the Venier family kept lions here! Peggy herself preferred the company of dogs – many of them are buried alongside her own grave in the sculpture garden.

The bulk of the collection is housed in the east wing of the palazzo. It is the pleasing result of an eclectic collector's whim. Early Cubist paintings include Picasso's *The Poet* (1911) and *Pipe, Glass, Bottle of Vieux Marc* (1914), and Georges Braque's *The Clarinet* (1912). But the list of greats of 20th-century art is long. There are a couple of Kandinskys, including his *Upward* (1929). Interesting works from Spain include Dali's *Birth of Liquid Desires* (1932) – a classic example of his rather psycho-sick 'eroticism' – and Miró's *Seated Woman II* (1939).

It wouldn't be right if Max Ernst, Guggenheim's husband and doyen of Surrealism, were not represented. Among his paintings is the disturbing *The Antipope* (1942). Other names to look for include: Jackson Pollock, Mark Rothko, Willem de Kooning, Paul Delvaux, Alexander Calder, Juan Gris, Kurt Schwitters, Paul Klee and Man Ray. Some stunning small sculptures by Henry Moore and Jean Arp are also on view. Outside in the sculpture garden are a few more.

The rear of the mansion hosts a separate collection of Italian Futurists and other modern artists from the peninsula collected by Gianni Mattioli and now incorporated into the Guggenheim collection. Artists include Giorgio Morandi, Giacomo Balla and one early work by Amedeo Modigliani.

Temporary exhibitions are held in the new wing on the west side of the garden. A very agreeable cafe overlooks the garden.

The collection is open daily except Tuesday from 11 am to 6 pm; admission costs L12,000.

Palazzo Dario (Map 5)

Back on the street, we keep moving east. The next little bridge brings us into a charming, shady square. The exuberant gardens dripping over the walls, seemingly in an attempt to drop down into the water of the Rio delle Toreselle, belong to the Palazzo Dario. You can get some impression of this late Gothic mansion from the rear, but really to appreciate it you need to see the facade from the Grand Canal – a unique Renaissance marble facing that was taken down and then later reattached in the 19th century.

Former Chiesa di San Gregorio (Map 5)

After all the bustle of the grand art galleries, it is a real pleasure to arrive in the tranquil Campo San Gregorio. The Gothic facade of the deconsecrated church of the same name boasts a graceful doorway with a Venetian pointed arch. The straggly garden on the northern flank of the square belongs to the Palazzo Genovese, built over part of what was once the church's abbey.

Chiesa di Santa Maria della Salute (Map 6)

As you wander under the rough-hewn portico of Calle dell'Abbazia, Longhena's dazzling white monolith fills your entire field of vision. It is possibly the city's most familiar silhouette (seen from Piazzetta San Marco or the Ponte dell'Accademia), but seen from so close up it's difficult to take in.

Longhena got the commission to build the church in honour of the Virgin Mary, to whose intervention was attributed the end of an outbreak of plague in 1630 that had wiped out more than one-third of the population. The ranks of statues that festoon the

outside of the church culminate in one of the Virgin Mary atop the dome.

The octagonal form of the church is unusual. Longhena's idea was to design it in the form of a crown for the Mother of God. The interior is flooded with light pouring through windows in the walls and dome. Dominating the main body of the church is the extraordinary baroque *altar maggiore* (high altar), in which is imbedded an icon of Mary brought to Venice from Crete. The altar was hidden by restorers' scaffolding at the time of writing.

Of the paintings in the church proper, only Titian's *Pentecoste* is of particular note, but the L2000 admission price to the sacristy is worth shelling out: the ceiling is bedecked with three remarkable Titians. The figures depicted are so full of curvaceous movement they almost seem to be caught in a washing machine! The three scenes are replete with high emotion, depicting the struggles between *Caino e Abele* (Cain and Abel), *David e Golia* (David and Goliath) and finally between Abraham and his conscience in *Il Sacrificio di Isaaco* (The Sacrifice of Isaac). The eight medallions by Titian depicting saints are small but intriguing. The closer you look, the more human his saints appear. St Mark seems to be winking in amusement to himself, while you could swear that, under his swirling beard, San Girolamo is having a quiet chuckle.

The other star of the sacristy is Tintoretto's *Le Nozze di Cana* (The Wedding Feast of Cana), filled with an unusual amount of bright and cheerful light by Tintoretto's rather dark standards.

Every year, on 21 November, a procession takes place from Piazza San Marco to the church to give thanks for the city's good health. The last part of the march takes place on a pontoon bridge thrown out between the Santa Maria del Giglio *traghetto* (ferry) stop and the church. The church is open daily from 9 am to noon and 3 to 6 pm.

Dogana da Mar (Map 6)

The customs offices that occupy the low-slung Dogana are due to be transferred elsewhere by the end of 1999. When they go, the city plans to establish a new art gallery in conjunction with the Guggenheim Foundation.

To stand at dawn on the Punta della Dogana, which marks the split between the Grand Canal and the Canale della Giudecca, is to feel oneself on the prow of a proud fighting vessel putting out to sea. Waxing lyrical, do you think? Not really. Giuseppe Benoni, who designed it in 1677, was hoping for just that effect. Atop the little tower behind you at the tip of the Dogana da Mar buildings, two bronze Atlases bend beneath the weight of the world. Above them twists and turns capricious Fortune, an elaborate weather vane.

The Zattere to I Gesuati (Maps 5, 6 & 10)

The Fondamenta Zattere runs the length of the south side of Dorsoduro along the Canale della Giudecca from Punta della Dogana to the Stazione Marittima. Not surprisingly, it is a popular spot to indulge in a lingering *passeggiata* (the afternoon or Sunday stroll that is something of an institution in Italian life). The first stretch, almost as far as Rio di San Vio, is for the time being rather ugly due to all the 'roadworks' going on behind temporary hoardings.

Saloni Ex-Magazzini del Sale (Map 10)

The first buildings of any note as you begin to walk west are the city's one-time salt warehouses. Although the facade (hard to appreciate from the street because you are standing so close) is a neoclassical job from the 1830s, the warehouses were built in the 14th century. It was only in the early 1900s that the salt was moved elsewhere. The buildings are now used in part by rowing clubs and as exhibition space for the Biennale.

Chiesa di Santo Spirito (Map 10) The

modest Renaissance facade of this small church is not overly remarkable. But it is from here that boats are lined up to create a bridge across the Canale della Giudecca for the Festa del Redentore in July (see Public Holidays & Special Events in the Facts for the Visitor chapter).

Ospedale degli Incurabili (Map 5)

Raised in the 16th century, this is where syphilis sufferers with no hope of cure ended up. People with this disease generally ended up quite potty. Later it was used as an orphanage and it is now the seat of the Minors Court.

Chiesa dei Gesuati (Map 5)

After crossing a couple of bridges, you wind up before the imposing 18th-century church built for the Dominicans by a collective of architects led by Giorgio Massari. Also known as the Chiesa di Santa Maria del Rosario, the church contains ceiling frescoes by Tiepolo telling the story of St Dominic. The statues lining the interior are by Gian Maria Morlaiter (1699–1781). The church is open daily from 8 am to noon and 5 to 7 pm.

The little-visited **Chiesa di Santa Maria della Visitazione** next door has a curious 15th-century chequerboard timber ceiling bearing row upon row of scenes depicting the Visitation and a series of portraits of saints and prophets.

Rio di San Trovaso (Map 5)

One of the most attractive of Venice's waterways, the Rio di San Trovaso is also home to the most important of the few remaining gondola workshops – the **Squero di San Trovaso** – in the city. From the right bank you look across and see vessels in various states of (dis)repair.

The leafy square behind the *squero* is backed by the **Chiesa di San Trovaso**, rebuilt in the 16th century on the site of its 9th-century predecessor. The associated *scuola* was home to the confraternity of *squerarioli*, or gondola-builders. Inside the church are a couple of Tintorettos. It's open daily from 3.30 to 6.30 pm between June and mid-September.

Before continuing with the itinerary, a brief stroll west along Fondamenta Bontini towards the former Chiesa di Ognissanti (now part of a medical centre) is worthwhile, if only to get a glimpse across the canal into the pretty gardens of the mansions that front the Zattere.

Chiesa di San Barnaba (Map 5)

A walk of a few hundred metres north brings you to this fairly unprepossessing 18th-century reconstruction. The church hosts a handful of paintings, including one Veronese and a couple by Palma il Giovane. It opens daily from 10 am to noon.

Ca' Rezzonico (Map 5)

This 17th- to 18th-century mansion, facing onto the Grand Canal, houses the **Museo del Settecento Veneziano** (Museum of the 18th Century). Designed by Longhena and completed in the 1750s by Massari, it was home to several notables over the years, including the poet Robert Browning, who died here.

The museum houses a collection of 18th-century art and furniture and is also worth visiting for the views over the Grand Canal.

A broad staircase by Massari ascends from the ground floor to the *piano nobile* (main floor). This leads you to the Sala del Ballo (Ballroom), a splendid hall dripping with frescoes and richly furnished with 18th-century couches, tables and statues in ebony.

There follows a series of rooms jammed with period furniture and *objets d'art*, and plenty of paintings. Particularly noteworthy is Tiepolo's ceiling fresco in the Sala del Trono (Throne Room), the *Allegoria del Merito tra Nobiltà e Virtù* (Allegory of Merit Between Nobility and Virtue). Tiepolo contributed several other frescoes and paintings, as did his son Giandomenico. Other artists include Pietro Longhi, Francesco Guardi and Canaletto.

Unfortunately, Ca' Rezzonico has been closed for some time and no-one seems to know when this state of affairs might change. What it will look like when it finally does reopen is anyone's guess.

Ca' Foscari (Map 5)

This late-Gothic structure was commissioned by Doge Francesco Foscari and is now the seat of the university. Although one of the finest mansions in the city, it has fallen into quite a state of disrepair. In mid-1999 a deceptively realistic mock facade was unveiled to hide restoration work that will take until at least 2002 to complete. For years, ugly hoardings seemed to indicate that someone was trying to stop the rot, although by all accounts it had done little more than hide from public view a feverish absence of even the slightest sign of activity. Only time will tell if things will start happening now.

Campo Santa Margherita (Map 5)

This is a real people's *Platz*. Sure, any number of tourists or foreign students can be heard at the tables of the many restaurants and bars, but in the afternoon, when all the local kids come out to play, it takes on a special, *living* air.

The square is headed at its northern end by what little is left of a former church, long ago swallowed up by residential building. The squat little object at its southern end was one of the city's many *scuole*, or religious confraternities.

Scuola Grande dei Carmini Proceed west of the square, as it tapers away from the buzz. Just before you bump into the church of the same name, you pass on the right the Scuola Grande dei Carmini, with paintings by Tiepolo inside.

The facades have been attributed to Longhena (but they were well hidden by scaffolding at the time of writing). In its heyday, this was probably the most powerful of the religious confraternities, with a membership in 1675 of 75,000 – not bad in a city where the entire population was not much more than twice that! For more on scuole, see the boxed text 'When School Was Cool' in the next section.

Of its numerous works of art, the nine ceiling paintings by Tiepolo in the Salone Superiore (upstairs) depict the virtues surrounding the Virgin in Glory. The scuola is open from 9 am to 6 pm Monday to Saturday and from 9 am to 1 pm on Sunday. Admission costs L7000.

Chiesa dei Carmini What remains of the 14th-century Byzantine and then Gothic original sits a little uneasily side by side with the richer, and perhaps less digestible, ornament of the 16th and 17th centuries. Among the paintings on view are several works by Cima da Conegliano.

The church is open to visitors daily from 7.30 am to noon and 3 to 7.10 pm (to 4.30 pm on Sunday).

Palazzo Zenobio (Map 5)

Stride across the small campo before the main facade of the church and head southwest along Fondamenta del Soccorso. The dominating mansion on your left is the **Palazzo Zenobio**, since the mid-19th century the headquarters of the Collegio Armeno dei Padri Mechitaristi (Armenian College of Mecharist Fathers). The baroque structure is the handiwork of Antonio Gaspari, but apart from the grand curved tympanum, the exterior of the building tells you little. Tourist visits are not welcome, but if you could only sneak in and see the Sala della Musica, you would witness Gaspari's voluptuous decor at its baroque extreme.

Chiesa di San Sebastiano (Map 5)

Continue past the Armenian College and round the canal to the left. Cross at the second bridge and you have before you the Renaissance reconstruction (Scarpagnino's work?) of Paolo Veronese's parish church, which became his final resting place too.

Veronese went to town here, decorating the inside of the church with frescoes and canvases that cover a good deal of space on the ceiling and walls. The organ is his work too, with depictions of scenes from Christ's life on its shutters. The ceiling paintings together seem to exude a pallid, yellowish light. The sacristy, which also contains some of his work, was tightly shut at the time of writing.

Titian left a notable item behind here too – his *San Nicolò*, first up on the right as soon as you enter the church.

The church is part of the Chorus scheme (see the boxed text 'A Chorus Line' earlier in this chapter). It's open from 10 am to 5 pm Monday to Saturday and 1 to 5 pm on Sunday. Admission costs L3000.

Santa Marta Area & Back to Campo Santa Margherita (Map 5)

When you walk out of the church, don't do what just about everyone else does and head back towards Zattere or Campo Santa Margherita. Wander around the back through interlinked squares that take you to the Chiesa di San Basilio, better known as **Angelo Raffaele**. The uneven squares, with clumps of grass pressing up between the flagstones, are intriguingly quiet during the day, but take on an evening buzz as locals take their places at the local *trattoria*.

As you cross the bridge north of Angelo Raffaele and look left (west), you'll espy the bell tower of the **Chiesa di San Nicolò dei Mendicoli**. Although it has been fiddled with over the centuries, the church still preserves elements of the 13th-century original. The portico attached to one side was used to shelter the poor. The whole area was fairly downtrodden and known for its *mendicoli*, or beggars. The tiny square, bounded in by the canals and featuring a pylon bearing the winged lion of St Mark (one of the few not to be destroyed under Napoleon), is at the heart of one of the oldest parishes in Venice. They say it was established in the 7th century.

Across the Rio delle Terese was the **Chiesa di Santa Teresa** and its attached convent, of which nothing much can be seen. A stroll up to Fondamenta Santa Marta and west into the quarter of the same name reveals a curious contrast to the Venice of monuments. It's a working-class district with orderly housing blocks and broad walkways. Just beyond, across the Canale Scomenzera (Map 2), you can watch the desultory activity of Venice's commercial port, now much overshadowed by the monster of Marghera.

You could then follow our suggested route back towards Campo Santa Margherita via Fondamenta delle Procuratie. Along here and the parallel Fondamenta dei Cereri, rental housing was built as early as the 16th century by the Procurators of St Mark for the less well off. It has remained largely unchanged since.

Campo San Pantalon (Map 5)

A short walk north of Campo Santa Margherita along Calle della Chiesa and over the bridge will bring you into Campo San Pantalon (which leads you on to the Scuola Grande di San Rocco and the Chiesa di Santa Maria Gloriosa dei Frari in Sestiere di San Polo – see the following section).

The stark, unfinished and now seriously cracked brick facade of the **Chiesa di San Pantalon** dominates the small square. It dates from the 17th century, although a church was here as early as the 11th century. Inside, the greatest impact comes from the 40 canvases representing the *Martirio e Gloria di San Pantaleone* (Martyrdom and Glory of St Pantaleone) painted for the ceiling by Giovanni Antonio Fumiani. The artist died in a fall from the scaffolding as he was finishing the painting and is buried in the church. Veronese, Vivarini and Palma il Giovane have works in here too. Head for the Cappella del Sacro Chiodo (Chapel of the Holy Nail) to see the greatest concentration of works. The church is open daily except Saturday from 4 to 6 pm. To observe the ceiling and Veronese's *San Pantaleone*

Risana un Fanciullo (St Pantaleone Heals a Boy) better, stick L500 into the slot machine to turn on the lights.

SESTIERI DI SAN POLO & SANTA CROCE (SANTA CROSE)

These two sestieri have been lumped together because they form a neat whole – more than with any other two sestieri, you will probably find yourself crossing from one to the other frequently.

From San Pantalon (see the previous section), follow the *calle* (street) around to the right of the church and keep heading north over the next bridge. You will emerge in Campo San Rocco. In front of you rises up the brooding Gothic apse of the Chiesa di Santa Maria Gloriosa dei Frari. On your left, the Scuola Grande di San Rocco and the church of the same name face each other at an angle. Between them they represent a formidable concentration of Venetian art.

Scuola Grande di San Rocco (Map 5)

Antonio Scarpagnino's (c.1505–49) Renaissance facade (with a hint of the baroque to

---

When School Was Cool

The name *scuola* (school) as applied to the great confraternities in Venice is perhaps misleading to a modern reader. In an era when the welfare state had not even been dreamt of, the scuola served as a kind of community association. Its lay members formed a brotherhood (*confraternita*) under a patron saint and, apart from acting as a sort of religiously based club, it dealt with such matters as financial assistance to the families of members fallen on hard times. The scuola, along with the parish church, formed the backbone of local social life.

The division between the big six (the Scuole Grandi, dedicated to San Marco, San Rocco, San Teodoro, San Giovanni Evangelista, Santa Maria della Misericordia and Santa Maria della Carità – the latter swallowed up into the Accademia in the 18th century) and the rest (the Scuole Minori) was decreed in the 15th century. The smaller scuole totalled about 400, many without a church or even a fixed headquarters. Pretty much all the city's workers' and artisans' guilds had their scuola and patron saint, with which they identified strongly. As club, welfare centre and rallying point for the big parades and religious events in the city, their role in Venetian society cannot be underestimated.

Early in the 19th century, most of the scuole, as religious institutions, were suppressed by Napoleon's administrators. Some of the richer ones (and they were indeed rather well endowed) lost a good number of their works of art and precious artefacts. Only a few of the scuole were later resurrected. Some are now used, among other things, to host exhibitions and concerts.

---

come), with its white marble columns and overbearing magnificence, seems uncomfortably squeezed into the tight space of the narrow square below it. Whatever you make of the exterior of this scuola dedicated to St Roch, nothing can prepare you for what lies inside.

St Roch, by the way, was born in 1295 in Montpellier (France) and at the age of 20 began wandering through Italy and southern France helping plague victims. He died in 1327 and a cult soon grew around him. His body was transferred to Venice in 1485.

After winning a competition (one of the other competitors was Veronese), Tintoretto went on to devote 23 years of his life to decorating the school. The overwhelming concentration of more than 50 paintings by the master is altogether too much for the average human to digest. Chronologically speaking, you should start upstairs (Scarpagnino designed the staircase) in the Sala Grande Superiore. Here you can pick up mirrors to carry around to avoid getting a sore neck while inspecting the ceiling paintings (which depict Old Testament episodes). Around the walls are scenes from the New Testament. A handful of works by other artists (such as Titian, Giorgione and Tiepolo) can also be seen. To give your eyes a rest from the paintings, inspect the woodwork below them – it is studded with curious designs, including a false book collection.

Downstairs, the walls of the confraternity's assembly hall feature a series on the life of the Virgin Mary, starting on the left wall with the *Annunciazione* and ending with the *Assunzione* opposite.

The scuola is open daily from 9 am to 5.30 pm from Easter to the end of October (from 10 am to 4 pm in winter). Admission costs L8000.

Chiesa di San Rocco (Map 5)

You are likely to wander out of the Scuola Grande di San Rocco wondering what hit you. Maybe that's why there's no charge to enter the church across the street. Although built at about the same time as the scuola, the church was completely overhauled in the 18th century – hence the baroque facade

(easily identified by all the statues in niches and wall sculpture). It has a somewhat neglected feel inside, but several paintings of interest to those who have not overdosed. These include some by Tintoretto on the main-entrance wall and around the altar.

Detour to Campo San Tomà (Map 5)

A brief walk towards the Grand Canal from the Campo San Rocco along Calle Larga Prima brings you to this charming little square, closed off at the far end by the **Chiesa di San Tomà**, whose facade dates from 1742 (closed). On the San Rocco side of the square is the **Scuola dei Calegheri**, the shoemakers' confraternity. Veering around to the right of the church you reach the San Tomà vaporetto stop.

Across Rio di San Tomà, at Calle Nomboli 2793, is **Palazzo Centani**, in which Venice's greatest playwright, Carlo Goldoni, was born in 1707.

Chiesa di Santa Maria Gloriosa dei Frari (Map 5)

If you have seen Notre Dame in Paris, Cologne's Dom or even Milan's Duomo, you will probably be asking yourself what is so Gothic about the Frari. Built for the Franciscans in the 14th and 15th centuries of brick rather than stone, and bereft of flying buttresses, pinnacles, gargoyles and virtually any other sign of decoration inside or out, it is indeed a singular interpretation of the style. Nevertheless, some features give it away, among them the Latin-cross plan (with three naves and a transept), the high vaulted ceiling and its sheer size. In any case, you should not let appearances deceive you – even if you are not struck by the church, a visit inside is a must on any art lover's tour of the city.

A curious element is the presence in the centre of the central nave of the *coro* (or choir stalls). A common feature in Spain, the stalls in most churches beyond the Iberian Peninsula tend to be kept out of the way (behind the altar, off to the side or high up at the bottom end of the cross floor-plan). Was the idea an import or is it coincidence?

The simplicity of the interior (red and white marble floor, with the same colours dominating the walls and ceiling) is more than offset by the extravagance of decoration in the form of paintings and funereal monuments.

Let's get to the point. While Tintoretto is the star of San Rocco, Titian is the main attraction of the Frari. His dramatic *Assunta* (Assumption; 1518) over the high altar represents a key moment in his rise as one of the city's greatest artists, praised unreservedly by all and sundry as a work of inspired genius.

Another of his masterpieces, the *Madonna di Ca' Pesaro* (Madonna of Ca' Pesaro), hangs above the Pesaro altar (in the left-hand aisle, near the choir stalls). Also of note are: Giovanni Bellini's triptych, in the apse of the sacristy; Donatello's statue of *Giovanni Battista* (John the Baptist), in the first chapel to the right of the high altar; and Vivarini's *Sant'Ambrogio in Trono e Santi* (St Ambrose Enthroned and Saints), in the second-last chapel to the left of the high altar.

The church is open from 9 am to 6 pm Monday to Saturday and from 1 to 6 pm on Sunday. Admission costs L3000.

Archivio di Stato (Map 5)

Next to the Frari spread the buildings and peaceful cloisters of the former Convento dei Frari, suppressed in 1810 by Napoleon and co. Since 1815 it has housed the Archivio di Stato, the city's archives. It is a treasure trove, containing some 15 million documents covering the breadth of Venice's history from the 9th century on. Wandering in is not a problem during office hours, but you are unlikely to make it even to the first of the three cloisters unless you are here on official business.

Scuola Grande di San Giovanni Evangelista (Maps 3 & 5)

Cross the Rio dei Frari, turn left and cross the next bridge. Veer right around the block and you end up in the nondescript Campo San Stin. Take the western exit off the campo and turn right. Almost immediately on the left you will be struck by what seems

like an iconostasis. Behind it two impressive facades give onto a courtyard.

On the southern side is the **Chiesa di San Giovanni Evangelista** (Map 5), first built in 970 but subsequently rebuilt several times. Opposite is one of the six major Venetian scuole, dedicated to the same saint (Map 3). Codussi designed the interior. Like San Rocco, the plan is typical of the big schools, with an assembly hall (here divided in two by a line of columns) and a grand staircase leading up to the 1st-floor hall, which contains an altar used for religious services. This hall was sumptuously restyled by Massari in 1727. Many of the major works of art once housed here have been moved to the Gallerie dell'Accademia. It's open to the public from 10 am to 4 pm on Sunday and Monday. You must join a guided tour, which costs L5000.

From Rio Marin to Piazzale Roma (Map 3)

Back on Calle dell'Olio, we proceed north to the rio and turn left (you have no choice about this). Cross the first bridge over the Rio Marin and head up to Calle della Croce. Our itinerary will take us right down this street and on to Campo San Giacomo dell'Orio.

Beforehand, a few words on some minor but noteworthy items between here and the western end of the Sestiere di Santa Croce. Right across Rio Marin you are facing the boarded-up **Palazzo Soranzo-Cappello**, a 16th-century mansion graced with what must have been a beautiful (but is now an unruly) garden. From the same period is the **Palazzo Gradenigo**, farther north, by the last bridge over the rio and obscured by scaffolding. Were you to walk up to that bridge and look east, you'd see the tiny **Chiesa di San Simeon Grande**. Of ancient origins, it was heavily restored in the 18th century. Inside you can see an *Ultima Cena* (Last Supper) by Tintoretto.

Across the bridge, you end up on Calle Bergami. Turn right at its end and head for the **Ponte dei Scalzi**, one of three bridges across the Grand Canal. Built in 1934, it replaced an iron bridge built by the Austrians in 1858. Following Fondamenta San Simeon Piccolo south-west, you'll pass the **church** of the same name (the present version was built from 1718 to 1738). Its outstanding feature is the bronze dome. At the bridge, turn left down Fondamenta dei Tolentini. The modern facade on the bend is the entrance to the **IUAV** (Istituto Universitario di Architettura di Venezia), designed by Carlo Scarpa. The institute is one the country's most prestigious architecture schools. Beside it, the late-16th-century **Chiesa di San Nicolò da Tolentino** houses quite a few works by Palma il Giovane.

The Giardini Papadopoli across the canal seems almost an afterthought. The park was actually quite a deal more impressive until in 1932 the Rio Nuovo was slammed through the city here. Opening hours are from 8 am to 7.30 pm (5.30 pm in winter). Beyond the park lies Piazzale Roma, home to the unlovely bus station and car parks. A wander around it and along Canale di Santa Chiara is a sobering reminder of how even the most beautiful of cities contain pockets of neglect.

Beyond the canal lies the now little-used merchant-shipping harbour and then the Isola del Tronchetto – a giant car park and temporary home to the Fenice theatre.

Chiesa di San Giacomo dell'Orio (Map 3)

Let's say you decided against going west of Rio Marin. Head east down Calle della Croce, turn right and left into Campo San Nazario Sauro, and keep heading east down Ruga Bella, which takes you into Campo San Giacomo dell'Orio.

This charming, leafy square is graced by the modest outline of one of Venice's few good examples of Romanesque architecture (see also Architecture in the Facts about Venice chapter). The initial 9th-century

A Bridge of Sighs

The Sestiere di Santa Croce just peters out glumly as you reach Piazzale Roma. The stretch of the Grand Canal down to Rio Nuovo is gloomy and depressing and the whole area stands in stark contrast to the rest of the lagoon city. Venice mostly escaped bombing in WWII; where it did suffer damage was around here. It has long been a pious wish, for which no-one has found the money, to resurrect the area, with modern buildings that fit into the local context – a tall order perhaps. For the moment, it is just plain scrappy.

Enter the curve ball. In May 1999 the local government under Mayor Massimo Cacciari decided to go ahead with planning for a fourth bridge across the Grand Canal. Designed by the Swiss-based Spanish architect Santiago Calatrava, the graceful arch in Istrian marble and glass would link Piazzale Roma with the waterfront in front of the railway administration buildings. Calatrava is a name – he has designed more than 60 bridges and built 40 of them.

The decision was taken, but few apart from Cacciari were convinced. Opposition was vocal and even the majority in favour divided. Nice bridge, some said, but what's the point of it? Most people arriving at Piazzale Roma (by car or bus) and at the train station head for the centre of town, not to the other transport terminal.

The plan sees the bridge crossing the canal diagonally, thus increasing its length and cost. And has anyone thought about the aesthetic impact on the canal? If it is built, the chances of reconstructing the whole area as a viable new quarter of Venice might be placed in jeopardy. Cacciari dismissed all of this as the usual conservative Venetian carping.

One local commentator suggested that, if the city council really felt it had to spend the eight billion lire and wanted to have the Calatrava touch, they could finally replace the 'temporary' wooden bridge at Accademia that is still awaiting its permanent successor.

The politicians have voted 'sì', but no-one is holding their breath just yet.

Food for Thought

From Calle della Croce you can make a detour to one of the rare strips of footpath actually on the Grand Canal. Turn left (north) up Calle Larga dei Bari, right along Lista dei Bari and left (north) along Ramo Zen then Calle Zen to the Riva di Biasio. A couple of the mansions here are interesting enough to behold and the views to the other side of the canal are more impressive still.

But the prize goes to a tale we all hope is taller than true. A sausage-maker by the name of Biagio (Biasio) Cargnio had a store here in the 16th century. They say he was sent to the next world on charges of having sausages made of – wait for it – children.

church was replaced in 1225. The main Gothic addition (14th century) is the remarkable wooden ceiling *a carena di nave* (in the style of an upturned ship's hull). It is one of several examples in Venice and, for anyone who has tramped around the great churches of Spain, starkly reminiscent of the Muslim-influenced *artesonado* ceilings.

Among the intriguing jumble of works of art are a 13th-century baptismal font, a Byzantine column in green marble and a Lombard pulpit perched on a 6th-century column from Ravenna. In front of the main altar is a wooden crucifix by Veronese and on the wall at the rear of the central apse a rare work by Lorenzo Lotto, *Madonna col Bambino e Santi* (Madonna with Child and Saints).

The church is part of the Chorus scheme (see the boxed text 'A Chorus Line' earlier in this chapter). It's open from 10 am to 5 pm Monday to Saturday and 1 to 5 pm on Sunday. Admission costs L3000.

From San Giacomo dell'Orio to Rialto via Campo San Polo (Maps 3, 5 & 6)

At this point, two separate routes suggest themselves to get you to the Ponte di Rialto. This first one follows a trail largely ignored by tourists. The other (see the following

section) is busier, but still loaded with interest. You can also join them together into a circular route that would bring you right back into this square. From here you could then backtrack to Rio Marin and go on to the Ponte dei Scalzi to pick up our route through Cannaregio.

From Campo San Giacomo dell'Orio follow Calle del Tintor south, cross the bridge and continue until you hit a T-junction. As you turn left into Rio Terrà Secondo note on the right-hand side, opposite the Gothic **Palazzo Soranza-Pisani**, the building in which Aldo Manuzio got his **Aldine Press** started up and so revolutionised the world of European letters (Map 3). His was an address much frequented by learned fellows from across the Continent.

Head north-east and turn right into Calle del Scaleter. At Da Fiore (one of only two restaurants with a Michelin star in all Venice), turn left into Calle del Cristo, cross the bridge and take the second right (Ramo Agnello). Follow it straight over the bridge and stop at the second bridge.

It's hard to tell now, but this was long the centre of Venice's cheaper red-light zone. The bridge is known as **Ponte delle Tette** (Tits Bridge; Map 3), because a city ordinance stipulated that the whores who worked here should hang about in windows and doorways bare-breasted to encourage business. Pardon? Back in the 14th century, the city fathers had in fact tried to clamp down on prostitution in Venice, but by the late 15th century found it the only hope of reviving the ardour of Venetian men, who were apparently adopting imported Eastern habits of sodomising each other. La Serenissima took a far dimmer view of this than prostitution, so much so that anyone successfully prosecuted for sodomy, under a law of 1482, found themselves executed and incinerated between the two columns on Piazzetta San Marco.

Beyond the bridge is Rio Terrà delle Carampane. The name originally came from a noble family's house in the area (Ca' Rampani), and at some point the ladies of the night working here came to be known as *carampane*. The word is now a colourful part

The Oldest Profession

Accounts of prostitution in Venice make interesting reading. Although generally allowing it to go on, and in some cases encouraging it, the attitude towards the practice and its practitioners was always somewhat ambiguous.

In 1358, local authorities were instructed to select an area of Rialto to set aside for prostitution. This they did and a group of houses was soon occupied by prostitutes and their *matrons*, who took care of the till and paid the women a wage at the end of the month. They were not allowed on the streets after a certain hour and were forbidden to work on religious holidays. This restricted area of houses of ill repute, kept under surveillance by six guardians, came to be known as Il Castelletto (the Little Castle). The atmosphere must have been oppressive, for prostitutes began to spread out across the city, especially to the Carampane area. At first, attempts were made to force them back into Il Castelletto, but in the end the authorities gave in to the situation and even proclaimed laws obliging the girls to display their wares to attract business.

By the 1640s, however, various regulations were in place to put a brake on prostitution. All sorts of restrictions were placed on prostitutes. They could not enter churches or potter around in two-oared boats (only 'ladies' could be taken about in such a manner). They were not to adorn themselves with gold or other jewellery. They could not testify in criminal court cases, nor could they prosecute when services rendered were not paid for (which was generally where pimps came in). Your average street whore was made to feel very much like a second-class citizen.

Different strokes for different folks: there was a whole other class of prostitution. In the 16th century the myth of the *cortigiane* (courtesans) began to take shape. These were women of distinction, not simply better-paid, better-looking bimbos. Schooled in the arts, fluent in Latin, handy with a harpsichord, they were women of keen intellect and talent not fortunate enough to have been born into nobility. For such daughters of middle-class families, working for a high-class escort service seemed the only way to acquire independence and wellbeing.

In 1535, when the Venetian populace totalled about 120,000 and some 11,000 prostitutes were registered, a very handy tourist guide was published: *Questo si è il Catalogo de tutte le principal, et più honorate Cortigiane di Venetia* (This Is the Catalogue of the Main and Most Honoured Courtesans of Venice). It contained names, rates and useful addresses. No wonder the city had such a lascivious reputation.

of standard Italian and describes the mutton-dressed-up-as-lamb brand of loose woman.

From the Ponte delle Tette, look south down Rio di San Cassiano and you will notice a high wrought-iron walkway linking **Palazzo Albrizzi** (Map 3) to its own private gardens. Inside the 16th-century mansion, Isabella Teotochi Albrizzi held her literary salon around the end of the 18th century, with sculptor Antonio Canova and writer Ugo Foscolo among the lucky guests.

We now backtrack to Da Fiore. Here turn left (south-east) across the bridge and along Calle Bernardo (the fine Gothic mansion of the same name is best seen from the bridge), which brings you into the broad and leafy expanse of Campo San Polo, one of the most attractive squares in the city. Among the several fine mansions facing onto the square are the **Palazzo Corner**, designed by Michele Sanmicheli in the 16th century, and the Gothic **Palazzi Soranzo** (both Map 5).

Chiesa di San Polo (Map 5) Although of Byzantine origin, the church has lost much of its attraction through repeated interference and renovation. Worst of all, the pile-up of houses between it and the Rio di San

Polo has completely obscured its facade. It is, however, worth your time to wander inside if you enjoy the art of Tiepolo. A whole cycle of his, the *Via Crucis* (Stations of the Cross), has been stacked rather unceremoniously along the walls of the sacristy.

The church is part of the Chorus scheme (see the boxed text 'A Chorus Line' earlier in this chapter). It's open from 10 am to 5 pm Monday to Saturday and 1 to 5 pm on Sunday. Admission costs L3000.

On to Rialto A glance at the map will show we have almost completed a circuit to the Frari. You could head down that way and beyond into Dorsoduro (see earlier in this chapter) or stroll eastwards towards Rialto and the Grand Canal.

From Campo San Polo, take Calle della Madonetta and follow it to Campo Sant'Aponal. On the way, duck down Calle Malvasia to peer enviously through the gates at the gardens of the **Palazzo Papadopoli** (Map 5). It seems almost unfair that such luxuriant greenery should be the preserve of the Istituto per lo Studio della Dinamica delle Grandi Masse (Institute for the Study of the Dynamics of Large Masses)!

The former **Chiesa di Sant'Aponal** (Map 5) has a simple Gothic facade topped by five statues, and its free-standing bell tower is Romanesque. From here Calle dell'Olio takes you around the right side of the church. Turn right down Rio Terrà San Silvestro and you pass the unremarkable early-20th-century facade of the **Chiesa di San Silvestro** (Map 5). Turn onto the former wine docks on the Grand Canal, the Fondamenta del Vin, and the Ponte di Rialto is clearly in view ahead. The restaurants along here make a tempting spot for a break, but you'll pay L5000 for a cup of coffee. For more on the Rialto area, see later in this chapter.

From San Giacomo dell'Orio to Rialto via Campo San Stae (Maps 3, 4 & 6)

Follow the signs north from the square along Calle Larga (turning off at the rio) to reach the **Fondaco dei Turchi** (Map 3), a 12th-century building used as a warehouse by Turkish merchants and now housing the Museo Civico di Storia Naturale (Natural History Museum).

In Venice and across the Middle East and beyond, this kind of establishment was set up to house foreign merchants and store their goods. The word fondaco spread, and where Western merchants stayed and worked came to be known in Arabic as a *funduq*, from Aleppo in Syria to Alexandria in Egypt. The Venetian dialect word, which you may also encounter, is *fontego*. In Arab countries, funduq has come simply to mean hotel.

The building was only rented out to the Turkish trading community in 1621 (they remained until 1858, long after the demise of La Serenissima). Previously it had belonged to a series of private owners and the dukes of Ferrara. Although it dates back to the 12th and 13th centuries, the place was restored in appalling taste in the mid-19th century. It was a little like plastic surgery gone wrong. Original features in the facade were sacrificed to the architectural fancies of the time – the towers and crenellations are, for example, an unhappy addition. Much of it was hidden behind scaffolding at the time of writing.

The museum has been closed for years – if it ever reopens take the kids there to see the impressive 12m-long crocodile.

Palazzo Mocenigo & San Stae (Map 3)

Backtrack from the fondaco to the rio, cross it and follow Calle del Tintor east (you pass the excellent Osteria La Zucca on the right). There are a few interesting shops along this main trail between La Zucca and Campo San Cassiano.

At Salizzada di San Stae, turn left (north). On the right is the **Palazzo Mocenigo**, which belonged to one of the most important families of the Republic. It now houses a modest museum, with clothes, period furnishings, accessories and the like. It is interesting for the hints it gives you of how the other half lived in the twilight years of La Serenissima. Admission is included in the combined ticket described under Special Tickets at the start of this chapter. The museum is open daily except Sunday from 8.30 am to 1.30 pm.

At the end of the street is the tiny canal-side Campo San Stae (St Eustace Square) and vaporetto stop, named after the baroque **church** that closes off the southern end of the square. It is a fairly simple little house of worship, although the facade (finished in 1709) might lead you to think otherwise. Among its art treasures are Tiepolo's *Il Martirio di San Bartolomeo* (The Martyrdom of St Bartholomew).

The church is part of the Chorus scheme (see the boxed text 'A Chorus Line' earlier in this chapter). It's open from 10 am to 5 pm Monday to Saturday and 1 to 5 pm on Sunday. Admission costs L3000.

Next door to the left (No 1980) is the **Scuola dei Tiraoro e Battioro**, the former seat of the goldsmith confraternity's scuola.

Ca' Pesaro (Map 3) From Campo San Stae, cross the bridge, turn right then left, cross another bridge and you arrive directly at the land entrance to this Renaissance mansion. Its main facade faces the Grand Canal and inside it has housed the **Galleria d'Arte Moderna** on the ground floor since 1902. The collection includes works purchased from the Venezia Biennale art festival and is one of the largest collections of modern art in Italy. The only problem is that the gallery has been firmly shut since 1983 and no-one knows when it will open again. If you could get in, you might enjoy works by De Chirico, Miró, Chagall, Kandinsky, Klee, Klimt, Moore and others.

The **Museo d'Arte Orientale**, in the same building on the top floor, *is* open and features Asian and Eastern oddments, including important collections of Edo-period art from Japan and Chinese porcelain. It's open daily except Monday from 9 am to 2 pm and admission costs L4000.

The building itself is considered one of the more important ones on the Grand Canal, started by Longhena and completed in 1710 by Gaspari. Longhena died worrying about the cost!

To Campo delle Beccarie (Map 3) Walk south away from Ca' Pesaro and on the corner of the second street on the right you could be forgiven for completely missing the **Chiesa di Santa Maria Mater Domini**. Sansovino supposedly had a hand in it and inside is an early work by Tintoretto, the *Invenzione della Croce* (Invention of the Cross). It's open to visitors daily except Sunday from 10 am to noon.

Campo Santa Maria Mater Domini is an intriguing little square, with well-preserved late-Byzantine and Gothic buildings. No 2174 dates from the 13th century. Cross the square and turn left (north) into Calle della Regina. At the end of the street, looking on to the Grand Canal, is the **Palazzo Corner della Regina**. The Corners, one of the most powerful trading families in Venice, had mansions all over town. On this site lived Caterina, a woman who ended up on the throne of Venetian-controlled Cyprus in the late 15th century, only to be unceremoniously obliged by the schemers of San Marco to abdicate. In exchange she got Asolo and its lovely countryside (see the Excursions chapter). The building as it stands today was actually remodelled in the early 18th century.

Tintoretto fans may want to stop off at the **Chiesa di San Cassiano** in the campo of the same name. The sanctuary is decorated with three of his paintings, the *Crocifissione* (Crucifixion), the *Risurrezione* (Resurrection) and the *Discesa al Limbo* (Descent into Limbo). It's open to visitors from 10 am to noon and 5.30 to 7 pm Tuesday to Saturday, and from 6 to 7 pm only on Sunday and Monday. Make a quick detour towards the Grand Canal along Calle del Campanile and duck into Corte de Ca' Michiel. This was once known as Calle del Teatro, reputedly the site of one of the city's first theatres in 1580. It didn't last too long, as the Inquisition (not an overly popular institution in Venice) shut it down for what it claimed were the lewd goings-on.

Rialto (Map 4)

A couple of streets on from the church you arrive at Campo delle Beccarie. Welcome to the nerve centre of Venice. Rivoalto (later contracted), the highest spot in the collection of islets that formed the initial nucleus of the lagoon city, was the area of first settlement. It became a centre of trade and banking for the Republic, and while political power resided over in San Marco, this is where dosh traded hands, voyages were bankrolled and news (sometimes hard to disentangle from fishwives' gossip) was exchanged. While in Campo delle Beccarie, spare a thought for the Querini family. One wing of their house still looks onto the square, but the rest was demolished in 1310 in reprisal for having backed the revolt against Doge Pietro Gradenigo.

Today, the area continues to buzz with the activity of the daily produce and fish markets – why break the habit of 1000 years? The **Fabbriche Vecchie**, along the Ruga degli Orefici and in the shadow of the **Palazzo dei Dieci Savi** (Palace of the 10 Wise Men), were created by Scarpagnino in 1522. They were designed to accommodate markets at ground level and house offices in the upper levels. The Dieci Savi administered taxes (the building now houses the Magistrato alle Acque, the water administration). The **Fabbriche Nuove**, running along the Grand Canal, went up in 1555 to designs by Sansovino and became home to magistrates' courts. Other magistrates, the 'chamberlains', were housed in a separate Renaissance edifice, the **Palazzo dei Camerlenghi**, designed by Guglielmo dei Grigi. At ground level were prisons for common offenders.

The **Pescaria**, the site of the fish market (which extends into Campo Beccarie), was rebuilt in neo-Gothic style in 1907. They have been selling fresh fish here since 1300.

From the docks all around here, Crusader fleets set sail. While men and provisions were gathered, various knights and other notables stayed in hostels just behind the Fabbriche Nuove. Many others camped out on Giudecca or around the Chiesa di San Nicolò on the Lido. Before heading off, they heard their last Mass on land for some time in the **Chiesa di San Giacomo di Rialto**. Virtually in the middle of the market, off the Ruga degli Orefici, it was supposedly founded on 25 March 421, the same day as the city.

Ponte di Rialto (Map 4) Given Rialto's importance from the earliest days of the Republic, it is hardly surprising that the city's first bridge over the Grand Canal was built here.

The crossing had quite a chequered history before Antonio da Ponte (Anthony of the Bridge) built this robust marble version. Commissioned in 1588, the present bridge cost 250,000 ducats, which was an enormous sum in those days. When it was finally completed in 1592, all concerned must have been happy with the result – which has lasted very nicely in the four centuries since.

The first bridge was little more than a dodgy pontoon arrangement thrown across the canal in 1175 (some think in 1180). A more permanent wooden structure was built in 1265, but it was cut in two in 1310 as Baiamonte Tiepolo and his fellow rebels beat a hasty retreat on horseback (see the boxed text 'Knocking Rebellion on the Head' earlier in this chapter). It was repaired, but collapsed in a heap in 1444 under the weight of a crowd straining to watch the wedding procession of the marquis of Ferrara. It was again rebuilt, as a timber dra wbridge, before finally being dismantled and replaced by da Ponte's version. You can cross here into the Sestiere di San Marco.

Alternatively, as mentioned earlier, you can follow one of the two above routes between Rialto and Campo San Giacomo dell'Orio back to the latter square, and then make a brisk dash for Rio Marin and the Ponte dei Scalzi to cross the Grand Canal and arrive in Cannaregio.

SESTIERE DI CANNAREGIO

This was long the swampiest part of Venice and unpleasantly malarial to boot. It owes its name to the reeds *(canna)* that grew in abundance here.

Most people first arrive here off the train, but for the sake of argument, let's assume you have just stumbled over Ponte dei Scalzi after following our routes around Santa Croce and San Polo. A glance at the map will confirm that it virtually amounts to the same thing anyway.

Stazione di Santa Lucia to Ponte delle Guglie (Map 3)

The long thoroughfare connecting the train station and Piazza San Marco crawls with tourists heading from one to the other – few venture off it into the peaceful back lanes.

The first sight of any significance you lay eyes on is the Carmelite **Chiesa dei Scalzi** (literally 'barefoot'), virtually next to the train station. There are damaged frescoes by Tiepolo in the vaults of two of the side chapels. Longhena designed the church but the baroque facade was done by Giuseppe Sardi. The abundance of columns and statues in niches is a deliberate echo of the particularly extravagant baroque style often employed in Rome. Apparently the Carmelites, who had moved here from Rome several years before, specifically requested that it be so. The voluptuous decorative spin continues within – the altar is a good example of baroque clearly heading for the extremes of rococo. The church is open daily from 6.45 to 11.45 am and 4 to 6.45 pm.

At the end of the Lista di Spagna, the otherwise uninspiring 18th-century **Chiesa di San Geremia** contains the body of Santa Lucia (St Lucy), who was martyred in Siracusa in AD 304. Her body was stolen by Venetian merchants from Constantinople in 1204 and moved to San Geremia after the Palladian church of Santa Lucia was demolished in the 19th century to make way for the train station. The bell tower is a Romanesque leftover from an earlier church on the same spot. Facing the square at right angles to the church, the **Palazzo Labia** is a fine 17th-century residence. Now the Venice office of the RAI, Italy's national radio and TV organisation, it boasts some Tiepolo frescoes inside. You have to phone ahead (☎ 041 524 28 12) to arrange a visit from 11 am to noon, Wednesday to Friday only.

At the **Ponte delle Guglie**, so called because of the obelisks at each end, the itinerary splits into two. The first option takes us to the Sestiere di San Marco via the Ghetto. The second is a more meandering stroll through many of the back streets and canals of Cannaregio that brings us to Campo SS Giovanni e Paolo in Castello.

Itinerary I: Ponte delle Guglie to Sestiere di San Marco

The Ghetto (Map 3) Cross the Ponte delle Guglie and turn left. Just before you do, you may want to poke around the daily **fish and produce market** on Rio Terrà San Leonardo.

Turn off the Fondamenta di Cannaregio at Calle del Ghetto Vecchio (you'll recognise it by the Gam Gam kosher restaurant). On emerging into the small square, you will see two of the Ghetto's five synagogues, also known as *schole* because they were also used for scripture studies. The existence of five places of worship within the Ghetto reflected in part the density of the Jewish population and also liturgical variations between the different communities. The **Schola Spagnola** is at the southern end of the square (look for the plaque commemorating Italian Jewish victims of the Holocaust). It and the **Schola Levantina**, opposite, were erected by Jews from the Iberian Peninsula. You can visit the latter as part of a tour starting at the Museo Ebraico (see towards the end of this section). The interior betrays a hefty rococo influence, best seen in the decor of the pulpit. The Schola Levantina is used for Saturday prayers in winter (it has heating) while the Schola Spagnola (which can't be visited) is used in summer.

Calle del Ghetto Vecchio proceeds northeast over a bridge into the heart of Venice's Jewish community, Campo di Ghetto Nuovo.

It's worth getting acquainted with an outline of the Ghetto's history. The first records of Jews in Venice go back to the 10th century. Even at this early point, acquiring Venetian citizenship was all but impossible, and so outsiders had to content themselves with regularly renewing their residence permits. The early Jews were Ashkenazi of German and Eastern European origins. In 1382 the Maggior Consiglio decreed that Jews could operate as moneylenders. In fact it encouraged them.

As refugees of various nationalities crowded into Venice during the dark days of the League of Cambrai, the Republic decided on 29 March 1516 that all Jews residing in Venice should be moved to one area.

The Getto Novo (New Foundry) was considered ideal, being far from the city's power centres and surrounded by water – a natural prison. The Ashkenazis' harsh Germanic pronunciation gave us the word ghetto.

Jews could move freely through the city only if they wore a yellow cap or badge. At midnight gates around the Ghetto Nuovo were shut by Christian guards financed by the Jewish community, and reopened at dawn.

Deliberately excluded from most professions, Jews had few career options. Most tried to get along as moneylenders or in the rag trade. Two of the 'banks' from which moneylenders operated remain in evidence on Campo di Ghetto Nuovo, the Banco Rosso and Banco Verde. A third option was medicine. Jews who had lived in Muslim Spain or in the Middle East had benefited from the advances in the Arab world on this front and were considered better doctors than their Christian counterparts. Jewish doctors were allowed, in emergencies, to leave the Ghetto during curfew. It sounds bad, but everything is relative. Jews who made it to Venice were not persecuted and were free to practise their religion. Compared with their brethren in much of the rest of Europe, Venice's Jews were doing OK.

A quick look around you will show how small the Ghetto was. And the population, in its thousands, was growing. In 1541 waves of Levantine Jews from Spain and Portugal finally made their way into Venice. Here there was a difference – they came with money, as many were wealthy and successful merchants with contacts in the Near East.

Extreme overcrowding, combined with building-height restrictions, had already turned the buildings around the Campo di Ghetto Nuovo into Venice's 'skyscrapers' – some apartment blocks have as many as seven storeys, but with very low ceilings. Atop three of them were built three modest schole. The **Schola Tedesca** (German Synagogue) is above the building that now houses the Museo Ebraico. Virtually next door is the **Schola Canton** (Corner Synagogue) and farther around is the **Schola Italiana**. This latter is the simplest. The largely destitute Italian Jews concerned had come

from Spanish-controlled southern Italy. From the outside, the synagogues could be distinguished from the residential housing by the small domes that indicate the position of the pulpit. In the case of the German and Italian ones, the rows of five larger windows are another giveaway sign.

When the Levantine Jews began to arrive, even the town authorities had to admit there was no more space and ceded another small area to the Jews – the Getto Vecio (Old Foundry). So of course it came to be known as the Old Ghetto, although the converse was true (the foundry was old but the Jewish community was new). Here the Spanish and Portuguese built their two synagogues, already mentioned above. They are considered the most beautiful synagogues in northern Italy.

A final small territorial concession was wrung from the town authorities when a street south of the Ghetto Nuovo, subsequently known as the Calle del Ghetto Nuovissimo (Very New Ghetto Street), was granted to the Jews.

From 1541 until 1553 the Jewish community thrived. Their money and trade were welcome in Venice, and the community also built a reputation for book printing. Then Pope Julian banned such activities. From then on things started to go downhill. To top it off, the plague of 1630 left fewer than 3000 Jews alive.

In 1797 Napoleon abolished all restrictions on Jews. Later, under the Austrians, they enjoyed considerable freedom, if not completely free of prejudice. After Venice was annexed to the Italian kingdom in 1866, all minorities were guaranteed full equality before the law and freedom of religious expression.

Mussolini's rise to power spelt trying times for the Jews in Italy. The 1938 race laws imposed restrictions, but the real torment came in November 1943, when the puppet Fascist government of Salò declared Jews enemies of the state. Of Venice's 1670 remaining Jews, quite a few were rounded up and sent to the Italian concentration camp of Fossoli (outside Modena). They were even marched out of the Casa Israelitica di

Riposo (rest home) on Campo di Ghetto Nuovo. The home's wall bears a memorial to the victims. The next stop for about 200 was a death camp in Poland. Altogether, about 8000 Italian Jews were killed in the Holocaust.

Of the 500 or so Jews still living in Venice, only about 30 remain in the Ghetto. You can contact the local Jewish community on ☎ 041 71 52 84.

The **Museo Ebraico** (Jewish Museum) in Campo di Ghetto Nuovo is open daily (except Saturday and Jewish holidays) from 10 am to 4.30 pm and admission costs L5000. It contains a modest collection of Jewish religious silverware. Guided tours (in Italian or English; other languages if booked in advance) of the Ghetto and three of its synagogues (Schola Canton, Schola Italiana and Schola Levantina) leave from the museum hourly between 10.30 am and 3.30 pm daily except Saturday and cost L12,000 (which includes the museum). The tour is highly recommended.

To Ca' d'Oro (Map 3) Leave the Ghetto by the portico that leads across the canal to Calle Farnese. This was one of the Ghetto gates that used to be locked at midnight. Proceed straight to Rio Terrà Farsetti and turn right, then duck down Rio Terrà del Cristo to have a quick look at the **Chiesa di San Marcuola** and the Grand Canal. Although a church has been here since the 9th century, what you see was cobbled together (and not quite completed) in the 18th century by Massari and Gaspari. Inside (you may only be able to get in during Mass) is an *Ultima Cena* (Last Supper) by Tintoretto. His Christ and apostles are spotlighted against a black background that gives the meal an extraordinary air.

Heading east across Rio di San Marcuola you will come up against the **Palazzo Vendramin-Calergi**. The canalside facade is a masterpiece of restrained Renaissance elegance. The composer Richard Wagner expired here in 1883. It's now the winter home of the casino: you can wander into the ground-floor area but will have to shell out to see the gaming rooms.

From here, return to the main drag (at this point called Rio Terrà della Maddalena – you'll know you've hit it when you are sucked up into the crowds again). Proceed a couple of blocks then head off to the right (south): in a quiet little campo is the quite unique, circular **Chiesa della Maddalena**, largely covered by scaffolding at the time of writing. The pretty square is flanked by houses with their upper parts poking over heavy timber barbicans. Notice anything yet? Like you are about the only one to have sufficient curiosity to get off the strip and have a quick look here? Try jumping back into the flood of passers-by and then jumping out again. Amazing, right?

Now you could go around the back of the church and follow Calle del Forno around to a dead end right on the Grand Canal. It's a little mucky but it is always interesting to get another view of the canal.

Backtracking and then taking Calle Correr you end up back on the strip. The bronze statue on the square opposite you is of Paolo Sarpi, La Serenissima's greatest philosopher (some might suggest only). He took on the papacy in 1606 and won (see History in the Facts about Venice chapter). You could make a little detour at this point and scurry northwards across a couple of bridges to get to the **Chiesa di San Marziale**. If it's open, have a peek in at all the baroque baubles.

Otherwise skip it and make for the east along the main street. It's called Strada Nova (or Nuova) here and was bulldozed through the area some years after the rail link was opened in the 19th century. On your right you pass a veritable parade of Venetian mansions, but you'd never know it – they only present their photogenic profile to the Grand Canal. The second of them after you cross the Rio di San Felice (named after the church you pass on the left just before the bridge) is the Ca' d'Oro.

Ca' d'Oro (Map 4) This magnificent Gothic structure, built in the 15th century, got its name (Golden House) from the gilding that originally decorated the sculptural details of the facade. The facade, which is visible from the Grand Canal, stands out quite remarkably from the remainder of the edifice, which is rather drab by comparison.

Ca' d'Oro houses the **Galleria Franchetti**, an impressive collection of bronzes, tapestries and paintings. The 1st floor is devoted mainly to religious painting, sculpture and bronzes from the 15th and early 16th centuries. One of the first items you see is a polyptych recounting the martyrdom of San Bartolomeo (St Bartholomew). Take a closer look at the detail. The violence is quite remarkable, as is the saintly indifference with which Bartholomew seems to accept his torment! Much of what you see on this floor is Venetian, but one room has been set aside principally for Tuscan art.

On the 2nd floor you can see a series of fragments of frescoes saved from the outside of the Fondaco dei Tedeschi (see the earlier Sestiere di San Marco section). All but one are by Titian. The other, a nude by Giorgione, is the most striking, however. Also on this floor is a mixed collection, including works by Tintoretto, Titian, Carpaccio, Mantegna, Vivarini, Signorelli and van Eyck.

A big incentive for visiting is the chance to lean out from the balconies over the Grand Canal on the 1st and 2nd floors. The Ca' d'Oro is open daily from 9 am to 2 pm, although they start hustling you out from around 1.40 pm. Admission costs L6000.

To Sestiere di San Marco (Map 4) The Strada Nuova leads into the pleasing **Campo dei SS Apostoli**. The church of the same name is worth visiting for the 15th-century Cappella Corner by Mauro Codussi, which features a painting of Santa Lucia by Tiepolo (undergoing restoration).

Keep following the crowd over the next two bridges and on the left is the rather curious **Chiesa di San Giovanni Crisostomo**. It was remodelled on a Greek-cross plan by Codussi in 1504. Since 1977 it has housed an icon of the Virgin Mary that attracts a lot of the local faithful. What with burning incense and candles, to wander in here is to feel yourself in a mysterious church of the Orthodox East. Notable is Giovanni Bellini's *San Gerolamo e Due Santi* (St Jerome and Two Saints).

Around the back, Corte Prima del Milion leads into a chain of brief streets, *sotoporteghi* and squares. At No 5845 in Corte Seconda del Milion you are supposedly looking at **Marco Polo's house**. That's one theory. Another suggests the Polo family house disappeared to make way for the 17th-century Teatro Malibran (now undergoing restoration). Return to the Chiesa di San Giovanni Crisostomo and head south. The next canal marks the boundary between the sestieri of Cannaregio and San Marco. The building you are looking at is the Fondaco dei Tedeschi (see the earlier Sestiere di San Marco section).

Itinerary II: Ponte delle Guglie to Castello

To Chiesa della Madonna dell'Orto
(Map 3) For this second ramble, we don't even cross the Ponte delle Guglie, choosing instead to head north along Fondamenta Venier, named after the late-18th-century neoclassical mansion of the same name. Farther up, Palazzo Savorgnan's big draw is its garden, now a public park with slides and other traditional amusements for the kiddies.

Beyond the palace, the character of the area changes quickly – it is clearly a working-class district. It was perhaps not always thus. Across the canal, just before you reach the last bridge (Ponte di Tre Archi), the 17th-century **Palazzo Surian** stands out. During the last century of the Republic, the French moved their embassy in here and Jean Jacques Rousseau managed to blag his way into a job as secretary to the ambassador.

To the left, down along Rio di San Giobbe, the rather ordinary church of the same name boasts a remarkable ceiling faced with multicoloured glazed terracotta. Of the one-time neighbouring convent little remains but one portico.

Before crossing the Ponte di Tre Archi, you might like to stroll to the end of Fondamenta di San Giobbe. The enormous complex at the end here was the **Macello Comunale**, the city's abattoir. Le Corbusier designed a hospital for the site, but (much to the annoyance of many citizens) it got the thumbs down in 1964. Since then not a lot has been made of the site. The Università Ca' Foscari operates in part of it and rowing clubs use the lagoon side as a launch pad.

Across the bridge, towards the end of Fondamenta di Cannaregio, the former **Chiesa di Santa Maria delle Penitenti** was one of the seemingly abundant religious institutions set up to take in wayward women who were anxious to put their wicked past behind them.

The winding walk along Calle Ferau and through the Sacca di San Girolamo area, an unpretentious residential district, takes you past the barely noticeable **Chiesa delle Cappuccine** on the left and the ugly hulk of the **Chiesa di San Girolamo** on the right across the canal. Apart from soaking up the peace and quiet of the area, your objective is the **Chiesa di Sant'Alvise**. Built in 1388, it plays host to a noteworthy Tiepolo, the *Salita al Calvario* (Climb to Calvary), a distressingly human depiction of one of Christ's falls under the weight of the cross. The ceiling frescoes are an unexpected riot of colour. The church is part of the Chorus scheme (see the boxed text 'A Chorus Line' earlier in this chapter). It's open from 10 am to 5 pm Monday to Saturday and 1 to 5 pm on Sunday. Admission costs L3000.

To reach the next stop, there is no choice but to make a detour across the canal and then a little way along Fondamenta della Sensa and back up Calle Loredan to Fondamenta Madonna dell'Orto. The long courtyard on the left as you head east is called Corte del Cavallo (Horse Court) because here the bronze was melted down for the great equestrian statue to Colleoni in Campo SS Giovanni e Paolo (see the following Sestiere di Castello section).

Chiesa della Madonna dell'Orto (Map 3) Architecture fans should find the exterior of this church intriguing. Elements of Romanesque remain (the inner arch over the main entrance, for instance) in what is largely a 14th-century Gothic structure in brick. That changes were made a century later is fairly clear from the series of statues in niches above the two lower wings of the facade and from the triangular finish at the

top. The five statues crowning the facade were actually added in the 18th century.

Tintoretto was a local parishioner and although he used a good deal of his creative genius filling the Scuola di San Rocco (in San Polo) with his paintings, he found the time to execute some works for this church too. Among them are the *Giudizio Finale* (Last Judgement), *Adorazione del Vitello d'Oro* (Adoration of the Golden Calf) and the *Apparizione della Croce a San Pietro* (Vision of the Cross to St Peter). On the wall at the end of the right aisle is the *Presentazione di Maria al Tempio* (Presentation of the Virgin Mary in the Temple). Tintoretto is buried with other family members in the church.

In the Cappella di San Mauro is the white stone statue of the *Madonna col Bambino* (Madonna and Child) after which the church is named. The statue was supposedly found in a nearby garden in 1377 and brought here amid considerable excitement.

The church is part of the Chorus scheme (see the boxed text 'A Chorus Line' earlier in this chapter). It's open from 10 am to 5 pm Monday to Saturday and 1 to 5 pm on Sunday. Admission costs L3000.

If you cross the first bridge east of the church, you will end up in Calle dei Mori. Follow it to the next canal and turn left down Fondamenta dei Mori. Almost immediately you will see on your left a plaque noting that Tintoretto lived here (No 3399) until his death. The strange statue of a man with a huge turban that sticks out of the wall next door on Palazzo Mastelli is one of four spread out along here and around the corner on Corte dei Mori. The street names here (dei Mori) mean 'of the Moors' and refer to these strange statues, traditionally said to represent members of the Mastelli family, 12th-century merchants from the Morea (one of La Serenissima's most important Greek possessions). The building on which they appear is also known as the Palazzo del Cammello, because of the distinct bas-relief depicting this animal on the facade overlooking Rio della Madonna dell'Orto.

[continued on page 153]

ALONG THE GRAND CANAL

JOHN HAY

Main St Venice is a river, or rather the extension of one. Centuries before people realised that the islets of Rivoalto would be a cosy place to found a city, the Brenta river (it is believed) had been carving a path through the mud flats and shallow waters of the Venetian lagoon towards the Adriatic Sea. After ducking and weaving its way past the islets, it widens into what the Venetians subsequently called the Canale di San Marco or Canal Grande (Grand Canal), and then heads on to the sea.

Like any self-respecting central boulevard, the Grand Canal is lined with classy hotels, grand old churches and, above all, fine mansions dating from the 12th to the 18th centuries. An inverted 'S' 3.5km long, the canal is only 6m deep. Its width ranges from 40m to 100m. In the glory days of La Serenissima, the warehouses along its banks were constantly busy with the loading and unloading of goods from all over the known world. Back in the 15th century, the French writer Philippe de Commines declared the Grand Canal 'the finest street in the world, with the finest houses'.

Today, the trading may have stopped, but the canal is as busy as ever. Traffic jams are not as much of a problem as in other cities, but the riot of colour and noise as *vaporetti*, private runabouts, taxis, ambulances, fire department vessels, delivery boats and gondolas churn their way up, down and across it makes the Grand Canal hectic enough.

Prime Venetian real estate has always included canal views. It follows that many of the jewels of centuries of Venetian architecture face the canal. Often, the only way to see them up close is from the water. On the assumption that you don't walk on the stuff and don't wish to shell out a sizeable wad of notes for a gondola, the best way to get a look is on *vaporetto* No 1 – the all-stops Grand Canal 'omnibus'.

The pages that follow briefly detail the bridges, churches and *palazzi* of note along the way, starting at the uninspiring top (north-western) end, by the train station, and winding down towards Piazza San Marco. The number refers to the map location, while an asterisk indicates that there is more detailed information in the Things to See & Do chapter, where we will sidle up to the buildings on foot as best we can!

Top: An unusually quiet moment on Venice's Grand Canal.

All you need to do now is jump on board the No 1 at Ferrovia and try to grab a deck seat at the back.

LEFT BANK

As you pull away from the landing, you leave behind (for a while anyway) the lowering form of **Stazione di Santa Lucia (1)**. Originally built in 1865 on the site of a convent dedicated to the same saint, the station was remodelled in 1954.

The baroque chocolate-cake facade just beyond the station fronts the **Chiesa dei Scalzi (2*)**. On the other side of the **Ponte dei Scalzi (3*)** is the **Palazzo Calbo-Crotta (4)**. Much remodelled, it retains some of the original 15th-century Gothic elements. A couple of smaller buildings to its right are also late Gothic.

TERESA GAUDIO

RIGHT BANK

As on the left bank, things get off to a desultory start, but that's probably a good thing: it'll give you time to get yourself sorted out for the visual feast farther down the line.

Palazzo Emo-Diedo (5) is a modest late-17th-century building attributed to Andrea Tirali. A couple of streets on is the unmistakable outline of the **Chiesa di San Simeon Piccolo (6*)**. Shortly after, **Palazzo Foscari-Contarini (7)** is a 15th-century reconstruction of a 12th-century mansion, in which it is thought Doge Francesco Foscari was born in 1375.

BETHUNE CARMICHAEL

Top Left: Chiesa dei Scalzi

Bottom Left: The southern reaches of the canal

LEFT BANK

Just before you pass the hulk of the 18th-century **Chiesa di San Geremia (9*)** is the four-storeyed **Palazzo Flangini (8)**, designed by Giuseppe Sardi and finished in 1682. A string of 17th- and 18th-century palazzi then stand rollcall up to the **Chiesa di San Marcuola (10*)**. After this house of God, you pass the *rio* of the same name and then a house of the devil, the Renaissance **Palazzo Vendramin-Calergi (11*)**, winter seat of the casino.

On the left (western) corner of Rio di Noale, **Palazzo Gussoni-Grimani della Vida (12)** has been attributed to Sanmicheli. Tintoretto added frescoes that have since faded away.

RIGHT BANK

Shortly after you pass Canale di Cannaregio on the left, **Palazzo Giovanelli (13)**, an elegant 15th-century Gothic mansion, emerges on the right. Next follows **Casa Correr (14)**, a modest 17th-century house where Teodoro Correr first started to put together the collection that would become the basis of the Museo Correr in Piazza San Marco.

Well hidden by scaffolding (at the time of writing) is the **Fondaco dei Turchi (15*)**. Across the rio, the 15th-century **Deposito del Megio (16)** was long the main grain silo of La Serenissima. The serious-looking lion of St Mark is a later copy of the one removed after Napoleon arrived in 1797 (Venice had been covered in lions, but the Corsican felt such symbols out of place in his brave new world and ordered them all destroyed). The following building, topped by what look like the tips of two spears, is a 17th-century creation of the very busy Longhena, **Palazzo Belloni Battaglia (17)**. **Ca' Tron (18)** went up a century earlier and is now part of the university. Farther along, you'll find it hard to miss the baroque facade of the **Chiesa di San Stae (19*)**.

Ca' Pesaro (20*) is an important example of canalside baroque, started by Longhena and finished by Gaspari.

Right: Palazzo Vendramin-Calergi

DAMIEN SIMONIS

LEFT BANK

The pink **Palazzo Fontana-Rezzonico (21)** was built in the style of Sansovino's buildings. In 1693 Carlo Rezzonico was born here – he went on to become Pope Clement XIII. A couple of houses along is **Ca' d'Oro (22*)**. **Ca' Pesaro (23)**, just on the other side of the vaporetto stop, is a nicely restored 15th-century Gothic house, immediately followed by the still older **Palazzo Sagredo (24)**, built in the Byzantine style and later given a Gothic overhaul.

Just past the Rio dei Santi Apostoli, approaching the bend, stands the medieval **Ca' da Mosto (25)**, once home to one of the oldest hotels in Venice.

When you've almost reached the **Ponte di Rialto (27*)**, you'll see the one-time trading house and present-day central post office, the **Fondaco dei Tedeschi (26*)**.

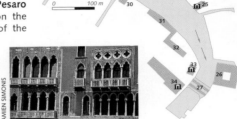

RIGHT BANK

Begun in 1724, the present version of **Palazzo Corner della Regina (28*)** appeared centuries after Caterina Corner, short-lived queen of Cyprus, had passed into history. The bijou 14th-century **Casa Favretto (29)** is now a hotel.

When you chug by the neo-Gothic arches of the **Pescaria (30*)**, you have reached what was long the commercial heart of Venice – Rialto. The produce markets still do a brisk trade, but the bankers have long since been replaced by tourist tat stalls. The long buildings are the **Fabbriche Nuove (31*)** and **Fabbriche Vecchie (32*)**. They are followed by the Renaissance **Palazzo dei Camerlenghi (33*)**, just before the Ponte di Rialto, and the **Palazzo dei Dieci Savi (34*)**, just after it.

Top Left: Ca' d'Oro

Top Right: Ca' Pesaro and Palazzo Sagredo

Bottom Right: Ca' da Mosto

Bottom Left: Ponte di Rialto

LEFT BANK

A couple of blocks south of the bridge are **Palazzo Dolfin-Manin (35*)**, designed by Sansovino, and **Palazzo Bembo (36*)**. Look for the narrow, early-Gothic **Palazzo Dandolo (37*)**, four houses along. On the right of Calle del Carbon stand two fine Veneto-Byzantine trading houses, **Palazzo Loredan (38*)** and **Ca' Farsetti (39*)**. They now house the city council.

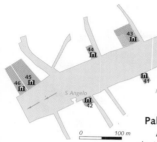

The third building along from here is the imposing Renaissance **Palazzo Grimani (40*)**.

Across Rio di San Luca are clustered several Gothic edifices, among them the 15th-century **Palazzo Tron (41)**, followed farther down by **Palazzo Corner-Spinelli (42*)**, which was the work of Codussi.

RIGHT BANK

When the No 1 leaves the San Silvestro stop, **Palazzo Papadopoli (43*)** is the mansion after the first canal on the right. More than anything else, it is locally renowned for its lush gardens. Just past the

next rio, **Palazzo Bernardo (44)** is a fine Gothic structure. Also worthy of note is **Palazzo Pisani-Moretta (45)**, dating from about the same period. Next door, the 16th-century **Palazzo Tiepolo (46)** still boasts some original (if faded) frescoes.

Top: Palazzo Bembo

Middle: Palazzo Grimani

Bottom: View of the right bank of the Grand Canal

LEFT BANK

Shortly before the next bend in the canal, four mansions, the **Palazzi Mocenigo (47)**, belonging to the powerful family of the same name, abut one another. The two outside houses were originally Gothic, but all four were substantially made over in the following centuries. The detached **Palazzo Contarini dalle Figure (48)** is a fine Renaissance house where Palladio lived for a while.

A couple of Gothic mansions lie between Palazzo Contarini and **Palazzo Moro-Lin (49)**, a stout house raised by the Tuscan architect Sebastiano Mazzoni in 1670. Larger still is the **Palazzo Grassi (50*)**. In a back street next to the **Palazzo Malipiero (51*)**, Giacomo Casanova was born in 1725. **Ca' del Duca (52*)** is the next major building down the canal. It is swiftly followed by **Palazzo Giustinian-Lolin (53)**, a 14th-century pile reworked by Longhena in 1630.

0   100 m

RIGHT BANK

Down at **Palazzo Balbi (54)**, on the northern side of Rio di Ca' Foscari, we can see some tentative early baroque touches on an essentially Renaissance structure. Across the rio is **Ca' Foscari (55*)**. It's been covered in scaffolding for years, but in mid-1999 a deceptively realistic mock facade was erected to hide restoration work that will take until at least 2002 to complete.

At the next vaporetto stop is the 17th-century **Ca' Rezzonico (56*)**. The fourth mansion along from here, **Palazzo Loredan dell'Ambasciatore (57)**, is so called because in the 18th century Hapsburg imperial ambassadors lived here.

Just across Rio di San Trovaso, **Palazzo Contarini degli Scrigni**

(58) is an interesting hybrid composed of a late-Gothic structure with an early-17th-century add-on. The original nucleus of the art collection that would later end up in the Gallerie dell'Accademia was housed here. Moving it can't have been too onerous, as the **Gallerie dell'Accademia (59*)** are about 100m to the south-east. In front of the Gallerie, the last of the Grand Canal's three bridges, the **Ponte dell'Accademia (60*)**, links Dorsoduro with the Sestiere di San Marco

BETHUNE CARMICHAEL

Left: Chiesa di Santa Maria della Salute from the Ponte dell'Accademia

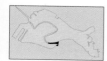

LEFT BANK

Past the Ponte dell'Accademia, the next edifice of substance is Sansovino's imposing **Palazzo Corner (61*)**, also known as Ca' Grande. The 15th-century Gothic **Palazzo Pisani-Gritti (62)** was altered in the 19th century and is now a luxury hotel. The rather narrow **Palazzo Contarini-Fasan (63*)** is an ornate Gothic building raised in the second half of the 15th century. **Palazzo Giustinian (64)** was built in 1474 in late-Gothic style. At this point, the No 1 ferry calls in at the San Marco stop.

RIGHT BANK

What distinguishes **Palazzo Barbarigo (65*)** are the mosaics added towards the end of the 19th century. Next up is the Palazzo Venier dei Leoni, which houses the **Peggy Guggenheim Collection (66*)**, followed a block later by the lopsided **Palazzo Dario (67*)**, with its early Renaissance marble facade.

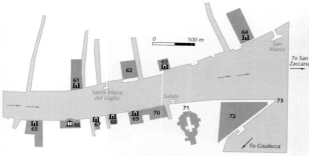

DAMIEN SIMONIS

Just on the other side of the next rio, **Palazzo Salviati (68)**, with its exuberant mosaic decoration, is hard to miss. The Salviati glass firm added this touch, recently by Venetian standards (in 1924).

Don't be fooled by the seemingly Gothic grandeur of **Palazzo Genovese (69)**. It is actually a neo-Gothic whim erected late in the 19th century. Much of the former **Abbazia di San Gregorio (70)** was destroyed to make way for it. What is left dates from the 12th century, although it has been so often remodelled that you'd never know. It presents a rather forlorn picture on the canal today. All the more so since this part of Dorsoduro is completely dominated by the baroque splendour of Longhena's **Chiesa di Santa Maria della Salute (71*)**.

Next to it are former seminary buildings and then the long low structure of the **Dogana da Mar (72*)**, where for centuries traders paid customs duty on seaborne imports. Like a ship's prow, Dorsoduro ends here in a point known as the **Punta della Dogana (73*)**.

The No 1 vaporetto continues on its way to San Marco, San Zaccaria and beyond.

Right: Palazzo Dario

Following page: Palazzo Salviati and the Punta della Dogana

DAMIEN SIMONIS

BETHUNE CARMICHAEL

Top: Glass mosaics adorn the Palazzo Salviati

Bottom: Journey's end: the Punta della Dogana seen here from the Campanile in Piazza San Marco

[continued from page 144]

To the Gesuiti (Map 4) Backtrack to the Chiesa della Madonna dell'Orto and continue east along Fondamenta Gasparo Contarini, named after the **Palazzo Contarini del Zaffo**, which extends to the end of the street. A narrow wooden quay protrudes out into the little protected bay off the lagoon. Locals use it for sunbathing and from here you enjoy good views across to the islands of San Michele and Murano. Behind the palazzo spread luxuriant private gardens leading to an isolated little building on the lagoon, the so-called **Casino degli Spiriti**, where in the 16th century students, literati and glitterati with the right contacts would gather for learned chit-chat and a few drinks.

There is little choice here but to cross Rio Madonna dell'Orto and follow Corte Vecchia south to Rio della Sensa. Before turning left to continue east, turn around to the right and you'll see a rare (and run-down) example of a squero, or gondola-building yard, complete with slipways into Rio dei Muti.

The next stop of importance is the Gesuiti, the massive hulk erected by the Jesuits. To get there, we pass down Fondamenta dell'Abbazia under the portico of the **Scuola Vecchia della Misericordia**, once the seat of one of the city's grand religious confraternities. It later moved into the immense **Scuola Nuova della Misericordia**, designed by Sansovino in the 1530s, on the southern side of Rio della Sensa. Next to the Scuola Vecchia on the pretty little campo that overlooks the busy Canale della Misericordia is the **Chiesa di Santa Maria della Misericordia**, established in the 10th century and altered in the 13th.

A series of bridges takes you into Calle della Racchetta. To get to the Gesuiti, follow this street north to Fondamenta Santa Caterina and head east until you reach Campo dei Gesuiti.

The Gesuiti & Around (Map 4) The Jesuits took over the church here in 1657 and ordered its reconstruction in the Roman baroque style. The conversion was completed by 1730. The facade is impressive enough – in fact, as is often the case with such sights in Venice (see also the Scuola di San Rocco in San Polo), it seems out of place, as though it were bursting for more space to allow a greater appreciation of its splendour.

Still, the real frills and thrills come inside. No-one could accuse the Jesuits of modest or sober tastes. Barely a square centimetre has been spared from the lust for decoration, with white and gold stucco, white and green marble floors and marble flourishes filling in any empty slots.

Tintoretto's *Assunzione della Vergine* (Assumption of the Virgin) is a remarkable exception to the rule – think of the darkness of his images in the Scuola di San Rocco and you wonder where all the lightness and joy came from in this representation of the Assumption. Maybe there was some role-swapping going on, as Titian's *Martirio di San Lorenzo* (Martyrdom of St Lawrence) is an uncharacteristically stormy and gloomy piece. Of course the subjects of each painting make the respective results quite logical.

The Gesuiti was closed for restoration at the time of writing.

On the subject of Titian, fans can find his house by walking up to the Fondamente Nuove, heading east as far as Calle delle Croci and penetrating the web of lanes in search of Corte della Carità. North of this square, a narrow dead-end lane is your objective – at the end of it on the right is Titian's place.

Chiesa di Santa Maria dei Miracoli (Map 4) From Corte della Carità you can trace a path down along Calle del Fumo, past the 17th-century **Palazzo Widman** and down the narrow calle of the same name. You will emerge on Campo Santa Maria Nova. Off to the right (west) is the **Chiesa di San Canciano**. Although here since the 9th century, what you see is the result of intervention by Massari and Gaspari.

The real stunner around here is off to the left (east). The **Chiesa di Santa Maria dei Miracoli** looks like an elaborate box containing the most refined of all imaginable chocolates. Pietro Lombardo was responsible for this Renaissance jewel, which is fully cara-paced inside and out in marble, bas-reliefs and statues. The result is intense, but lacks the flowery motifs that would come later with baroque. The timber ceiling is also eye-catching. Pietro and Tullio Lombardo executed the carvings on the choir.

The church is part of the Chorus scheme (see the boxed text 'A Chorus Line' earlier in this chapter). It's open from 10 am to 5 pm Monday to Saturday and 1 to 5 pm on Sunday. Admission costs L3000.

From the church you can turn left (east) along Calle Castelli (which continues over the rio as Calle delle Erbe). Once over the next bridge, you are obliged to swing left and arrive in Campo SS Giovanni e Paolo. You are now in the city's easternmost ses-tiere: Castello.

SESTIERE DI CASTELLO
Chiesa dei SS Giovanni e Paolo & Around (Map 4)

This huge Gothic church, founded by the Dominicans, rivals the Franciscans' Frari in size and grandeur. Work started on it in 1333, but it was not consecrated until 1430. The similarities between the two are all too evident. The use of brick and modest white stone refinements around windows and doorways is a clear point they have in com-mon. A particular departure here, however, is the way in which three chapels, each of different dimensions, have been tacked – it seems almost willy-nilly – onto the church's southern flank.

The vast interior, like that of the Frari, is divided simply into an enormous central nave and two aisles, separated by graceful, soaring arches. The red and white chequer-board floor is a further demonstration of the contemporaneity of the two buildings.

A beautiful stained-glass window made in Murano in the 15th century fills the south-ern arm of the transept with light. A host of artists contributed to its design, including Bartolomeo Vivarini, Cima da Conegliano and Girolamo Mocetto. It owes some of its brilliance to restoration carried out in the 1980s. Below the window and just to the right is a fine *pala* (altarpiece) by Lorenzo Lotto. On the opposite aisle wall, below the organ, is a triptych by Bartolomeo Vivarini. Noteworthy, too, are the five late-Gothic apses, graced by long and slender windows. Look out for Giovanni Bellini's polyptych

The Infamy of Famagusta

Keep an eye out for the monument to Marcantonio Bragadin in the Chiesa dei SS Giovanni e Paolo. It is on the wall of the south aisle, virtually opposite the westernmost pillar. The monument is singular for its content, rather than any artistic merit.

Bragadin was the commander of the Famagusta garrison in Cyprus that was the last to fall to the Turks in 1570. Promised honourable terms of surrender after having endured a long siege, Bragadin decided to call on the Turkish commander Mustafa and present him the keys of the city. Mustafa lost, as it were, his head, and lopped off Bragadin's ears and nose. Sev-eral hundred Christians in the vicinity also lost their heads, rather more literally. The post-battle massacre that until now had been avoided suddenly swept like a storm across the town.

While the population of Famagusta was decimated, Bragadin rotted for a couple of weeks in prison. He was then hauled about the town under the crushing weight of sacks of stone and earth. After various other humiliations, he was tied to a stake in the execution square and skinned alive. According to one account he only passed out when they reached his waist. The corpse was then beheaded and quartered, and the skin stuffed with straw and paraded about town. Mustafa then took it home as a trophy to present to the sultan. Some years later a Ven-etian trader with considerable courage managed to steal it from the arsenal of Constantinople and return it to the Bragadin family in Venice. The remains have been in this church since 1596.

of San Vincenzo Ferreri (St Vincent Ferrer) over the second altar of the right aisle.

In the Cappella del Rosario, off the northern arm of the transept, is a series of paintings by Paolo Veronese, including ceiling panels and an *Adorazione dei Pastori* (Adoration of the Shepherds) on the west wall.

The church is a veritable ducal pantheon. Around the walls, many of the 25 tombs of doges were sculpted by prominent Gothic and Renaissance artists, in particular Pietro and Tullio Lombardo. The church is open daily from 7 am to 12.30 pm and 3.30 to 7.30 pm.

At right angles to the main facade of the church is the rather more eye-catching marble frontage of the former **Scuola Grande di San Marco**. Pietro Lombardo and his sons all worked on what was once one of the most important of Venice's religious confraternities. Codussi put the finishing touches on this Renaissance gem. Have a closer look and, apart from the predictably magnificent lions, you will notice the sculpted trompe l'oeil perspectives covering much of the lower half of the facade. Nowadays the scuola is the entrance to the Ospedale Civile. You are free to enter the scuola itself – the timber beams of the ceiling are held up by two ranks of five columns. The staircase to the upper storey is closed. Beyond, in what were the Convento dei Domenicani and the Chiesa di San Lazzaro dei Mendicanti, is the hospital proper.

Presiding over the Campo di SS Giovanni e Paolo is the most impressive of the city's few equestrian statues, by the Florentine Verrocchio (1435–88). It is dedicated to the *condottiero* **Bartolomeo Colleoni**, who from 1448 commanded mercenary armies in the name of the Republic. Although he was of the school of mercenaries that tended to organise things so that they lived to fight another day, he remained faithful to La Serenissima. On his death in 1474, Colleoni bequeathed 216,000 gold and silver ducats and considerably more in property to Venice, on one condition – that the city erect a commemorative statue to him in Piazza San Marco. The Senato took the money but cheated, placing the grand statue here in-

stead. Still, Colleoni can rest easy that the Republic didn't scrimp on the statue itself.

Ospedaletto (Map 7)

Just east of the campo, Longhena's baroque Chiesa di Santa Maria dei Derelitti (also known as the Ospedaletto, or Little Hospital) is the focal point of a hospital for elderly and poor patients that was built in the 17th century. In an annexe is the elegantly frescoed **Sala da Musica**, where patients performed concerts. It's open from 4 to 7 pm (3 to 6 pm in winter). Admission to the Sala da Musica costs L2500.

Chiesa di San Francesco della Vigna (Map 7)

After a quiet stroll east along residential streets, you emerge in Campo San Francesco della Vigna, where the sudden appearance of the massive Palladian facade of this church comes as a bit of a shock.

The remainder of the church, which takes its name from the vineyard that once thrived on the site, was designed by Sansovino for the Franciscans. Out the back is the bell tower – to all intents and purposes the twin of the Campanile in Piazza San Marco.

Inside, just to the left of the main door, is a triptych of saints by Antonio Vivarini. The Cappella dei Giustiniani, to the left of the main altar, is decorated with reliefs by Pietro Lombardo and his school (undergoing restoration). Off the left (northern) arm of the transept you can enter the Cappella Santa, which houses a *Madonna col Bambino e Santi* (Madonna and Child with Saints) by Giovanni Bellini. From here you can admire the leafy cloisters too. The church is open from 9 am to noon and 3 to 7 pm.

Scuola di San Giorgio degli Schiavoni (Map 7)

Proceeding east around the south flank of San Francesco della Vigna, you'll end up in Campo della Celestia. Follow the only lane exiting off it across the rio and into Campo San Ternità. Calle Dona veers to the left (east) off this square. After the rio turn right (south) and almost immediately on your left is **Casa Magno**, a fairly unique example of

Gothic housing. Now head straight down to and across Campo Do Pozzi. You'll end up on Calle degli Scudi, at which point you turn right (north-west) and cross the rio into Campo delle Gatte. A quick dogleg and you will run into Rio di San Lorenzo. Just before the bridge, on the right, is the Scuola di San Giorgio degli Schiavoni.

Venice's Dalmatian community established this religious school in the 15th century and the building was erected in the 16th century. The main attraction is on the ground floor, where the walls are graced by a series of superb paintings by Vittore Carpaccio depicting events in the lives of the three patron saints of Dalmatia: George, Tryphone and Jerome. The image of St George dispatching the dragon to the next life is a particularly graphic scene. Scattered about before the dragon are remnants of its victims – various limbs, the half-eaten corpse of a young woman and an assortment of bones.

Members of the scuola gathered upstairs for meetings and religious services. The delicate timber decor and the heavy exposed beams of the ceilings complete the scene. It's open daily except Monday from 9.30 am to 12.30 pm and 3.30 to 6.30 pm. Admission costs L5000.

From here proceed south along the rio and at the Chiesa Sant'Antonin follow the main street south into Campo Bandiera e Moro.

Campo Bandiera e Moro (Map 7)

This quiet square is named after the brothers Bandiera and the Venetian Domenico Moro, who were executed by troops of the Bourbon Kingdom of the Two Sicilies after a hopelessly failed pro-unity insurrection in Cosenza (Calabria) in 1844. It is fronted in the south-eastern corner by the **Chiesa di San Giovanni in Bragora**, where Antonio Vivaldi was baptised.

Among the works of art inside is a restored triptych by Bartolomeo Vivarini, the *Madonna in Trono tra I Santi Andrea e Giovanni Battista* (Enthroned Madonna with St Andrew and John the Baptist). In the peaceful square just south of the church,

Campiello del Piovan, the architect Giorgio Massari was born at No 3752.

Arsenale (Maps 7 & 8)

From the Chiesa di San Giovanni in Bragora, follow Calle Crosera to the east. About the shortest route to what was once the military powerhouse of the Republic takes us up Calle Erizzo past the Renaissance palazzo of the same name and across the bridge to the **Chiesa di San Martino** (Map 7). The church is a 16th-century Sansovino design on the site of a 7th-century predecessor that was built by mainland refugees fleeing Lombard invaders. Across the canal are the walls of the Arsenale. To reach its entrance, walk along Fondamenta di Fronte until you run into the Rio dell'Arsenale.

The city's huge dockyards are traditionally thought to have been founded in 1104, although some historians think it may have happened a century later. What became known as the Arsenale Vecchio (Old Arsenal) is the core of the whole complex. Within it was a special storage area for the *bucintoro*, the great ceremonial galley used by the doge on important occasions, such as the Sposalizio del Mar (see the boxed text 'With This Ring I Thee Wet' in the History section of the Facts about Venice chapter).

As the Republic's maritime needs grew and shipbuilding requirements changed, so the Arsenale was enlarged. In 1303–4 came the first expansion, known as La Tana. It occupies almost the whole length of the southern side of the Arsenale (it was refashioned in 1579 by Antonio da Ponte). The Arsenale Nuovo (New Arsenal; Map 8) was added in 1325, followed in 1473 by the Arsenale Nuovissimo (Very New Arsenal; Map 2). When, in the 16th century, production of much larger war vessels with a deeper draught *(galeazze)* got under way, further workshops and sheds were added, along with the Canale delle Galeazze. The whole was unsurprisingly walled in and top secret. The *arsenaloti*, or shipyard workers, were relatively well paid and tended throughout the history of the Republic to be faithful to the doge and the State. This was proven on several occasions when they were called to arms in times of unrest or rebellion.

The Arsenale was as close as Venice (or anyone for that matter, until the 18th century) came to industrial production. And to late medieval eyes it must have made an enormous impression, with all its boiling black pitch, metalworking and timber cutting. Dante was so awestruck he used it as a model scene for Hell in his *Divina Commedia* (Canto XXI, 7–21).

The Arsenale had another function. An emergency reserve fleet of at least 25 vessels was always to be kept ready to sail from inside it, either as a war fleet or as merchant ships. As the centuries progressed, although the shortage of raw materials (especially timber) became a problem, more often than not the Republic's difficulty was finding crews. Eventually, it was obliged to employ slaves, prisoners and press gangs to fill the personnel gaps.

The Arsenale at its peak covered 46 hectares, was home to 300 shipping companies and employed up to 16,000 people. In 1570, when requested to produce as many ships as possible for an emergency fleet, the Arsenale put out an astounding 100 galleys in just two months. The following year at the Battle of Lepanto, which was the last great sea struggle fought mainly with oar power and which concluded in a stunning defeat of the Turks, more than half the allied Christian fleet (which included such powers as Imperial Spain) was provided by Venice.

For most of its history Venice relied on one form or other of rowing vessel, often combined with sail. In battle, such galleys were often more manoeuvrable. By the 17th century, however, the nimble, all-sail vessels being produced in England and Holland began to show their superiority. The Arsenale never fully made the switch and when it tried its products often proved inferior. By this time Venetians were increasingly turning away from the sea anyway, and the practice of buying or renting foreign vessels (and sometimes their crews) grew more common. Venice was growing soft and its people becoming landlubbers. By

the time La Serenissima fell in 1797, naval production had all but ceased. Various minor modifications were made in the course of the 19th century and the whole area is now naval property, although they do little with it.

The land gateway, surmounted by the lion of St Mark, is considered by many to be the earliest example of Renaissance architecture in Venice; it was probably executed in 1460. Later, a plaque was installed commemorating the victory at Lepanto in 1571. The fenced-in terrace was added in 1692. At the foot of the statues (each with allegorical meaning) is a row of carved lions of varying size and type. The biggest of them, in regally seated pose, was taken as booty by Francesco Morosini from the Greek port of Piraeus. This must have required quite an effort. On its right flank is a series of Viking runes. Unfortunately, Swedish experts have failed to decipher them.

There was a time when the No 52 vaporetto plied the Rio dell'Arsenale Darsena, Arsenale Vecchio and Canale delle Galeazze, but alas no more. On the way through you could see 15th- and 16th-century workshops and the storage area for the *bucintoro*. The best you can do today is enter the vestibule at the pedestrian entrance and peer through. It can be open as early as 7 am and is generally shut by 5 pm. It is only open at all to let navy personnel in and out.

Museo Storico Navale & Beyond (Maps 7 & 8)

A short walk down Fondamenta dell'Arsenale towards the Canale di San Marco brings us to this former grain silo (Map 7).

Spread over four floors, this museum traces the maritime history of the city and of Italy. There are some wonderfully complex models of all sorts of Venetian vessels, but also ancient triremes, Asian warships, WWII battleships and ocean liners. The ground floor is devoted mainly to weaponry (the usual stuff – cannons, blunderbusses, swords and sabres). Most curious are the 17th-century diorama maps of Venetian ports and forts across its one-time Adriatic and Mediterranean possessions.

On the 1st floor is a model of the sumptuous *bucintoro*, the doge's ceremonial barge. Napoleon's French troops destroyed the real thing in 1798. The 2nd floor is mostly given over to Italian naval history and memorabilia, from unification to the present day. Up on the 3rd floor is a room containing a few gondolas, including Peggy Guggenheim's. A small room set above the 3rd floor is given over to – wait for it – Swedish naval history. Curious.

The museum is open from 8.45 am to 1.30 pm Monday to Saturday (except Thursday, when it opens from 2.30 to 5 pm) and admission costs L3000.

If you proceed east you are entering Very-Few-Tourists Territory. Follow the street round behind the museum and past the ugly Palazzetto dello Sport to Campo della Tana. Here you are again faced by the walls of the Arsenale. Follow them, cross the bridge and take Fondamenta della Tana, turning right down Calle di San Francesco di Paola – you'll hit the broad Via Giuseppe Garibaldi. The **Chiesa di San Francesco di Paola** (Map 8) is a fairly uninteresting 18th-century remake of the 16th-century original.

Follow the road east and cross the last bridge northwards across the Rio di Sant'Anna (named after the ruined church that looks out over the Canale di San Pietro). Proceed north across Campo di Ruga and take the last lane on the right (east). The bridge at the end of it takes you across to the Isola di San Pietro.

There is no need to rush through this part of the itinerary. An aimless wander through the simple grid pattern of residential streets allows you to immerse yourself in the simple, gritty, everyday life of ordinary Venetians. No sights, just life.

San Pietro (Map 8)

Although overshadowed by the Basilica di San Marco in the heart of town, the **Cattedrale di San Pietro di Castello**, on the island of San Pietro, was in fact Venice's cathedral from 1451 to 1807. Indeed, the island was among the first areas to be inhabited.

In 775 the original church here was the seat of a bishopric. Between then and the 16th century, the church underwent several transformations. Its present appearance is basically a post-Palladian job, taking its cue in part from Giudecca's Chiesa del Redentore. Inside, various hands were at work at one point or another, including Longhena, responsible among other things for the baroque main altar.

Although this was officially Venice's cathedral for so long, the Basilica di San Marco to all intents and purposes was the senior church. The doges no doubt liked it that way. The splendour of their chapel, as it were, thus outshone even ecclesiastical power. The Church never really did get its own way in the Republic.

Today San Pietro rests in easy retirement on this quiet islet, its blinding white campanile (bell tower), made of Istrian stone by Codussi, leaning at an odd angle and the former patriarchate dosily crumbling away next door. The latter was for a while used as a barracks.

San Pietro is part of the Chorus scheme (see the boxed text 'A Chorus Line' earlier in this chapter). It's open from 10 am to 5 pm Monday to Saturday and 1 to 5 pm on Sunday. Admission costs L3000.

Giardini Pubblici & Biennale (Map 8)

The only other way off the Isola di San Pietro is the southern of the two bridges, which brings us back to the ruins of Sant'Anna. Walk past them (heading west) and duck down Calle Correra. Cross the broad Secco Marina, keep on down Corte del Solda and cross the bridge. A stroll past the **Chiesa di San Giuseppe di Castello** will bring us into the somewhat tatty Giardini Pubblici, one of the city's few public parks. You may have noticed during your Venetian strolls that a surprising amount of greenery shoots out at all sorts of angles (except in winter), but it is mostly in the form of private gardens (so much so that someone has even published a coffee-table book entitled *Secret Gardens in Venice*).

There are few opportunities for enjoying parks, and about the best on offer are the Giardini Pubblici and their extension across to Sant'Elena (see the next section). In the gardens you'll find shaded benches, a few *giostre* (swings and other kids' rides) and a snack bar.

Also here are the pavilions of the **Biennale Internazionale d'Arte**. The various national pavilions of the Biennale, an arts fest held every two years from June to the end of the year, together form a kind of mini-compendium of 20th-century architectural thinking. Standing well away from the historic centre and thus uninhibited by concerns about clashing with it, the site's pavilions are the work of a veritable legion of architects. Carlo Scarpa contributed in one way or another from 1948 to 1972, continually updating the Italian Pavilion and building the Venezuelan one (1954). He also did the Biglietteria (ticket office) and entrance courtyard. Other interesting contributions are James Stirling's 1991 Padiglione del Libro (Book Pavilion), Gerrit Rietveld's Dutch Pavilion (1954), Josef Hoffman's Austrian Pavilion (1934) and Peter Cox's Australian Pavilion (1988).

Sant'Elena (Maps 2 & 8)

From the Biennale you can wander over the Rio dei Giardini to what is probably the quietest and leafiest residential corner of Venice. Housing construction began in 1925, before which there was little here but an abandoned pilgrims' hospice and the closed Chiesa di Sant'Elena. The arrival of riot police and armies of football supporters occasionally snap it out of its usual (and not unpleasant) torpor. The crowds make for the **Stadio Penzo** (Map 2) to see Venice, a mediocre 1st-division side, do battle so as not to end up in the 2nd division.

Just past the stadium is the humble **Chiesa di Sant'Elena** (Map 2). It's a small Gothic number that was abandoned in 1806 and reopened in 1928 when people started moving into the new residential district nearby.

Towards San Marco (Maps 7 & 8)

At this point the weary could get the No 42 or 52 circle line vaporetto from the Sant'Elena stop to San Zaccaria to continue this itinerary, or the No 1 and up the Grand Canal to do something else altogether.

Otherwise, it is a pleasant and leafy walk from the Chiesa di Sant'Elena through the Parco delle Rimembranze and then the Giardini Pubblici along the waterfront. If you do choose to amble, you will approach Venice almost as it should be done – by sea (that is, you are coming from the appropriate direction – it's just that you are on land rather than seaborne). The idea is a borrowed one: cheers Thomas Mann et al!

The waterside walkway west from Rio Ca' di Dio and on to the Palazzo Ducale in San Marco is known as the **Riva degli Schiavoni** (Map 7), a word for Slavs that referred to Dalmatian fishermen who, from medieval times, used to cast their nets around here. For centuries, vessels would dock here amid all the chaos you might expect from a busy harbour. Boat crews, waterfront merchants, nobles, gendarmes and crooks, dressed in all manner of garb reflecting the passing parade of Greeks, Turks, Slavs, Arabs, Africans and Europeans, all jostled about here. It is perhaps hard to imagine the sight of seemingly chaotic rows of galleys, galleons and, later on, sailing vessels competing for dock space or moored farther out in the Canale di San Marco. Or the confusion of rigging and containers of all sorts, the babel of languages, the clang and clatter of arms and cooking pots as locals or seafarers prepared impromptu meals for those just arrived. The assault on all the senses must have been quite something.

Today it remains busy, but the actors have changed. The galleons of yore have been replaced by ferries, the exotic crews and merchants by gondoliers and not-so-exotic tourists. Instead of impromptu food stalls and the smell of cooking meat, there are ice cream stands and tourist tat. The babble of languages remains as confusing as ever. And now some of the grand old mansions function as pricey hotels for the well-heeled out-of-towner.

One of Italy's greatest writers, Francesco Petrarca (Petrarch), for a time found lodgings at No 4175, east of Rio della Pietà.

Just at the point where we will turn inland, away from the lagoon, is the Chiesa di Santa Maria della Pietà (Map 7), simply known as **La Pietà**, where concerts are held regularly. Vivaldi was concert-master here in the early 18th century. Look for the ceiling fresco by Tiepolo.

San Giorgio dei Greci (Map 7)

A short walk north brings you to the rear side of the Chiesa di San Giorgio dei Greci. Walk around it to reach the main entrance alongside Rio dei Greci.

Here, Greek Orthodox refugees were allowed to raise a church in 1526, interesting for the richness of the Byzantine icons, iconostasis and other works inside. Attached to it is the **Museo di Dipinti Sacri Bizantini** of the Istituto Ellenico, where you can further explore the curiosities of Byzantine-era Orthodox religious art. The complex was closed at the time of writing.

Campo San Lorenzo (Map 7)

As you leave San Giorgio and cross the bridge to the west, take Fondamenta di San Lorenzo north. At the second bridge across the rio is Campo San Lorenzo, dominated by the rather shaky-looking brick facade of the church of the same name. It is an odd structure, divided down the middle to form a section for the general public and another for members of a Benedictine nunnery that has long since ceased to exist. The church is closed for restoration.

Campo Santa Maria Formosa & Around (Map 6)

This square is one of the most appealing in Venice, full of local life, eateries, benches where you can take the weight off your feet and some interesting buildings. There was a time when all sorts of popular festivals were played out here (chasing bulls around the square was one of the less sensible activities). Veronica Franco, one of the city's best-remembered courtesans, lived in a house on this campo. Poet, friend of Tintoretto and lover, however briefly, of France's King Henry III, Miss Franco was listed in the city's 16th-century guidebook to high-class escorts as: *Vero. Franco a Santa Mar. Formosa. Pieza so mare. Scudi 2.* The last bit is the base price for her services, which ranged from intelligent conversation to horizontal folk-dancing.

Perhaps there was always a little ribaldry in the air around here. The **Chiesa di Santa Maria Formosa** was rebuilt in 1492 by Mauro Cordussi on the site of a 7th-century church. The name stems from the legend behind its initial foundation. San Magno, bishop of Oderzo, is said to have had a vision of the Virgin Mary on this spot. Not just any old vision, however. In this instance she was *formosa* (beautiful, curvy). The inside was damaged when an Austrian bomb went off in 1916. Among the works of art on display is an altarpiece by Palma il Vecchio depicting St Barbara.

The church is part of the Chorus scheme (see the boxed text 'A Chorus Line' earlier in this chapter). It's open from 10 am to 5 pm Monday to Saturday and 1 to 5 pm on Sunday. Admission costs L3000.

Among the ageing mansions facing onto the square, **Palazzo Vitturi** is a good example of the Veneto-Byzantine style, while the buildings making up the **Palazzi Donà** are a mix of Gothic and late Gothic. While you're here, a further quick circuit suggests itself. Leave the square and head north-west. Don't cross the canal – veer right instead along Calle del Dose and then left along Calle Pindemonte. You end up in Campo Santa Marina (Map 4), faced by the 13th-century **Palazzo Dolfin Bollani** and the Lombard-style **Palazzo Loredan**. A side lane of the square leads you to the 15th-century **Palazzo Bragadin-Carabba**, restored by Sanmicheli.

Coming out of the square to the west, head south along Calle Carminati, which brings you into the Campo San Lio. A brief detour farther south down Calle della Fava brings you to the campo of the same name and the **Chiesa di Santa Maria della Fava**. It was begun by Gaspari and finished off in 1753 by Massari. Inside, the first painting on your right after you enter is Tiepolo's *Educazione della Vergine* (The Virgin's Education). Back outside, you can get a good view across Rio della Fava of the late

The Palazzo Ducale and the lion of St Mark, the emblem of Venice, dominate Piazzetta San Marco.

The courtyard of the Palazzo Ducale, the political heart of Venice for nine centuries

The Palazzo Ducale boasts works by Titian and Tintoretto.

Chiesa di SS Giovanni e Paolo

Tetrarchs, Basilica di San Marco

Synagogue in the Ghetto

The 15th-century Torre dell'Orologio clock on Piazza San Marco

Gothic **Palazzo Giustinian-Faccanon**, over in the Sestiere di San Marco.

Scurrying back to Campo San Lio, turn right (more or less east) down the busy Salizzada di San Lio. The street retains some intriguing examples of Byzantine housing. More interesting still, though, is **Calle del Paradiso**, which branches off it back in the direction of Campo Santa Maria Formosa. It is marked by the Gothic arch beneath which you enter this street, which gives you a pretty good idea of what a typical Gothic-period street in Venice looked like. On the ground floor were shops of various types. Jutting out above them on heavy timber barbicans are the upper storeys, which were offices and living quarters. At the end of the street is another arch, this one more elaborate. Known as the **Arco del Paradiso** (Heaven's Arch), it depicts the Virgin Mary and bears the standards of the families who financed it.

Palazzo Querini-Stampalia (Map 6)

Once back in Campo Santa Maria Formosa, walk around the church. Behind it, a private bridge leads you to this mansion. The outside shell dates from the first half of the 16th century. The last of this branch of the Querini ordained that the building should be home to a foundation of the same name, and it has been since the 1860s.

The inside of the mansion could not be more surprising. Carlo Scarpa was commissioned in the 1940s to design the entrance and garden, and again in 1959 to rethink the first floor (which houses the foundation's library). Scarpa decided to have some disciplined fun with shape and in the garden, in particular, took some inspiration from the Arab emphasis on geometrical patterns. It may or may not appeal, but it does make a refreshing change in one sense – there is very little that is 'modern' in Venice.

Of Floors & Walls

As you wander about the Palazzo Querini-Stampalia observe the floor. The smooth speckled surface, a classic *terrazzo alla Veneziana*, could almost be a mottled carpet if it weren't a little more solid than pile. In fact it's the result of combining finely fragmented marble chips with plaster and then laying this mixture down.

Why not straight marble floors? Virtually the entire city is built on foundations of timber pylons and has all the resulting problems of subsidence that you would expect. Movement is often greater than in more stable mainland environments. Great slabs of marble have no give – they would just crack open. This mixture, when hardened, has all the feel and solidity of marble, but greater elasticity. And when cracks do appear, all you need to do is mix up a batch of the marble-plaster goo, smooth it over and allow it to dry. You don't want it to dry *out*, though. At least once-yearly treatment with linseed oil is needed to keep it in good shape and to allow it to be polished up.

You will no doubt have noticed this type of floor in the Palazzo Ducale, Museo Correr and some other sites – you may even have it in your hotel room!

It is not so apparent in this building, but if you get to see inside other houses or manage to stay in a hotel or mansion of sufficient history, you will often see how much these floors undulate with time – a lot better than breaking up altogether.

While on the subject of home handyman issues, you may also have noticed that the classic Venetian colour is a reddish-burnt orange. Innumerable houses are 'painted' this way. Except it isn't really paint. A straight coat of red paint quickly fades and streaks with all the rain and humidity inevitable in the lagoon. Traditionally, the outside walls of houses, when painted, were coated in a mixture of paint and crushed up red bricks. Once applied and dry, it lasts much longer than standard wall paint.

On the 2nd floor is the **Museo della Fondazione Querini-Stampalia**. The core of the collection is made up of period furniture that mostly belonged to the family, portraits of some of the more illustrious members of the family and various family papers. The collection of paintings consists mostly of minor works, although there is an interesting *Presentazione di Gesù al Tempio* (Presentation of Jesus in the Temple) by Giovanni Bellini. The poor child looks like a long-suffering mummy, standing up improbably in his tightly wrapped swaddling clothes. And what's the guy on the right looking at? Well you, actually.

Just before you get to the Bellini is a small annexe of a large hall. It is given over to a long series of paintings by Gabriele Bella (1730–99) depicting *Scene di Vita Veneziana* (Scenes of Venetian Life). The style of painting is rather naive, if not downright childlike, but the series does provide an intriguing set of snapshots of life under the doges. It is a curious exercise to try to blend these images in your mind's eye with places you have seen to capture some idea of what Venice must have been like in the last decadent century of the Republic.

Another room towards the end of the permanent exhibition is devoted to works of Pietro Longhi. It also contains some good examples of traditional Venetian furniture, characteristic for its engraved and lacquered wood with painted floral motifs. Not a few hotels around town have adopted a watered-down version of the style to furnish their rooms.

The museum is open from 10 am to 1 pm and 3 to 6 pm Tuesday to Sunday (to 10 pm on Friday and Saturday in summer). Admission is a somewhat steep L12,000. On Friday and Saturday evenings in summer short concerts are put on at 5 and 8.30 pm. They are free to those visiting the museum.

Museo Diocesano d'Arte Sacra (Map 6)
From Palazzo Querini-Stampalia, our route winds south past the former **Chiesa di San Giovanni Novo** (now used occasionally as exhibition space) and eventually across the Rio del Vin to the Chiesa di San Zaccaria. A quick detour to the Museo Diocesano d'Arte Sacra, in the opposite direction, is worthwhile, especially for fans of Romanesque architecture.

Housed in a former Benedictine monastery dedicated to Sant'Apollonia, the museum has a fairly predictable collection of religious art. More interesting is the little Romanesque cloister you cross in order to get to the museum. It is a rare example of the genre in Venice. The museum is open daily except Sunday from 10.30 am to 12.30 pm. Admission is free (although a voluntary contribution is welcomed). The cloister is often open much longer hours.

The building next door was a church until 1906. It now houses various exhibition spaces.

Back on the main street, instead of turning left (west) for Piazza San Marco, head in the opposite direction down Salizzada San Provolo.

Chiesa di San Zaccaria (Map 7)
You'll know you've struck pay dirt when you pass beneath a Gothic arch depicting the Virgin Mary and Jesus, thought to have been crafted by a sculptor from Tuscany in around 1430.

Beyond it, you arrive in the Campo San Zaccaria. The Renaissance facade of the church before us is the handiwork of Antonio Gambello and Codussi. Gambello started off in a Gothic vein but was already influenced by Renaissance thinking. The lower part of the facade in marble is his work. When Codussi took over, he favoured white Istrian stone and the clean curves at the top that mark his take on the Renaissance.

Inside, the mix of styles could not be clearer. Against a backdrop of classic Gothic apses, the high cross vaulting of the main body of the church is a clear leap of faith into the Renaissance.

On the second altar to the left after you enter the church is Giovanni Bellini's *La Vergine in Trono col Bambino, un Angelo Suonatore e Santi* (The Virgin Enthroned with Jesus, an Angel Musician & Saints). You cannot miss it. It exudes a light and freshness that the surrounding paintings seem deliberately to lack.

For L2000 you can enter the Cappella di Sant'Atanasio off to the right. It holds some works by Tintoretto and Tiepolo, as well as some magnificently crafted choir stalls. You then pass through another chapel to reach the Cappella di San Tarasion (also called Cappella d'Oro) in the apse. Its vaults are covered in frescoes and the walls are decorated with Gothic polyptyches. You can wander downstairs to the Romanesque crypt, left over from an earlier church on the site.

To Piazzetta San Marco (Map 6)

When you exit the church, head south off the square and you emerge through a sotoportego onto Riva degli Schiavoni again, not far from where we left it earlier.

Turn right (west) to cross the Ponte del Vin; the building immediately on the right is the Palazzo Dandolo, better known to most of us as the **Danieli**, one of the city's most prestigious hotels. For a curious story about the origins of the hideous Danieli extension on the other side of Calle delle Rasse, see the boxed text 'A Dogey Death' in the Places to Stay chapter.

Calle delle Rasse takes its name from the word *rascia* or *rassa*, a rough woollen material sold along this street for use as protective covers for gondolas. The material came from what is now Serbia, known to the Venetians centuries ago as Rascia. The next street, Calle degli Albanesi, was so named because an Albanian community lived on and around it. Interesting choice of address when you consider that the prisons line its western side.

Walking past the prisons, which you may have visited while touring the Palazzo Ducale (see the earlier Sestiere di San Marco section), we arrive at the bridge that marks the boundary between the sestieri of San Marco and Castello. Look north at the unassuming closed passage linking the Palazzo Ducale with the prisons. Yes folks, this is it, the bridge you've all been waiting for: the **Ponte dei Sospiri**, or Bridge of Sighs. Now you can breath a sigh of relief that you have seen it. Some people walk

away inconsolably despondent that the bridge in no way corresponds to all their romantic imaginings.

The pink and white walls of the Palazzo Ducale lead us back to the Piazzetta San Marco, the gateway to Venice, where we finally complete our long and tortuous circuit of the lagoon city that for more than 1000 years was the Most Serene Republic. Perhaps now is an opportune moment to again gaze out over the Bacino di San Marco and let your by now well-primed imagination do a little wandering.

On the other hand, maybe it's time for a drink. Why not loosen the old purse strings and pop across to Harry's Bar for a soothing cocktail?

AROUND THE LAGOON

Venice goes beyond the six sestieri. Indeed, it did not even begin on the islands that constitute them. Although the bulk of the city's visitors don't bother, it is a more than worthwhile exercise to get out to at least some of the islands and even onto the mainland. The remainder of this chapter and the Excursions chapter towards the end of the book should set you on your way.

Giudecca (Maps 9 & 10)

Originally known as *spina longa* (long fishbone) because of its shape, Giudecca's present name probably derives from the word Zudega (from *giudicato* – the judged), applied to rebellious nobles banished from Venice proper. There are variations on this story – the most likely seems to be that as early as the 9th century, families that had been exiled earlier (and one assumes unjustly) were given land on Giudecca by way of compensation. Until that time, the only inhabitants had been a handful of fishermen and their families.

By the 16th century, the island had been extended through land reclamation to reach something approaching its present form. Merchants set up warehouses and a flourishing local commercial life made Giudecca a prime piece of real estate. Elite families (such as the Dandolos, Mocenigos and Vendramins) bought up land to build their homes-away-from-home facing Venice to the north and ending in luxuriant gardens looking south to the open lagoon. Several religious orders also established convents and monasteries here.

With the fall of the Republic in 1797, everything changed. The noble families gradually slipped away as their fortunes declined. The religious orders were suppressed and the convents closed. The face of the island gradually changed through the 19th century. Replacing the pleasure domes and religious retreats came prisons, barracks and factories, and, with the latter, working-class housing grids. Descendants of the workers who powered the factories remain in the modest low-level housing, but most of the factories have long been closed down.

Giudecca is a strangely melancholy place. A few boatyards keep busy with repair work, while a handful of shops and eateries survive on a modest local trade and the few tourists who stop long enough to want to eat here. The women's prison (until 1857 it had been a convent for reformed prostitutes) is still in operation. Mild building activity suggests that perhaps more life will some day come to Giudecca.

Chiesa del Redentore (Map 10) With the passing of the plague in 1577, the Senato commissioned Palladio to design a church of thanksgiving. The following year the doge, members of the Senato and a host of citizens made the first pilgrimage of thanksgiving, crossing from Zattere on a pontoon bridge of boats and rafts.

Work on this magnificent edifice was completed under Antonio da Ponte (better known for his Ponte di Rialto) in 1592. The long church was designed to accommodate the large numbers of pilgrims who, from 1578 on, made the annual excursion. Even now, on the third Saturday in July the pilgrimage takes place and it remains one of the most important events on Venice's calendar.

Inside are a few works by Tintoretto, Veronese and Vivarini, but it is the powerful facade that most inspires observers. Indeed, although it is uncertain why the site was chosen, there is no doubt that its open

position makes the church easy to observe and admire from just about anywhere on the Fondamenta Zattere across the Canale della Giudecca. The simple cleanness of the design reminds one, if on a considerably grander scale, of the Venetian villas on the mainland (see the Excursions chapter). The church was closed at the time of writing.

Chiesa delle Zitelle (Map 10) Also designed by Palladio in the late 16th century, the Chiesa di Santa Maria della Presentazione, known as the Zitelle, was conceived as a church and hospice for poor young women (*zitelle* means 'old maids', which is presumably what many of these unfortunates remained). It is now used as a conference centre.

Chiesa di Sant'Eufemia (Map 9) A simple Veneto-Byzantine structure of the 11th century, the church's main portico was actually added in the 18th and 19th centuries. Down Fondamenta Rio Sant'Eufemia are the one-time church and convent of **SS Cosma e Damiano**. They were turned into a factory and the bell tower into a smokestack!

Molino Stucky (Map 9) The striking hulk of the best-known factory complex on the island, the Molino Stucky, was built in the late 19th century. The windowless brick structure looks for all the world like a cathedral to industry and is hard to miss when looking across to Giudecca from the western end of the Zattere. It was shut in 1954 and has long sat in dignified silence. The buildings have been saved from the wrecking ball and are being restored in a project destined to convert them into a complex of 120 apartments with a hotel and a congress centre.

San Giorgio Maggiore (Map 10)

On the island of the same name, Palladio's **Chiesa di San Giorgio Maggiore** has one of the most prominent positions in Venice and, although it inspired mixed reactions among the architect's contemporaries, it had a significant influence on Renaissance architecture. Built between 1565 and 1580, it is possibly Palladio's most imposing structure in Venice. The facade, although not erected until the following century, is believed to conform with Palladio's wishes. The massive columns on high plinths, crowning tympanum and statues contain an element of sculptural chiaroscuro, if such a term is permissible, casting strong shadows and reinforcing the impression of strength. Indeed, facing the Bacino di San Marco and the heart of Venice, its effect is deliberately theatrical.

Inside, the sculptural decoration is sparse, the open space regimented by powerful clusters of columns and covered by luminous vaults.

San Giorgio Maggiore's art treasures include works by Tintoretto: an *Ultima Cena* (Last Supper) and the *Raccolta della Manna* (Shower of Manna) on the walls of the high altar, and a *Deposizione* (Deposition) in the Cappella dei Morti. Take the lift to the top of the 60m-high bell tower for an extraordinary view (L3000).

Opening hours are from 9.30 am to 1 pm and 2.30 to 5 pm daily (to 10.30 am only on Sunday and holidays).

Behind the church extend the grounds of the former monastery. Established as long ago as the 10th century by the Benedictines, it was rebuilt in the 13th century and then restructured and expanded in a series of projects that spanned the 16th century, finishing with the library built by Longhena in the 1640s. Unfortunately, little or none of this can be seen, as the Fondazione Cini bought it in 1951 (saving it from a slow death by neglect, it should be added). The foundation operates various scholarly centres here. The open-air Teatro Verdi, at the bottom end of the islet, has been off limits for many years.

San Michele (Map 2)

The city's cemetery was established on Isola di San Michele under Napoleon (even the Venetians can't complain that the diminutive Corsican did nothing for them) and is maintained by the Franciscans. The **Chiesa di San Michele in Isola**, begun by Codussi in 1469, was among the city's first Renaissance buildings. Among those pushing up daisies here are Ezra Pound, Sergei Diaghilev and Igor Stravinsky.

The grave of the famous Russian ballet dancer Sergei Diaghilev (1872–1929) is well tended.

Vaporetto lines 12 and 13 from Fondamente Nuove stop here, as do the circle line vaporetto Nos 41 and 42.

Murano (Map 11)

The people of Venice have been making crystal and glass (the difference between the two lies in the amount of lead used) since as early as the 10th century, when the secrets of the art were brought back from the East by merchants. The bulk of the industry was moved to the island of Murano in 1291 because of the danger of fire posed by the glass-working furnaces.

Venice had a virtual monopoly on the production of what is now known as Murano glass and the methods of the craft were such a well-guarded secret that it was considered treason for a glass-worker to leave the city.

The incredibly elaborate pieces produced by the artisans can range from the beautiful to the grotesque – but, as the Italians would say, *i gusti son gusti* (each to his own). Watching the glass-workers in action in shops and factories around the island is certainly interesting.

The **Museo Vetrario** contains some exquisite pieces and is open daily except Wednesday from 10 am to 5 pm. Admission costs L8000, or you can buy one of the combined tickets allowing you to visit a number of museums – see Special Tickets at the start of this chapter. Across Canale di

San Donato is one of the few private mansions of any note on the island, the 16th-century **Palazzo Trevisan**.

The nearby **Chiesa dei SS Maria e Donato** is a fascinating example of Veneto-Byzantine architecture. Looking at the apse, however, it is impossible not to see Romanesque influences too. Founded in the 7th century and rebuilt 500 years later, the church was originally dedicated to the Virgin Mary. It was rededicated to St Donato after his bones were brought here from Cephalonia, along with those of a dragon he had supposedly killed (four of the 'dragon' bones are hung behind the altar). The church's magnificent mosaic pavement (a very Byzantine touch) was laid in the 12th century, and the impressive mosaic of the Virgin Mary in the apse dates from the same period.

Palazzo da Mula, just over the only bridge to span the Canal Grande di Murano, is sometimes host to exhibitions. More often than not the subject is ... glass.

The island can be reached on vaporetto Nos 12, 13 or 42 (41 the other way) from Fondamente Nuove (No 42 also leaves from San Zaccaria and Piazzale Roma). No 62 (61 the other way) also chugs there from Piazzale Roma.

Burano (Map 12)
Famous for its lace industry, Burano is a pretty fishing village, its streets and canals lined with bright, pastel-coloured houses. They say the bonbon colours have their origins in the fishermen's desire to be able to see their own houses when heading home from a day at sea. Regardless of the reasons, the bright, gay colours are engaging. Given the island's distance from Venice (around 40 minutes by ferry) you really do get the feeling of having arrived somewhere only fleetingly touched by La Serenissima.

If you go to the effort of coming (most people couple the excursion with stops in Murano and Torcello), try to give yourself time to wander into the quietest corners and shady parks. Walk over the wooden bridge to neighbouring **Mazzorbo**, a larger island with little more than a few houses, a couple of *trattorie* and open green space. A snooze

in the grass takes you light years away from the marvels of Venice and somehow puts them into a harmonious perspective.

The **Museo del Merletto di Burano** is a lace-making museum open daily except Tuesday from 9 am to 5 pm (ticket window shut from 3.30 pm). Admission costs L8000, or you can buy one of the combined tickets allowing you to visit a number of museums – see Special Tickets at the start of this chapter. If you plan to buy lace on the island, choose with care and discretion, as these days much of the cheaper stuff is imported from Asia (see also the Shopping chapter). That said, you can still occasionally see women working away at lace-making in the shade of their homes and in the parks.

Take vaporetto No 12 from Fondamente Nuove (Cannaregio). Note that this ferry stops at Murano, San Michele, Mazzorbo, Burano and Torcello. That same ferry on the way back doesn't generally stop at Burano, but it does call in at Mazzorbo (from where you can walk to Burano). This priceless piece of information is for those who want to go to Torcello first and then Burano.

Torcello (Map 12)
This delightful little island, with its overgrown main square and sparse, scruffy-looking buildings and monuments, was at its peak from the mid-7th century to the 13th century, when it was the seat of the bishop of Altinum and home to some 20,000 people. Rivalry with Venice and a succession of malaria epidemics systematically reduced the island's splendour and population. Today, fewer than 80 people call Torcello home.

When you get off the vaporetto, you have little choice but to follow the path along the canal that leads to the heart of the island in a leisurely 10 minutes. Around the central square is huddled all that remains of old Torcello – the lasting homes of the clergy and the island's secular rulers.

To get here take vaporetto No 12 from Fondamente Nuove (via Murano and Burano; see the previous Burano section for details).

Cattedrale di Santa Maria Assunta
The island's Veneto-Byzantine cathedral

was founded in the 7th century and was Venice's first. Visitors to Venice tend to forget that the first important settlement in the lagoon was right here in Torcello. In its now abandoned state the island gives us some idea of how things must have looked at the outset of settlement on the other islands too.

What you see of Santa Maria Assunta today dates from the first expansion of the church in 824 and rebuilding in 1008. It is therefore about the oldest Venetian monument to have remained relatively untampered with. This we probably owe to the fact that by 1008 the settlement was already well on the road to decline.

The three apses (the central one dates back to the original 7th-century structure) could be Romanesque and a certain intermarriage of building styles seems likely. A jewel of simple, early-medieval architecture, the interior is still more fascinating for its magnificent Byzantine mosaics.

On the western wall of the cathedral is a vast mosaic depicting the Last Judgement. Hell (lower right side) doesn't look any fun at all. Late-20th-century sceptics may grin, but such images probably inspired sheer terror in the average resident of Torcello back in the 12th and 13th centuries when the mosaics were put together.

The greatest treasure is the mosaic of the Madonna in the half-dome of the central apse. Starkly set on a pure gold background, the figure is one of the most stunning works of Byzantine art you will see in Italy. And if you needed more confirmation of the church's Eastern influences, have a look at the iconostasis set well before the altar.

The cathedral is open daily from 10 am to 5.30 pm. Admission costs L5000, which includes an informative audio tape. You can also climb the bell tower (L3000).

Around Santa Maria Assunta The adjacent tiny **Chiesa di Santa Fosca** was founded in the 11th century to house the body of Santa Fosca. Across the square, in the Palazzo del Consiglio, is the **Museo di Torcello**, which tells the history of the island. Part of the collection is in the adjacent **Palazzo dell'Archivio**. Both buildings date

from the 13th centur the nerve centre of cello. The museur 12.30 pm and 2 tc Admission costs L30

The rough-hewn stone known as the **Sedia di Attila** (Att Why is anyone's guess and even the us which the seat was put is a bit of a mystery. It is surmised that magistrates sat here to pass judgement.

Lido di Venezia (Maps 13 & 14)

The main draw here is the beach, but the water ain't great and the public areas of the waterfront can be less than attractive. You pay a small fortune (between L20,000 and L80,000) to rent a chair, umbrella and changing cabin in the more easily accessible and cleaner areas of the beach. This said, it is not entirely clear what, if anything, is done if you choose to plonk your towel close to the water's edge (a town ordinance technically forbids obstruction of the open beach area between the rows of cabins and the water).

The Lido forms a land barrier between the lagoon and the Adriatic Sea. For centuries, the doges trekked out here to fulfil Venice's Marriage to the Sea ceremony by dropping a ring into the shallows, celebrating the city's close relationship with the sea. This was done just off the **Chiesa di San Nicolò**, at the northern end of the island. After the ceremony, everyone headed to the church to hear Mass. The church today is a relatively uninteresting 17th-century structure. Nearby was one of the city's defensive forts.

The Lido became a fashionable seaside resort at the end of the 19th century and its more glorious days are depicted in Thomas Mann's novel *Der Tod in Venedig* (Death in Venice). A wander around the streets between the Adriatic and the vaporetto stop will turn up occasional Art Nouveau (what the Italians refer to as 'Liberty style') and even Art Deco villas. Today the island is fairly laid back for most of the year, although it can get crowded on summer weekends with local and foreign sun-seekers. The beaches are better on the northern coast of

land (Cavallino, Jesolo and farther
the coast as far as Bibione), but the
is easier to reach. The place fills up
the Mostra del Cinema di Venezia in
August–September. The cinema-fest is hosted in the snappy **Palazzo della Mostra del
Cinema** and the ugly **casino** does a brisk
summer business (both Map 13).

On the lagoon side you can see the
nearby Isola di San Lazzaro degli Armeni
(see the following Minor Islands section).
Closer to the shore is the former leper
colony of **Lazzaretto Vecchio** (Map 13).

Bus B from Gran Viale Santa Maria
Elisabetta or your bicycle will take you to
Malamocco, in the south of the island, one
of the oldest settlements in the lagoon.
Arranged across a chain of squares and
some canals, the old heart of this town
seems more reminiscent of Venice than the
turn-of-the-century seaside conceits at the
northern end of the island.

You can reach the Lido by vaporetto Nos
1, 6, 14, 51, 52, 61, 62 and 82 and the
vehicle ferry from Tronchetto (No 17). The
first thing you should do is hire a bicycle at
the hire place just off Gran Viale Santa Maria
Elisabetta, a couple of minutes from the main
vaporetto stop (Map 14). It costs L15,000 a
day and will allow you to explore the whole
island, as well as (for the energetic) Pellestrina and even Chioggia, to the south.

Pellestrina

Separated from the southern tip of the Lido
by the Porto di Malamocco, one of the three
sea gates between the Adriatic and the lagoon, Pellestrina is shaped like an 11km-
long razor blade.

Small villages of farmers and fishing
families are spread out along the island,
protected on the seaward side by the
Murazzi, a remarkable feat of 18th-century
engineering, although they don't look much
to the modern eye. These sea walls, designed
to keep in check the power of the sea over
the lagoon, once extended without interruption some 20km from the southern tip of
Pellestrina to a point well over halfway up
the coast of the Lido. The Pellestrina stretch
and part of the Lido wall remain. They were

heavily damaged during the 1966 floods
and partially restored in the 1970s. Long
stretches of sparsely populated grey sand
beaches separate the Murazzi from the sea
on calm days.

You get to Pellestrina using the No 11
Lido-Chioggia bus-and-ferry line. If you've
hired a bicycle you can take it across on the
ferry for L2000 (plus the passenger fare of
L6000 if you haven't got a day ticket).

Minor Islands
San Francesco del Deserto (Map 1)
The Franciscans built themselves a monastery (☎ 041 528 68 63) on this island about
1km south of Burano to keep away from it
all. The island is otherwise deserted and it
makes an enchanting detour while exploring the islands of the lagoon. Legend has it
that Francis of Assisi himself landed here,
seeking shelter after a journey to Palestine
in 1220. The Franciscans left in 1420, as
conditions were difficult and malaria was
rampant. Pope Pius II then granted the island to another order, the Minori Osser-
vanti. Except for an interruption under
Napoleon, they have remained ever since.

The monastery opens its doors to visitors
daily from 9 to 11 am and 3 to 5 pm. The
only way there is to hire a private boat or
taxi from Burano. Ask around along the
canal behind the Chiesa di San Martino.

Le Vignole & Sant'Erasmo (Map 1) To-
gether these islands almost equal Venice
in size, but any comparison ends there.
Sparsely inhabited, they offer nothing in
terms of sights, but for those curious
enough to get a glimpse of little-known
sides of Venice and its lagoon, they are not
without interest. Both are largely rural, and
covered in fields and groves.

The south-western part of Le Vignole is
owned by the military and contains the best
preserved of a scattering of old forts, the
Forte Sant'Andrea. It can only be seen from
the sea.

Like Le Vignole, Sant'Erasmo has never
been densely inhabited. About 1000 people
are resident on the island, many around the
Chiesa ferry stop. Historically, it has always

been agricultural, although the Roman chronicler Martial records the presence of holiday villas belonging to the well-to-do of the now disappeared mainland centre of Altino. If you can get your hands on a hire bicycle, a spin among the fields takes you about as far from the atmosphere of Venice as is possible.

The No 13 ferry runs to Le Vignole and Sant'Erasmo from Fondamente Nuove and Murano (Faro stop).

San Clemente, San Servolo and San Lazzaro degli Armeni (Map 1)

The **Isola di San Clemente** (vaporetto No 10 from San Zaccaria) was once the site of a hospice for pilgrims returning from the Middle East. Later, a convent was built and from 1522 it was a quarantine station for people thought to be infected with contagious diseases (along with the Lazzaretto Vecchio off the Lido). The plague that devastated Venice in 1630 was blamed by some on a carpenter who worked on San Clemente, became infected and brought the disease over to the city. The Austrians turned the building into a mental hospital for women and until recently it still operated in part as a psychiatric hospital.

The **Isola di San Servolo** (vaporetto Nos 10 and 20 from San Zaccaria) shared these mental hospital functions from the 18th century until 1978. From the 7th to the 17th centuries Benedictine monks had a monastery here, bits of which still remain in the former hospital. Now the island is home to various cultural institutions.

Of the islets scattered about south of Venice, the most important is the **Isola di San Lazzaro degli Armeni** (vaporetto Nos 10 and 20 from San Zaccaria). In 1717 the Armenian order of the Mechitarist fathers was granted use of the island, which centuries before had been a leper colony. The Mechitarists founded a monastery that became an important centre of learning, which it remains to this day. Visitors can see the 18th-century refectory, church, library, museum and *pinacoteca* (art gallery). A mix of Venetian and Armenian art is on show, along with a room dedicated to Lord Byron, who frequently stayed on the island. Considerable damage was done to the complex by fire in 1975. At the time of writing it was closed for restoration. When open, you can visit daily (by guided tour) from 3 to 5 pm only.

Poveglia Lying less than 1km off Malamocco, at the southern end of the Lido, this long-abandoned island could in the coming years be brought back to life with an original plan by the CTS. It hopes to have a youth tourism centre established on the island in 2001, with hostels, activities and a communications centre to allow cultural exchanges between young people in Venice and elsewhere in the world. The project seems a decent alternative to the only other plan on the table until mid-1999 – to put the island up for sale to the first comer.

Chioggia

The most important town in the Comune di Venezia after Venice itself, Chioggia lies at the southern end of the lagoon.

Invaded and destroyed by the Venetian Republic's maritime rival, Genoa, in the late 14th century, the medieval core of modern Chioggia is a crumbly but not uninteresting counterpoint to its more illustrious patron to the north. In no way city like Murano or Burano, Chioggia is a firmly practical town, its big sea-fishing fleet everywhere in evidence.

In May 1999 a couple of fishermen became victims of the NATO assault on Kosovo. One of the six Adriatic zones set aside for warplanes in difficulty to unload bombs was in line with Chioggia. Fishing trawlers 'caught' hundreds of bombs in their nets and in one incident two fishermen were injured in an explosion. NATO at first claimed the bomb was a WWII relic, but later sent in minesweepers to clean the area up and mollify the irate seamen.

Information The APT office (☎ 041 554 04 66) is on the waterfront towards the northern end of Sottomarina. In summer it's open from 8.30 am to 7.15 pm Monday to Saturday, and from 9 am to noon and

3 to 6 pm on Sunday and holidays. Hours are reduced in winter.

Things to See & Do On the assumption you come down via the Lido and Pellestrina – by far the most enchanting way to arrive – then you are at the northern end of Main St Chioggia as soon as you set foot on dry land.

A brisk walk down this cobblestoned and largely pedestrianised thoroughfare, Corso del Popolo, and you are in the heart of old Chioggia. It is in fact an island and transferred here from its original position in what is today Sottomarina, on the coast, after the Genoese siege of 1379–80. The reasoning was simple enough. Just as water was Venice's best defence, so it would be for Chioggia. People only began to populate the Sottomarina area again three centuries later.

Through the middle of the island runs the ever-so-Venetian Canale della Vena, complete with little bridges. On either side it is protected by the Canale Lombardo and Canale di San Domenico. Beyond the latter (after crossing another narrow islet), the Ponte Translagunare bridges the lagoon to link Chioggia with Sottomarina and thus the Adriatic beaches.

As soon as you get off the boat, head left down Calle della Santa Croce to the **Chiesa di San Domenico**, whose main claim to fame is the painting of *San Paolo*, said to be Vittore Carpaccio's last known work.

Back on Corso del Popolo, you can walk the length of it down to the **Cattedrale**. Rebuilt in the 17th century to a design by Longhena, about all that remains of the earlier structure is the Campanile (bell tower), raised in 1350.

More interesting than the monuments is simply pottering about, ducking down the alleys that branch off like ribs to the east and west from the spinal cord of Corso del Popolo. The fish market (*mercato ittico*), alongside Canale di San Domenico where the Ponte Translagunare reaches into Chioggia, is an eye-opener if you can get there at about 6 am (closed Sunday and Monday mornings).

If you want a swim, the **beaches** at Sottomarina are pretty clean, although the water can be murky. It's a typical seaside scene, with cheap hotels, bouncy castles for kids, snack bars, tat and even the odd tacky disco.

Getting There & Away If your time is limited in Venice, you can live without seeing Chioggia – the trip can take about two hours each way.

Bus No 11 leaves from Gran Viale Santa Maria Elisabetta, outside the tourist office on the Lido; it boards the car ferry at Alberoni and then connects with a steamer at Pellestrina that will take you to Chioggia. Or you can catch a bus from Piazzale Roma.

Once you're in the town, city bus Nos 1, 2, 6 and 7 connect Chioggia with Sottomarina (a 15-minute walk), the town's beach.

ACTIVITIES
Swimming
If you feel the need to do a few laps rather than wallow in the Adriatic, try the Piscina Comunale di Sacca Fisola (Map 2; ☎ 041 528 54 30), on Sacca Fisola, west of Giudecca. The hours are limited and complicated and it's closed in July and August. A swim costs L7500. Another pool, with even tighter hours, is the Piscina Comunale di Sant'Alvise (Map 2; ☎ 041 71 35 67), Campo Sant'Alvise, Cannaregio 3161. It's closed from mid-July to mid-September.

Jogging
If you can't live without a run, the best place to do it is around the Giardini Pubblici and Isola di Sant'Elena (Castello).

COURSES
Study Visas
Non-EU citizens who want to study at a university or language school in Italy must have a study visa. These visas can be obtained from your nearest Italian embassy or consulate. You will normally require confirmation of your enrolment and payment of fees, as well as proof of adequate funds to support yourself before a visa is issued. The visa will then cover only the period of the enrolment. This type of visa is renewable

within Italy but, again, only with confirmation of ongoing enrolment and proof that you are able to support yourself – bank statements are preferred.

Language Courses

The Istituto Italiano di Cultura (IIC; Italian Cultural Institute), a government-sponsored organisation aimed at promoting Italian culture and language, is a good place to research courses in Italy. It has branches all over the world, including Australia (Sydney), Canada (Montreal), the UK (London) and the USA (Los Angeles, New York and Washington).

The Società Dante Alighieri (Map 7; ☎ 041 528 91 27), Palazzo Zorzi, Castello 3405, offers intensive and longer-term Italian-language courses between September and June. Month-long courses start at around L350,000.

The Istituto Zambler (Map 5; ☎ 041 522 43 31, fax 041 528 56 28), on Campo Santa Margherita, Dorsoduro 3116/a, offers language and one- to two-week cooking courses. It also does a course in Venetian history and art, involving 12 guided tours of the city. Check out their Web site at www .virtualvenice.net/zambler.

Other Courses

InformaGiovani (see Tourist Offices in the Facts for the Visitor chapter) can provide some ideas on the kinds of course available in Venice.

Fondazione Cini (Map 10; ☎ 041 528 99 00), Isola di San Giorgio Maggiore, organises seminars on subjects relating to the city, in particular music and art.

Università Internazionale dell'Arte (Map 10; ☎ 041 528 70 90, email uiave@tim.it), Calle Michelangelo 54, Giudecca, 30033 Venice, runs full courses on art. Foreigners are welcome. For more information write or email.

Places to Stay

It will come as no great surprise to hear that Venice is an expensive place to stay, in spite of the huge choice of accommodation. Even in the depths of the low season, you're unlikely to pay less than L65,000/95,000 for a single/double without private bathroom. In the high season, only a handful of hotels offer such prices. Expect to pay from L150,000 upwards for a halfway decent budget double with bathroom (which generally means shower, washbasin and toilet).

Lone travellers are particularly penalised. Most hotels have few, if any, single rooms. When they do, such rooms are usually rather poky. One upset tourist complained of having found herself shoved into a hastily reconverted storage room (the hotel concerned is not in this guide). You will generally be offered a double at two-thirds to three-quarters of the price two people would pay.

Many places offer triple, quad and even quintuple rates. What this usually means is extra beds in a fairly spacious double. Still, if you are in a group, it works out more economically. Most hotel proprietors pad out the bill by including a compulsory breakfast in the price. The (in)famous Continental breakfast in these cases generally consists of a lavishly laid out stale bread roll, accompanied by little packets of butter and jam and a pot of weak instant coffee. If you have the cash, you may as well view this as an optional arrangement and get a proper cup of coffee in a bar.

Hotels go by various names. An *albergo* is a hotel. A *pensione* or *locanda* is generally a smaller, simpler, family-run establishment, although frequently there is little to distinguish them from lower-end hotels.

Budget travellers have the choice of the youth hostel on Giudecca or a handful of other dormitory-style possibilities, some of them religious institutions. They are mostly open in summer only.

Most of the top hotels are around San Marco and along the Grand Canal, but it is still possible to find 'bargains' (the concept is, of course, relative) tucked away in tiny streets and on side canals in the heart of the city. There are lots of hotels near the train station, but it is a good 30-minute walk from here to San Marco. The Dorsoduro area is quiet and relatively free of tourists.

Inflation continually sends prices up, but in Venice more than elsewhere hotel rates vary wildly for a range of other reasons. Some hotels have the same prices year-round, while others drop them when things are slow (rare). 'Low season' for the average Venetian hotelier means November, early December and January. That's it. Some of the more expensive hotels operate further price differentials: weekend rates can be higher than weekday rates and rooms with views (especially of the Grand Canal) are generally more expensive than others. If you are there in the low season and/or staying several days, it never hurts to ask for a discount before simply agreeing to a room price. Of course, in busy periods the only reaction you're likely to get is a pitying smile.

The prices that follow should be regarded as a guide and are high season (which at most places is pretty much year round anyway).

If things are looking tight, you could consider using Padua as a base (it's only 37km, or 30 minutes on most trains, away), perhaps for a day or two while you get oriented in Venice, and so give yourself time to find and book a place that suits.

Seasons & Reservations

It is advisable to book in advance year round in Venice, particularly for Christmas, Easter and Carnevale, in May and September and for weekends. Remember that, unless you pay a deposit, many smaller hotels won't feel obliged to hold a room for you all day unless you call to confirm on the day. Some hoteliers have been known to overbook in the way airlines do. If you haven't sent a fax with confirmation and/or made some form of deposit payment, you risk losing the room if you turn up late in the evening.

The Associazione Veneziana Albergatori (☎ 041 71 50 16, 041 71 52 88, fax 041 523 49 41) has offices at Santa Lucia train station, in Piazzale Roma and at the Tronchetto car park, where staff can book you a room in a wide range of hotels. You pay a booking fee, ranging from L1000 at the train station to L4000 at Piazzale Roma. The train station branch is the main one, open daily from 8 am to 10 pm in summer (understood as Easter to the end of October). It closes one hour earlier in winter. They also have 'last-minute' booking numbers: from within Italy the number is ☎ 800-843 006 toll free; from abroad dial ☎ 041 522 22 64.

The Consorzio Alberghi della Terraferma Veneziana (☎ 041 93 01 33, fax 041 93 15 70) is a separate organisation based in Mestre train station (platform 1). If you arrive in Mestre and are worried Venice may be full, these people can put you in a hotel in Mestre – be warned, though, that they have been known to be a little less than frank about the situation in Venice. They have about 40 Mestre hotels on their books. The booking fee here is L3000 and the office is open from 8.30 am to 8.10 pm Monday to Saturday.

PLACES TO STAY – BUDGET

You have already been warned. Cheap options are close to non-existent. Apart from camping, hostels and other dorm possibilities, only a handful of places charge 'low' rates. We have included places running up to as much as L200,000 or so for a double with toilet and shower/bath in this category. That may sound absurd, but wait until you see the prices for mid-range and top-end digs!

Camping

There are numerous camp sites, many with bungalows, on the Litorale del Cavallino, the coast along the Adriatic Sea, north-east of the city. You can also stay at one of several along the rather tacky beach at Sottomarina, Chioggia. Neither of these options puts you very close to Venice. If you want to camp or park your trailer a little nearer to the city, there are several possibilities. None are truly great, but some are OK. The tourist office in Piazza San Marco has a full list.

In all cases you will be paying roughly L10,000 per person and L20,000 per car and tent space. Add the inconvenience of getting to and from Venice and you may find this is not really such a hot option.

You could try the **Marina di Venezia** (☎ 041 530 09 55, fax 041 96 60 36, Via Montello 6), at Punta Sabbioni (Map 1), which is open from late April to the end of September. It has just about everything, from a private beach through to a shop, cinema and kiddies' playground. It even has a Web site at www.cavallino.net/marinave. You can get the No 12 vaporetto to Fondamente Nuove (Cannaregio) via Burano and Murano or the No 14 to San Zaccaria via the Lido.

If you do want to stay closer to Venice, **Serenissima** (Map 1; ☎ 041 92 02 86, fax 041 92 02 86, Padana 334/a, Località Oriago) is possibly the best bet. Set in a fairly leafy locale on the Venice–Padua bus route (No 53 from Piazzale Roma), the camp site has a shop, restaurant, laundry facilities and table tennis. It's open from mid-April to mid-November.

The good thing about **Campeggio Fusina** (Map 1; ☎ 041 547 00 55, fax 041 547 00 50, Via Moranzani 79, Località Fusina), apart from the fact that it's open year round, is that you can get the LineaFusina vaporetto (L8000 one way, L15,000 return, L35,000 for a three-day ticket for all vaporetti) straight into Venice (Zattere).

Hostels

The Hostelling International (HI) **Ostello Venezia** (Map 10; ☎ 041 523 82 11, fax 041 523 56 89, Fondamenta delle Zitelle 86) is on Giudecca. It's open to members only, although you can buy a card there (see Documents in the Facts for the Visitor chapter). B&B costs L25,000 and evening meals are available for L14,000. Take vaporetto No 41, 42 or 82 from the train station or Piazzale Roma to Zitelle. The hostel is open from 7 to 9.30 am and 1.30 pm to midnight. It is on HI's computerised International Booking Network (IBN).

Nearby, the **Istituto Canossiano** (Map 9; ☎/fax 041 522 21 57, Fondamenta di Ponte Piccolo 428) has beds for women only from

L21,000 a night. Take vaporetto No 41, 42 or 82 to Sant'Eufemia on Giudecca.

Foresteria Valdese (Map 4; ☎/fax 041 528 67 97, Castello 5150) is in an old mansion near Campo Santa Maria Formosa (Map 6). Head east from the square on Calle Lunga, cross the small bridge and the Foresteria is in front of you. It has a couple of dorms with beds for L30,000 per night, breakfast included. Doubles cost from L84,000 to L120,000, depending on the room and whether or not it has a bathroom. Book well ahead.

Domus Civica (Map 5; ☎ 041 72 11 03, fax 041 522 71 39, Calle Campazze 3082) is open from mid-June to early September and charges L45,000 for student-dorm-style beds. Doubles cost L80,000.

Hotels & Pensioni

Cannaregio There is plenty to choose from here, with many hotels just a stone's throw from the train station.

About the cheapest place in this *sestiere* is *Archies (Map 3; Rio Terrà del Cristo 1814/b)*. They don't like to give out their phone number, which is OK because they probably won't take phone bookings anyway. Very basic singles/doubles/triples cost L50,000/66,000/75,000. A bed in a dorm costs about L20,000. Run by a Chinese family (with ads up for cheap Chinese food around town), it's a crumbling place, reminiscent of dives on the overland trails in Asia or Africa. It's hard to argue with the price though.

Off the Lista di Spagna, *Hotel Santa Lucia (Map 3; ☎/fax 041 71 51 80, Calle della Misericordia 358)* is in a newish building with clean, spacious and well-kept rooms. A lone traveller can pay L80,000 for a room without bathroom. Doubles with/without bathroom cost L160,000/130,000.

Just up the road, *Hotel Villa Rosa (Map 3; ☎ 041 71 65 69, fax 041 71 65 69, email villarosa@ve.nettuno.it, Calle della Misericordia 389)* has 33 comfortable rooms with bathroom, TV and phone. Out the back is a quiet little garden terrace where you can take your compulsory breakfast. You will pay as much as L150,000/170,000 for a

single/double, although a single could be as low as L80,000 in slow periods.

The *Hotel Minerva & Nettuno (Map 3; ☎ 041 71 59 68, fax 041 524 21 39, Lista di Spagna 230)* is a tad more economical. Singles/doubles start at L75,000/95,000. If you want a bathroom, it's L95,000/145,000. The rooms are generally a good size, some looking onto the noisy street, others over internal courtyards. Some are actually in a building across the road.

Hotel Rossi (Map 3; ☎ 041 71 51 64, fax 041 71 77 84, Calle delle Procuratie 262) is in a tiny lane off the Lista di Spagna. Singles/doubles start at L75,000/120,000 (L120,000/150,000 with bathroom) including breakfast. The rooms are pleasant enough, with wood panelling, fans and heating. The location is nice and quiet while still handy for the train station.

At *Hotel al Gobbo (Map 3; ☎ 041 71 50 01, fax 041 71 47 65, Campo San Geremia 312)* singles/doubles cost L105,000/145,000 with bathroom, L80,000/115,000 without. The rooms are pleasantly decorated and comfortable.

Hotel San Geremia (Map 3; ☎ 041 71 62 45, fax 041 524 23 42, Campo San Geremia 290/a) is a friendly establishment. The rooms are standard, with phone and TV. Some have views of the square and a couple up top have little terrace arrangements, although these are usually rented as triples. Doubles with/without bathroom cost L220,000/150,000. The prices are inflated in comparison with neighbouring places, but if you have no luck finding a place around here, it is a reasonable option for people travelling in pairs.

The pick of the crop on this square for a simple, budget deal is a twin-family act. *Alloggi Calderan* and *Casa Gerotto (Map 3; ☎ 041 71 53 61, Campo San Geremia 283)* have combined to offer a whole range of rooms. Small but rather cute, bright singles, of which there are admittedly only a handful, cost L50,000. Dorms (single sex) cost on average L30,000 a head. Doubles cost L140,000 with bathroom, L100,000 without. Triples are also available and most rooms have pleasing views over the square.

Prices can drop by about one-third in slow periods.

Hidden away in a narrow lane leading into the Ghetto, **Hotel Silva & Ariel** *(Map 3; ☎ 041 72 03 26, fax 041 71 47 73, Calle della Masena 1391/a)* is not a bad little place. Double rooms cost L165,000/143,000 with/without bathroom (about L40,000 less if taken as singles) and there's a little back garden to sit in. The owners also rent out apartments at L350,000 for up to six people.

San Marco Despite being the most heavily touristed part of Venice, Sestiere di San Marco contains a few places that offer comparatively good value for money.

Just off Piazza San Marco is **Hotel ai do Mori** *(Map 6; ☎ 041 520 48 17, fax 041 520 53 28, Calle Larga San Marco 658)*. It has pleasant rooms, many of which have been refurbished. Some offer views of the basilica, but the pick of the crop is without doubt the cosy little double at the top that comes with a terrace attached. Prices for doubles start at L180,000/135,000 with/without bathroom. The hotel also offers accommodation for groups of three, four and five.

Al Gambero *(Map 6; ☎ 041 522 43 84, fax 041 520 04 31, email hotgamb@tin.it, Calle dei Fabbri 4685)* is in a great location off Piazza San Marco and can be recommended. Clean, comfortable rooms come with TV, phone and that very Italian consideration, a hairdryer in the bathroom. Singles/doubles cost L165,000/210,000 with bathroom, L85,000/140,000 without.

Hotel Noemi *(Map 6; ☎ 041 523 81 44, fax 041 277 10 05, Calle dei Fabbri 909)* is another good choice on the bottom rung. Good-sized singles/doubles with phone and satellite TV go for L100,000/140,000. None have a bathroom, although the owners are planning to convert a few rooms. To get here from Piazza San Marco, take the *sotoportego* next to Caffè Quadri and then turn left into Calle dei Fabbri.

One of the nicest places to stay in this area is **Locanda Casa Petrarca** *(Map 6; ☎ 041 520 04 30, fax 041 520 04 30, San Marco 4386)*, with singles/doubles for L80,000/120,000 without bathroom. Doubles with

toilet and shower cost L150,000. Breakfast is extra (L10,000). It's a bit of a family affair and the cheerful owner speaks English. To get here, find Campo San Luca, follow Calle dei Fuseri, take the second left and then turn right into Calle Schiavone.

Pensione al Gazzettino *(Map 6; ☎ 041 528 65 23, fax 041 522 33 14, San Marco 4971)* is not as good but is quite acceptable. The position by the canal is enticing and they have a decent restaurant (see the Places to Eat chapter). They offer straightforward, comfortable doubles with bathroom for L180,000. The only single is a fairly tiny affair on the top floor and without bathroom. It costs L80,000.

Locanda Fiorita *(Map 5; ☎ 041 523 47 54, fax 041 522 80 43, email locafior@ tin.net, San Marco 3457/a)* is set on a wonderful little square a spit away from the broad Campo Santo Stefano. The rooms in this old Venetian pile are simple but well maintained and it is hard to complain about the prices: up to L100,000 for a single without bathroom and L170,000 for a double with. This is one of those inexplicable gems that makes you ask why they can't all be so.

Castello This area to the east of San Marco, although close to the piazza, is less heavily touristed. From the train station catch vaporetto No 1 and get off at San Zaccaria.

A stone's throw east of San Marco is a delightful little establishment to rival the Fiorita (see the previous section). **Hotel Doni** *(Map 6; ☎ 041 522 42 67, fax 041 522 42 67, Fondamenta del Vin 4656)* is an 18th-century mansion (although they say the ground floor is 200 years older still). It has been a hotel for more than a century, originally as the Minerva until it changed hands in 1947. It is well maintained and a pleasure to be in. The 12 rooms are mostly spacious and in one the ceiling is adorned with a fine fresco dating from 1850. Singles/doubles without bathroom go for L80,000/120,000. A double with bathroom costs L160,000.

Albergo Corona *(Map 6; ☎ 041 522 91 74, Calle Corona 4464)* is an odd place. You climb mountains of stairs to get to indifferent rooms that cost L72,000/110,000 for a single/double (although the electric baggage-carrier may take a load off your shoulders if it works). The breakfast area is quirkily decorated (check out the wooden parrot). What can you say? It's about as cheap as it gets around here.

One preferable rival is **Locanda Silva** *(Map 6; ☎ 041 522 76 43, fax 041 528 68 17, Fondamenta del Rimedio 4423)*, south of Campo Santa Maria Formosa. It doesn't have any of the odd character, but the modest rooms are clean and pleasant enough. A few look onto the narrow canal. Singles/doubles without bathroom go for L70,000/110,000 and doubles with shower and toilet cost L165,000. Next door, **Locanda Canal** *(Map 6; ☎ 041 523 45 38, fax 041 241 91 38, Fondamenta del Rimedio 4422/c)* is perhaps a smidgen less inviting, but fine if the Silva is full. Doubles (no singles) range from L120,000 without bathroom to L170,000 with toilet and shower. A few of the rooms could do with a good paint job.

Hotel Riva *(Map 6; ☎ 041 522 70 34, Ponte dell'Angelo 5310)* is on a lovely side canal. Doubles with/without amenities cost L170,000/140,000. With a little persuasion you can get the rate shaved a little for single occupancy.

The loquacious (if you speak Italian) proprietor of **Casa Linger** *(Map 7; ☎ 041 528 59 20, fax 041 528 48 51, Salizzada Sant'Antonin 3541)* lends this fairly pedestrian locanda a little animation. If you like climbing stairs this is definitely the spot for you. Still it's not too bad and the place is quiet. Double rooms with/without bathroom cost L180,000/130,000. Forget about the rabbit hole they call a single room (L140,000).

The big advantage of **Pensione Bucintoro** *(Map 7; ☎ 041 522 32 40, fax 041 523 52 24, Riva San Biagio 2135)* is that you are right on the lagoon. Singles/doubles cost L140,000/250,000 with bathroom, L110,000/200,000 without. All rooms look onto the lagoon and are well kept. They shave off about L10,000 per person in slack periods.

Locanda Sant'Anna *(Map 8; ☎ 041 528 64 66, fax 041 528 64 66, Corte del Bianco 269)* is hidden away right in the east of Castello. You can't get much farther away from the heart of Venice and still be there! This is a real residential quarter and may appeal to some for that reason alone. Modest but comfortable single/double rooms cost up to L115,000/155,000.

Santa Croce The **Hotel al Gallo** *(Map 5; ☎ 041 523 67 61, fax 041 522 81 88, Corte di Amai 197/g)* is a couple of minutes' walk from Piazzale Roma. It has just seven rooms (five with bathroom), all with TV and phone. About the best price you can hope to get as a lone traveller is L70,000 in low season. Doubles cost L155,000/130,000 (subtract L35,000 to L40,000 in slack periods) with/without bathroom. This is one of the few places where breakfast is not included (although you might think for the prices it should be!).

Locanda Salieri *(Map 5; ☎ 041 71 00 35, fax 041 72 12 46, Fondamenta Minotto 160)*, just south of the al Gallo, has clean, comfortable singles/doubles from L65,000/110,000. To the east, **Albergo Casa Peron** *(Map 5; ☎ 041 528 60 38, fax 041 71 10 38, Salizzada San Pantalon 84)* has singles/doubles for L75,000/110,000 with shower, but the toilet's in the corridor. It's a small but characterful place, with rooms tucked around corners and up stairs. Another L30,000 will get you a room with your own toilet.

Hotel dalla Mora *(Map 5; ☎ 041 71 07 03, fax 041 72 30 06, Santa Croce 42/a)* is on a small canal just off Salizzada San Pantalon, near the Casa Peron. It has clean, airy rooms, some (like No 5) with lovely canal views, and there is a terrace. Singles/doubles cost L85,000/140,000 with bathroom, but they have some doubles without bathroom for L100,000. A quad with toilet and shower costs L220,000. Bookings are a must.

San Polo The **Pensione Guerrato** *(Map 4; ☎ 041 522 71 31, fax 041 528 59 27, Ruga due Mori 240/a)*, in amid the Rialto markets, is a gem. This is one of only two one-star places to have rooms with at least glimpses of the Grand Canal. It is housed in a former convent, which before had served as a hostel for knights heading off on the Third Crusade. The friendly managers run a tight ship. Doubles (there are no singles) cost L180,000 with bathroom, L130,000 without. Or you can get a family room for up to five people for L300,000. They are usually booked pretty solid.

Dorsoduro Ezra Pound favoured the *Antica Locanda Montin* (Map 5; ☎ 041 522 71 51, fax 041 520 02 03, Fondamenta di Borgo 1147). It is small and comfortable, with singles/doubles for L110,000/130,000 without bathroom (and doubles with bathroom for L150,000), and has a popular if pricey restaurant.

The *Albergo Antico Capon* (Map 5; ☎ 041 528 52 92, fax 041 528 52 92, Campo Santa Margherita 3004/b) is right on a lovely square and has a variety of rooms for anything up to L150,000. The beds are wide and firm, the rooms in which they stand bright and airy.

Hotel Galleria (Map 5; ☎/fax 041 520 41 72, Accademia 878/a) is the only one-star hotel right on the Grand Canal, near the Ponte dell'Accademia. The place was an old private mansion before being converted into the modest and warm-feeling hotel it is now. Space is a little tight, but the decor is welcoming. If you can get one of the rooms on the canal, how can you possibly complain? Rates start at L95,000/135,000 for a single/double. Their biggest doubles cost L195,000.

Lido The *Pensione La Pergola* (Map 14; ☎ 041 526 07 84, Via Cipro 15), just off Gran Viale Santa Maria Elisabetta, has a range of rooms. Singles/doubles with bathroom cost L70,000/140,000 in the high season and as little as half that in the low season. The rooms are simple but pleasant enough. It's about as cheap as you'll find on the Lido in summer.

Burano The *Locanda Al Raspo de Ua* (Map 12; ☎/fax 041 73 00 95, Via Galuppi 560) is a modest place on the island's main drag and has doubles starting at L80,000 without bathroom. It is the only place to stay

here and could make your Venetian visit a quite different experience. After the last of the tourists head back to Venice at night, it's just you and the locals on this pretty islet.

Mestre Only 10 to 15 minutes away on city bus Nos 7 and 2 (the latter passes Mestre train station) or by train, Mestre is a drab, if sometimes necessary, alternative to staying in Venice. There are a number of good hotels, as well as plenty of cafes and places to eat around the main square.

Albergo Roberta (Map 15; ☎ 041 92 93 55, fax 041 93 09 83, Via Sernaglia 21) has good-sized, clean singles/doubles for L105,000/160,000. Singles without bathroom come in at L85,000. A cheaper alternative is the *Giovannina* (Map 15; ☎ 041 92 63 96, fax 041 538 84 42, Via Dante 113), which charges a maximum of L80,000/ 100,000. A single without bathroom costs L55,000.

Similar in price and also close to the station, but in a quiet residential street, is *Hotel Monte Piana* (Map 15; ☎ 041 92 62 42, fax 041 92 28 55, Via Monte San Michele 17). It has some on-site parking.

PLACES TO STAY – MID-RANGE
Cannaregio

The *Hotel Abbazzia* (Map 3; ☎ 041 71 73 33, fax 041 71 79 49, Calle Priuli detta dei Cavalletti 68) is in a restored abbey, a one-minute walk from the train station. Many of the lovely rooms face onto a central garden. Singles/doubles cost up to L295,000/ 330,000, with bathroom and breakfast. Prices drop considerably out of season.

The *Locanda Leon Bianco* (Map 4; ☎ 041 523 35 72, fax 041 241 63 92, Campiello Leon Bianco 5629) is a fine option, although your initial impression may not be too positive as you enter the tiny, lightless courtyard. To find it, cross Rio dei SS Apostoli (heading towards San Marco) and turn right. Pass the high staircase on your left and head straight into the dead-end courtyard. Up two flights of stairs in which medieval-style flaming torches would be at home and you are 'home'. The best three rooms (of eight) look right onto the Grand

PLACES TO STAY

Canal. The undulating *terrazzo alla Veneziana* floors (see the boxed text 'Of Floors & Walls' in the Things to See & Do chapter) and heavy timber doors with their original locks lend the rooms real charm. All but one have bathrooms. Doubles cost L250,000, or L205,000 for the small rooms without canal views. Breakfast is served in the rooms. The house next door is the 12th-century Ca' da Mosto. Owned from the beginning by a renowned family of Venetian navigators, from the 16th to the 18th centuries it also housed Venice's first and most famed hotel, Del Leon Bianco.

San Marco

The Sestiere di San Marco is generally not so great for good-value mid-range hotels, and in any case is so thronged with tourists that it is hard to think of a reason for staying in the area. Attractive alternatives abound in other parts of town that really aren't so far away.

Still, if you must stay here, the **Serenissima** *(Map 6; ☎ 041 520 00 11, fax 041 522 32 92, Calle Goldoni 4486)*, tucked away in the area between San Marco and the Ponte di Rialto, is not a bad option. Singles/doubles cost L190,000/250,000.

Castello

Castello offers a broad palette on the accommodation front in this range, with a couple of noteworthy gems and some worthy runners-up.

Comparatively new, but not overly spacious, is *Hotel Bridge (Map 6; ☎ 041 520 52 87, fax 041 520 22 97, Calle Rimpeto la Sacrestia 4498)*. It is not a bad choice at this level, but you can find better alternatives for less. Room rates vary pretty wildly with the seasons, but as usual you should count on paying top dollar, which means L230,000 for a standard double with bathroom, or up to L336,000 for a room furnished in typical period Venetian style (anaemic-looking creamy painted woodwork with floral decorations).

Locanda Al Piave (Map 6; ☎ 041 528 51 74, fax 041 523 85 12, email hotel.alpiave@iol.it, Ruga Giuffa 4838–4840) has fine and,

in most cases, spacious rooms, furnished with muted elegance. All have shower and TV and are spotlessly clean. Your average double will cost from L220,000 to L240,000. Singles cost L170,000.

Hotel da Bruno (Map 6; ☎ 041 523 04 52, Salizzada San Lio 5726), just west of Campo Santa Maria Formosa, has singles/doubles/triples costing L200,000/250,000/330,000. The rooms are a reasonable size and have bathroom and TV.

Albergo al Nuovo Teson (Map 7; ☎ 041 520 55 55, fax 041 528 53 35, Ramo Pescaria 3980) is secreted away on a square with a real local flavour. Sure, there is a passing trade in tourists, but here you feel you have moved away from the glitz and into a grittier side of Venice. There's nothing particularly gritty about the rooms, elegantly furnished and equipped with shower, TV and phone. Again, loners get a rough deal. Singles/doubles cost up to L210,000/230,000.

A good deal if you get one of the three waterfront rooms is *Albergo Paganelli (Map 7; ☎ 041 522 43 24, fax 041 523 92 67, Riva degli Schiavoni 4182)*. This place has been a hotel since the mid-19th century. Singles/doubles/triples start at L170,000/270,000/320,000 with bathroom and breakfast. For views over the lagoon you must shell out more.

If you can live without watery views, head inland for *La Residenza (Map 7; ☎ 041 528 53 15, fax 041 523 88 59, Campo Bandiera e Moro)*. This delightful 15th-century mansion is also known as Palazzo Gritti-Badoer, after two of the families who have owned it. The main hall upstairs makes quite an impression with its candelabras, elaborate decoration and distinguished furniture. The rooms are rather more restrained, but fine value at up to L160,000/240,000 for a single/double.

Locanda Remedio (Map 6; ☎ 041 520 62 32, fax 041 521 04 85, Calle Rimedio 4412) is indeed something of a remedy ... after the streaming, screaming masses of visitors thronging around San Marco just a few minutes away. It's hard to imagine them so close to the tranquil little courtyard in which this inn is hidden. The building dates from the 16th century and belonged to the Rimedio family. In the same courtyard was a *malvasia*, a tavern where wine of the same name, imported from the Venetian-controlled Greek islands, could be had. In a nice play of words the building came to be known by the name 'remedio' (remedy) towards the end of the 16th century – a massive outbreak of plague had ripped through the city, but the medicinal qualities of malvasia wine were thought to ward off the pestilence. Try for the front double, the ceiling of which is graced with a mid-16th-century fresco by Andrea Medolla. You'll pay up to L150,000/ 280,000 for the peace of a single/double in this place (and the chance to wade into the frenzy at any moment you choose!).

Although run by a chain (Tulip Inns), the 15th-century mansion converted into the *Hotel Scandinavia (Map 6; ☎ 041 522 35 07, fax 041 523 52 32, Campo Santa Maria Formosa 5240)* is not a bad choice. The heavy timber beams and period furnishings give the rooms a cosy touch – the best ones look onto the square. All rooms have bathroom and TV (with in-house movie channels). Rates vary considerably. A double can cost from L250,000 to L500,000 (as usual, however, count on the bad news rather than the good). They have a few not-so-inspiring singles for L150,000.

Santa Croce

Although this area is not the most picturesque in Venice, the *Hotel Canal (Map 3; ☎ 041 523 84 80, fax 041 523 91 06, Fondamenta San Simeon Piccolo 553)*, a few minutes' walk from Piazzale Roma, overlooks the Grand Canal. Singles/doubles with bathroom, TV and phone cost L220,000/300,000 including breakfast. Chop off one-third in the low season.

A prettier and more tranquil option is *Hotel Ai Due Fanali (Map 3; ☎ 041 71 84 90, fax 041 71 83 44, Campo San Simeon Grande 946)*. The square ends on the Grand Canal and is close to being a private courtyard. From rooms at the front you have limited canal views. Singles/doubles cost L180,000/330,000.

San Polo

The *Locanda Sturion (Map 6; ☎ 041 523 62 43, fax 041 522 83 78, email sturion@ tin.it, Calle Sturion 679)* is two minutes from the Ponte di Rialto. It has been a hotel on and off since the 13th century and has superb singles/doubles starting at L200,000/310,000.

Dorsoduro

Albergo Accademia Villa Maravege (Map 5; ☎ 041 521 01 88, fax 041 523 91 52, Fondamenta Bollani 1058) is set in lovely gardens, with views of the Grand Canal. This popular hotel has singles/doubles for up to L185,000/345,000.

Pensione Seguso (Map 5; ☎ 041 528 68 58, fax 041 522 23 40, Fondamenta Zattere ai Gesuati 779) is in a lovely quiet position facing the Canale della Giudecca. Singles/ doubles cost up to L195,000/250,000 with bathroom and breakfast. Book ahead.

La Calcina (Map 5; ☎ 041 520 64 66, fax 041 522 70 45, Fondamenta Zattere ai Gesuati 780) is where John Ruskin wrote *The Stones of Venice*. Singles/doubles cost L160,000/280,000.

Hotel Messner (Map 5; ☎ 041 522 74 43, fax 041 522 72 66, Rio Terrà del Spezier 216) is tucked away on a tiny street. It was fairly recently overhauled and boasts an inviting bar and courtyard. You'll pay up to L220,000 for a double.

Albergo agli Alboretti (Map 5; ☎ 041 523 00 58, fax 041 521 01 58, Rio Terrà Antonio Foscarini 884) is a charming hotel that almost feels like an inviting mountain chalet when you step inside. In its category, it is one of Venice's star choices. The management is friendly and the rooms tastefully arranged. Singles/doubles cost up to L160,000/250,000. The restaurant is also of a high standard.

Mestre

Hotel Vivit (Map 15; ☎ 041 95 13 85, fax 041 95 88 91, Piazza Ferretto 75) is a somewhat drab and cumbersome-looking place, but the functional rooms are quite OK. If you have to be in Mestre, at least you are in the heart of town and on a lively pedestrianised square. Singles/doubles cost L90,000/146,000.

The three-star *Tritone (Map 15; ☎ 041 93 09 55, fax 041 93 00 79, email htltritone@ tin.it, Viale Stazione 16)* has singles/doubles costing up to L160,000/200,000. It is quite comfortable and has the obvious advantage of being right by the station – ideal for quick getaways to the lagoon.

PLACES TO STAY – TOP END

A cut above and apart, *Grand Hotel Palazzo dei Dogi (Map 3; ☎ 041 220 81 11, fax 041 72 22 78, email hotels@boscolo .com, Fondamenta Madonna dell'Orto 3500)* stands in splendid isolation right up in the north-west of the city. The rooms are well appointed and if you want luxury while feeling nicely out of the way, this could be the place for you. Singles/doubles cost L480,000/700,000.

San Marco

The luxury *Gritti Palace (Map 5; ☎ 041 79 46 11, fax 041 520 09 42, Campo Santa Maria del Giglio 2467)*, the facade of which

fronts the Grand Canal, is one of the most famous hotels in Venice. If you can afford to pay up to L1,600,000 for a double, you'll be mixing with royalty.

The *Bauer Grünwald & Grand Hotel (Map 6; ☎ 041 520 7022, fax 041 520 7557, Campo San Moisè, San Marco 1459)* is, for some people, a better address still. Don't mind the awful 1949 Soviet-style entrance – the canalside neo-Gothic frontage of the *palazzo* is sufficiently elegant. Views from some rooms across the Grand Canal towards Santa Maria della Salute are hard to beat and you're a stone's throw from Piazza San Marco. The elegant rooms of the 2nd floor drip Carrara marble and Murano glass. Doubles start at L790,000, but canal views will push the price up to L1,100,000.

Castello

Some of the city's finest hotels are on the Riva degli Schiavoni. The four-star *Londra Palace (Map 7; ☎ 041 520 05 33, fax 041 522 50 32, email info@hotellondra.it, Riva*

A Dogey Death

When Doge Vitale Michiel returned to Venice with the sorry remains of his fleet in May 1172, he must have known things weren't going to go well for him. He had set off in September of the year before with a war fleet of 120 vessels to avenge assaults on Venetians carried out in Constantinople. Unfortunately, he decided to agree to talks.

While his negotiators got bogged down in ultimately fruitless chitchat, his idle fleet at the Greek island of Chios collapsed as plague broke out. By the time it had become clear that Constantinople had no intention of continuing serious talks, the fleet was in no condition to fight. And so Michiel had little alternative but to go home – taking the plague with him.

As he gave his sorry report to the assembly in the Palazzo Ducale, he realised from the mounting anger that he would have to flee. He didn't get very far. Scampering east along the Riva degli Schiavoni, he was met by the mob and killed. (A conflicting version of events says Michiel was on his way to the Chiesa di San Zaccaria for the Easter service when he was struck down.)

At any rate, when things had calmed down a little, the city's leaders searched for, tried and executed the assassin. If anyone was going to do the killing around here, it was the State. The man's house was found to be at Calle delle Rasse, virtually next to the spot where Michiel met his end, and was flattened. It was decreed that in future no building of stone should be raised on the site.

The decree was respected until 1948. When it was finally repealed, the silent vacuum of reproach was filled with the rather Mussolini-esque expansion of the Hotel Danieli, an ugly sister that sits rather uncomfortably beside Palazzo Dandolo, the hotel's main home.

degli Schiavoni 4171) has doubles for anything up to L1,000,000 and most rooms have views over the water. Renovated in 1998, the rooms feature 19th-century period furniture, Jacuzzis and marble bathrooms.

The *Hotel Danieli (Map 6; ☎ 041 522 64 80, fax 041 520 02 08)*, nearby on Riva degli Schiavoni, has singles/doubles for up to L700,000/1,350,000, most of them looking out over the canal. It opened as a hotel in 1822 in the Palazzo Dandolo, built in the 14th century.

Giudecca

The *Cipriani (Map 10; ☎ 041 520 77 44, fax 041 520 39 30, email cipriani@gpnet.it, Giudecca 10)* is set in the one-time villa of the Mocenigo family and surrounded by lavish grounds, with unbeatable views across to San Marco. In the high season you will need to shell out up to L1,750,000 for a princely suite. Prices drop considerably in the low season. The hotel runs a private boat from San Marco.

Lido

Villa Mabapa (Map 14; ☎ 041 526 05 90, fax 041 526 94 41, email mabapa@mbox .vol.it, Riviera San Nicolò 16) is a pleasant hideaway handy for the vaporetto stop. Singles/doubles cost up to L312,000/420,000.

Otherwise, the top two addresses are the *Grand Hotel Des Bains (Map 14; ☎ 041 526 59 21, fax 041 526 01 13, Lungomare Guglielmo Marconi 17)*, for Thomas Mann fans, and the fanciful Moorish-style *Excelsior (Map 13; ☎ 041 526 02 01, fax 041 526 72 76, Lungomare Guglielmo Marconi 41)*. Doubles at either cost between L800,000 and L900,000.

LONG-TERM RENTALS

Not too many of us can afford to hang around even the cheapest hotel indefinitely. You could try striking a deal with an *affittacamere* (the APT has a list). These are private households that rent out rooms and operate more or less as little *pensioni*.

A cheaper option, but not an easy one to set up, is to share an apartment. In Italy, only students tend do this, so start by heading to the Università Ca' Foscari notice boards at Calle Larga Foscari in San Polo and next to Chiesa di San Sebastiano in Dorsoduro (both Map 5). You can put up your own ad here. You could also try for an apartment to rent alone. As a rule, it's possible to get a room in a shared place for about L500,000 a month, sometimes less. To rent even a studio for yourself, you could be looking at L2,000,000. Another approach is to ask pensione owners if they know of anything – sometimes they can quickly find a place for you to rent.

In the UK, Venetian Apartments (☎ 020-8878 1130, fax 8878 0982), 413 Parkway House, Sheen Lane, London SW14 8LS, arranges accommodation in flats, starting at around UK£550 for two people per week.

Finally, another route to go might be time-share. You buy time in a property (minimum one week) for annual use. You don't have to use it yourself, but could sublet or simply not bother with it. Theoretically at least, it should be like investing in property – you could sell your share further down the line. One time-share company doing this is Immobiliare Sviluppo (☎ 041 523 01 24, fax 041 522 67 16), Campo SS Apostoli, Cannaregio 4438 (Map 4). They call their programme Perle Veneziane and you can email them at info@perleveneziane.it.

Places to Eat

FOOD

If you've enjoyed the cuisines of Tuscany and Emilia-Romagna, the 'down home' style of a Roman meal or the Sicilians' gift for seasoned fantasies, you might find the fare in Venice a bit disappointing. Indeed, other Italians tend to be rather disparaging about La Serenissima's attempts in the kitchen, lamenting that *si spende tanto e si mangia male* (you spend a lot and eat badly), but then they are rather fastidious about their food. For the rest of us, Venice isn't really that bad – even that august collective of self-appointed foodies in Italy, Slow Food, were able to find about 20 places to stick into their annual *Osterie d' Italia* guide. Chowing down in Venice is, however, rather pricey.

Search out the little eateries tucked away in the side streets and squares, since many of the restaurants immediately around San Marco and near the train station are tourist traps. Read the fine print if you want to eat seafood, as most fish is sold by weight. When considering a set-price menu, make sure you know whether or not all service charges are included – often they are not.

When to Eat

Breakfast *(colazione)* is generally a quick affair, taken on the hop in a bar on the way to work.

For lunch *(pranzo)*, restaurants usually open from 12.30 to 3 pm, but many are not keen to take orders after 2 pm. In the evening, opening hours for dinner *(cena)* vary, but people start sitting down to dine around 7.30 pm. You'll be hard pressed to find a place still serving after 10.30 pm.

Bars (which in Italy also serve hot drinks and sandwiches) and cafes generally open from 7.30 am to 8 pm, although some stay open after 8 pm and turn into pub-style drinking and meeting places.

Restaurants and bars are generally closed one day each week; the day varies between establishments.

Where to Eat

The standard name for a restaurant is *ristorante*. Often you will come across something known as a *trattoria*, by tradition, at least, a cheaper, simpler version of a ristorante. In Venice in particular you will also come across another phenomenon, the *osteria*, originally a wine bar offering snacks and a small selection of dishes. For specific examples see the boxed text 'Osteria 'Opping' later in this chapter. The *pizzeria* needs no explanation.

The problem with all this is that nowadays the names seem to have become interchangeable. It would appear that restaurant owners consider it more enticing to punters to call their places *osterie* (or even *hostarie*, reflecting an olde-worlde approach). Don't judge an eatery by its tablecloth. You may well have your best meal at the dingiest little establishment you can find.

In all cases, it is best to check the menu, usually posted by the door, for prices. Occasionally you will find places with no written menu. This usually means they change the menu daily. Inside there may be a blackboard or the waiter will tell you what's on – fine if you speak Italian, a little disconcerting if you don't. Try to think of it as a surprise. If you encounter this situation in an overtly touristy area, you should have your rip-off antennae up.

Most eating establishments have a cover charge, ranging from L1500 up to L10,000 at places like Quadri. On top of this you have to factor in the service charge of 10 to 15%.

Better areas to look for places to eat include the back streets of Cannaregio, Santa Croce, San Polo and Castello.

Where Not to Eat

Feeding tourists second-rate meals is something of a sport in Venice. As a rule, places with a set-price *menù turistico* are to be avoided if you want to eat at all well (see the next section). Places displaying a menu in languages other than Italian can be dodgy too, although this is not always the case. One fairly clear warning signal is whole tour groups chomping together on identical meals – usually a sorry-looking plate of pasta with a tomato sauce, a side order of wilting salad and maybe even chips. Anyone who takes up a waiter/tout's invitation to step inside and enjoy their food deserves everything they get.

The worst areas are in Cannaregio – along the route from the train station towards San Marco – and in the San Marco zone itself. This is not to say you can't find good places in either of these areas – just that they have more than their fair share of bad 'uns.

What to Eat

Breakfast Italians rarely eat a sit-down breakfast. They tend to drink a cappuccino, usually *tiepido* (warm), and eat a croissant *(cornetto)* or other type of pastry (generically known as *pastine*, which elsewhere in northern Italy you'd call *brioches*) while standing at a bar.

Snacks Many bars serve filling snacks with lunch-time and pre-dinner drinks. Most also have a wide range of *panini* (sandwiches or filled bread rolls), with every imaginable filling. *Tramezzi* (sandwich triangles) and huge bread rolls cost from L1500 to L5000 if you eat them standing up. You'll also find numerous outlets where you can buy pizza by the slice *(a taglio)*.

Another option is to go to an *alimentari* (delicatessen) and ask them to make a *panino* with the filling of your choice. At a *pasticceria* you can buy pastries, cakes and biscuits.

A further alternative are osterie (also known in their more straightforward, old-fashioned bar form as *bacari*). They serve local wines by the glass *(ombra)* and snacks *(cichetti)*, mostly of the seafood variety. Some also act as restaurants (see the boxed text 'Osteria 'Opping' later in this chapter).

Lunch & Dinner Lunch is traditionally the main meal of the day and some shops and businesses close for two or three hours every afternoon to accommodate it.

A full meal will consist of an *antipasto*, which can vary from fried vegetables to a small offering of fried seafood. Next comes the *primo piatto*, generally a pasta or risotto, followed by the *secondo piatto* of meat or fish. This does not usually come with vegetables and Italians will order a *contorno* (vegetable dish) to go with it. Salads *(insalate)* have a strange position in the order here. They are usually ordered as separate dishes and in some cases serve as a replacement for the primo piatto. Although there is nothing to stop you ordering a salad as a side order to a main (second) course, Italians don't seem to do so as a rule.

Although most restaurants offer a range of desserts, Italians sometimes prefer to round off the meal with fruit then *caffè*, often at a bar on the way back to work.

Numerous restaurants offer a *menù turistico* or *menù a prezzo fisso*, a set-price lunch costing an average of L20,000 to L30,000 (not including drinks). Generally choice is limited and the food is breathtakingly unspectacular. Sometimes it's bloody awful. From your taste buds' point of view (and as long as you are not overly hungry), you'd be better off settling for a plate of pasta, some salad and wine at a decent restaurant.

The evening meal, which follows a similar pattern, was traditionally a simpler affair, but habits are changing because of the inconvenience of travelling home or going out for lunch every day.

Note It appears certain culinary stereotypes have gone too far. Many people seem to believe that *parmigiano* (parmesan cheese) should be scattered on top of all pasta dishes, no matter what the sauce. Nothing could be further from the truth. You should never use it with any kind of seafood sauce, for the simple reason that the cheese kills the flavour rather than enhancing it! If your waiter doesn't offer you the cheese, 99 times out of 100 there will be a perfectly good reason for this. It seems some dinner guests feel they are being ripped off if they don't get their parmesan and badger their waiters into providing the cheese against their own better judgement!

Gelati At the tail end of lunch and dinner you can opt for a house dessert, but at least once or twice a day you should head for the nearest *gelateria* (ice-cream parlour) to round off the meal with a *gelato*, followed perhaps by a *digestivo* (digestive liqueur) at a bar. Italians tend to see ice cream as a summertime treat and/or something for the kids. But that's their problem. Recent studies published in Italy affirm that a gelato a day can actually be good for you – now that's good news!

Food Vocabulary For essential food vocabulary, see the Language chapter at the end of this book.

Venetian Cuisine

Some commentators, such as Venice's own Alvise Zorzi (an historian and writer of some note in the lagoon city), claim that true Venetian cuisine has all but disappeared. Whether or not this is quite accurate is open to debate, and one hopes that Zorzi's faith in the rebirth of interest in good cooking (and eating!) will save any traditions that might have been on the verge of extinction. At any rate, his introduction to *A Tavola con I Dogi*, an elaborate tome devoted to fine Venetian cuisine, makes interesting reading.

Staples The basic staple in north-eastern Italian cuisine is a very humble thing indeed – *polenta*. This corn-based stodge is to Venetians what couscous is to North Africans. It comes in different forms, although generally it arrives at the table in yellow slabs, lightly grilled. A less common version is made of a fine maize and has the colour and consistency of porridge. By itself it really is a little sad, but used to soak up sauces and the like during a meal it can be quite tasty.

No-one could be expected to live on polenta alone. Two dishes form the next basic rung up not only in Venice but across the Veneto, and you will see them often on the menu. *Risi e bisi* is a kind of risotto broth with peas. Despite the often lurid green appearance, it is really very tasty when prop-

In Praise of Polenta

If you have any doubts about what the natives think of that rather stodgy culinary invention of theirs, polenta, just have a read of Carlo Goldoni's 1743 play *La Donna di Garbo*. He considered it important enough to lift it to literary heights, as one character, Rosaura, explains to Arlecchino (Harlequin) how to prepare a slap-up dish of the stuff. Mmm.

erly prepared. Sometimes it's served with ham and parmesan cheese. In the Veneto, people take their peas seriously – some towns even stage Pea Parties *(sagra dei bisi)*. It takes all sorts.

Perhaps even more common is *pasta e fagioli* (in Venetian dialect, *pasta e fasioi*). This is 'poor' cuisine, a peasant dish par excellence that people unable to afford much meat have been munching for centuries. It is not restricted to the Veneto – indeed, you can find it all over Italy and across the Adriatic in the former Yugoslavia. To the basic mix of short pasta, dry fava beans, onion, olive oil and salt and pepper, you can add pretty much what you want to make it more interesting. Other vegetables (carrots, peas, potatoes) and various kinds of sausage and meat are all options.

Snacks & Starters *Cichetti* and *antipasti*, or snacks and starters, are Venetian specialities. A classic snack or starter is *sarde in saor*, sardines fried up in an onion marinade, a favourite since the 13th century. Anything fishy fried up in saor tastes pretty good. The secret is in the saor marinade, which comes out extra tasty with a few pine nuts thrown in. Onions played a big part in traditional Venetian cuisine, especially for those at sea, as a preventative measure against scurvy.

Variations on the *baccalà* (dried cod) theme are also legion. Served up with polenta it is good – the polenta absorbs some of the fish's natural saltiness. A classic cod dish is *baccalà mantecato*, cod prepared in garlic and parsley.

Another delicacy, at their best from October to December, are *granseole*, large crabs that live at the bottom of the Mediterranean and the Adriatic. *Cape sante*, or *coquilles St Jacques*, often feature with pasta, but as a snack are fried in olive oil and garlic, with parsley, lemon and a little white wine added at the last minute. *Peoci* (mussels, known as *cozze* in Italian) and other shellfish all feature prominently and the list of bite-size seafood items served up as cichetti is long as the sea is deep. The Venetians also tend to have their own names for everything – the best advice is to get in there and pick and choose. Among the meat starters are *cotechino*, a type of pork sausage served up with mustard.

Vegetables fried in breadcrumbs *(verdure fritte)* are also good. A particular Venetian obsession is artichokes (*carciofi* in Italian, *articiochi* in Venetian dialect). If you hang around produce markets, you may well see buckets of carefully cut out artichoke hearts (*fondi di articiochi*) in water. Locals swear that, fried up with parsley and garlic and accompanied by a slab of steak, articiochi will send your taste buds to heaven.

Primi Piatti Beyond the two classics named above (risi e bisi and pasta e fagioli), you will come across a wide range of first courses, split fairly evenly between risotto and pasta.

Risotto, basically a rice-based stew (think of the Spanish paella and you'll begin to get the idea), comes in many varieties in the Veneto. Among the possible ingredients served up with your risotto are mushrooms, zucchini, sausage, quail, trout and other seafood, chicken and spring vegetables. Not to be missed is *risotto nero*, coloured and flavoured with the ink of cuttlefish *(seppia)*. Many restaurants that offer risotto will only serve it to a minimum of two people. So, yet again, the lone traveller gets it in the neck.

One thing to note about pasta is that only a few types really have any long standing in the Venetian tradition. In Venetian restaurants today you can eat good pasta first courses, but often they have their origins in other regions. So although *spaghetti alle vongole* (spaghetti with clams) may be a delicious dish readily available in many restaurants, it is not strictly Venetian. In fact, it is Neapolitan.

One type of pasta that is Venetian is *bigoli*, a kind of rough, thick spaghetti. Its texture makes it ideal for seafood sauces, which stick to it better than to other pastas. A classic is bigoli or spaghetti *alla busara* – with scampi and a very mild red sauce. Unfortunately, if you talk to the Milanese about bigoli they will giggle like school kids – for them a bigolo is slang for a boy's naughty bit. *Gnocchi*, made of potato, are strictly speaking a Veronese speciality, but have been absorbed into the Venetian tradition.

Among the soups, the best known is *sopa de pesse* (which in Italian is *zuppa di pesce*, or fish soup). When it's good, it's very good, especially on a cold winter's night.

Secondi Piatti Seafood is very popular, but also often expensive. Try seppia with polenta. The most common fish types you will be offered include *branzino* (sea bass, good when boiled), *orata* (bream) and *sogliola* (sole). *Masanete* and *moleche* are variations on the crab theme (both of which just translate to *granchio* in Italian).

Of land-going critters, pork and its derivatives figure high in the more traditional foods, along with items such as liver *(fegato)* and even spleen (*milza*, an acquired taste) or cow udder *(mammella di vacca)*. Don't worry, all the more standard cuts of beef *(manzo)*, lamb *(agnello)*, veal *(vitello)* and so on are available. Or try boiled meats with bitter red lettuce *(radicchio trevisano)* eaten baked, in risotto or with pasta.

If you were to try only one meat dish in Venice that you had never had before (or even if you had), it would have to be *carpaccio*. We all know that the Bellini was invented in Harry's Bar (see the boxed text 'The Cocktail Circuit' in the next section), but less well known is that the idea to serve up plates of very finely sliced raw beef in a simple sauce was also 'cooked' up chez Cipriani. The sauce is a mix of mayonnaise, crushed tomato, cream, mustard and a dash of Worcestershire sauce. The Ciprianis named it after Vittore Carpaccio, because at

PLACES TO EAT

the time the artist was the subject of a big exhibition in Venice. A common variation on the theme sees the beef slices bathed in lemon, *rucola* (rocket) and shavings of *grana* cheese.

Dolci Apart from the classic gelati (see the earlier What to Eat section), you will find no shortage of house desserts *(dolci)*.

Tiramisù, a rich dessert with mascarpone, is a favourite here and supposedly comes from Venice. All sorts of light biscuits have been dreamed up over the centuries in Venice – start looking in pasticceria windows. They come with such names as *baicoli*, *ossi da morto* and *bigarani* and are supposed to be taken with dessert wine.

In Venice, more than elsewhere in Italy, you may well be offered *sorbetto* (a lemon sorbet, sometimes with a drop of alcohol) at the end of the main course. It is designed to clean your palate before dessert, but for many makes a good dessert on its own account.

Foreign Cuisine

The availability of non-Italian cuisine in Venice is conspicuous by its almost total absence, aside from the ubiquitous Chinese option.

Among the restaurants listed in this chapter you will notice one Indian, a couple of Arab spots and others where you can munch on tacos. That's really about as far as it goes here.

Vegetarian Food

Vegetarian restaurants as such seem nonexistent in Venice. This may not cause huge problems, as many starters, pasta dishes and side orders *(contorni)* are all-vegetable affairs (Osteria La Zucca, in particular, has wonderful and generous contorni – see Santa Croce & San Polo in the Budget section later in this chapter).

DRINKS
Nonalcoholic

Water While tap water is reliable, most Italians prefer bottled mineral water *(acqua minerale)*. It comes either sparkling *(frizzante* or *gasata)* or still *(naturale)* and you will be asked in restaurants and bars which you prefer. If you want a glass of tap water, ask for *acqua dal rubinetto*.

Coffee The first-time visitor to Italy is likely to be confused by the many ways in which the locals consume their caffeine. As in other Latin countries, Italians take their coffee seriously. Consequently they also make it complicated!

First, there's the pure and simple *espresso* – a small cup of very strong black coffee. A *doppio espresso* is a double shot of the same. You could also ask for a *caffè lungo*, but this may end up being more like the watered-down, instant version with which foreigners will be more familiar. If you want to be quite sure of getting the watery version, ask for a *caffè americano*.

Enter the milk. A *caffè latte* is coffee with a reasonable amount of milk. To most locals it is a breakfast drink only. The stronger version is a *caffè macchiato*, basically an espresso with a dash of milk. Alternatively, you can have *latte macchiato*, a glass of hot milk with a dash of coffee. *Cappuccino* is a frothy version of caffè latte. You can ask for it *senza schiuma* (without the froth, which is scraped off the top). It tends to come lukewarm, so if you want it hot, ask for it to be *molto caldo*.

In summer, the local version of an iced coffee is a *caffè freddo*, a long glass with cold coffee, sometimes helped along with ice cubes.

To warm up on those winter nights, a *corretto* might be for you – an espresso 'corrected' with a dash of grappa or some other spirit. Some locals have it first thing in the morning.

After lunch and dinner it wouldn't occur to Italians to order either caffè latte or cappuccino – espresso, macchiato and corretto are perfectly acceptable. Of course, if you want a cappuccino there's no problem – but you might have to repeat your request a couple of times to convince disbelieving waiters that they have heard correctly.

An espresso or macchiato can cost from an Italy-wide standard of L1400 or L1500 standing at a bar to L3000 sitting at your average outside table. Along the Grand Canal (around Ponte di Rialto) the price will be more like L5000, and expect L10,000 or more in a place such as Caffè Florian on Piazza San Marco.

Tea Italians don't drink a lot of tea *(tè)* and then generally only in the late afternoon, when they might take a cup with a few *pasticcini* (small cakes). You can order tea in bars, although it will usually arrive in the form of a cup of warm water with an accompanying tea bag. If this doesn't suit your taste, ask for the water *molto caldo* or *bollente* (boiling). Good-quality packaged teas, such as Twinings tea bags and leaves, as well as packaged herbal teas, such as camomile, are often sold in alimentari (grocery stores) and sometimes in bars. You can find a wide range of herbal teas in a herbalist's shop *(erboristeria)*, which will sometimes also stock health foods.

Granita *Granita* is a drink made of crushed ice with fresh lemon or other fruit juices, or with coffee topped with fresh whipped cream. It is a Sicilian speciality, but you'll see it in Venice in the summer months.

Soft Drinks The usual range of international soft drinks is available in Venice, although they tend to be expensive. There are some local versions too, along with the rather bitter Chinotto, an acquired taste.

Alcoholic

Beer The main Italian brands are Peroni, Dreher and Moretti, all very drinkable and cheaper than the imported varieties. If you want a local beer, ask for a *birra nazionale*, which will be either in a bottle or on tap. Italy imports beers from throughout Europe and the rest of the world. Several German beers, for instance, are available in bottles or cans; English beers and Guinness are often found on tap *(alla spina)* in *birrerie* (bars specialising in beer). You can even find Australia's XXXX, if you are so inclined. The UK and Irish cause is being spread with the growth of the pseudo-Irish-pub phenomenon, to which not even Venice is immune.

The Cocktail Circuit

Back in the 1950s, behind the bar at Harry's, a new sensation was born. It was deceptively simple: mix prosecco with peach nectar, and you have a Bellini. Of course, they will tell you there is more to it than that – the quality of the ingredients and, more importantly, the proportions. Whatever – it is good.

You don't have to shell out the L18,000 for one at Harry's Bar, as Bellinis and other cocktails are popular at *aperitivo* time (that loose early-evening, pre-dinner period) all over town. Still, if you can afford a drink or two at Harry's, it's worth it. Apart from the Bellini they do some other mean mixes. These guys have been practising the art of the Martini for as long as they have been open.

Truman Capote called a good Martini a Silver Bullet. What's in it? Good gin and a drop of Martini Dry. But of course the amount of the latter varies according to taste: for a strong, dry Martini, 'rinse' the glass with Martini and then pour in freezing gin. Hemingway, who set part of his book *Across the River and into the Trees* at Harry's, had his own recipe: pour freezing-cold gin into a glass dipped in ice and sit it next to a bottle of Martini for a moment before drinking!

More emblematic of everyday Venice is the *spritz*. This is one part sparkling white wine, one part soda water and one part bitter (Campari, Amaro, Aperol or Select), topped with a slice of lemon and, if you wish, an olive. They say this drink dates from the days of the Austrian occupation in the 19th century.

Wine Wine *(vino)* is an essential accompaniment to any Italian meal. Italians are justifiably proud of their wines and it would be surprising for dinner-time conversation not to touch on the subject, at least for a moment.

Prices are reasonable and you will rarely pay more than L15,000 for a good bottle of wine, although they can range up to more than L40,000 for the better stuff. Wine tends to be more expensive in Venice than elsewhere in Italy because of added transport costs.

Wine is graded according to three main classifications – DOCG *(denominazione d'origine controllata e garantita)*, DOC *(denominazione di origine controllata)* and table wine *(vino da tavola)* – which are marked on the label. A DOC wine is produced subject to certain specifications, although the label does not certify quality. DOCG is subject to the same requirements as normal DOC, but it is also tested by government inspectors.

Your average trattoria will generally stock only a limited range of bottled wines, but quite a few of the better restaurants (some of which are listed in this chapter) offer a carefully chosen selection of wines from around the country. Most people order the house wine *(vino della casa)* or the local wine *(vino locale)* when they go out to dinner and generally this is perfectly fine.

For fairly obvious reasons, Venice itself produces no wines. Nor is the Veneto Italy's prime wine-making region. That said, some good ones are produced around Verona, including Soave (white), Valpolicella (red) and Bardolino (red and rosé). Nosiola, another white, is not bad. The Vicenza area is also dotted with wineries. Wines from Friuli-Venezia Giulia, Italy's easternmost region, are often good and are readily available. The Pinot Grigio (white) and Pinot Nero (red) are both promising.

A Venetian wanting a quick drink in a bar will quite likely ask for a *prosecco*, a lightly bubbly white wine, produced all over the Veneto. The average price is L2500. Otherwise, a simple *ombra* (small glass) of local house *bianco* (white) or *rosso* (red) will do.

Another regional curiosity is the very sweet *fragolino*. This strawberry-flavoured red isn't strictly wine and cannot be sold as such commercially, though you'll occasionally come across it in bars in Venice and elsewhere in the Veneto. You can sometimes find a white version too. You can be fairly sure you are drinking the real thing if it is served in unlabelled bottles. Many stores have taken to selling a fizzy 'wine' they call fragolino. This is a travesty – it is little more than poor wine with strawberry flavouring added – it is *not* the real McCoy (if it were, they couldn't sell it).

Liquors & Liqueurs For an after-dinner digestivo, try a shot of grappa, a strong, clear brew made from grapes. It comes from the nearby Grappa region, on the mainland. Or you could go for an *amaro*, a dark liqueur prepared from herbs. If you prefer a sweeter liqueur, try an almond-flavoured *amaretto* or the sweet aniseed *sambuca*.

PLACES TO EAT – BUDGET

One diner's idea of a budget meal will be the next guy's once-a-month splurge, so it's a little difficult to come up with a hard-and-fast category. The bad news is that truly dirt-cheap places are thin on the ground here.

This category covers you up to around L50,000 – you could easily spend more at most of these places, which thus could equally be considered mid-range. On the

Getting Your Foot in the Door

For much of the year Venice is heaving with visitors, so for many restaurants you should consider booking ahead. You can, of course, often get a table when you walk in off the street, but you can by no means bank on it. Some of the places listed in this chapter have been clearly identified as ones where you can virtually be guaranteed of finding no room at the inn without a reservation. At many others it can be touch and go, so if you have your heart set on any one place, call ahead.

other hand, if you stick to one course and a side order, combined with house wine, you can often get away with spending around L30,000 or less, which also goes for those places listed as mid-range.

At lunch time, in particular, sticking to pizzas or other snacks, such as sandwiches, can save you loads. The average panino, often with ham, cheese and salad, with a can of coke can cost you around L13,000 – a filling and inexpensive way to kill midday growls. You can stick to the pizza formula at night (the average pizza will cost from L8000 to L12,000 depending on place and size of pizza). By the slice it is cheaper still.

If you want to have a full meal (starter, pasta, main course and dessert with wine), you really cannot hope to spend under L40,000 unless you get a set-price meal. However, as mentioned earlier, they are not the thing to go for if you are hoping for any serious culinary satisfaction.

By the way, when looking at menus and working out what you might spend, remember that almost invariably you will pay separately for vegetables or salad to go with your main course. So a main advertised at L22,000 will be more like L30,000 when you add in a mixed salad.

A final tip. If you are scrimping and scraping but would like to splurge, you can save pennies by cutting down on the frills. A post-prandial cup of coffee in a restaurant will cost double or more than you would pay for the same thing at a bar across the street. The same goes for dessert. If you want gelato, go to a gelateria – the walk will do you good anyway!

Snack Bars & Restaurants

Cannaregio Numerous bars along the main thoroughfare between the train station and San Marco serve sandwiches and snacks.

For restaurants, it is best to head for the side streets to look for little trattorie and pizzerie, but there are a couple of OK spots on the main thoroughfare. *Trattoria alla Palazzina (Map 3; ☎ 041 71 77 25, Cannaregio 1509)* serves good pizza for L8000 to L10,000 and memorable home-made desserts. It's closed Wednesday.

Fondamenta della Misericordia is something of foodies' street where locals crowd into several trattorie and bars. Young people will enjoy *Paradiso Perduto (Map 3; ☎ 041 72 05 81)*, at No 2539, a restaurant/bar with live music and tables outside in summer. The *lasagne ai carciofi* (artichoke lasagne) is great. The bar snacks are also enticing. It gets pretty packed and is closed Sunday and Wednesday.

For a Middle Eastern touch, try *Sahara (Map 3; ☎ 041 72 10 7)*, at No 2520. They serve up good Syrian food and you can even clap along to a not-so-authentic display of belly dancing. It's closed Monday evening. Next door, at No 2515, you could opt for the Mexican flavour at Venice's first Latin American experiment, *Iguana (Map 3; ☎ 041 71 35 61)*. The low, wood-beam ceiling makes for a warm atmosphere and the food is OK and moderately priced. It's closed Monday.

Pizzeria Casa Mia (Map 4; ☎ 041 28 55 90, Calle dell'Oca 4430) has pizzas and pasta for around L10,000 and main courses for around L18,000. It's closed Tuesday.

Gam Gam (Map 3; ☎ 041 71 52 84, Ghetto Nuovo 2884) is great for your taste buds if you like Israeli-style falafels and other Middle Eastern delicacies. This place is fully kosher and presents a diverse menu, ranging from Red Sea spaghetti to couscous (with choice of meat, fish or vegetable sauce) and from houmous to that arch-Venetian side order of *fondi di carciofi*. Pasta courses cost around L15,000 and mains L22,000. It's closed on Friday night and Saturday.

On the 'frontier' with Sestiere di Castello, the aptly named *Ostaria Al Ponte (Map 4; ☎ 041 528 61 57, Calle Larga G Gallina 6378)* is a highly recommended and rather tiny spot to snack on cichetti and indulge in good wines. It's closed Sunday.

San Marco For a great range in mini-panini, pop into *Ai Rusteghi (Map 6; ☎ 041 523 22 05, Calletta della Bissa 5529)*. They also offer good wines. There's nothing better than an ombra or two and a couple of panini as a quick lunch-time snack. It's closed Sunday.

PLACES TO EAT

Vino Vino (Map 6; ☎ 041 523 70 27, Calle del Cafetier, San Marco 2007) is a popular bar/osteria at Ponte Veste, near Teatro La Fenice. The menu changes daily and the pre-prepared food is of a reasonable quality. A pasta or risotto dish costs L8000, a main dish L15,000 and there is a good selection of vegetables. Wine is sold by the glass for L2000. It's closed Saturday.

Trattoria Fiore (Map 5; ☎ 041 523 53 10, Calle delle Botteghe 3460) also has a bar. The latter is a cheerful spot for a glass of wine and cichetti that locals seem to appreciate, while foreigners tend to occupy the sit-down eating part. The whole place is closed Tuesday.

Tavernetta San Maurizio (Map 5; ☎ 041 528 52 40), just off Campo San Maurizio, is a surprisingly economical place to munch away. Try their *risotto alla pescatora*, a fishy affair at L10,000. Mains will set you back around L15,000 – not bad at all by Venetian standards. It's closed Sunday.

Santa Croce & San Polo This is a great area for small, cheap places to eat. *Brodo di Giuggiole (Map 5; ☎ 041 524 24 86, Fondamenta Minotto 159)* is small and family run and offers a fine set-price menu for L45,000 – the *degustazione di cucina veneziana* – or a choice of various traditional dishes. Irina, who runs the place, is what every restaurateur should be – a lover of fine food. Her kitchen does a good job with classics like home-made *gnocchi alla granseola* (gnocchi with crab). It's closed Monday.

Arca (Map 5; ☎ 041 524 22 36, Calle San Pantalon 3757) serves pasta and pizza for L8000 to L10,000. On Tuesday nights there's live music, usually of a light jazz variety. It's closed Sunday.

At *Trattoria al Ponte (Map 3; ☎ 041 71 97 77, Ponte del Megio 1666)* arrive early and try to grab one of the few canal-side tables. This simple, down-home little eatery tends to specialise in fish, but other options are available. The food is solid and the prices reasonable – a full meal will probably see a L50,000 note leave your possession. It's closed Saturday evening and Sunday.

Light on the Heart of Darkness

If you pass under the sotoportego to the east of the Vecio Fritolin, you'll notice on the left an altar in the wall. In fact, you may already have seen them scattered about town; there are some 500 in all. Their purpose was not just to encourage passers-by to stop for a moment of prayer and contemplation. Apart from helping to bring light to the darkness of tormented souls, the candles or oil lamps kept alight in them also served as a form of street lighting from medieval times.

If that fails, *Osteria La Zucca (Map 3; ☎ 041 524 15 70, Calle del Tintor 1762)*, just over the bridge, is an excellent alternative. It seems like just another Venetian trattoria, but the menu (which changes daily) is an enticing mix of Mediterranean themes. The vegetable side orders alone are inspired (try the *peperonata alle melanzane*, a cool stew of capsicum and aubergine), while the mains are substantial. You won't need to order pasta as well. It's closed Sunday.

At *Vecio Fritolin (Map 3; ☎ 041 522 28 81, Calle della Regina 226)* you can sit down for a meal of fried seafood or just munch cichetti at the bar over an ombra. They have a good wine list from regions as far apart as Piedmont and Tuscany. A *fritolin* traditionally was an eatery where diners sat at a common table bedecked with bits of fried seafood and polenta and simply dug in. Things are not quite so messy here nowadays. In fact, the phenomenon seems to have disappeared from Venetian life – a great loss. It's closed Sunday and Monday lunch time.

Dorsoduro You'll find several choices for snacks and drinks on Campo Santa Margherita, including the *Green Pub (Map 5; ☎ 041 520 59 76, Campo Santa Margherita 3053/a)*, which is also good for a Guinness (considered by many to be a substantial meal on its own). It's closed Thursday.

Caffè (Map 5; ☎ 041 528 79 98, Campo Santa Margherita 2693) is a lively student bar with snacks. Definitely a hip hang-out, it is known to locals as the *caffè rosso* because of the red sign. It's closed Sunday.

For a more substantial meal, *Al Sole di Napoli* (Map 5; ☎ 041 528 56 86, Campo Santa Margherita 3023) is one of the best pizza joints in town. Try the huge *pantera rosa* (pink panther), smothered in a thick tomato paste, then slathered with prawns in a cocktail sauce and finally topped with a forest of rucola (L16,000). It's closed Thursday.

Osteria da Toni (Map 5; ☎ 041 528 68 99, Fondamenta San Basilio 1642) is a popular workers' haunt. You can eat great seafood at relatively low prices or just sip wine. When the sun shines, take your place by the canal. It's closed Monday.

Trattoria ai Cugnai (Map 5; ☎ 041 528 92 38, Piscina Forner 857) is a simple little place with solid home cooking – their various soups are great in winter. Expect to part company with about L50,000 a head for a full meal. It's closed Monday.

Castello Between Riva degli Schiavoni and Campo SS Filippo e Giacomo is *Al Vecchio Penasa* (Map 6; ☎ 041 523 72 02, Calle delle Rasse, Castello 4587), which offers an excellent selection of sandwiches and snacks at reasonable prices.

One of the few restaurants near Piazza San Marco that can be recommended is *Alla Rivetta* (Map 6; ☎ 041 528 73 02, Ponte San Provolo 4625). It has long been on the tourist list of must places to eat, but you can still get edible seafood for not unreasonable prices. It's closed Monday.

Pizzeria da Egidio (Map 6; ☎ 041 528 91 69, Campo Santa Maria Formosa 5245) serves generous pizzas costing from L9000 to L12,000, and you can sit in the piazza. It's closed Wednesday.

For cheap and cheerful food, *Trattoria agli Artisti* (Map 6; ☎ 041 277 02 90, Ruga Giuffa 4625) is an acceptable stop. They have one set menu going for L18,000 and another, slightly better one, for L24,000. You can't complain about the prices! It's closed Wednesday.

It is not often you find a restaurant that in the early evening can post a sign in the window saying *Completo* (full), as though it were a hotel. Well *Trattoria da Remigio* (Map 7; ☎ 041 523 00 89, Salizzada dei Greci 3416) can. Pasta costs about L9000 and main courses L18,000. It has a mixed menu, featuring Venetian fish dishes and some meat options. It's clearly busy and you'll need to book to be sure of a spot. It's closed Monday evening and Tuesday.

If you end up in the eastern end of Castello, past the Arsenale, you will be in a distinct minority. The only spot in this neighbourhood really worth considering is the homely little *Hostaria da Franz* (Map 8; ☎ 041 522 08 61, Fondamenta San Giuseppe 755). A full meal will probably set you back about L60,000, but you could settle for pasta at around L12,000. They specialise in crustaceous creatures. It's closed Tuesday. Otherwise, your only option is a cheap pizza at the nameless *pizzeria* (Map 8; Paludo San Antonio 876) in the back lanes near the Biennale Internazionale d'Arte complex. They cost from L6000 to L9000. It's closed Tuesday.

Sant'Elena The *Trattoria dal Pampo* (Map 8; ☎ 041 520 84 19, Calle Gen Chinotto) is a real locals' place for ombre and cichetti, but you can sit down and have a full meal for around L40,000. Set opposite a charming little park in this, the quietest end of the city, it comes well recommended. It's closed Friday. If you have made the effort to get here and find it's closed, about your only choice is *Trattoria al Diporto* (Map 2; ☎ 041 528 59 78, Calle Cengio 25–27), which is quite OK but nothing special. It's closed Monday.

Giudecca On this island there's a pseudo-Mexican culinary islet, *Los Murales* (Map 10; ☎ 041 523 00 04, Fondamenta della Zitelle 70). Here, you can have a very Italian set meal for L20,000 (which is not bad for lunch) or tapas type things in the evening. It's closed Wednesday.

Ai Tre Scaini (Map 10; ☎ 041 522 47 90, Calle Michelangelo 53/c) is *the* popular local eatery. It's a no-nonsense place for seafood and other goodies and you can dine

PLACES TO EAT

in the garden out the back. You should be able to get away with around L40,000 (which will include copious amounts of house wine). It's closed Sunday.

Lido The island is not particularly known for its great cuisine. One down-to-earth exception to the rule is *Bar Trento (Map 13; ☎ 041 526 59 60, Via San Gallo 82)*. For around L30,000 you can tuck into a hearty full meal. On offer are tempting cichetti and a series of baccalà dishes, several variations on risotto (changing with the season) and other Venetian specialities. Except for the two weeks of the cinema festival, Bar Trento opens for lunch only. It's closed Sunday.

Trattoria da Scarso (☎ 041 77 08 34, Piazzale Malamocco 4) is a simple trattoria with a pleasant pergola. Set in the tiny old Venetian settlement of Malamocco, it isn't too heavily frequented by *foresti* (foreigners). The local colour alone makes it an attractive stop. It's closed Monday.

Murano The *Osteria dalla Mora (Map 11; ☎ 041 527 46 06, Fondamenta Manin 75)* looks out over one of the island's canals and is worth considering for lunch or dinner. A meal will cost around L55,000. The *frittura mista*, or mixed fried seafood dish, is a popular request. It's closed Friday.

Chioggia Several options suggest themselves in central Chioggia, all just off or near Corso del Popolo. *Ristorante Vecio Foghero (☎ 041 40 46 79, Calle Scopici 91)* has good pizzas and seafood. The *tagliolini al salmone* (pasta with salmon sauce) is tempting. This is one of a few cheap restaurant options that put its Venetian counterparts to shame, at least in relative terms of quality and wallet damage. It's closed Tuesday.

Another good one to look for is *Trattoria Y Nada Mas (☎ 041 40 47 95, Calle Fattorini 255)*. They have half a dozen tables in air-con comfort upstairs and another six on the lane. The limited seafood menu is very good. Try the *gnocchetti al sugo di pesce*, tiny gnocchi bathed in a tangy fish sauce. It's closed Monday. In both places you should get a full meal for around L40,000.

A little brassier but equally popular is *Ristorante El Fontego (☎ 041 550 09 53, Piazzetta XX Settembre 497)*. It offers a broad range of vegetarian pizzas and 'cream pizzas' (with a brie cheese base). Actually, they're not bad. It's closed Monday.

Osteria Penzo (☎ 041 40 09 92, Calle Larga Bersaglio 526) is a slightly pricier option. This place once offered no more than wine and basic cichetti, but now presents local cuisine based entirely on the fleet's catch. Expect to pay around L50,000, exclusive of wine. It's closed Tuesday.

Mestre A couple of blocks from the train station, *Da Bepi Venesian (Map 15; ☎ 041 92 93 57, Via Sernaglia 27)* serves traditional dishes. A meal could cost L50,000. The place is huge – with four dining areas – and specialises in fish. Try the *seppie con polenta* (cuttlefish with polenta). It's closed Monday.

At *Osteria La Pergola (Map 15; ☎ 041 97 49 32, Via Fiume 42)* you could be served a delicious plate of *pappardelle all'anatra* (a thick pasta with duck) below the vines of the garden pergola. You can get away with L40,000. It's closed Saturday lunch time and Sunday.

Chains

Those on a tight budget in particular may want to keep an eye out for these cheaper eateries. Several Italian firms have taken the fast-food concept and put a local spin on it. The result is a cut way above the McDonald's of this world (we have indicated one of these in Cannaregio, on Map 4, for those who need a fix – three others lurk in Sestiere San Marco and one at Mestre train station), at an affordable price.

The bad news is that you won't find many outside Mestre – and however good the value, it is hard to recommend a special trip to Mestre! Since chains have a habit of spreading, you may run into others by the time you read this.

At *Brek (Map 15; Via Carducci 54, Mestre)* first courses cost about L5000 and seconds L7000. *Spizzico (Map 4; Strada Nova 3834/a)*, in Cannaregio, does pizza

The island of Burano, in the north of the lagoon, attracts visitors with its striking facades.

Lido di Jesolo, one of the Veneto's top beaches

A *peata* on the Canal Grande di Murano

Cafe society on Piazza San Marco: elegant and extravagant

A quiet moment in the piazza

Dining by the Grand Canal

Damigiane – Italian wine kegs

A shady spot on the Canal Grande di Murano

slices for around L5000. It's open until 11 pm and sometimes closed on Sunday.

Self-Catering

Putting your own snacks together is the cheapest way to keep body and soul together. The best *markets* take place on the San Polo side of the Ponte di Rialto (Map 7).

For salami, cheese and wine, shop in alimentari or *salumerie*, which are a cross between grocery stores and delicatessens. Fresh bread is available at a *forno* or *panetteria* (bakeries which sell bread, pastries and sometimes groceries) and usually at alimentari. You'll find a concentration of these around Campo Beccarie, which happens to lie next to the city's main fish market (Map 4).

There is a *Standa supermarket* (Map 3) on Strada Nova, Cannaregio, and another Standa at the corner of Calle Magazen and Calle Goldoni (Map 6), near Campo San Luca in Sestiere di San Marco. *Billa Billa supermarket* (Map 5), down on the Zattere near the Stazione Marittima, is a big place where you can stock up before hitting the high seas for Greece. The *Coop supermarket* (Map 4), at Rio Terrà dei Santi Apostoli 4662, in Cannaregio, and the *Mini-Coop* (Map 3), at Campo San Giacomo dell'Orio 1492, are also good places to hunt for nutrients and other useful items.

PLACES TO EAT – MID-RANGE

We take this to mean a fairly broad range, up until around L100,000 a head. By London standards, for instance, this is not an unreasonable sum to pay, especially if the chow on offer is good. If you've landed in Venice from the United States or Australasia and haven't acclimatised your purse to the European fiscal free-for-all, this may seem a little shocking. Such is life.

Restaurants

Cannaregio The *Trattoria al Vagon* (Map 4; ☎ 041 523 75 88, Cannaregio 5596), overlooking the Rio dei SS Apostoli, is wonderful for its canalside dining under the porticoes. The food is OK without being spectacular and the prices are a little ele-

vated – you are paying for the location rather than the salivation here. It's closed Tuesday.

Vini da Gigio (Map 4; ☎ 041 528 51 40, Fondamenta della Chiesa 3628/a) is a wine drinker's home away from heaven. A selection of fine whites (the crisp Soave Classico 1996 is good) and reds from the Veneto and beyond (ranging from L35,000 to L60,000 a bottle) help wash down some fine cooking – how about the *gnocchi con burro fuso e ricotta affumicata* (little dumplings bathed in melted butter and smoked ricotta cheese)? It's closed Monday.

San Marco The *Ristorante da Ivo* (Map 6; ☎ 041 528 50 04, San Marco 1809) specialises in seafood and is recognised as one of Venice's best restaurants. Consequently it's not cheap: a full seafood meal will cost around L80,000 to L100,000. It's closed Sunday.

Ristorante ai Barbacani (Map 6; ☎ 041 521 02 34, Calle del Paradiso 5746), right by a canal bridge, is a delightful spot if you can grab a waterside seat – but don't fall in! As for the food, it's fine without being Venice's best. Prices are moderate. It's closed Monday.

Since 1953, *Ristorante al Gazzettino* (Map 6; ☎ 041 522 33 14, San Marco 4971), below the pensione of the same name, has been a well-known favourite in central Venice. Until 1977, journos and printers from *Il Gazzettino* newspaper, then based in the nearby Ca' Faccanon, made it their regular. As if in tribute to the good ol' days, the present owners have plastered the walls with pages from *Il Gazzettino* past – if you can read Italian, you'll find it hard not to let your food go cold. It's closed Monday.

The *Fiaschetteria Toscana* (Map 4; ☎ 041 528 52 81, Calle Crisostomo 5719) is about as Tuscan as a gondola. Rather they serve up Venetian food to be washed down with a choice of wines from an impressive list which includes tipples from around the country. The *frittura della Serenissima*, a mixed fried seafood platter, is memorable. It's closed Monday lunch time and Tuesday.

PLACES TO EAT

Santa Croce & San Polo The *Trattoria alla Madonna (Map 6; ☎ 041 522 38 24, Calle della Madonna, San Polo 594)*, a few streets west of the Rialto off Fondamenta del Vin, is an excellent trattoria specialising in seafood. Prices are reasonable, but a full meal will cost L60,000 or more. It's closed Wednesday.

Al Nono Risorto (Map 3; ☎ 041 524 11 69, Sotoportego de Siora Bettina). Stop in here if only to luxuriate in the canalside garden. *Pesce ai ferri* (grilled fish) is tasty at L25,000. You can precede it with various pasta dishes at around L13,000. It's closed Wednesday.

Trattoria dalla Zanze (Map 3; ☎ 041 522 35 55, Fondamenta dei Tolentini 231) is a mid-priced spot popular with locals in search of seafood platters. The *grigliata mista* (L40,000 with vegetable side order) is not bad at all. It's closed Sunday.

Fancy a quick curry? Forget it. But a good slow one can be had on the pleasant little canalside terrace of **Shri Ganesh** *(Map 3; ☎ 041 71 90 84, Rio Marin, San Polo 2426)*. Danilo and his charmingly chaotic staff serve up authentic dishes at reasonable prices – particularly pleased guests have scribbled their appreciation on the walls. They even do takeaways. It's closed Wednesday.

Dorsoduro Typical regional fare is served at *L'Incontro (Map 5; ☎ 041 522 24 04, Rio Terrà Canal 3062)*, between Campo San Barnaba and Campo Santa Margherita. The menu alters daily and a full meal will cost around L40,000. It's closed Monday.

The restaurant at the *Antica Locanda Montin* hotel *(Map 5; ☎ 041 522 71 51, Fondamenta di Borgo 1147)*, near Campo San Barnaba, has generally good food and a shady garden. If you want quantity for money this is perhaps not the place to come, as it is rather pricey and appeals to gourmands. They offer some fine wines to go with the meal, so you will be looking at around L80,000 a head. It's closed Wednesday.

Castello Closer to the centre of things is *Al Covo (Map 7; ☎ 041 522 38 12, Campiello della Pescaria 3968)*. Anyone who

can afford to shut their doors twice a week must feel pretty confident about their product. The place has quite a name among Venetians. Cuisine is resolutely local and with main courses at over L25,000, you can expect to pay around L70,000 for a full meal. For lunch there's a special L50,000 job set meal. Credit cards are not accepted. It's closed Wednesday and Thursday.

Hidden well away off even the unbeaten track is *Trattoria Corte Sconta (Map 7; ☎ 041 522 70 24, Calle Pestrin 3886)*. The chefs prepare almost exclusively seafood, served up to you inside or in a charming little garden. The owners cannot guarantee that on any given day all the dishes on the menu will be available for the simple reason that they use only the fish and other sea critters they find fresh at the market that day. Who can carp at such a policy? You will pay around L75,000 for a full meal with wine. It's closed Sunday and Monday.

Al Nuovo Galeon (Map 8; ☎ 041 520 46 56, Via Garibaldi 1308) not only has a boat jammed inside it, but it feels as if you are in the cabin of a great Venetian merchant ship. There aren't too many fine dining choices around this part of town, so it can get a little packed – booking ahead is advisable. It specialises in fish dishes and you can expect to part with around L60,000 a head. It's closed Tuesday. Just out of interest, next door is the recently restored entrance to the former Ospeal de le Pute. It seems to be Venetian for Whores' Hospice. Venice was known for its courtesans, but the mind boggles.

Giudecca Run by the Hotel Cipriani, *Harry's Dolci (Map 9; ☎ 041 522 48 44, Fondamenta San Biagio 773)* has fantastic desserts (which is the main reason for stopping by). Should you want a full meal they can also accommodate you. It will cost L80,000 or more. There's a snack bar too. It's closed Tuesday, and open from April to October only.

For the average pocket, the best deal on the island is *All'Altanella (Map 9; ☎ 041 522 77 80, Calle delle Erbe 268)*. Seafood is the speciality. Romantic candle-lit dinners in winter or outside by the canal in summer are the order of the evening. It's closed Monday and Tuesday.

Burano The island is pretty, but the restaurant prices are less so. One of the better choices is *Ristorante Galuppi (Map 12; ☎ 041 73 00 81, Via B Galuppi 470)* – look for the dolls in the windows. A meal will cost about L40,000 a person. It's closed Thursday, except in summer.

Torcello Unless you plan to blow your budget at the famous Locanda Cipriani (see the next section), try *Al Trono di Attila (Map 12; ☎ 041 73 00 94, Fondamenta Borgognoni 7/a)*, between the ferry stop and the cathedral, where a full meal will cost around L40,000. The atmosphere is suitably bucolic and you will want to dine in the charming garden with pergola. Try the *gnocchetti con rucola e scampi* (small

Osteria 'Opping

Venice's osterie (also known as *bacari*) are a cross between bars and trattorie, where you can sample *cichetti* (small snacks of finger-food such as stuffed olives and vegetables deep-fried in batter). The little glass of wine you quaff to wash these down is often referred to also as an *ombra*. They say the name, which means 'shade', comes from the days when people would go to stands set up in the shade in the local square for an afternoon tipple. Locals often choose to bar hop from osteria to osteria, munching cichetti as they go. They are a great way to experience a more down-to-earth side of Venice.

Some osterie serve full meals. *Osteria al Mascaron (Map 6; ☎ 041 522 59 95, Calle Lunga, Castello 5525)*, east of Campo Santa Maria Formosa, is a bar/osteria and trattoria. The cichetti are good, but a meal is overpriced. It's closed Sunday. The *Osteria dalla Vedova (Map 4; ☎ 041 528 53 24, Calle del Pistor 3912)*, off Strada Nova in Cannaregio, is also called Trattoria Ca d'Or and is one of the oldest osterie in Venice. The food is excellent and modestly priced – L40,000 will cover you. It's closed Sunday and Thursday.

In the San Marco area, near Campo San Luca, *Enoteca Il Volto (Map 6; ☎ 041 522 89 45, Calle Cavalli 4081)*, has an excellent wine selection and good snacks. It's closed Tuesday. Another good little place along these lines could easily slip your notice. *Osteria da Carla (Map 6; ☎ 041 523 78 55, Ramo Primo Corte Contarini 1535)* is tucked away just west of Piazza San Marco. It's largely a locals' place to snack and sip wine. You could make a full meal of *sarde in saor, baccalà* (a creamy cod concoction) and other seafood dishes, but the place is a little overpriced for this kind of thing – stick to the bar. It's closed Sunday.

On the San Polo side of the Ponte di Rialto, *Cantina do Mori (Map 4; ☎ 041 522 54 01, Sotoportego dei do Mori)* is something of a traditional institution. Unfortunately, the local consensus is that the new managers have upped the prices and dropped the quality. Shame, because it is an enticing place, oozing history and character. It's closed Sunday. A few steps away, the *Cantina do Spade (Map 3; ☎ 041 521 05 74, Calle do Spade 860)* is Venice's oldest eating house – L60,000 should see you through dinner. It's closed Sunday. Nearby, the choice for cichetti is probably *All'Arco (Map 4; ☎ 041 520 56 66, Calle Arco, San Polo 436)*. It's closed Sunday.

Osteria alla Patatina (Map 5; ☎ 041 523 72 38, Calle Saoneri 2741/a) is a straight-up-and-down local eatery where the cichetti are tasty and the simple first courses go down well with a glass of red or two. It retains a traditional air. It's closed Saturday evening and Sunday.

Another hidden Venetian jewel along similar lines is *Osteria da Alberto (Map 4; ☎ 041 523 81 53, Calle Gallina 5401)*, in Cannaregio. Be aware that they close the kitchen by about 9 pm here. The baccalà is good. It's closed Sunday.

gnocchi with rocket and shrimps). Generally it opens for lunch only, unless you book ahead for dinner. It's closed Monday. The only other option on the island is *Osteria al Ponte del Diavolo (Map 12; ☎ 041 73 04 01, Fondamenta Borgognoni 10–11)*. It's closed Wednesday.

Gelaterie
Gelateria Millefoglie da Tarvisio (Map 5; San Polo 3034), behind the Chiesa di Santa Maria Gloriosa dei Frari, is an excellent ice cream stop.

The best ice cream in Venice is from *Gelati Nico (Map 5; Fondamenta delle Zattere 922)*. The locals take their evening stroll along the fondamenta while eating their gelati. *Gelateria il Doge (Map 5; Campo Santa Margherita)* also has excellent gelati.

Pasticceria
One of Venice's better cake shops is *Pasticceria Marchini (Map 5; Calle Spezier 2769)*, just off Campo Santo Stefano.

PLACES TO EAT – TOP END
Using L100,000 a head as the artificial marker, wherever you can be reasonably sure of busting that limit without trying has been slotted in here.

Restaurants
San Marco A quick stroll west of Piazza San Marco, *Harry's Bar (Map 6; ☎ 041 528 57 77, Calle Vallaresso 1323)* is off Salizzada San Moisè. The Cipriani family, who started the bar in 1931, claims to have invented many Venetian specialities, including the Bellini cocktail (L18,000).

A meal at the restaurant upstairs will cost you at least L150,000 but it is one of only two restaurants in the city to have been awarded a Michelin star. Toscanini, Chaplin and just about everyone who was anyone (and quite a few who were definitely no-one) have eaten and drunk here. It's open daily.

San Polo The other recipient of a Michelin star is *Da Fiore (Map 3; ☎ 041 72 13 08, Calle del Scaleter 2202)*. The unprepossessing shopfront appearance belies an Art Deco interior and some killer dishes, such as *risotto di scampi* and *bigoli in salsa*. They have a good wine selection and you can easily hit the L120,000 mark. This doesn't deter people though, and the place can easily be booked out for dinner weeks in advance. It's easier to get in for lunch. Da Fiore is closed Sunday and Monday.

Closer to Rialto, *Trattoria Poste Vecie (Map 4; ☎ 041 72 10 37, Pescaria 1608)* claims to be the oldest eating house in Venice. It is definitely inviting, but the L100,000 or more you spend will be for the location more than the food. It's closed Tuesday. The name, which means 'old post office', refers to the days when many states and cities took care of their own post and thus had offices across Venice at the service of their own citizens. After the fall of the Republic, many offices were converted to wine cellars.

Torcello The *Locanda Cipriani (Map 12; ☎ 041 73 01 50, Piazza Santa Fosca 29)* has been an exclusive culinary hideaway since 1946. Ernest Hemingway, more readily associated with Spain, set down his bags here in 1948 and wrote part of his *Across the River and Into the Trees*. They don't let out rooms in this rustic retreat anymore, but it's an enticing place to splash out on your rumbling tum. Expect to part with at least L100,000 a head. It opens for lunch only, except on Saturday, when you can also do dinner, and it's closed Tuesday.

Cafes & Bars
If you can cope with the idea of paying upwards of L10,000 for a cappuccino (some lucky people have reported being charged as much as L20,000), spend an hour or so sitting at an outdoor table at Florian or Quadri, enjoying the atmosphere in Piazza San Marco, the world's most famous square.

Caffè Florian (Map 6) is the more famous of the two – its plush interior has seen the likes of Lord Byron and Henry James taking breakfast (separately) before they crossed the piazza to *Caffè Quadri (Map 6; ☎ 041 522 21 05, San Marco 120)* for lunch.

The restaurant at Quadri is closed Monday and Tuesday.

A little less renowned, but in the same vein, is **Lavena** (*Map 6; ☎ 041 522 40 70, San Marco 133*). Wagner was among its more visible customers, but historically gondoliers and codegas (see the boxed text on this page) also hung out here. It's closed Tuesday from October to March.

All three cafes have bars, where you can pay less extravagant prices for a coffee or drink (taken on your feet) and still enjoy the elegant surroundings.

In summer they go to the trouble of having quartets playing under awnings on the square – they seem to compete with one another for attention, one striking up some stirring Vivaldi and the other countering with a little modern stuff. They usually have the courtesy of playing in turns – if you stand in the middle of the square when they aren't being so gentlemanly, the effect is

Shining Path

Until street lighting began to make an appearance in 1732, anyone game enough to venture into the streets at night would, if they had any sense, hire the services of a *codega*. This fellow has traditionally been depicted as a mere lantern-bearer who would precede you down the twisting *calli* to your destination and so light your way. Nocturnal crime was something of a problem in Venice (as in most other cities), so it seems logical to assume that these fellows were fairly well versed in the gentle art of street brawling should the need arise.

more cacophonous than melodious. Which is reassuring – even when trying to outdo itself in refined elegance, Venice can occasionally be humanly lacking in finesse.

Entertainment

The Venice Carnevale (see Festivals under Public Holidays & Special Events in the Facts for the Visitor chapter) is one of Italy's best-known festivals, but exhibitions, theatre and musical events continue throughout the year. Information is available in *Un Ospite di Venezia*, and the tourist office also has brochures listing events and performances for the entire year.

BARS
San Marco
The *Black Jack Bar* (Map 6; Campo San Luca) serves a decent Bellini, among other cocktails, for L3500. It's closed Sunday. In the market area at Campo Beccarie is *Vini da Pinto* (Map 4), a small bar frequented by stallholders.

Vino Vino (see the Places to Eat chapter) is great just for sipping wine if you want to forget the food.

The *Devil's Forest* (Map 6; ☎ 041 520 00 23, Calle Stagneri 5185) is a reasonable imitation of a UK pub, complete with old red telephone box and Irish beers on tap (Kilkenny and Harp). It's open until 1 am, but is closed Sunday.

The *Irishark* (Map 6; Calle Mondo Nuovo 5788), closed Sunday, is yet another little twist on the Irish pub theme. 'Nuff said.

At *Bacaro Jazz* (Map 6; ☎ 041 528 52 49, Salizzada San Giovanni Crisostomo 5546) you can enjoy happy hour from 7 to 10 pm. The place likes to sell itself as an eatery too – a rather pricey one. It won't be to everyone's taste, being a little brash and too close to the tourist route for comfort, but at least it's open until 2 am. It's closed Wednesday.

If you like the piano-bar scene, maybe *Martini Scala* (Map 6; ☎ 041 522 41 21, San Marco 1501) is for you. It's a little cheesy and very pricey, but then the options aren't bountiful, are they? The bar opens from 9 pm to 3.30 am and is closed Tuesday.

Morozi (Map 5; Campo Santa Stefano 2801) attracts a mixed crowd of locals and *foresti* (foreigners). You can drink on the *campo* (square) until 2 am and they keep the kitchen open for food until 11 pm and sometimes later – unheard of in Venice. It's closed Monday.

As well as being one of the city's more notable restaurants, *Harry's Bar* (see the Places to Eat chapter) is, of course, first and foremost known as a bar. Everyone who is anyone and passing through Venice usually ends up here sooner or later. The Aga Khan has lounged around here and other characters as diverse as Orson Welles, Ernest Hemingway and Truman Capote have all sipped on a cocktail or two at Harry's.

Cannaregio
The nameless *wine bar* (Map 3), by the bridge at Rio Terrà della Maddalena in Cannaregio, is great for a drink or three. It tends to be a local hang-out. *Paradiso Perduto* (see the Places to Eat chapter) is a hip joint with live music.

On the Irish scene, *The Fiddler's Elbow* (Map 4; Corte dei Pali 3847) is representative of the genre. It's closed Wednesday.

Oodles of wine and 120 types of bottled beer in one knockabout little place? Perhaps you should get along to *Osteria agli Ormesini* (Map 3; ☎ 041 71 38 34, Fondamenta degli Ormesini 2710), open for whistle-wetting until 2 am. It's something of a student haunt and tipplers spill out on to the fondamenta to enjoy their ambers. It's closed Sunday. *Le Notti d'Oriente* (Map 3; ☎ 041 71 73 15), at No 2578, is a not so great North African restaurant, but later in the evening people tend to use it as a bar – at least in summer when you can sit out by the canal. It's open daily.

Dorsoduro
Caffè Blue Music (Map 5; ☎ 041 523 72 27, Dorsoduro 3778) is a coolish student bar with live music on Friday. It's open until 2 am, but it has to be said it can be a little quiet on some evenings. It's closed Sunday.

Fill 'Er Up

Yes, it's all very fine sitting about posturing in fine restaurants and paying high prices, but sometimes you just want some plonk to have at home. And there's the question of cost – not everyone can afford to go out and invest in great-name labels.

Fortunately, apart from the wonderful option of sipping wines in a local osteria or bacaro, a fine take-home tradition persists in Venice. Every now and then you will stumble across a wine shop. You'll know you've hit one if you find it crammed with huge glass containers (the kind of 'bottle' even Hercules would have trouble slugging from) known as *damigiane*. From these monsters, each containing a sea of simple and quite acceptable Veneto table wine, you make a choice and have it poured into whatever you bring – used wine or mineral-water bottles – it's up to you. The stuff is siphoned (much as you would siphon petrol from a car) into your bottle and you will be charged, on average, L3800 per litre.

A chain called Nave de Oro has four branches in Venice (listed below) and one each on the Lido and Murano. A handful of other places along the same lines can also be found:

Cantina dal Baffo
(Map 3; Fondamenta degli Ormesini, Cannaregio 2678) Open daily from 8.30 am to 1 pm and 5 to 7.30 pm (afternoon only on Wednesday)
Nave de Oro
(Map 3; Rio Terrà San Leonardo, Cannaregio 1370) Open daily from 8 am to 1 pm and 4.30 to 7.30 pm (afternoon only on Wednesday)
(Map 4; Calle dei SS Apostoli 4657) Open daily except Sunday from 9 am to 1 pm and 5 to 8 pm (morning only on Wednesday)
(Map 5; Campo Santa Margherita, Dorsoduro 3664) Open from 9 am to 1 pm and 5 to 7.30 pm (morning only on Wednesday)
(Map 6; Calle Mondo Nuovo, Castello 5786/b) Open from 9 am to 1 pm and 5 to 7.45 pm (morning only on Wednesday)
Wine Shops (Nameless)
(Map 3; Fondamenta di Cannaregio 1116) Open daily from 8.30 am to 1 pm and 4.30 to 7.30 pm (morning only on Wednesday)
(Map 5; Campo Santa Margherita, Dorsoduro 2897) Open from 9 am to 12.30 pm and 5 to 7.30 pm (morning only on Wednesday)

A couple of steps east, **Café Noir** *(Map 5; ☎ 041 71 09 25, Calle dei Preti 3805)* was about to reopen as writing was finished. It's the only true Internet cafe in the city, so is worth checking out for that reason alone.

Cantinone Già Schiavi *(Map 5; Fondamenta Maravegie 992)* is a fusty old wine bar across from the Chiesa di San Trovaso. Wander in for a glass of *prosecco* (a lightly bubbly Venetian white wine) beneath the bar's low-slung rafters and in the wavering light provided by dodgy bulbs. Alternatively, you could just buy a bottle of whatever takes your fancy and take it away. It's closed Sunday.

Santa Croce
Ai Postali *(Map 3; ☎ 041 71 51 76, Fondamenta Marin 821)* is a buzzy little locals' bar along the Rio Marin. Roberto gave up flying for Alitalia to pilot this place until 2 am and sometimes later. It's closed Sunday.

CLUBS & DISCOS
The club and dancing scene in Venice is virtually zero. One or two possibilities are available, but if you are looking for action, do not come to Venice.

Things look up a little in summer, when a handful of places open on the Lido, but the real action goes on at Jesolo, on the coast to

euro currency converter L10,000 = €5.16

the north-east of Venice. Remember that although the word *discoteca* may conjure up images of bell-bottoms and big hair, it's the Italian equivalent of what others think of as clubs. A 'club' to an Italian could be anything from a local bingo association to a sleazy night spot where people with bald pates, bad-smelling cigars and chest carpets buy drinks for themselves and their recently acquired girlfriends.

In Italy, the in clubs for the young, student-age set tend to be placed well out of the way, in the countryside or small towns. Generally, the only way to get to them is to drive, and you need to be right up to date with what's in and what's out. The same is true in Venice and around. Get a hold of *Press Music* or *Venezia News* for some specific ideas.

Expect to pay from around L10,000 to L20,000 to get into a club. This may include the first drink. A few options are given here.

Dorsoduro

Piccolo Mondo (Map 5; ☎ 041 520 03 71, San Marco 1506) is a little on the slimy side, but perfectly all right in its own, wide-lapel fashion. It does have the merit of being open until 4 am (closed Monday). It attracts a 30s-plus crowd.

Mestre

The best offering here is *Zoo (☎ 041 541 51 00, Via Ca' Zorzi 2)*, out in Tessera, near San Marco airport. In three dance spaces you can weave from house to Latin rhythms or mainstream pop. It's open Wednesday, Friday and Saturday from 11 pm to 4 am. In the centre of town, you can sip cocktails and listen to good music at *Metrò (Map 15; Via Einaudi)*. It's open daily from 10 pm to 4 am.

Chioggia

In summer, especially, a row of beach-front discos cranks up for the local holiday crowd in Sottomarina. It's not really practical from Venice, though.

Jesolo

About one hour's drive from Venice, this seaside resort is where the nightlife really is, from June to September. ATVO bus No 10a

from Piazzale Roma takes about 70 minutes and costs L6000 (or L10,600 return, valid for three days). The problem is getting back home. Even in summer, the last bus leaves at 11.20 pm. Locals seem to compete to see who will be killed first on the roads. Perhaps sleeping the night off on the beach would be safer! If you find a taxi, you are looking at L140,000 or more, depending on the traffic.

Top of the list is *Movida (☎ 0421 96 17 19, Viale Belgio 149)*, which throws its doors open from 11 pm to 5 am on Saturday (June to September), with the latest in house music and all its derivatives.

Down on the beach, *AIDA/Elastique (Via Mameli 105)* keeps the same hours and in three different rooms presents a variety of music, with the latest in club sounds dominating. Another place, along similar lines although without quite the same profile, is *Matilda (☎ 0421 37 07 68, Via Bafile 342)*. It's open Wednesday, Friday and Saturday from 11 pm to 5 am. Another half-dozen clubs/discos keep Jesolo fairly busy, but as you might have guessed from reading the above, it really only hops on weekends.

Sound Garden (Via Aleardi/Piazza Mazzini), open nightly from 10 pm to 4 am, concentrates on rock (sometimes of the hard variety) and features live bands on Friday.

MUSIC
Classical & Baroque

Several groups of musicians perform regular concerts of classical or baroque music throughout most of the year. These are aimed at tourists and can be a little cheesy, but the quality is really not bad.

A popular venue for classical music recitals over the past few years has been the Chiesa di Santa Maria della Pietà, or La Pietà (Map 7), on the Riva degli Schiavoni. Others are the Chiesa di San Bartolomeo (Map 6) near the Ponte di Rialto, the Chiesa delle Zitelle on Giudecca (Map 10), the Scuola Grande di San Teodoro (Map 6) in San Marco and the Scuola Grande di San Giovanni Evangelista (Map 3).

The two standard Venetians, Vivaldi and Albinoni, figure in the repertoire of the

Interpreti Veneziani. Rondò Veneziano go the period-costume route. Don't let that distract you, as their interpretations of 18th-century baroque music have won plaudits around the world. It may not be seriously highbrow, but it certainly is not lacking class. Following Rondò down the period-costume path is the Orchestra di Venezia (☎ 041 522 81 25).

Information and tickets for performances by pretty much any of these groups can be had from Agenzia Kele & Teo (Map 6; ☎ 041 520 87 22), Ponte dei Baratteri, San Marco. Expect typically to pay L35,000 to L40,000 a head.

Contemporary
With the exception of jazz, blues and the like, intermittently on offer at a handful of places such as Paradiso Perduto (see the earlier Bars section), there's not much happening.

Occasionally you can see bands play in Venice, but very occasionally. If you really want to see bands, you'll need to go to Mestre or even Padua. If you can get hold of the monthly booklet *Press Music* (you can sometimes find it lying around in Caffè – see the Places to Eat chapter), you will see that most of the action takes place well beyond the city limits. Even in Mestre the offerings aren't fabulous.

On the Lido you can sometimes catch live music in summer. *Piazza Caffè (Map 14; Lungomare Marconi 22)* quite often has dance ranging from underground to salsa. It's closed Monday. Right down the other end of the island, at Alberoni, *Energy Darshan* also puts on live music occasionally. *Il Gazzettino* newspaper seems to keep up with both of them.

Because the true university town in the region is Padua, that's where there is most likely to be some action – and even there, mostly out in the suburbs rather than in town itself.

In summer, occasional concerts are organised in Jesolo – watch the local press. A big rock event (in its fifth year in 1999) is Jesolo Beach Bum, (the Italian rendering of the English 'boom'), usually held over a weekend at the beginning of July. In Mestre's

Forte Marghera area, the big annual event is Al Fresco, a programme of nightly live music, from rock to ethnic, that runs from late June right through the summer. Admission on any given night costs L5000.

A Contemporary Music Festival is held annually in October at the Teatro Goldoni (see the Theatre section).

CINEMAS
The city doesn't have an English-language cinema. *Summer Arena*, a cinema-under-the-stars in Campo San Polo open during July and August, features British and American films, but they are generally dubbed. The time to see foreign cinema in the original language is during the Venice International Film Festival in September (see Festivals under Public Holidays & Special Events in the Facts for the Visitor chapter).

If you do have a hankering for the movies and can cope with dubbing into Italian, several cinemas screen decent movies.

Cinema Accademia d'Essai (Map 5; ☎ 041 528 77 06, Calle Corfu, Dorsoduro 1018) is a fusty old place with indifferent screen quality, but they choose quality flicks. Full price is L12,000; students/seniors pay L8000.

Cinema Giorgione Movie d'Essai (Map 4; ☎ 041 522 62 98, Cannaregio 4612) is new and quite a deal better. It also screens decent films. Tickets are L11,000.

In Mestre, the best bet is *Cinema Dante d'Essai (Map 15; ☎ 041 538 16 55, Via Sernaglia 12)*.

THEATRE
The main theatre in the centre of town is, unsurprisingly, the *Teatro Goldoni (Map 6; ☎ 041 520 75 83, Calle Teatro Goldoni 4650/b)*, named after the city's greatest playwright. It's not unusual for Goldoni's plays to be performed here – after all, what more appropriate location?

OPERA & BALLET
La Fenice
Until it was destroyed by fire in January 1996 (see the boxed text 'Faltering Phoenix' on the next page), *Teatro La Fenice*

ENTERTAINMENT

Faltering Phoenix

From as far off as the Ponte della Libertà, the bridge linking Venice to the mainland, scarlet flames could be seen shooting into the night sky as the pride of the city, the Teatro La Fenice, burned to the ground on 29 January 1996.

The blaze began at about 8 pm and five fire-brigade squads were rushed in to avert disaster – in vain. Fate would have it that the canals in the immediate area had been temporarily drained so that they could be unsilted. This lack of water close to hand proved fatal. Firemen managed to prevent the blaze spreading, but the theatre was utterly destroyed.

It had been closed since the previous August for refurbishment and was due to be reopened shortly. In May 1999 two electricians went on trial for arson. It is claimed they started the fire because they feared fines of L50 million for being late with their work. If it all went up in smoke, no-one would ever know they were behind schedule. Eight other people were also ordered into the dock, including mayor Massimo Cacciari. As chairman of the theatre's board, he was charged with negligence, along with other theatre administrators. Police say fire alarms had been turned off and highly inflammable materials left around the theatre. As far as the police are concerned, Cacciari and the others contributed to the swiftness and completeness of the destruction.

Built in 1792, the theatre was a tangible link with the final days of the Venetian Republic. The horseshoe-shaped seating created exquisite acoustics. Prior to a fire in 1836, various opera greats had made their mark here – Rossini, Bellini and Donizetti, to name a few. Rebuilt within two years, the theatre's halcyon days came with the years of close association between La Fenice and Giuseppe Verdi, who presented many of his most outstanding operas here in the 1850s. As the 19th century wore into the 20th, a more international flavour came to pervade the Venetian operatic scene, with works by such diverse composers as Britten and Prokofiev staged. All the greats have graced its stage, from Callas to Pavarotti.

(Map 5; Campo San Fantin, San Marco 1970) was Venice's premier opera stage. Performances of opera and ballet are still organised but held in alternative venues.

Among the more commonly used alternative venues are the hastily erected circus-style big top called the **PalaFenice** *(Map 2; ☎ 041 520 40 10, Isola del Tronchetto)*, the Scuola Grande di San Giovanni Evangelista (Map 3), Teatro Goldoni (Map 6) and the Chiesa di Santo Stefano (Map 5). Tickets are available from the Biglietteria del Teatro La Fenice outlet in the Cassa di Risparmio di Venezia bank (Map 6; ☎ 041 521 01 61), on Campo San Luca, or the Pala-Fenice (accessible by *vaporetto* No 82). You can look up the programme on the Web at www.tin.it/fenice and book online. At the same online address, you can also find details of booking agents in your country. The cost of tickets ranges up to L60,000 for a

decent seat at the opera. The performances are frequently by quality international artists, although we are not at the heights of Milan's La Scala here.

CASINO

The **Casinò Municipale di Venezia** *(☎ 041 529 71 11)* has two locations. In winter (October to May) it is on the Grand Canal at the Palazzo Vendramin-Calergi, Cannaregio 2040 (Map 3). It's open daily from 3 pm to 3 am. Take vaporetto Nos 1 or 82 and alight at the San Marcuola stop. All the old gamblers' favourites, from slot machines to black jack, are available to contribute to your fiscal demise.

In summer (June to September), the casino moves to the Palazzo del Casinò, Lungomare Marconi, the Lido (Map 13). It's open daily from 4 pm to 3 am. Vaporetto Nos 61/62 take you to/from the summer

Faltering Phoenix

If the manner of the theatre's demise in 1996 was lamentable, the story of its return to brilliance is perhaps even more so. Massimo Cacciari and just about everyone who is anyone in Venetian politics vowed to have the theatre back in action *dov'era, com'era* ('where it was and as it was') in time for the opera season in 2000. (The bon mot was a phrase borrowed from the 1902 collapse of the Campanile in Piazza San Marco – which was, in fact, rebuilt exactly as it had been.)

NICKY CAVEN

Burnt to the ground in 1996, La Fenice has yet to take after its namesake.

There is no chance of the theatre making that date now. After interminable delays, rebuilding work began only in February 1998. It lasted six months before 'irregularities' in the awarding of the building contracts were discovered. A new contract was only signed in May 1999. The latest estimate on when this Phoenix might again rise from the ashes is September 2002 ... at the earliest. The court case that had begun in May also ground to a halt – a quorum of judges with no remote involvement in the theatre cannot be found before the end of 1999.

In the meantime, opera-goers have to content themselves with the 'big top' circus tents known as the PalaFenice, on the Isola del Tronchetto, as the interim alternative theatre.

---

version, departing from San Zaccaria. The Casinò Express ferry also leaves from Tronchetto and Piazzale Roma. You can buy a *Coupon Casinò* at the car parks at Tronchetto and Piazzale Roma. The coupon covers the cost of parking, the ferry and admission to the game rooms. Normal full-price admission costs L10,000. People under the age of 18 are not allowed in.

FOOTBALL

Like anywhere else in Italy, *il calcio* reigns supreme in the hearts and minds of many a Venetian. The *arancioneroverde* (orange, black and greens) are a mid-level team rarely touched by the ultimate pleasure of competition victory. They play at the Stadio Penzo, on Isola Sant'Elena (Map 2), at the far eastern end of the lagoon city. The uniqueness of the team's home town makes for some interesting logistics when the side

plays at home. Special ferry services are laid on between Tronchetto car park and Sant'Elena – normally a quiet little place with hardly a soul to disturb the leafy peace. All buses arriving in Venice on a match day are diverted first to Tronchetto to disgorge their loads of fans before reaching Piazzale Roma.

Tickets are available at the stadium itself or from branches of the Banca Antoniana Popolare Veneta. An average seat will cost around L35,000. The bank used as a ticket outlet can change from year to year, so you may want to ask at the tourist office or call Venezia Calcio (☎ 041 95 81 00). Because Venice is not a top-flight team, getting tickets on match day is rarely a problem, even when Verona, the only other Veneto team currently in Serie A, comes to town. This tends to be a fun game, regardless of where the teams are placed on the ladder, as it excites passions as only a local derby can.

ENTERTAINMENT

euro currency converter L10,000 = €5.16

Shopping

The main shopping area for clothing, shoes, accessories and jewellery is in the narrow streets between San Marco and the Rialto, particularly the Mercerie and around Campo San Luca. The more upmarket shops are west of Piazza San Marco.

For arty stuff, ranging from Carnevale masks and costumes through ceramics and on to model gondolas, San Polo is the place to hunt. Another Venetian speciality is marbled paper – you'll find people doing this all over town.

Many places open on Sunday during the tourist season. For more on opening hours, see Business Hours in the Facts for the Visitor chapter.

ANTIQUES
Laboratorio del Gerva (Map 7; ☎ 041 523 67 77), in Campo Bandiera e Moro, is a higgledy-piggledy workshop with enough goods to whet the appetite of any antiques collector, but if you are a serious purchaser, ask about the warehouse (which you can, if genuinely interested, arrange to see by appointment). Michele Gervasuti is continuing the work of his father, Eugenio, a master craftsman who opened the shop here in 1959. They concentrate on restoration and are involved in important projects across the city.

ART GALLERIES
Many shops (and artists in the city's numerous squares) sell simple watercolours of typical Venetian scenes. Several small art galleries are also dotted about the city.

The single biggest concentration of galleries, with all kinds of stuff, is on the streets that lie between the Gallerie dell'Accademia and the Peggy Guggenheim collection. A few stragglers line Calle del Bastion on the approach to the former Chiesa di San Gregorio (just east of the Guggenheim). Another area to look is Calle delle Carrozze, close to Palazzo Grassi (Map 5).

San Marco
Veneziartigiana (Map 6; ☎ 041 523 50 32), Calle Larga 412, is a collective selling works by Venetian artists, along with a host of other stuff more directly aimed at the passing tourist trade.

The Bugno Samueli Art Gallery (Map 6; ☎ 041 523 13 05), Campo San Fantin 1996/a, has some works by contemporary artists on permanent display, although money is the object. While you might not be able to afford a Miró or De Chirico, there's plenty of other material for the modern art collector. Needless to say, this is not a hobby for impecunious backpackers (or anybody else short of Rockefeller status).

Studio Aoristico di Matteo lo Greco (Map 6; ☎ 041 521 25 82), Campo San Fantin 1998, is a one-man show with some interesting sculpture and paintings.

Galleria Traghetto (Map 5; ☎ 041 522 11 88), Calle delle Ostreghe 2457, is another place with a curious mix of sculpture and paintings.

ART PRINTS & POSTERS
One way to remember a visit to Venice is by taking home some images of the city. Several shops produce high-quality prints and etchings. So long as you don't bend them on the way home, they can make a good, lightweight souvenir or gift.

The BAC Art Studio (Map 5; ☎ 041 522 81 71), Campo San Vio 862, has paintings, aquatints and engravings signed Cadore and Paolo Baruffaldi that can make fine gifts. You'll have seen cheaper depictions of Venice street and canal scenes at street stalls (and there is nothing wrong with a lot of them), but this stuff is a cut above those. Cadore concentrates his commercial efforts on Venetian scenes, while Baruffaldi depicts masked people. The store is a good place for quality postcards too. There is another branch in San Polo.

Graffiti (Map 5; ☎ 041 522 88 43), Salizzada San Rocco 3045, has some fine depictions of Venice (though the best come attached with high prices), as well as some excellent postcards.

BOOKS

There are several good bookshops in Venice, but English-language titles can be pricey compared with the UK and US.

San Marco

San Marco Studium (Map 6; ☎ 041 522 23 82), Calle de la Canonica 337/a, off Piazza San Marco, has a good selection of English-language guides and books on Venice. If you read Italian, Libreria al Fontego (Map 6; ☎ 041 520 04 70), San Marco 5361, is a pleasingly topsy-turvy bookstore over a couple of floors. Libreria Emiliana (Map 6; ☎ 041 522 07 93), Calle Goldoni 4484, has a broad range of books dealing with Venice in a several languages. Themes range from art to Pinocchio.

Libreria Goldoni (Map 6; ☎ 041 522 23 84), Calle dei Fabbri 4742, is one of the city's establishment bookshops. It has an impressive range of material on Venice in Italian, English and French.

Libreria Cassini (Map 5; ☎ 041 523 18 15), Via XXII Marzo 2424, has rare books and valuable prints, and will interest the discerning bibliophile with notes to burn.

Libreria al Ponte (Map 6; ☎ 041 522 40 30), Calle Cortesia 3717/d, is a small but useful shop offering a solid range of guides and other books on Venice, as well as children's books, many in English.

Cannaregio

Liberia Demetra (Map 3; ☎ 041 275 01 52), Campo San Geremia 282, is open until midnight and stocks a limited range of paperbacks and material on Venice.

Castello

Editore Filippi (Map 6; ☎ 041 523 56 35), Calle Casselleria 5763, is a den of books on all manner of subjects related to Venice, many published and only on sale here. The Filippis have been in the book business for nearly a century. Scholars search them out for their tomes and encyclopaedic knowledge.

CARNEVALE MASKS & COSTUMES

Carnevale masks make beautiful souvenirs. Again, quality and price are uneven. You can find people selling masks on just about every canal corner, but for serious craftsmanship you have to look a little closer. The cheap touristy rubbish is manufactured industrially (in Padua, for instance) and worthless. The ceramic masks have absolutely nothing to do with the genuine article, which are carefully crafted objects in papier-mache (*cartapesta*) or leather. The places listed here are all specialists and should give you a decent range of options.

Dorsoduro

Ca' Macana (Map 5; ☎ 041 520 32 29), Calle delle Botteghe 5176, is one of several places where you can see how the masks are made.

San Polo

Atelier Pietro Longhi (Map 5; ☎ 041 71 44 78), Rio Terrà 2604/b, is the place to come if you've ever fancied buying a helmet and sword to go with your tailor-made Carnevale costume.

L'Arlecchino (Map 3; ☎ 041 71 65 91), Calle dei Cristi 1722–1729, claims that their masks are made only with papier-mache to their own designs. To prove it you can inspect their workshop. The quality of masks is evident, but they aren't cheap. There's another store (Map 6; ☎ 041 520 82 20) at Ruga del Ravano 789.

La Zanze Veneixana (Map 5; ☎ 041 523 79 83), Ponte dei Frari 2566, is a small workshop whose owner, Laura Pinato, offers a mishmash of things, ranging from masks to bookmarks. Some of the stuff is attractive, but this is not one of the main recognised *mascherai* (mask-makers).

Tragicomica (Map 5; ☎ 041 72 11 02), Calle Nomboli, San Polo 2800, is one of the city's bigger mask and costume merchants. They also organise costume parties during Carnevale. The place is quite overwhelming at first sight.

You can also check out Laboratorio Artigianale di Decorazione Artistica, listed in the Crafts section later in this chapter.

SHOPPING

Who Are You Calling Big Nose?

NICKY CAVEN

At once sinister and amusing, the Doctor is a familiar Carnevale figure.

The fun of the fair at Venice's Carnevale was re-injected only after WWII, but the tradition is, in fact, a long one. In the languid years preceding the Republic's rather limp-wristed surrender to that Corsican upstart, Napoleon, back in 1797, Venetians had been known to party on for as long as six months. People came just to gawk at the costumed excess of the one-time merchant empire.

Perhaps the best known of the costumes has its wearer looking somewhat like an awkward flightless bird. Its origins, however, inspire anything but hilarity. Back in 1630, Venice lay prostrate as a singularly virulent epidemic of plague carried off as much as two-thirds of the population. Some of the doctors who hung about to care for the sick – not that there was much they could do – took to wearing some very odd vestments indeed. They donned head-to-foot cloaks coated in wax, gloves, a hat and a stick that they used to lift sheets or clothing from patients for a visual examination.

The *piece de resistance* was, however, the mask with glasses. The long protuberance, looking for all the world like a beak, contained various 'medical' essences considered helpful in avoiding infection (this was for the wearer's sake, not anyone else's). Whether or not they worked is not known, but the mask of the Medico della Peste (Plague Doctor), also known as the Medico della Morte (Doctor Death) is among the most famous of all.

Castello

Ca' del Sole (Map 7; ☎ 041 528 55 49), Fondamenta dell'Osmarin 4964, makes and sells costumes and masks that are aimed at both the public and the theatre.

CERAMICS

You'll see occasional shops selling pottery, tiles and various other ceramic items around town. Although this can't really be claimed to be a traditional Venetian art form, some pieces are particularly arresting.

The designs at Arca (Map 3; ☎ 041 71 04 27), Calle del Tintor 1811, are powerful, and for some tastes the colours are possibly a little strong. Teresa della Valentina paints her tiles and other ceramic objects in bold, bright, deep colours. Red here is deep blood red. You can organise to have your selections shipped directly home.

The contrast at Ceramiche (Map 3; ☎ 041 72 31 20), Sotoportego de Siora Bettina 2345, couldn't be greater. Margherita Rossetto's kitchen pots, clocks and other hand-painted items are all tranquil designs in soft blues and yellows – an altogether sunnier look.

CLOTHING & TEXTILES

Central Venice, especially the Sestiere di San Marco, has all the big fashion names. A small selection to get started is listed under Fashion. A couple of other places that merit attention follow here.

The window of Fiorella Gallery (Map 5; ☎ 041 520 92 28), Campo Santo Stefano 2806, contains transsexual Doge mannequins that in themselves make this unusual clothing store stand out – and a little difficult to classify under Fashion. Make of it what you will.

La Viola (Map 5; ☎ 041 523 71 20), Salizzada San Polo 2103, is the place for Lanvin silk ties and scarves (and leather bags). Its prices are reasonable.

CRAFTS
San Marco
Livio de Marchi (Map 5; ☎ 041 528 56 94), Salizada San Samuele, with wooden sculptures of underpants, socks and shirts, is rather weird. But endearing all the same.

Dorsoduro
Legno e Dintorni (Map 5; ☎ 041 522 63 67), Fondamenta Gherardino 2840, sells wonderful little wooden models of various monuments and facades that are akin to simple 3-D puzzles. They make rather refined gifts for kids, but wouldn't go amiss with many an adult.

Loris Marazzi (Map 5; ☎ 041 523 90 01), Campo Santa Margherita 2903, like Livio de Marchi (see San Marco in this section), has sculptures on a weird wooden theme, but is perhaps better known.

San Polo
Laboratorio Artigianale di Decorazione Artistica (Map 5; ☎ 041 275 01 48), Ruga Cassetti 2581, is an original cast on the mask and paper-decorating theme. The masks (from L70,000) are quite a novel and eye-catching variation on the standard fare and the other objects are in general a playful bunch of items.

All goods at A Mano (Map 5; ☎ 041 71 57 42), Rio Terrà 2616, are handmade. Quirky lampshades, mirrors and other odds and sods give this place a special attraction.

DEPARTMENT STORES
There are no department stores in Venice itself. For this kind of thing you will need to head for Mestre. There, right in the heart of town, off Piazza XXII Marzo, is Le Barche shopping complex (Map 15), home to several of the country's leading stores, including Feltrinelli (the bookshop chain), Ricordi Mediastore (for CDs and music), Coin (a leading budget department store) and PAM (particularly noted for its value-for-money food department). For clothes you could try Belfe & Belfe on the ground floor.

FASHION
The streets leading away west from Piazza San Marco towards the Teatro La Fenice are flanked by all the fashion names you need. If you can't make it to Milan, you'll probably find a good selection right here. It has to be said, however, that Milan is cheaper. If you're into Benetton, make for the heartland – Treviso (see the Excursions chapter). There's no need to go into great detail here – the label-collectors among you will know what all the following mean and what you want from them. You'll notice that quite a few are linked (they have the same phone number). They all appear on Map 6.

Agnona
   (☎ 041 520 57 33) Calle Vallaresso 1307
Armani
   (☎ 041 523 78 08) Calle dei Fabbri 989
Dolce & Gabbana
   (☎ 041 520 57 33) Calle Vallaresso 1313
Fendi
   (☎ 041 520 57 33) Salizzada San Moisè 1474
Gucci
   (☎ 041 520 74 84) Calle Vallaresso 1317
Kenzo
   (☎ 041 520 57 33) Ramo Fuseri 1814
Laura Bigiotti
   (☎ 041 520 34 01) Calle Larga XXII Marzo 2400
Louis Vuitton
   (☎ 041 522 45 00) Campo San Moisè
Missoni
   (☎ 041 520 57 33) Calle Vallaresso 1312/b
Prada
   (☎ 041 528 39 66) Salizzada San Moisè 1464–1469
Roberto Cavalli
   (☎ 041 520 57 33) Calle Vallaresso 1316
Valentino
   (☎ 041 520 57 33) Salizzada San Moisè 1473
Versace
   (☎ 041 520 00 57) Campo San Moisè

FOOD & DRINK
Giacomo Rizzo (Map 4; ☎ 041 522 28 24), Salizzada S Giovanni Crisostomo 5778, just north of the post office, has been keeping the locals in pasta since 1905. Take a look if you want to buy handmade pastas – they

produce quite a range, all made with natural products – or unusual pasta, for instance Curaçao blue tagliatelle. You'll find anything from *tagliolini con curry indiano* to *tagliolini con cacao amaro* (with bitter cocoa). They also sell imported specialities, such as olive oil from Modena and some pastas from Puglia.

The nameless delicatessen (Map 3; Kosher Delicatessen) at Calle del Ghetto Vecchio 1142 sells kosher food and wine.

For details of shops where you can fill up your own containers with wine, see the boxed text 'Fill 'Er Up' in the Entertainment chapter.

FURNITURE

Segno di Lorenzo Usicco (Map 3; ☎ 041 71 09 75), Calle del Tintor 1809, is worth a look, if only out of curiosity. The furniture is hand-painted and quite exquisite (for instance, a fine chest of drawers of hand-decorated cherry wood comes in at a cool L1,500,000) – for those with lots of dough.

GLASS & CRYSTAL

When people shop in Venice they tend to think of Murano glass and there is no shortage of workshops and showrooms full of the stuff, particularly between San Marco and Castello and on the island of Murano. Much of it is designed for tourists, so shop around. Quality and prices vary dramatically.

Always haggle, as the marked price is usually much higher than what the seller expects. If you decide to buy, the shop will often ship it home for you. Remember, though, that this can take a long time and you are likely to have to pay duty when it arrives.

You can see glass being blown in some of the glass shops on Murano. Look for the sign *fornace*, which means oven or furnace. You do not, however, need to go to Murano to buy glassware. Indeed, there is far more of the stuff readily available in Venice itself and prices tend to be similar.

San Marco

L'Isola (Map 6; ☎ 041 523 19 73), Campo San Moisè 1468, has glass objects by Carlo Moretti that are much appreciated for their elegance and finesse. The prices aren't exactly low, however.

Galleria Marina Barovier (Map 5; ☎ 041 522 61 02), Calle delle Carrozze 3216, is damn expensive, but wander down here to see the latest creations of some of the most outstanding artists in glass in Venice.

Daniele Bardella (Map 6; ☎ 041 520 70 51), at Fondamenta Orseolo, San Marco 1166, is not as classy as Barovier, but nonetheless remarkable for some of the flights of fantasy on display – astonishing as much for their sheer physical size as their inventiveness – and again for the price tags (not that we want to appear stingy or anything).

Murano

The bulk of the glass stores are congregated, as they should be, along Fondamenta dei Vetrai. Ever since the *vetrai*, or glassmakers, were transferred to the island at the close of the 13th century, this is where they have practised their art. Quite a few occupy Fondamenta Manin, across the canal, and others can be found on Viale Garibaldi and Fondamenta Andrea Navagero – strategically placed by the vaporetto stops to intercept visitors to the island.

Barovier & Toso (Map 11; ☎ 041 527 43 85), Fondamenta dei Vetrai 28, is, as you may have already guessed from the San Marco entry, one of the leading names in quality artistic glassware. They have a colourful Web site at www.barovier.com. Your cheque book will tremble on entering.

Venini (Map 11; ☎ 041 73 99 55), Fondamenta dei Vetrai 47–50, is the place to come to browse the top-shelf stuff before wandering off to poke your nose into less-exalted glass factories and shops. Again, independent wealth comes in handy. For a sneak preview, check out the Web site at www.venini.it.

Berengo (Map 11; ☎ 041 527 63 64), Fondamenta dei Vetrai 109/a, is one of those places that has abandoned almost completely any pretence at functionality. This is glass for art's sake. If you are into the idea of glass as sculpture, this is one of a couple of places that could interest you. See also the Web site at www.berengo.com.

Venice is a shopper's paradise. Carnevale masks and outfits may be uppermost in your mind, but Burano is famous for its lace, while grappa (grape liqueur) and ceramics are produced in Bassano del Grappa.

DAMIEN SIMONIS

There's been a fish market in Rialto for centuries.

JON DAVISON

An extravagant display of Murano glass

DAMIEN SIMONIS

Unlimited pasta possibilities at Giacomo Rizzo's

JULIET COOMBE

Choose a mask to suit your mood.

JULIET COOMBE

Venetian pizza – not just deep pan or thin crust

DAMIEN SIMONIS

Commerce on the canals – a floating greengrocer

JEWISH GOODS

In the Ghetto in Cannaregio you'll find a few interesting places. On the western side of the museum is a nameless little shop selling Jewish art (Map 3). Some of the porcelain is very attractive.

On Calle del Ghetto Vecchio you'll find a couple of shops purveying an odd mix of souvenirs and religious stuff. David's Shop (Map 3; ☎ 041 71 62 78), Campo del Ghetto Nuovo 2880, is the place to pick up your Jewish souvenirs with a Venetian spin. Some of the stuff is nice, but some a little tatty. How about a mezuzah made of Murano glass for L12,000 (10% off for cash)? Or another 'made by my mother'?

La Stamperia del Ghetto (Map 3; ☎ 041 275 02 00), Calle del Ghetto Vecchio 1185/a, has a pleasing collection of prints with general scenes of Venice, not only the Ghetto or Jewish themes.

LACE

The Isola di Burano traditionally lived off two activities – fishing and lace-making. The former is rapidly losing importance and the latter has been converted into the main attraction for the tourist dollar.

You will find any number of shops along and near Via Galuppi on the island. Inspect the wares closely – although you can often see some of the island's more venerable ladies busily creating these products in quiet corners, the stuff on sale is often of uneven quality and/or imported from Asia. The reason? It's a lot cheaper to import imitations than to make the real thing and most tourists aren't prepared to spend money on the genuine article. You don't need to get to Burano to buy lace – several stores sell it in Venice too.

Jesurum (Map 6; ☎ 041 520 60 85), Merceria del Capitello 4856, has been in business since 1860, when Michelangelo Jesurum opened a lace school on the Isola di Burano, then a deeply poor backwater. The quality and complexity of the women's work was such that Jesurum's laces won a prize at the 1878 Universal Exposition. Since then, it has been *the* name in lace – and the prices are commensurate.

MARBLED PAPER

Venice is noted for its *carta marmorizzata* (marbled paper). It has become something of a hit with visitors and is used for all sorts of things, from expensive giftwrap to book covers.

San Marco

Legatoria Piazzesi (Map 5; ☎ 041 522 12 02), Campiello della Feltrina 2551/c, is the oldest shop purveying these materials; they employ time-honoured methods to turn out high-quality (and high-priced) items.

Il Papiro (Map 5; ☎ 041 522 30 55), Calle del Piovan 2764, is another classic stop on the paper chase.

Dorsoduro

Il Pavone (Map 5; ☎ 041 523 45 17), Fondamenta Venier dai Leoni 721, is also a quality store for marbled paper, veering away from the traditional and indulging in a little fantasy. They also have a branch at San Marco 3287.

San Polo

Legatoria Polliero (Map 5; ☎ 041 528 51 30), Campo dei Frari 2995, is a traditional exponent of the art of Venetian bookbinding with (and without) marbled paper.

METALWORK

Valese (Map 6; ☎ 041 522 72 82), Calle Fiubera 793, is where, since 1918, the Valese family have been casting figures in bronze, copper and other metals. Their reputation is unequalled in the city. Although not all the items might suggest themselves as souvenirs as much as the horses that adorn the flanks of the city's gondolas, there is some interesting stuff here.

MODELS

Gilberto Penzo (Map 5; ☎ 041 71 93 72), Calle Saoneri 2681, is owned by Mr Penzo, who long ago got passionate about gondolas. So much so that he began to build models of them and collect detailed plans of them and all other lagoon and Adriatic vessels. He founded an association aimed at keeping all this ancient knowledge fresh, and to finance it all he opened a shop. Here you can buy exquisite wooden models of various Venetian vessels, hand built. He also takes in old ones for restoration. For the kids, you can fork out L45,000 on gondola model kits (or buy them ready-made and painted). Poster-size technical drawings of Venice's floating symbol sell for L20,000. And round the corner, you can have a peek at his workshop. This place is a gem.

MUSIC
Nalesso (Map 5; ☎ 041 520 33 29), Calle del Spezier 2765/d, in a small courtyard off the street, specialises in CDs of music in some way connected with Venice, concentrating on classical, Renaissance, baroque and opera. This is the place to come if you want any CDs by Rondò Veneziano (see Music in the Entertainment chapter).

PHOTOGRAPHY
Color Team (Map 6; ☎ 041 522 39 85), Riva del Vin 529, is tucked away discreetly back from the Grand Canal, near the Ponte di Rialto, and is a handy place to pick up film and have prints or slides developed quickly.

SHOES
Manuela Calzature (Map 5; ☎ 041 522 66 52), Ruga Rialto 1046, is a small shoe shop with a nice range, including more expensive footwear that they make under their own name. Don't judge it by the cheap junk outside. Bruno Magli (Map 6; ☎ 041 522 72 10), Calle Vallaresso 1302, has fashionable footwear for men and women.

SILVERWARE
At Argenteria (Map 5; ☎ 041 520 33 99), Campo San Tomà 2863, you can find an interesting array of silverware objects, from tiny bibelots to offset your Schwarowski glass collection to plates and other tableware and larger items you might find a little difficult to take home.

TEDDY BEARS
Il Baule Blu (Map 5; ☎ 041 71 94 48), Campo San Tomà 2916/a, is the place to come for a luxury bear. The owners of this shop have turned cuddly bears into a business for aficionados. If you really can't live without your bear and have brought it along to Venice, then you can be assured that the shop also operates a Teddy Hospital.

Excursions

The greater part of the Veneto, the region of which Venice is the capital, is plains country, stretching away from the mighty Po river. To the north, ranks of hills rise up gradually into the Dolomite mountains.

All of it was at one stage or another under the control of the Venetian Republic. Indeed, the surrounding regions of Friuli-Venezia Giulia and Trentino (part of the joint region known as Trentino-Alto Adige) are often lumped together with the Veneto and called the Triveneto.

The destinations covered in this chapter are all do-able as day trips from Venice, with no need to spend even a night outside the lagoon city if you do not wish. The Dolomites, splendid skiing and hiking country, are not covered, as you really need to set aside several days for such a trip.

Highlights include the cities of Padua (Padova) and Verona, to the west, and the hilltop village of Asolo to the north-west. Architecture enthusiasts will want to consider touring the Riviera del Brenta and beyond. Palladio is an architectural theme unto himself – apart from villas along the Brenta and outside the city of Vicenza, that city itself is a rich repository of his work.

For some local sun and sand you could try the beaches of Jesolo and beyond, on the coast curving away north-east of Venice.

RIVIERA DEL BRENTA

Dotted along the Brenta river, which passes through Padua and spills into the Venetian lagoon, are more than 100 villas built by wealthy Venetian families as summer homes.

Many of the them are closed to the public, but some of the more outstanding ones can be visited. Among them are **Villa Foscari** (1571), built by Palladio at Malcontenta, and **Villa Pisani**, also known as Villa Nazionale, at Strà. The latter, built for Doge Alvise Pisani, was later used by Napoleon and hosted Hitler's first meeting with Mussolini. Details of the principal villas open to the public follow.

ACTV buses running between Padua and Venice stop at or near the villas. For the latest information on all the villas open to the public, ask at the Venice APT office. Bear in mind that their information may not always be accurate – since most of the villas are privately owned, opening times and prices can vary capriciously.

The luxurious *Burchiello* barge plied the Brenta river between Venice and Padua in the 17th and 18th centuries. Today's version, a rather drab and anything but luxurious old thing, lumbers up and down the river between Venice and Strà ferrying tourists for about L120,000 one way, including lunch and short tours. There are connecting shuttles buses between Strà and Padua. Call ☎ 049 66 09 44 for information or try travel agents in Venice, for example Intras (Map 6), Piazza San Marco 145. At least two other ferries ply the Brenta – ask at the Padua APT office.

Apart from the villas covered in this section, several others occasionally open, in some cases only if you book ahead by phone – check with the APT office in Venice.

See the Around Vicenza section later in this chapter for information on other Venetian villas.

Villa Foscari

No sooner do you roll out of the nightmare industry-scape of Marghera than you find yourself headed for Malcontenta (ACTV bus No 53; ask for the bus to Padua via Malcontenta). Here, the Foscari family commissioned Palladio to construct a pleasure dome on the Brenta river. The result was a Palladian trademark: the riverside facade, with its ionic columns and classical tympanum, echoes the ancients that inspired him. The villa is also known as La Malcontenta (the malcontent), supposedly because a female family member was exiled here for fooling around with people other than hubby. Its interior is remarkable only for the frescoes with which it is covered.

EXCURSIONS

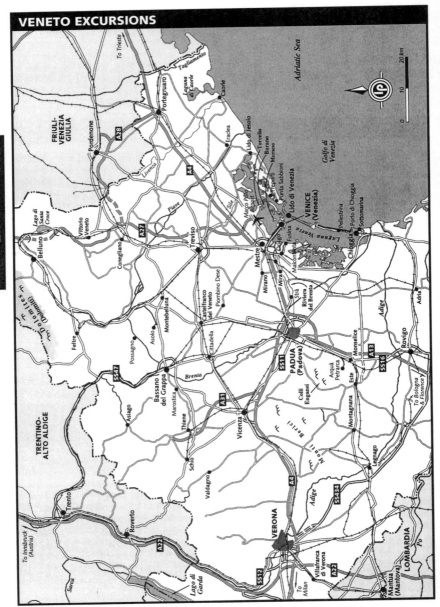

VENETO EXCURSIONS

They mostly depict scenes from classical literature.

The villa (☎ 041 547 00 12) is open on Tuesday and Saturday between April and October. It may be open on other days if you are lucky, but if you want to be sure, you must book ahead. Admission costs a very steep L15,000 – you really have to want to see it at this price.

Villa Widmann Foscari

An 18th-century rococo caprice just west of Oriago, this villa (☎ 041 42 41 56) is open daily from 10 am to 6 pm between June and September. In April, May and October its hours are from 10 am to 5 pm and it is closed altogether on Monday. It opens on Sunday only in March and is shut for the rest of the year. Admission costs L8000.

Villa Barchessa Valmarana

Across the Brenta from Villa Widmann Foscari, this villa (☎ 041 510 23 41) was built a century earlier. Only part of it is ever open to the public, daily except Monday from 9.30 am to noon and 2 to 5.30 pm between late March and September. Admission costs L8000.

Villa Pisani

This is by far the most magnificent of the lot. Set in extensive gardens a few kilometres short of Strà, it was completed in 1760. It is quite an exercise in family trumpet blowing. From the outsize statues at the main entrance to Tiepolo's ceiling fresco (a pictorial eulogy to the Pisani clan), it is a flashy display of wealth. Outside, a close-cropped lawn and pond separate the main house from a lesser mansion. On either side, privacy is maintained by heavily wooded gardens.

The villa (☎ 049 50 20 74) is open daily from 9 am to 6 pm between April and September. The rest of the year it closes at 4 pm. Combined admission to the villa and grounds costs L10,000 (L5000 to the grounds alone).

TREVISO
postcode 31100 · pop 85,000
A small, pleasant city with historical importance as a Roman centre, Treviso is worth a

day trip from Venice, easily accomplished by train. You could also make a stopover if you are heading north for the Dolomites. People planning to stay overnight should note that there is no decent cheap accommodation in the city.

Treviso claims Luciano Benetton, the clothing manufacturer, as its favourite son. The company's factories can be found around the city and this is the place to do your Benetton shopping.

Information
The APT office (☎ 0422 54 76 32) is at Piazzetta Monte di Pietà 8, adjacent to Piazza dei Signori. It's open from 9 am to 1 pm Monday to Saturday and also from 3 to 6 pm Wednesday to Saturday.

Things to See & Do
The APT promotes Treviso as the *città d'acqua* (city of water) and compares it to Venice. While the Sile river, which weaves through the centre, is quite beautiful in parts, the comparisons are more touching than realistic.

The city's other claim to fame is as the *città dipinta* (frescoed city). Pick up a copy of *Treviso Città Dipinta* from the APT office and follow the fresco itinerary, taking in the **Cattedrale di San Pietro**, with frescoes by Il Pordenone (1484–1539), the **Chiesa di San Nicolò**, with frescoes by Tommaso da Modena (1326–79), and the deconsecrated **Chiesa di Santa Caterina**, where there is another fresco cycle by Tommaso.

In summer, you can take a boat cruise (☎ 0422 78 86 63, 0422 78 86 71) on the *Silis* or *Altino* down the Sile to the Venetian lagoon and back.

Places to Stay & Eat
You'll be looking at a minimum of around L85,000/120,000 for a single/double room at the handful of places in central Treviso – the best choice is *Albergo alle Beccherie* (☎ 0422 54 08 71, Piazza Ancilotto 8), near Piazza dei Signori. It's also known as the *Campeol* and has a good restaurant. *Ristorante al Dante* (☎ 0422 5 18 97, Piazza Garibaldi 6) has good budget options, with

EXCURSIONS

pasta from L8000. It's closed on Saturday lunch time and Sunday.

Getting There & Away

The bus station is on Lungosile Mattei, near the train station in Piazzale Duca d'Aosta. Lamarca Trevigiani buses link Treviso with other towns in the province and ACTV buses go to Venice. Trains go to/from Venice, Belluno, Padua and major cities to the south and west. By car, take the SS53 for Venice and Padua.

BELLUNO

postcode 32100 • pop 36,000

Belluno is a beautiful little town at the foot of the Dolomites. If you start early enough, you could just about combine it with Treviso in a day trip from Venice, either by train or bus. Better still, hang around for a few days and use it as a base to explore the mountains.

The tourist office, the Azienda di Promozione Turistica delle Prealpi e Dolomiti Bellunesi (☎ 0437 94 00 83), Via Rodolfo Psaro 21, produces a feast of information on walking, trekking, skiing and other sporting activities. You should pop in if you're planning to head into the Dolomites. The Comunità Montana Bellunese (☎ 0437 94 02 83), Via San Lucano 7, can assist with details on Alpine *rifugi* (mountain huts).

Places to Stay & Eat

The *Camping Park Nevegal* (☎ *0437 90 81 43, Via Nevegal 263*), open all year, is about 10km from the town, in Nevegal. Take the Autolinee Dolomiti bus from Belluno. The nearest youth hostel is the *Ostello Imperina* (☎ *0437 6 24 51*), 35km north-west at Rivamonte Agordino. B&B costs L25,000 and you can get there on the Agordo bus from Belluno. The *Casa per Ferie Giovanni XXIII* (☎ *0437 94 44 60, Piazza Piloni 11*), near the centre of Belluno, has singles for L39,000 and a few doubles for L69,000. They will knock off about L5000 if you stay several nights in a row. The *Albergo Taverna* (☎ *0437 2 51 92, Via Cipro 7*), has singles/doubles without bathroom for L30,000/55,000. Most of the town's restaurants are around the central Piazza dei Martiri.

Getting There & Away

Autolinee Dolomiti buses (☎ 0437 94 12 37) depart from the train station, on the western edge of town, for Agordo, Cortina d'Ampezzo, Feltre and smaller towns in the mountains and south of town. Trains are less regular to northern towns, but there are services to Cortina as well as to Treviso and Venice.

BASSANO DEL GRAPPA

postcode 36061 • pop 39,000

Known above all for its firewater, grappa, and to lesser degree for its production of ceramics, Bassano del Grappa sits astride the Brenta river just south of the first line of hills that are a prelude to the Dolomites. To art lovers, the name will ring another bell. The Da Ponte family of Renaissance painters, known to us now as the Bassano, came from here. The town's pretty centre and accessibility from Venice make it an enjoyable trip that takes you off the main tourist trails.

Information

The well-stocked APT office (☎ 0424 52 43 51) is at Largo Corona d'Italia, close to the train and bus stations.

Things to See

The centre of Bassano is composed of two sloping and interlinking squares, Piazza Garibaldi and Piazza Libertà. In the latter, the winged lion of St Mark stands guard on a pedestal to remind you of who was long in charge here.

In the **Museo Civico**, attached to the Chiesa di San Francesco on Piazza Garibaldi, you can see an assortment of items, ranging from paintings by members of the Bassano clan through to ancient archaeological finds.

Follow Via Matteotti north off Piazza Libertà towards the **Castello Ezzelini**, the remains of the stronghold that belonged to the medieval warlords of the same name.

Via Gamba slithers downhill from Via Matteotti to the Brenta river and the covered bridge known as the **Ponte degli Alpini**. It is named after the mountain troops who rebuilt it in 1948 after it was seriously damaged by retreating German soldiers at the tail end of WWII. Via Gamba and the bridge are lined with ceramics shops and a few grappa outlets. Throw in some bars and snack joints and it makes a pleasant stroll. The views across to old Bassano from the far riverbank alone make the walk from the centre worthwhile.

Places to Stay & Eat

If you want to stay, the cheapest option is *Ostello Don Cremona* (☎ 0424 52 20 32, fax 0424 52 23 62, Via Chini 6). A bed costs up to L28,000. The *Victoria* (☎ 0424 50 36 20, fax 0424 50 331 30, Viale Diaz 33) has comfortable single/double rooms for up to L80,000/140,000.

As far as eating is concerned, you can't go wrong at *Alla Riviera* (☎ 0424 50 37 00, Via San Giorgio 17). Here you will be served hearty traditional Veneto cuisine, such as *pasta e fagioli* (pasta and beans) or rabbit in a tangy sauce. It is closed Monday evening and Tuesday.

Getting There & Away

The easiest way to reach Bassano from Venice is by train on the Venice–Trento line. The trip takes about 1¼ hours. From here there are train and bus connections to Padua and buses to Vicenza.

AROUND BASSANO DEL GRAPPA

A half-dozen destinations are clustered around Bassano. Some are easily reached from Venice, while others could be considered in tandem with Bassano. Alternatively, you could make Bassano a base for a night or two. With the exception of Asolo, all these places can be considered of secondary interest. Those with limited time may want to concentrate on more important destinations like Padua, Vicenza and Verona (see later in this chapter). If you have a vehicle, you can get around all these spots easily and quickly.

Asolo

Its position high in the hills, surrounded by fields, farms and woods, makes Asolo an enchanting village. Caterina Corner, the ill-

fated Venetian queen of Cyprus, was given the town and surrounding county towards the end of the 15th century in exchange for her abdication (see the boxed text on the next page). The writer Pietro Bembo attended Caterina's salons. Perhaps in search of a hint of that atmosphere, Robert Browning also put in time in Asolo.

Things to See Piazza Garibaldi forms the centre of town, from where streets wind up in all directions between the tight ranks of golden-hued houses that lend this place so much of its charm. The **duomo** (cathedral) lies below and just to the south of the square. It contains a few paintings by Jacopo Bassano and Lorenzo Lotto. Caterina Corner lived in the **castello**, now used as a theatre. An arduous climb up Via Collegio from Piazza Brugnoli will get you up to the **rocca**, the town's medieval fortress. The walk north out of town to the **Cimitero di Sant'Anna** is rewarding for the views over the lush green countryside. Eleonora Duse, a whirlwind actress romantically involved with poet Gabriele d'Annunzio, was buried here in 1924.

Places to Stay & Eat Staying here is unfortunately the preserve of the better off. Of the three options, *Hotel Duse* (☎ 0423 5 52 41, fax 0423 95 04 04, Via Browning 190) has lovely rooms, but you will pay up to L250,000 for a double. If you don't stay, at least consider lunch at *Ca' Derton* (☎ 0423 52 96 48, Piazza d'Annunzio 11). They do a tempting *capretto alle erbe aromatiche* (kid meat in herbs) and have a fine wine list and dessert menu. It's closed Monday.

Getting There & Away Buses between Bassano and Treviso stop below Asolo. You need to get the little orange shuttle bus to reach the centre (otherwise it's a long walk).

Villa Barbaro

About 7km east of Asolo, at Maser, this Palladian villa is one of the best of the genre. Palladio built it in the late 1550s for the Barbari brothers – two eminent figures in Venetian public life – and it was decorated by

A Queen Cornered

As 14-year-old Caterina Corner was escorted in pomp out of the family mansion in San Polo to the Palazzo Ducale in 1468 she must have wondered what was coming next. *Niente di buono* (nothing good) would have been the response of wise onlookers. Betrothed to 28-year-old James, the usurper king of Cyprus, four years later Caterina found herself pregnant, widowed and surrounded by enemies in her new island home.

James' untimely (and suspicious) death left Venice in no doubt that it had to act to protect its growing interest in the island. Captain General Pietro Mocenigo was dispatched first to fortify Venetian strongholds and then later to reverse a coup against the queen. The Cypriots were none too enamoured with de facto Venetian rule on their island, but after the coup attempt government was effectively in the hands of two Venetian *consiglieri* (councillors), ostensibly in the service of the queen.

After the death of her infant son in 1474, Caterina's problems only increased. Plots against her by Cypriot nobles came thick and fast, and her protectors, the Venetians, virtually held her prisoner. In 1488 Venice decided enough was enough. Cyprus was threatened by Turkish invasion and the latest plots against Caterina were proving insufferable. It was decided to absorb the island into the Venetian empire and Caterina had to be persuaded to abdicate.

This she did with some reluctance, but she had little choice. As compensation, she was given a mainland fief centred on Asolo and a generous life pension. She only returned to her Venetian home in 1509, where she died the following year. She kept her title of queen until the end. Less than a century later Venice would lose Cyprus to the Turks anyway.

Veronese, whose remarkable fresco cycle adorns the upper floor. In the grounds stands Palladio's **Tempietto**. Based on the Pantheon in Rome, it was his last project. The villa is open from 3 to 6 pm on Tuesday, Saturday and Sunday. Admission costs L8000.

Possagno

Birth and resting place of Antonio Canova, Italy's master of neoclassical sculpture, Possagno is a good place to get an idea of how Canova worked. The **Gipsoteca** is home to a long series of clay models and other preparatory pieces for his finished work (you can see some statues and reliefs by Canova in Venice's Museo Correr). It is open daily except Monday from 9 am to noon and 3 to 6 pm (7 pm on Sunday) between May and September. Evening closing time is one hour earlier during the rest of the year. Admission costs L5000.

Before you even reach the Gipsoteca, you'll have been astonished by the rather outsize **tempio** (to all intents and purposes the parish church) Canova was considerate

enough to leave his town. Finished in 1832, it could be described as neo-mongrel-classical, as it is an amalgam of Greek and Roman models.

The best way to reach Possagno is by bus from Bassano – the trip takes around one hour.

Marostica

You know you have almost arrived here when the you see the jagged line of battlements that climbs the hill from Marostica's town centre to the upper castle.

Pretty enough to warrant a brief stop in its own right, Marostica comes into its own every other year in September for the colourful **Partita a Scacchi** (Chess Match). Back in 1454, two knights challenged each other to a duel for the hand of the fair Lionora, elder daughter of the town's ruler, Taddeo Parisio. The latter, not wanting to lose either warrior, banned the duel and ordered them to 'fight' it out in a grand game of chess using real people on a huge 'board' at the gates of the lower castle in the town centre.

The two knights ordered the moves and the winner got Lionora. The loser didn't come off too badly, since he wed Parisio's younger daughter, apparently just as radiant.

The event today is just as colourful as the original must have been, with an assembly of players and other characters in period costume. The game is choreographed in advance, using one of the classic matches between chess champions as the basis. If you can't be here for the second weekend of September in even years (2000, 2002, and so on), you can admire the costumes in the lower castle (Castello da Basso). The tourist office (☎ 0424 7 21 27) is in the entrance to the castle. For information on the chess match you can email the tourist office at promarostica@telemar.it.

There are five hotels in Marostica, but finding a place to stay during the Partita a Scacchi is virtually impossible. The town is about 30 minutes by bus from Bassano.

Cittadella

The main reason for getting to Cittadella, a 12km bus ride south of Bassano on the busy SS47 to Padua, is to inspect the towering red-brick walls and moat that still surround this one-time fortress town.

Padua raised the fort in the 13th century to face off the one built by Treviso at Castelfranco del Veneto (see the following section). In 1405 the small town that had grown up behind the 1.5km of walls came under the control of Venice.

There's not an awful lot to keep you busy here. Of the four gates, the northern Porta Bassano is the most elaborate. Look out for llamas grazing in the former moat at the southern end of town.

Castelfranco del Veneto

Treviso built the 'Free Fort' (free because the rulers of Treviso exempted from all taxes anyone prepared to move in) at the end of the 12th century. From then until 1339, when it was absorbed into Venice's mainland empire, Castelfranco del Veneto remained a hotly contested site and frequently changed hands. Indeed, Padua laid siege to the town barely 10 years after its construction.

The square-based walls of the fort are less impressive than the circular version at Cittadella, but the town has an extra claim to fame as the birthplace of the mysterious painter Giorgione. Little is known about his life and only half a dozen works can be definitely attributed to him, one of them the *Madonna col Bambino in Trono e Santi Francesco e Liberale* (Madonna and Child Enthroned with Saints Francis and Liberale), in the **duomo**.

In the unlikely event you want to stay, roughly half a dozen hotels offer doubles for around L120,000 or less. You can eat well at *Alle Mura* (☎ 0423 49 80 98, Via Preti 69), within the city walls. Don't expect much change from L80,000 for a full meal with wine. It's closed Tuesday.

Castelfranco is on the train line that connects Venice with Bassano del Grappa.

Piombino Dese

A little closer to Venice on the Bassano del Grappa train line, this nondescript town is home to the **Villa Cornaro** (☎ 049 936 50 17). The most impressive element of the mansion is its two-tiered portico, which you can see perfectly well from the street. It is open from 3.30 to 6 pm on Saturday between May and September. Admission costs L8000, which is silly for what you get to see.

PADUA (PADOVA)
postcode 35100 · pop 225,000

Although famous as the city of St Anthony and for its university, one of the oldest in Europe, Padua is often seen merely as a convenient and cheap place to stay while visiting Venice. However, the city offers a rich collection of art treasures, including Giotto's incredible frescoed chapel, and its many piazzas and arcaded streets are a pleasure to explore.

Padua's wealth grew during the 13th century, when it was controlled by the counts of Carrara, who encouraged cultural and artistic pursuits (when they weren't busy warring with all and sundry neighbours) and established the Studium, the forerunner of the university.

EXCURSIONS

EXCURSIONS

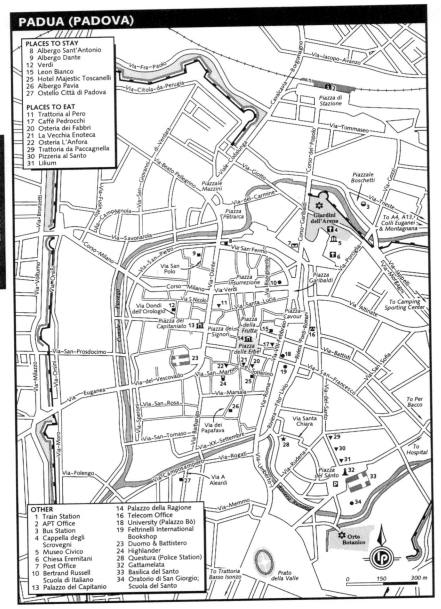

PADUA (PADOVA)

PLACES TO STAY
- 8 Albergo Sant'Antonio
- 9 Albergo Dante
- 12 Verdi
- 15 Leon Bianco
- 25 Hotel Majestic Toscanelli
- 26 Albergo Pavia
- 27 Ostello Città di Padova

PLACES TO EAT
- 11 Trattoria al Pero
- 17 Caffè Pedrocchi
- 20 Osteria dei Fabbri
- 21 La Vecchia Enoteca
- 22 Osteria L'Anfora
- 29 Trattoria da Paccagnella
- 30 Pizzeria al Santo
- 31 Lilium

OTHER
- 1 Train Station
- 2 APT Office
- 3 Bus Station
- 4 Cappella degli Scrovegni
- 5 Museo Civico
- 6 Chiesa Eremitani
- 7 Post Office
- 10 Bertrand Russell Scuola di Italiano
- 13 Palazzo del Capitanio
- 14 Palazzo della Ragione
- 16 Telecom Office
- 18 University (Palazzo Bò)
- 19 Feltrinelli International Bookshop
- 23 Duomo & Battistero
- 24 Highlander
- 28 Questura (Police Station)
- 32 Gattamelata
- 33 Basilica del Santo
- 34 Oratorio di San Giorgio; Scuola del Santo

0   150   300 m

Orientation

From the train station, it's a 10-minute walk across the square and up Corso del Popolo (later Corso Garibaldi) to the centre. Bus No 10 will also get you there. Piazza della Frutta and the adjoining Piazza delle Erbe form the lively heart of the old city, bustling with market activity – take some time to drool over all the fine foods. The Basilica del Santo and the vast Prato della Valle are a good 20-minute walk south from the train station.

Information

Tourist Office The APT office at the train station (☎ 049 875 20 77) is open from 9 am to 7.30 pm Monday to Saturday (9.15 am to 5.45 pm November to March) and 8.30 am to 12.30 pm Sunday (9 am to midday November to March).

Post & Communications The post office, Corso Garibaldi 33, is open from 8.15 am to 7 pm Monday to Saturday and 8.30 am to 6.30 pm Sunday. Address poste restante mail to 35100 Padua.

Telecom has an unstaffed phone office at Riviera Ponti Romani 38, open from 7 am to 10 pm Monday to Saturday.

Bookshops Padua is full of bookshops. If you're looking for anything in languages other than Italian, try Feltrinelli International at Via San Francesco 14.

Medical Services & Emergency Medical assistance is provided by the Complesso Clinico Ospedaliero (hospital; ☎ 049 821 11 11), Via Giustiniani 1. The *questura* (police station; ☎ 049 83 31 11) is at Via Santa Chiara, on the corner of Riviera Ruzante.

Things to See

A special ticket, Padova Arte, admits you to the main monuments. It's available from the APT office and ticket offices at the monuments concerned. (There's a similar ticket for lesser sights in the surrounding province.)

Cappella degli Scrovegni Many art lovers visit Padua just to see this chapel in the Giardini dell'Arena. It was commissioned in 1303 by Enrico Scrovegni as a resting place for his father, who had been denied a Christian burial because of his money-lending practices. Giotto's remarkable fresco cycle, probably completed between 1304 and 1306, illustrates the lives of Mary and Christ and is arranged in three bands. You can pick up an adequate guide to the frescoes as you enter. Among the most famous scenes in the cycle is the *Bacio di Giuda* (Kiss of Judas). The series ends with the *Ultima Cena* (Last Supper) on the entrance wall and the Vices and Virtues are depicted around the lower parts of the walls. Keep in mind when the frescoes were done – Giotto was moving well away from the two-dimensional figures of his medieval contemporaries and presaging greater things to come.

The chapel is often full and at busier times attendants enforce strict time limits, usually of 20 to 30 minutes. The chapel is open daily except Monday from 9 am to 6 pm (7 pm in summer) and admission costs L10,000. The ticket is also valid for the adjacent **Museo Civico**, whose collection of 14th- to 18th-century Veneto art and forgettable archaeological artefacts includes a remarkable crucifix by Giotto.

Chiesa Eremitani Completed in the early 14th century, this Augustinian church was painstakingly rebuilt after being almost totally destroyed by bombing in WWII. The remains of frescoes done by Andrea Mantegna during his 20s are displayed in a chapel to the left of the apse. Most were wiped out in the bombing, the greatest single loss to Italian art during the war. The *Martirio di San Jacopo* (Martyrdom of St James), on the left, was pieced together from fragments found in the rubble of the church, while the *Martirio di San Cristoforo* (Martyrdom of St Christopher), opposite, was saved because it had been removed before the war.

Historic Centre Via VIII Febbraio leads to the city's **university**, the main part of which is housed in the Palazzo Bò ('ox' in Veneto dialect – it's named after an inn that previously occupied the site). Established in 1222, the university is Italy's oldest after the one in Bologna. Europe's first anatomy theatre was opened here in 1594 and Galileo Galilei taught at the university from 1592 to 1610.

Continue along to Piazza delle Erbe and Piazza della Frutta, which are separated by the majestic **Palazzo della Ragione**, also known as the Salone for the grand hall on its upper floor. Built in the 13th and 14th centuries, the building features frescoes by Giusto de' Menabuoi and Nicolò Mireto depicting the astrological theories of Pietro d'Abano. It is open daily except Monday from 9 am to 7 pm (6 pm in winter). The cost of admission (usually around L7000) depends largely on the nature of the temporary exhibits.

West from here is the Piazza dei Signori, dominated by the 14th-century **Palazzo del Capitanio**, the former residence of the city's Venetian ruler. South is the city's **duomo**, built from a much-altered design by Michelangelo. The 13th-century Romanesque **battistero** (baptistry) features a series of frescoes of Old and New Testament scenes by Giusto de' Menabuoi, influenced by Giotto.

The cathedral is open daily except Monday from 7.30 am to noon and 3.45 to 7.30 pm (slightly longer hours on Sunday and public holidays), while the baptistry opens from 9.30 am to 1 pm and 3 to 6 pm (7 pm in summer) on the same days. Admission to the baptistry costs L3000.

Piazza del Santo The city's most celebrated monument is the **Basilica del Santo** (or di Sant'Antonio), which houses the corpse of the town's patron saint and is an important place of pilgrimage. Construction of what is known to the people of Padua as Il Santo began in 1232. The saint's tomb, bedecked by requests for his intercession to cure illness or thanks for having done so, is in the Cappella del Santo, in the left transept. There was a time when the area around the tomb was awash with crutches and other prosthetic devices of the grateful cured – these have been reduced to a symbolic few. Look out for the saint's relics in the apse. The sculptures and reliefs of the high altar are by Donatello. The church is open from 6.30 am to 7 pm daily (7.45 pm in summer).

In the piazza in front of the basilica is the *Gattamelata*, created by Donatello in 1453. This magnificent equestrian statue of the 15th-century Venetian *condottiero* (mercenary leader) Erasmos da Narni (whose nickname, Gattamelata, translates as 'Honeyed Cat') is considered the first great bronze of the Italian Renaissance.

On the south side of the piazza lies the **Oratorio di San Giorgio**, the burial chapel of the Lupi di Soranga family of Parma, with 14th-century frescoes. Next door is the **Scoletta** (or **Scuola**) **del Santo**, containing works believed to be by Titian. The former is closed for restoration; the latter is open from 9 am to 12.30 pm and 2.30 to 7 pm (5 pm in winter). Admission costs L3000.

Just south of Piazza del Santo, the **Orto Botanico** is purportedly the oldest botanical garden in Europe. It is open daily from 9 am to 1 pm and 2 to 6 pm (Monday to Saturday mornings only in winter) and admission costs L5000.

Courses
The Bertrand Russell Scuola di Italiano (☎ 049 65 40 51), Via E Filiberto 6, runs one-month language courses for foreigners costing around US$570. Accommodation is extra.

Organised Tours
For tours of Padua, get in touch with Xanadu Viaggi (☎ 049 66 42 55) or the tourist office.

Places to Stay
Padua has no shortage of budget hotels, but they fill up quickly in summer. The closest camp site, *Camping Sporting Center* (☎ 049 79 34 00, Via Roma 123), at Montegrotto Terme, about 15km from Padua, can be reached by city bus M. *Ostello Città di Padova* (☎ 049 875 22 19, Via A Aleardi 30) offers B&B for L20,000. Take bus Nos 3, 8 or 12 from the train station to Prato della Valle and then ask for directions.

The Koko Nor Association (☎ 049 864 33 94, Via Selva 5) can help you to find

B&B-style accommodation in family homes starting from around L40,000/70,000 for a single/double.

Verdi (☎ *049 875 57 44, Via Dondi dell'Orologio 7*) has basic, clean singles/doubles for L40,000/64,000. *Albergo Pavia* (☎ *049 66 15 58, Via dei Papafava 11*) offers similar rooms for L44,000/59,000.

Albergo Sant'Antonio (☎ *049 875 13 93, Via San Fermo 118*), at the northern end of Via Dante, has excellent singles/doubles, most with TV and phone, for L94,000/116,000 with bathroom, L58,000/82,000 without. Just nearby is the much simpler and cheaper *Albergo Dante* (☎ *049 876 04 08, Via San Polo 5*), with rooms for L40,000/57,000.

The three-star *Leon Bianco* (☎ *049 875 08 14; fax 049 875 61 84, Piazzetta Pedrocchi 12*), near Piazza della Frutta, has rooms costing from L130,000/169,000 in high season (which is most of the time!). A leafy alternative is *Hotel Majestic Toscanelli* (☎ *049 66 32 44, Via dell'Arco 2*), with rooms for up to L195,000/295,000.

Places to Eat

Daily *markets* are held in the piazzas around the Palazzo della Ragione, with fresh produce sold in the Piazza delle Erbe and Piazza della Frutta and bread, cheese and salami sold in the shops under the porticoes.

Trattoria al Pero (☎ *049 875 87 94, Via Santa Lucia 72*), serves regional dishes and a full meal will come to around L30,000. It's closed Sunday.

Osteria dei Fabbri (☎ *049 65 03 36, Via dei Fabbri 13*) is full of atmosphere, although more expensive. Try the *ravioloni di magro*, exquisite, light ravioli done in a butter and sage sauce. It's closed Sunday.

Getting a table isn't always easy at *Osteria l'Anfora* (☎ *049 65 66 29, Via dei Soncin 13*). This is a fine eatery with loads of atmosphere. You can expect to pay about L35,000 a head. It's also closed Sunday.

La Vecchia Enoteca (☎ *049 875 28 56, Via San Martino e Solferino 32*) is a swanky joint where mouth-watering mains cost around L25,000. It's closed Sunday and Monday lunch time.

Pizzeria al Santo (☎ *049 875 21 31, Via del Santo 149*) has good pizzas from L7000. It's closed Tuesday. Nearby, *Trattoria da Paccagnella* (☎ *049 875 05 49, Via del Santo 113*) is a comfortably elegant setting for fine Veneto cuisine – try the *coniglio in casseruola con verdure e origano* (casseroled duck with vegetables and oregano). It's closed Sunday. *Lilium* (Via del Santo 181) offers wonderful gelati and fine pastries.

Behind the blunt neoclassical facade of the newly refurbished *Caffè Pedrocchi*, just off Via VIII Febbraio, lay the meeting place for 19th-century liberals and one of Stendhal's favourite haunts. Today it's more posy than cosy.

A local favourite for simple, economically priced home-cooking is the *Trattoria Basso Isonzo* (☎ *049 68 08 13, Via Montepertica 1*), south-west of the centre. It's a bit of a pain to get to unless you opt for a cab from, say, Prato della Valle, but they do a mean creamy *baccalà* (cod). It's closed Monday.

For somewhat classier eating, you can't go past *Per Bacco* (☎ *049 802 23 27, Piazzale Pontecorvo 10*). You can expect to pay around L50,000. Try their *tagliatelle alla norcina con tartufo nero* (tagliatelle with black truffles), a classic of Umbrian cuisine. The wine list is also strong. The restaurant is closed Monday.

Entertainment

The city hosts the Notturni d'Arte festival from July to September each year, featuring concerts and outdoor events; many are free. The tourist office has details. Some opera and theatrical performances are held at the *Teatro Comunale Verdi* (☎ *049 876 03 39*), Via Livello 32.

Beer-lovers wanting a variation on the Irish theme could strike out for *Highlander* (Via San Martino e Solferino 71) – you guessed it, a 'Scottish' pub. For some tips on discos and the like, start with the tourist office's *Dove Andiamo Stasera* brochure.

Getting There & Away

Bus & Train SITA buses (☎ *049 820 68 34*) depart from Piazzale Boschetti, 200m south of the train station, and head for Montegrotto, the Colli Euganei, Venice (L5100), Este and Genoa. By train the city is connected to Milan, Venice (L4100 in 2nd class; L8100 on the fast InterCity trains) and Bologna.

Car & Motorcycle The A4 (Milan–Venice) passes to the north, while the A13, which connects the city with Bologna, starts at the southern edge of town. The two motorways are connected by a ring road.

AROUND PADUA
Colli Euganei
South-west of Padua, along the A13 or the SS16, the Colli Euganei (Euganean Hills) are dotted with vineyards and good walking trails: ask at the Padua APT office for information about the trails and accommodation. The Consorzio Vini DOC dei Colli Euganei (☎ 049 521 18 96), Via Vescovi 41 in Luvigliano, can provide details of the vineyards.

If you are driving (which you pretty much have to, as public transport is abysmal in the area), follow the signposted Strada dei Vini dei Colli Euganei (Euganean Hills Wine Road), which will take you on a tour of many vineyards. Pick up a map and itinerary from the APT in Padua. Most of the vineyards are open to the public and some offer accommodation.

Arquà Petrarca This quiet, hilly medieval village in the southern Colli Euganei was where Italy's great poet Petrarch (Petrarca) chose to spend the last five years of his life. You can visit his house, set in cheerful gardens, which is open daily except Monday from 9 am to 12.30 pm and 3 to 7 pm (2.30 to 5.30 pm between October and the end of January). Admission costs L6000. Buses run here from Este and Monselice, both a short distance to the south.

Monselice
An easy train trip south from Padua, Monselice was once wrapped in no less than five protective layers of fortifications. The main point of interest here is the 11th-century **castello**, which can be visited by guided tour only (L10,000). If you decide to stay, you have the choice of only two places.

Este
Heading west from Monselice along the road to Mantua (Mantova), this town is yet another in the chain of fortified strongholds in the area. Padua's Carrara clan were assiduous fortress builders – it seems they had a good number of enemies to keep at bay. Although the walls of their castle are in reasonable shape, the inside is pretty much a ruin. On the bumpy lane that climbs northward behind the castle is the **Villa Kunkler**, where Byron settled in for a year or so in 1817. Shelley also stayed here.

You'll find a couple of hotels here and the town is linked to Monselice by train.

Montagnana
The main attraction in this plains town is the remarkably well-preserved set of medieval defensive walls. Of all the Veneto's walled towns, this is the most impressive – from the outside. Once you get inside there's not an awful lot to see.

The fabulous youth hostel, *Rocca degli Alberi* (☎/fax 0429 807 02 66, *Castello degli Alberi*), is housed in a former castle and open from April to mid-October. B&B costs L16,000 and it is close to the town's train station. Montagnana is also on the Monselice–Mantua train line.

VICENZA
postcode 36100 • pop 109,000
Vicenza is the centre for Italian textile manufacture and a leader in the development and production of computer components, making it one of the country's wealthiest cities. Most tourists come to Vicenza to see the work of Palladio, who was particularly busy here. Vicenza flourished as the Roman Vicentia. In 1404 it became part of the Venetian Republic. Testimony to the close ties between the lagoon city and Vicenza are the many Venetian Gothic mansions here.

Orientation
From the train station, in the gardens of Campo Marzo, walk straight ahead along Via Roma into Piazzale de Gasperi. From here, the main street, Corso Andrea Palladio, leads to the duomo and the centre of town.

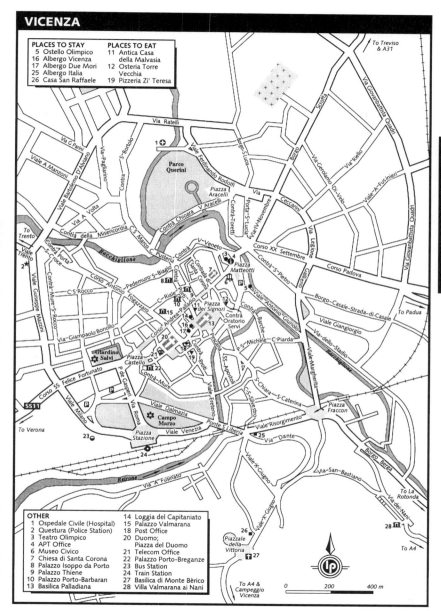

VICENZA

PLACES TO STAY
5 Ostello Olimpico
16 Albergo Vicenza
17 Albergo Due Mori
25 Albergo Italia
26 Casa San Raffaele

PLACES TO EAT
11 Antica Casa della Malvasia
12 Osteria Torre Vecchia
19 Pizzeria Zi' Teresa

EXCURSIONS

OTHER
1 Ospedale Civile (Hospital)
2 Questura (Police Station)
3 Teatro Olimpico
4 APT Office
6 Museo Civico
7 Chiesa di Santa Corona
8 Palazzo Isoppo da Porto
9 Palazzo Thiene
10 Palazzo Porto-Barbaran
13 Basilica Palladiana
14 Loggia del Capitaniato
15 Palazzo Valmarana
18 Post Office
20 Duomo; Piazza del Duomo
21 Telecom Office
22 Palazzo Porto-Breganze
23 Bus Station
24 Train Station
27 Basilica di Monte Bèrico
28 Villa Valmarana ai Nani

euro currency converter L10,000 = €5.16

Information

Tourist Office The APT office (☎ 0444 32 08 54) is at Piazza Matteotti 12. It's open from 9 am to 1 pm and 2.30 to 6 pm Monday to Saturday and from 9 am to 1 pm on Sunday.

Post & Communications The main post office is at Contrà Garibaldi, near the duomo. Address poste restante mail to 36100 Vicenza. There's a small, unstaffed Telecom office at Contrà Vescovado 2.

Medical Services & Emergency For urgent medical assistance, go to the Ospedale Civile (☎ 0444 99 31 11), Viale Ferninando Rodolfi 37, north of the city centre from Piazza Matteotti. The questura (police station; ☎ 0444 54 33 33) is at Viale Giuseppe Mazzini 24.

Things to See

Piazza Castello contains several grand edifices, including the **Palazzo Porto-Breganze** on the southern side, designed by Palladio and built by Scamozzi, one of the city's leading 16th-century architects. Corso Andrea Palladio runs north-east from the square and is lined with fine buildings.

Piazza dei Signori, nearby, is dominated by the immense **Basilica Palladiana**, on which Palladio started work in 1549 over an earlier Gothic building – the slender 12th-century bell tower is all that remains of the original structure. The basilica is open from 9.30 am to midday and 2.15 to 5 pm Tuesday to Saturday, and from 9 am to 12.30 pm Sunday. Palladio's **Loggia del Capitaniato**, at the north-western side of the piazza on the corner of Via del Monte, was left unfinished at his death. South-west from the basilica is the **duomo**, a dull church destroyed during WWII and later rebuilt (some of its works of art were saved).

Contrà Porti, which runs north off Corso Andrea Palladio, is one of the city's most majestic streets. The **Palazzo Thiene** at No 12, by Lorenzo da Bologna, was originally intended to occupy the entire block. Palladio's **Palazzo Porto-Barbaran** at No 11 features a double row of columns. Palladio also built the **Palazzo Isoppo da Porto** at No 21, which remains unfinished. His **Palazzo Valmarana**, at Corso Antonio Fogazzaro 18, is considered one of his more eccentric creations. Across the Bacchiglione river is the **Parco Querini**, the city's largest park.

North along Corso Andrea Palladio and left into Contrada di Santa Corona is the **Chiesa di Santa Corona**, established in 1261 by the Dominicans to house a relic from Christ's crown of thorns. Inside are the *Battesimo di Gesù* (Baptism of Christ) by Giovanni Bellini and *Adorazione dei Magi* (Adoration of the Magi) by Veronese.

Corso Andrea Palladio ends at the **Teatro Olimpico**, started by Palladio in 1580 and completed by Scamozzi after the former's death. Considered one of the purest creations of Renaissance architecture, the theatre design was based on Palladio's studies of Roman structures. Scamozzi's remarkable street scene, stretching back from the main facade of the stage, is modelled on the ancient Greek city of Thebes. He created an impressive illusion of depth and perspective by slanting the streets upward towards the rear of the set. The theatre was inaugurated in 1585 with a performance of *Oedipus Rex*, but soon fell into disuse – the ceiling caved in and it remained abandoned for centuries until 1934, when it was restored and reopened. Since then, the theatre has become a prized performance space for opera and drama – it is one of the few working theatres where the performers and audience are eyeball to eyeball. In summer, it is open from 9 am to 12.30 pm and 2.15 to 5 pm Monday to Saturday, and from 9.30 am to 12.30 pm Sunday and holidays. In winter, closing times are 15 minutes earlier. Admission costs L5000.

The nearby **Museo Civico**, in the Palazzo Chiericati, open the same hours, contains works by local artists as well as by the Tiepolos and Veronese. Admission costs L5000. If you want to see the theatre and museum, get a *biglietto cumulativo* (combined ticket) for L9000.

South of the city, the **Basilica di Monte Bèrico**, on Piazzale della Vittoria, set on top of a hill, presents magnificent views over the city. The basilica was built in the 18th

View along the Brenta river from Ponte degli Alpini, Bassano del Grappa, in the Veneto

Impressive defensive walls, built in the 13th century, encircle the town of Montagnana.

Fountain just off Piazza dei Signori, Verona

A house in the colourful town of Caorle, Veneto

The town hall in Piazza Brà, Verona

A glimpse of Verona from the Ponte Scaligero

Definitely no parking! A quiet street in Verona

century to replace a 15th-century Gothic structure, itself raised on the supposed site of two appearances by the Virgin Mary in 1426. An impressive 18th-century colonnade runs most of the way up Viale X Giugno to the church – very handy when it's pouring with rain in autumn. Or catch city bus No 9.

A 20-minute walk part of the way back down Viale X Giugno and then east along Via San Bastiano will take you to the **Villa Valmarana ai Nani**, featuring brilliant frescoes by Giambattista and Giandomenico Tiepolo. The 'ai nani' (dwarfs) refers to the statues perched on top of the gates surrounding the property. The villa is open every afternoon except Monday between mid-March and early November – check at the APT office or call ☎ 0444 54 39 76. Admission costs L10,000.

A path leads on to Palladio's Villa Capra, better known as **La Rotonda**. It is one of the architect's most admired – and copied – creations, having served as a model for buildings across Europe and the USA. The gardens (admission L5000) are open from 10 am to midday and 3 to 6 pm on Tuesday, Wednesday and Thursday between March and November, and the villa (admission L10,000) is open the same hours on Wednesday. Otherwise, groups of 25 or more can book a visit to the villa and gardens (L20,000 a person) on ☎ 0444 32 17 93. Bus No 8 stops nearby.

Places to Stay

Many hotels close during the summer, particularly in August, so book ahead. At other times you should have no problems getting a room.

The closest camp site, the *Campeggio Vicenza* (☎ 0444 58 23 11, Strada Pelosa 239) is near the Vicenza Est exit from the A4. The recently opened HI youth hostel, the *Ostello Olimpico* (☎ 0444 54 02 22, Viale Giuriolo 7–9) is in a fine building right by the Teatro Olimpico. It costs L25,000 per person.

The *Albergo Italia* (☎ 0444 32 10 43, Viale Risorgimento 3), near the train station, has singles/doubles with bathroom from L60,000/80,000 (but this can increase

enormously in high season). The *Albergo Vicenza* (☎ 0444 32 15 12, Stradella dei Nodari 5–7), near Piazza dei Signori, has singles/doubles with bathroom for up to L80,000/110,000. The *Albergo Due Mori* (☎ 0444 32 18 86), nearby at Contrà do Rode 26, has singles/doubles for up to L65,000/124,000 in the high season. One of the best choices is the *Casa San Raffaele* (☎ 0444 54 57 67, Viale X Giugno 10), in a former convent behind the colonnade leading to Monte Bèrico. Singles/doubles with bathroom cost L65,000/95,000.

Places to Eat

A large produce market takes place each Tuesday and Thursday in Piazza delle Erbe. *Pizzeria Zi' Teresa* (☎ 0444 32 14 11, Contrà San Antonio 1) has good pizzas costing from L8000. It's closed Monday.

They say the *Antica Casa della Malvasia* (☎ 0444 54 37 04, Contrà delle Morette 5) has been around since 1200. In those days, it was the local sales point for Malvasia wine imported from Greece by Venetian merchants. Nowadays it offers main courses for up to L13,000, accompanied by an array of 80 types of wine and 150 types of grappa! It's closed Monday.

Another good destination is the *Osteria Torre Vecchia* (☎ 0444 32 00 50, Contrà Oratorio Servi 23). This elegant old house with wooden ceilings offers fine eating at a highish price. You could try their *menù afrodisiaco* for L40,000. It's closed Sunday.

Entertainment

Concerts are held in summer at the Villa Valmarana ai Nani; check at the APT for details. For information about performances in the Teatro Olimpico, contact the APT or call ☎ 0444 22 21 11.

Getting There & Away

FTV buses (☎ 0444 22 31 15) leave from the bus station, just near the train station, for Padua, Thiene, Asiago, Bassano, Verona and towns throughout the nearby Monti Berici (Berici Hills). Trains connect the city with Venice, Milan, Padua, Verona, Treviso and smaller towns in the north.

EXCURSIONS

By car, the city is on the A4 connecting Milan with Venice. The SS11 connects Vicenza with Verona and Padua, and this is the best route for hitchhikers. There is a large car park near Piazza Castello and the train station.

Getting Around

The city is best seen on foot, but bus Nos 1, 2, 3 and 7 connect the train station with the city centre.

AROUND VICENZA

As Venice's maritime power waned in the 16th century, the city's wealthy inhabitants turned their attention inland, acquiring land to build sumptuous villas (see also the Riviera del Brenta section earlier in this chapter). Forbidden from building castles by the Venetian senate, which feared a landscape dotted with well-defended forts, Vicenza's patricians were among those to join the villa construction spree. Many of the thousands that were built still remain, although most are inaccessible to the public and run down.

The APT in Vicenza can provide reams of information about the villas, including a booklet entitled *Vicenza – the Villas*. The De Agostini map, *Ville Venete*, sells for about L8000 at newspaper stands and is one of the few complete maps.

Drivers should have little trouble planning an itinerary. If you don't have a car, take the FTV bus north from Vicenza to Thiene, passing through Caldogno and Villaverla, and then continue on to Lugo. The Villa Godi-Valmarana, now known as the **Malinverni**, at Lonedo di Lugo, was Palladio's first villa.

A good driving itinerary is to take the SS11 south to Montecchio Maggiore and continue south to Lonigo and Pojana Maggiore before heading north for Longare and back to Vicenza. A round trip of 100km, the route takes in about a dozen villas.

A few kilometres south of Pojana Maggiore, you'll find an HI youth hostel at Montagnana (see the Around Padua section earlier in this chapter for details).

Check with the APT in Vicenza for details of the Concerti in Villa Estate, a series of classical concerts held in villas around Vicenza each summer. You can also ask about accommodation, which is available in some villas.

VERONA
postcode 37100 · pop 250,000

Wander the quiet streets of Verona on a winter's night and you might almost be forgiven for believing the tragic love story of Romeo and Juliet to be true. Get past the Shakespearean hyperbole, however, and you'll find plenty to keep you occupied in what is one of Italy's most beautiful cities. Known as *piccola Roma* (little Rome) for its importance in the days of the Roman Empire, its truly golden era came during the 13th and 14th centuries under the Della Scala family (also known as the Scaligeri). The period was noted for the savage family feuding which Shakespeare wrote about in his play.

Orientation

Old Verona is small and easy to find your way around. There is a lot to see and it is a popular base for exploring surrounding towns. Buses leave for the centre from outside the train station; otherwise, walk to the right, past the bus station, cross the river and walk along Corso Porta Nuova to Piazza Brà, 15 minutes away. From the piazza, walk along Via Mazzini and turn left at Via Cappello to reach Piazza delle Erbe.

Information

Tourist Offices The main APT office (☎ 045 806 86 80) is in the Palazzo Maffei, at Piazza delle Erbe 38. It's open from 8 am to 2 pm Monday to Friday. The IAT office (☎ 045 806 86 80), in the same building as the Scavi Scaligeri, is open from 9 am to 7 pm Tuesday to Sunday (there can be seasonal variations). Another office (☎ 045 800 08 61) at the train station (to the right before you exit) is open from 8 am to 7.30 pm (6 pm in winter) Monday to Saturday.

Money Banks dot the town centre, including the Banca Popolare di Bergamo on Piazza Brà, one of several with a currency exchange machine. American Express is represented by Fabretto Viaggi (☎ 045 806 01 55),

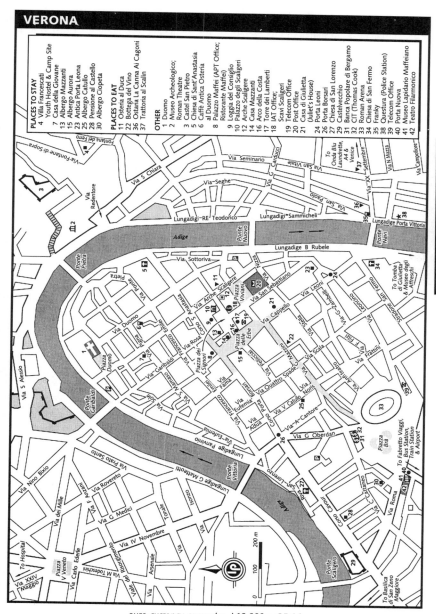

VERONA

PLACES TO STAY
4 Villa Francescati
Youth Hostel & Camp Site
7 Casa della Giovane
13 Albergo Mazzanti
15 Albergo Aurora
23 Antica Porta Leona
25 Albergo Catullo
28 Pensione al Castello
30 Albergo Ciopeta

PLACES TO EAT
11 Osteria al Duca
22 Bottega del Vino
36 Ostaria La Canna Ai Cagoni
37 Trattoria al Scalin

OTHER
1 Duomo
2 Museo Archeologico;
Roman Theatre
3 Castel San Pietro
5 Chiesa di Sant'Anastasia
6 Caffè Antica Osteria
al Duomo
8 Palazzo Maffei (APT Office;
Ristorante Maffei)
9 Loggia del Consiglio
10 Palazzo degli Scaligeri
12 Arche Scaligere
14 Casa Mazzanti
16 Arco della Costa
17 Torre dei Lamberti
18 IAT Office;
Scavi Scaligeri
19 Telecom Office
20 Post Office
21 Casa di Giulietta
(Juliet's House)
24 Porta Leoni
26 Porta Borsari
27 Chiesa di San Lorenzo
29 Castelvecchio
31 Banca Popolare di Bergamo
32 CIT (Thomas Cook)
33 Roman Arena
34 Chiesa di San Fermo
35 Franky
38 Questura (Police Station)
39 Telecom Office
40 Porta Nuova
41 Museo Lapidario Maffeiano
42 Teatro Filarmonico

EXCURSIONS

Corso Porta Nuova 11. Thomas Cook and MoneyGram are represented by CIT (☎ 045 59 17 88), at Piazza Brà 2.

Post & Communications The main post office, Piazza Viviani 7, is open from 8 am to 7 pm Monday to Saturday. Address poste restante mail to 37100 Verona. You'll find telephones at the train station, as well as Telecom offices on Piazza delle Erbe and Via Leoncino.

You can get onto the Internet at a spot by platform 1 at the train station or at Diesis, Via Sottoriva 15 (generally open from 11 am to between 10 pm and midnight).

Laundry There is an Onda Blu laundrette at Via XX Settembre 62/a.

Medical Services & Emergency The Ospedale Civile Maggiore (☎ 045 807 11 11) is at Piazza A Stefani, north-west from Ponte Vittoria. Otherwise, the city's Guardia Medica (☎ 045 807 56 27) provides medical services from 8 pm to 8 am and usually comes to you.

The questura (police station; ☎ 045 809 06 11) is at Lungadige Porta Vittoria, near Ponte Navi.

Things to See
As you will soon see, visiting all the monuments and museums of Verona can become an expensive business. For this reason the city is considering a *biglietto* that gives you access to all (or at least a decent selection) of them for a single reduced price. Ask at a tourist office before coughing up at each place.

Roman Arena This pink marble Roman amphitheatre, in the bustling Piazza Brà, was built in the 1st century AD and is now Verona's opera house. The third-largest Roman amphitheatre in existence, it could seat around 20,000 people. It is remarkably well preserved, despite a 12th-century earthquake that destroyed most of its outer wall. The arena is open daily except Monday from 9 am to 7 pm and admission costs L6000 (or L7000 if you wish to inspect the nearby

Museo Lapidario Maffeiano too). See the Entertainment section for information about opera and plays at the arena.

Casa di Giulietta Off Via Mazzini, Verona's main shopping street, is Via Cappello, with the Casa di Giulietta (Juliet's house) at No 23. Romeo and Juliet may have been fictional, but here you can swoon beneath what popular myth says was her balcony or, if in need of a new lover, approach a bronze statue of Juliet and rub her left breast for good luck. Others have made their eternal mark by adding to the slew of scribbled love graffiti on the walls of the house. It is, by the way, doubtful there was ever a feud between the Cappello and Montecchi families, on whom Shakespeare based the play. The house is open daily except Monday from 9 am to 6.30 pm and admission costs L6000.

If the theme excites you sufficiently, you could also search out the Tomba di Giulietta (Juliet's tomb), at Via del Pontiere 5. Also housed here is the Museo degli Affreschi. It's open from 9 am to 6.30 pm Tuesday to Sunday and admission costs L5000.

NICKY CAVEN

'But, soft! what light through yonder window breaks? It is the east, and Juliet is the sun!'

Piazza delle Erbe Originally the site of a Roman forum, this piazza remains the lively centre of the city today. Although the permanent market stalls in its centre detract from its beauty, the square is lined with some of Verona's most sumptuous buildings, including the baroque **Palazzo Maffei**, at the northern end, with the adjoining 14th-century **Torre del Gardello**. On the eastern side is **Casa Mazzanti**, a former Della Scala family residence. Its fresco-decorated facade stands out.

Separating Piazza delle Erbe from Piazza dei Signori is the **Arco della Costa**, beneath which is suspended a whale's rib. Legend says it will fall on the first 'just' person to walk beneath it. In several centuries, it has never fallen, not even on the various popes who have paraded beneath it. Ascend the nearby 12th-century **Torre dei Lamberti** by elevator (L4000) or on foot (L3000) for a great view of the city. It's open daily from 9 am to 6 pm.

Piazza dei Signori The 15th-century **Loggia del Consiglio**, the former city council building at the northern end of this square, is regarded as Verona's finest Renaissance structure. It is attached to the **Palazzo degli Scaligeri**, once the main residence of the Della Scala family.

Through the archway at the far end of the piazza are the **Arche Scaligere**, the elaborate tombs of the Della Scala family, which unfortunately may only be viewed from outside.

In the courtyard just behind the Arche you can now see some excavation work done on this part of Verona. You enter the **Scavi Scaligeri** through the same building as the IAT office. The excavations are not so exciting as to warrant a big detour, so to make them more attractive the building is used to host international photographic exhibitions. It's open daily except Monday from 10 am to 6 pm. Admission prices depend on the exhibition.

Churches North from the Arche Scaligere stands the Gothic **Chiesa di Sant'Anastasia**, started in 1290 but not completed until the late 15th century. Inside are numerous works of art including, in the sacristy, a lovely fresco by Pisanello of *San Giorgio che Parte per Liberare la Donzella dal Drago* (St George Setting out to Free the Princess from the Dragon).

The 12th-century **duomo** combines Romanesque (lower section) and Gothic (upper section) styles and has some very interesting features. Look for the sculpture of Jonah and the Whale on the south porch and the statues of two of Charlemagne's paladins, Roland and Oliver, on the west porch. In the first chapel of the left aisle is an *Assumption* by Titian, in an altar frame by Jacopo Sansovino.

At the river end of Via Leoni is the **Chiesa di San Fermo**, which is actually two churches: the Gothic church was built in the 13th century over the original 11th-century Romanesque structure. The **Chiesa di San Lorenzo** is near the Castelvecchio (see the following section) and the **Basilica di San Zeno Maggiore** (see the Basilica di San Zeno Maggiore section after Castelvecchio) is farther to the west.

A combined entrance ticket to all these churches costs L8000. Otherwise, admission to each costs L3000.

Opening times vary according to the season. Generally, the churches are open from 10 am to 1 pm and 1.30 to 4 pm Tuesday to Saturday.

Castelvecchio South-west from Piazza delle Erbe, on the banks of the Adige, is the 14th-century fortress of Cangrande II (of the Della Scala family). The fortress was damaged by bombing during WWII and restored in the 1960s. It now houses a museum with a diverse collection of paintings, frescoes, jewellery and medieval artefacts. Among the paintings are works by Pisanello, Giovanni Bellini, Tiepolo, Carpaccio and Veronese. Also of note is a 14th-century equestrian statue of Cangrande I. The museum is open daily except Monday from 9 am to 6.30 pm and admission costs L6000. The **Ponte Scaligero** spanning the Adige river was rebuilt after being destroyed by WWII bombing.

euro currency converter L10,000 = €5.16

Basilica di San Zeno Maggiore A masterpiece of Romanesque architecture, this church in honour of the city's patron saint was built mainly in the 12th century, although its apse was rebuilt in the 14th century and its bell tower, a relic of an earlier structure on the site, was started in 1045. The basilica's magnificent rose window depicts the Wheel of Fortune. Before going inside, take a look at the sculptures on either side of the main doors. The doors themselves are decorated with bronze reliefs of biblical subjects. The highlight inside is Mantegna's triptych of the *Madonna col Bambino tra Angeli e Santi* (Madonna and Child with Angels and Saints), above the high altar.

Across the River Across Ponte Pietra is a **Roman theatre**, built in the 1st century AD and still used today for concerts and plays. Take the lift at the back of the theatre to the convent above, which houses an interesting collection of Greek and Roman pieces in the **Museo Archeologico**. On a hill high behind the theatre and museum is the **Castel San Pietro**, built by the Austrians on the site of an earlier castle. Both the museum and theatre are open daily except Monday from 9 am to 3 pm. Combined admission costs L5000.

City Gates Near the Casa di Giulietta, in Via Leoni, is the **Porta Leoni**, one of the gates to Roman Verona. The other is **Porta Borsari**, at the bottom end of Corso Porta Borsari.

Places to Stay

If you are having problems finding a hotel room, you could try calling the Cooperativa Albergatori Veronesi (☎ 045 800 98 44). They start with two-star hotels and the service is free.

The beautifully restored HI youth hostel, *Villa Francescati* (☎ 045 59 03 60, Salita Fontana del Ferro 15) should be your first choice. B&B costs L21,000 a night. Next door is a *camp site*. To reserve a space, speak to the hostel management. Catch bus No 73 from the train station (bus Nos 70, 72 and 90 will also get you to the general area).

Casa della Giovane (☎ 045 59 68 80, Via Pigna 7), off Via Garibaldi, is for women only and costs up to L22,000 for a bed in a triple or quad. A bed in double or a double with bathroom costs L25,000. Catch bus No 70 and ask the driver where to get off.

About the cheapest place in a central location is *Albergo Catullo* (☎ 045 800 27 86, Via Valerio Catullo 1). Basic singles/ doubles without bathroom start at about L45,000/65,000, but can rise as high as L60,000/90,000. They also have more expensive doubles with bathrooms.

Pensione al Castello (☎ 045 800 44 03, Corso Cavour 43) has rooms with bathroom for as much as L90,000/120,000. *Albergo Ciopeta* (☎ 045 800 68 43, Vicolo Teatro Filarmonico 2), near Piazza Brà, is a great little place, but you'll need to book well in advance. Its singles/doubles cost L80,000/ 120,000.

One of the best-located hotels in the city is the *Albergo Aurora* (☎ 045 59 47 17, Piazzetta XIV Novembre 2). It has singles without bathroom for L70,000, but you'll be lucky to get this price. Singles/doubles with bathroom start at L110,000/130,000 and can rise another 40% depending on the season.

The *Albergo Mazzanti* (☎ 045 800 68 13, Via Mazzanti 6), just off Piazza dei Signori, is potentially a better deal. If you can get low-season prices, the rooms are small but clean and not too pricey at L77,000/97,000 for a single/double with bathroom, L47,000/ 67,000 without. Add up to 50% in the high season. *Antica Porta Leona* (☎ 045 59 54 99, Corticella Leoni 3) is an excellent hotel, not far from the Casa di Giulietta. Its lovely single/double rooms cost up to L180,000/ 250,000 in the high season.

Places to Eat

Known for its fresh produce, its crisp Soave (a dry white wine) and boiled meats, Verona offers good eating at reasonable prices.

The *Osteria al Duca* (☎ 045 59 44 74, Via Arche Scaligere 2), in the so-called Casa di Romeo (actually the former home of the Montecchis, one of the families on which Shakespeare's play is based), has a solid set menu for L20,000, but its reputation is greater than its cooking. It's closed Saturday evening and Sunday.

More expensive, but locally recommended, is the *Bottega del Vino* (☎ 045 800 45 35, *Vicolo Scudo di Francia 3/a*). The frescoes alone are worth seeing. It's closed Tuesday. *Ristorante Maffei* (☎ 045 801 00 15, *Piazza delle Erbe 38*), in the Palazzo Maffei, has pasta from L16,000 and main dishes from L25,000. They also do some vegetarian dishes. It's closed Sunday.

Head east across the river for a couple of other treats. *Ostaria La Canna Ai Cagoni* (*Via Scrimiari 5*) offers *spadellato* (pan-sauteed pasta with various meats, cheese and *rucola*, or rocket). *Trattoria al Scalin* (*Via San Vitale 6*) offers enticing Sicilian cooking.

Entertainment
Throughout the year, the city hosts musical and cultural events, culminating in the season of opera and drama from July to September at the *Arena*. Tickets cost from L28,000 to L290,000; bookings can be made on ☎ 045 800 51 51. For more information try the Web site at www.arena.it.

There is a programme of ballet and opera in winter at the 18th-century *Teatro Filarmonico* (☎ 045 800 28 80, *Via dei Mutilati 4*), just south of Piazza Brà, and Shakespeare is performed at the Roman theatre in summer. Information and tickets for these events are available at the Ente Lirico Arena di Verona (☎ 045 800 51 51), Via Dietro Anfiteatro 6–8.

Caffè Antica Osteria al Duomo (*Via Duomo 7*) is a cosy tavern with mandolins, balalaikas and other stringed instruments hanging on the wall. Pop in for a drop of *fragolino* (sweet strawberry wine).

For a brighter, more youthful ambience, you could try *Franky* (*Via San Paolo 5/b*). It has a grunge feel and occasionally you can hear live performances of anything from poetry to music.

Getting There & Away
Verona-Villafranca airport (☎ 045 809 56 66) is just outside the town and accessible by bus. Flights from all over Italy and some European cities arrive here.

The main intercity bus station is in front of the train station, in an area known as Porta Nuova. Buses leave for Mantua, Ferrara, Brescia and provincial destinations. The airport bus also leaves from here.

Verona has rail links with Milan, Venice, Padua, Mantua, Modena, Florence, Rome, Austria and Germany, and is at the intersection of the Serenissima A4 (Milan–Venice) and Brennero A22 autostradas.

Getting Around
Bus Nos 11, 12, 13 and 72 (bus Nos 91 or 98 on Sunday and holidays) connect the train station with Piazza Brà, and bus No 70 goes to Piazza delle Erbe (tickets cost L1600). Otherwise, it's a 15- to 20-minute walk along Corso Porta Nuova. Cars are banned from the city centre in the morning and early afternoon, but you will be allowed in if you are staying at a hotel. There are free car parks at Via Città di Nimes (near the train station), Porta Vescovo and Porta Palio, from where there are buses into the city centre. For a taxi, call ☎ 045 53 26 66.

EAST OF VENICE
The Adriatic coast spreading east and gradually north away from Venice is lined with popular local beach resorts. They tend to be pretty crowded on summer weekends but not quite so bad during the week. Quite a few foreigners flock to them too, using the resorts as the core of their summer holiday and chucking in the odd excursion to Venice as a diversion. These places are pleasant enough, but the northern Adriatic is not the place to plan a classic Mediterranean beach holiday.

Jesolo
Lido di Jesolo, the strand a couple of kilometres away from the main town, is far and away the Venetians' preferred beach. The sand is fine and clean, the water OK without being wonderfully crystal clear.

Jesolo marks the northern end of a long peninsula that becomes Litorale del Cavallino as you head south and culminates in Punta Sabbioni, which together with the northern end of the Lido forms the first of

EXCURSIONS

the three entrances into the Venetian lagoon from the Adriatic.

The beaches tend to be covered in umbrellas, recliners and the people using them, but it makes for a pleasant change from all the sightseeing in summer. The area also has camp sites and plenty of hotels of all classes. The whole lot is predictably short on character.

ATVO buses run from Piazzale Roma in Venice (70 minutes, L6000). Traffic can get horrendous, so try to make an early getaway. In summer, one or two ferries to Venice (L10,500 one way) are laid on.

Caorle

Nothing is left to remind you of the ancient roots of **Eraclea**, now a small agricultural town on the way from Jesolo to Caorle, itself around 30km east around the coast from Jesolo.

In the 1st century BC Caorle was a Roman port and it remains a busy fishing centre even today. Small but proud, it only actually dropped resistance to Venetian pressure and passed under the paws of St Mark's lion in the 15th century.

The centre of the medieval town is watched over by the extraordinary cylindrical bell tower of the 11th-century **cattedrale**. The cheerful streets present a pastel pageant. Although they haven't gone to quite the lengths of the people of Burano, the townsfolk take a special pride in keeping their houses gleaming with a fresh coat of paint in an array of bright colours.

The beaches are busy but OK and the whole place has a nice restrained vibe. It is quite popular with Germans.

If you want to stay, there is a handful of hotels and no shortage of restaurants in which to enjoy the local seafood. ATVO buses run from Piazzale Roma in Venice (from 1½ to two hours, L7700). In summer, ferry services to Venice (L20,500 one way) are available.

Language

Italian is a Romance language related to French, Spanish, Portuguese and Romanian. The Romance languages belong to the Indo-European group of languages, which includes English. Indeed, as many English and Italian words have common Latin roots, you will recognise many Italian words.

Modern literary Italian began to develop in the 13th and 14th centuries, predominantly through the works of Dante, Petrarch and Boccaccio, who wrote chiefly in the Florentine dialect. The language drew on its Latin heritage and many dialects to develop into the standard Italian of today. Although many dialects are spoken in everyday conversation, standard Italian is the national language of schools, media and literature, and is understood throughout the country.

Visitors to Italy with more than the most fundamental grasp of the language need to be aware that many Italians still expect to be addressed in the third person formal (*lei* instead of *tu*). Also, it's not considered polite to use the greeting *ciao* when addressing strangers unless they use it first; it's better to say *buon giorno* (or *buona sera*, as the case may be) and *arrivederci* (or the more polite form, *arrivederla*). We have used the formal address for most of the phrases in this guide. Use of the informal address is indicated by 'inf' in brackets. Italian also has both masculine and feminine forms (they usually ending in 'o' and 'a' respectively). Where both forms are given in this guide, they are separated by a slash, the masculine form first.

If you'd like a more comprehensive guide to the language, get a copy of Lonely Planet's *Italian phrasebook*.

If you have a reasonable command of Italian and find you don't understand a great deal of what is being spoken around you in Venice, what you're hearing is probably Venessian (or Veneziano), the local dialect (see the boxed text on the next page). Native Italian speakers have trouble with it too. At times you hear quite familiar words, then the flow seems to stream off into something that to the unaccustomed ear sounds like a strange mix of Portuguese and Spanish. Not only are the words different, the intonation is quite distinct as well.

Pronunciation

Italian pronunciation isn't difficult to master once you learn a few simple rules. Although some of the more clipped vowels, and stress on double letters, require careful practice for English speakers, it's easy enough to make yourself understood.

Vowels

Vowels are generally more clipped than in English:

a	as in 'art', eg *caro* (dear); sometimes short, eg *amico/a* (friend)
e	as in 'tell', eg *mettere* (to put)
i	as in 'inn', eg *inizio* (start)
o	as in 'dot', eg *donna* (woman); as in 'port', eg *dormire* (to sleep)
u	as the 'oo' in 'book', eg *puro* (pure)

Consonants

The pronunciation of many Italian consonants is similar to that of their English counterparts. Pronunciation of some consonants depends on certain rules:

c	as 'k' before 'a', 'o' and 'u'; as the 'ch' in 'choose' before 'e' and 'i'
ch	as the 'k' in 'kit'
g	as the 'g' in 'get' before 'a', 'o', 'u' and 'h'; as the 'j' in 'jet' before 'e' and 'i'
gli	as the 'lli' in 'million'
gn	as the 'ny' in 'canyon'
h	always silent
r	a rolled 'rr' sound
sc	as the 'sh' in 'sheep' before 'e' and 'i'; as 'sk' before 'a', 'o', 'u' and 'h'
z	as the 'ts' in 'lights', except at the beginning of a word, when it's as the 'ds' in 'suds'

Venice's Other Tongue

Some people do not take kindly to hearing their tongue referred to as a dialect. Such is the case with Venessian, the 'dialect' of Venice, which some linguists would instead identify as a variant of a regional language that takes in the whole Veneto region (and even some way beyond) – Venet.

Be that as it may, Venet and/or Venessian are generally, along with many other vestigial local languages spoken across Italy, dismissed as dialects of Italian. This can of worms is not worth opening here, but a couple of points should be considered.

Modern Italian has its roots in the medieval Tuscan Italian of Dante and has really developed as an amalgam ever since. Its primacy only came this century.

For 1000 years, the people of the Venetian Republic spoke Venessian, the local offshoot of Latin. Much influenced by Tuscan Italian over the centuries, Venessian nevertheless contains many Latin, Byzantine Greek and even Germanic words, and obeys different rules of pronunciation. Venetian linguists bristle at the suggestion that Venessian/Venet is merely a distortion of Italian. Given its 1000-year history, some place the local language on an equal footing with modern Italian, French and other Romance languages – all descendants, or dialects if you will, of Latin.

Evidence to support such claims can be found in Venessian vocabulary. From the Latin comes *pistor* (baker, which in Italian is *fornaio*) and from the Byzantine Greek *carega* (seat, in Italian *sedia*).

All this said, it is clear from Italian documents that Venessian was not the exclusive official language of the Republic; the use of certain spellings betrays the influence, but not the dominance, of the Venetian dialect.

Since WWII, internal migration and the spread of the electronic media have to a great extent 'Italianised' Venetians and their linguistic habits. A series of provincial varieties of Venet (of which Venessian would be the main one) can be identified, but the language is not as robust as those in some of the minority language areas of other European countries. The vigorous promotion of Catalan and Basque in the north of Spain, for instance, has no real equivalent in Italy, if you except the small minorities who speak French or German in the country's north. To what extent locals are even interested in resuscitating the use of Venet is an open question. Curiously, one of the leading recognised experts on the Venet language is a Welshman!

Nevertheless, Venet/Venessian is still spoken to some degree by most natives of the Veneto. This is true not only in rural areas, where one would expect linguistic conservatism to be more prevalent, but also in the towns. Hearing is believing – wander around less-touristed parts of Venice, like Castello, and you'll soon be convinced. Venessian is also alive in the public eye – in Venice, at least, street signs and other public notices are increasingly appearing in Venessian, and you'll often see Venessian words on menus.

Even forgetting Venessian, the Veneto accent itself is hard to miss, even when you hear many locals speaking Italian. Among its traits is the lack of double consonants and frequent dropping of consonants between vowels (*bela fia* for *bella figlia* – beautiful daughter). Another is the frequent inversion of feminine and masculine: *il latte* (the milk) in Italian is *la latte* for many Venetians. The list of curiosities is immense – if you want to know more, you could pick up a pocket Venessian dictionary during your stay. We have abstained from providing phrases in Venessian in this book, as most locals will already be considerably surprised if you manage to do anything more than blurt out a few 'sì's and 'no's in standard Italian!

Note that when **ci**, **gi** and **sci** are followed by **a**, **o** or **u**, the 'i' is not pronounced unless the accent falls on the 'i'. Thus the name Giovanni is pronounced joh-**vahn**-nee.

Word Stress
A double consonant is pronounced as a longer, more forceful sound than a single consonant. Stress generally falls on the second-last syllable, as in *spa-**ghet**-ti*. When a word has an accent, the stress falls on that syllable, as in *cit-**tà*** (city).

Greetings & Civilities

Hello.	*Buongiorno.*
	Ciao. (inf)
Goodbye.	*Arrivederci.*
	Ciao. (inf)
Yes.	*Sì.*
No.	*No.*
Please.	*Per favore/Per piacere.*
Thank you.	*Grazie.*
That's fine/	*Prego.*
You're welcome.	
Excuse me.	*Mi scusi.*
	Scusami. (inf)
Sorry (forgive me).	*Mi scusi/Mi perdoni.*

Small Talk

What's your name?	*Come si chiama?*
	Come ti chiami? (inf)
My name is ...	*Mi chiamo ...*
Where are you from?	*Di dov'è?*
	Di dove sei? (inf)
I'm from ...	*Sono di ...*
I (don't) like ...	*(Non) Mi piace ...*
Just a minute.	*Un momento.*

Language Difficulties

Please write it down.	*Può scriverlo, per favore?*
Can you show me (on the map)?	*Può mostrarmelo (sulla carta/pianta)?*
I understand.	*Capisco.*
I don't understand.	*Non capisco.*
Do you speak English?	*Parla inglese?*
	Parli inglese? (inf)
Does anyone here speak English?	*C'è qualcuno che parla inglese?*
How do you say ... in Italian?	*Come si dice ... in italiano?*
What does ... mean?	*Che vuole dire ...?*

Signs

INGRESSO/ ENTRATA	ENTRANCE
USCITA	EXIT
INFORMAZIONE	INFORMATION
APERTO/CHIUSO	OPEN/CLOSED
PROIBITO/VIETATO	PROHIBITED
POLIZIA/ CARABINIERI	POLICE
QUESTURA	POLICE STATION
CAMERE LIBERE	ROOMS AVAILABLE
COMPLETO	FULL/NO VACANCIES
GABINETTI/BAGNI	TOILETS
UOMINI	MEN
DONNE	WOMEN

Paperwork

name	*nome*
nationality	*nazionalità*
date of birth	*data di nascita*
place of birth	*luogo di nascita*
sex (gender)	*sesso*
passport	*passaporto*
visa	*visto*

Getting Around

What time does ... leave/arrive?	*A che ora parte/ arriva ...?*
the aeroplane	*l'aereo*
the boat	*la barca*
the (city) bus	*l'autobus*
the (intercity) bus	*il pullman/ la corriera*
the train	*il treno*
I'd like a ... ticket.	*Vorrei un biglietto ...*
one-way	*di solo andata*
return	*di andata e ritorno*
1st-class	*prima classe*
2nd-class	*seconda classe*
I want to go to ...	*Voglio andare a ...*
The train has been cancelled/delayed.	*Il treno è soppresso/ in ritardo.*
the first	*il primo*
the last	*l'ultimo*

platform number	binario numero
ticket office	biglietteria
timetable	orario
train station	stazione

I'd like to hire ...	Vorrei noleggiare ...
a bicycle	una bicicletta
a car	una macchina
a motorcycle	una motocicletta

Directions

Where is ...?	Dov'è ...?
Go straight ahead.	Si va sempre diritto.
	Vai sempre diritto. (inf)
Turn left.	Giri a sinistra.
Turn right.	Giri a destra.
at the next corner	al prossimo angolo
at the traffic lights	al semaforo
behind	dietro
in front of	davanti
far	lontano
near	vicino
opposite	di fronte a

Around Town

I'm looking for ...	Cerco ...
a bank	un banco
the church	la chiesa
the city centre	il centro (città)
the ... embassy	l'ambasciata di ...
my hotel	il mio albergo
the market	il mercato
the museum	il museo
the post office	la posta
a public toilet	un gabinetto/ bagno pubblico
the telephone centre	il centro telefonico
the tourist office	l'ufficio di turismo/ d'informazione

I want to change ...	Voglio cambiare ...
money	del denaro
travellers cheques	degli assegni per viaggiatori

beach	la spiaggia
bridge	il ponte
castle	il castello
cathedral	il duomo/la cattedrale
church	la chiesa

island	l'isola
main square	la piazza principale
market	il mercato
mosque	la moschea
old city	il centro storico
palace	il palazzo
ruins	le rovine
sea	il mare
square	la piazza
tower	la torre

Accommodation

I'm looking for ...	Cerco ...
a guesthouse	una pensione
a hotel	un albergo
a youth hostel	un ostello per la gioventù

Where is a cheap hotel?	Dov'è un albergo che costa poco?
What is the address?	Cos'è l'indirizzo?
Could you write the address, please?	Può scrivere l'indirizzo, per favore?
Do you have any rooms available?	Ha camere libere/C'è una camera libera?

I'd like ...	Vorrei ...
a bed	un letto
a single room	una camera singola
a double room	una camera matrimoniale
a room with two beds	una camera doppia
a room with a bathroom	una camera con bagno
to share a dorm	un letto in dormitorio

How much is it ...?	Quanto costa ...?
per night	per la notte
per person	per ciascuno

May I see it?	Posso vederla?
Where is the bathroom?	Dov'è il bagno?
I'm/We're leaving today.	Parto/Partiamo oggi.

Emergencies

Help!	*Aiuto!*
Call ...!	*Chiami ...!*
	Chiama ...! (inf)
a doctor	*un dottore/*
	un medico
the police	*la polizia*
There's been an	*C'è stato un*
accident	*incidente!*
I'm lost.	*Mi sono perso/a.*
Go away!	*Lasciami in pace!*
	Vai via! (inf)

Shopping

I'd like to buy ...	*Vorrei comprare ...*
How much is it?	*Quanto costa?*
I don't like it.	*Non mi piace.*
May I look at it?	*Posso dare*
	un'occhiata?
I'm just looking.	*Sto solo guardando.*
It's cheap.	*Non è caro/a.*
It's too expensive.	*È troppo caro/a.*
I'll take it.	*Lo/La compro.*
Do you accept ...?	*Accettate ...?*
credit cards	*carte di credito*
travellers	*assegni per*
cheques	*viaggiatori*
more	*più*
less	*meno*
smaller	*più piccolo/a*
bigger	*più grande*

Time, Date & Numbers

What time is it?	*Che ora è?/Che ore*
	sono?
It's (8 o'clock).	*Sono (le otto).*
in the morning	*di mattina*
in the afternoon	*di pomeriggio*
in the evening	*di sera*
today	*oggi*
tomorrow	*domani*
yesterday	*ieri*
Monday	*lunedì*
Tuesday	*martedì*
Wednesday	*mercoledì*
Thursday	*giovedì*
Friday	*venerdì*
Saturday	*sabato*
Sunday	*domenica*
January	*gennaio*
February	*febbraio*
March	*marzo*
April	*aprile*
May	*maggio*
June	*giugno*
July	*luglio*
August	*agosto*
September	*settembre*
October	*ottobre*
November	*novembre*
December	*dicembre*

0	*zero*
1	*uno*
2	*due*
3	*tre*
4	*quattro*
5	*cinque*
6	*sei*
7	*sette*
8	*otto*
9	*nove*
10	*dieci*
11	*undici*
12	*dodici*
13	*tredici*
14	*quattordici*
15	*quindici*
16	*sedici*
17	*diciassette*
18	*diciotto*
19	*diciannove*
20	*venti*
21	*ventuno*
22	*ventidue*
30	*trenta*
40	*quaranta*
50	*cinquanta*
60	*sessanta*
70	*settanta*
80	*ottanta*
90	*novanta*
100	*cento*
1000	*mille*
2000	*due mila*
one million	*un milione*

Health

I'm ill.	*Mi sento male.*
It hurts here.	*Mi fa male qui.*

I'm ...	*Sono ...*
asthmatic	*asmatico/a*
diabetic	*diabetico/a*
epileptic	*epilettico/a*

I'm allergic ...	*Sono allergico/a ...*
to antibiotics	*agli antibiotici*
to penicillin	*alla penicillina*

antiseptic	*antisettico*
aspirin	*aspirina*
condoms	*preservativi*
contraceptive	*anticoncezionale*
diarrhoea	*diarrea*
medicine	*medicina*
sunblock cream	*crema/latte solare (per protezione)*
tampons	*tamponi*

FOOD
Basics

breakfast	*prima colazione*
lunch	*pranzo*
dinner	*cena*
restaurant	*ristorante*
grocery store	*un alimentari*

I'd like the set lunch.	*Vorrei il menù turistico.*
Is service included in the bill?	*È compreso il servizio?*
I'm a vegetarian.	*Sono vegetariano/a.*
What is this?	*(Che) cos'è?*

Menu
Useful Words

affumicato	smoked
al dente	firm (as all good pasta should be)
alla brace	cooked over hot coals
alla griglia	grilled
arrosto	roasted
ben cotto	well done (cooked)
bollito	boiled
cameriere/a	waiter/waitress
coltello	knife
conto	bill/cheque

cotto	cooked
crudo	raw
cucchiaino	teaspoon
cucchiaio	spoon
forchetta	fork
fritto	fried
menù	menu
piatto	plate
ristorante	restaurant

Staples

aceto	vinegar
burro	butter
formaggio	cheese
limone	lemon
marmellata	jam
miele	honey
olio	oil
olive	olives
pane	bread
pane integrale	wholemeal bread
panna	cream
pepe	pepper
peperoncino	chilli
polenta	cooked cornmeal
riso	rice
risotto	rice cooked with wine and stock
sale	salt
uovo/uova	egg/eggs
zucchero	sugar

Soups & Antipasti

brodo	broth
carpaccio	very fine slices of raw meat
castraura	artichoke hearts
cotechino	pork sausage served with mustard
insalata caprese	sliced tomatoes with mozzarella and basil
insalata di mare	seafood, generally crustaceans
minestrina in brodo	pasta in broth
minestrone	vegetable soup
olive ascolane	stuffed, deep-fried olives
prosciutto e melone	cured ham with melon
ripieni	stuffed, oven-baked vegetables
stracciatella	egg in broth

Pasta Sauces

alla matriciana	tomato and bacon
al ragù	meat sauce (bolognese)
arrabbiata	tomato and chilli
carbonara	egg, bacon and black pepper
napoletana	tomato and basil
panna	cream, prosciutto and sometimes peas
pesto	basil, garlic and oil, often with pine nuts
vongole	clams, garlic, oil and sometimes tomato

Pizzas

All pizzas listed have a tomato (and sometimes mozzarella) base.

capricciosa	olives, prosciutto, mushrooms and artichokes
frutti di mare	seafood
funghi	mushrooms
margherita	oregano
napoletana	anchovies
pugliese	tomato, mozzarella and onions
quattro formaggi	four types of cheese
quattro stagioni	like a capricciosa, but sometimes with egg
verdura	mixed vegetables, eg courgette/zucchini, aubergine/eggplant, carrot and spinach

Meat & Fish

acciughe	anchovies
agnello	lamb
aragosta	lobster
bistecca	steak
calamari	squid
coniglio	rabbit
cotoletta	cutlet or thin cut of meat, usually crumbed and fried
cozze	mussels
dentice	dentex (type of fish)
fegato	liver
gamberi	prawns
granchio	crab
manzo	beef
merluzzo	cod
ostriche	oysters
pesce spada	swordfish
pollo	chicken
polpo	octopus
salsiccia	sausage
sarde	sardines
sgombro	mackerel
sogliola	sole
tacchino	turkey
tonno	tuna
trippa	tripe
vitello	veal
vongole	clams

Vegetables

asparagi	asparagus
carciofi	artichokes
carote	carrots
cavolo/verza	cabbage
cicoria	chicory
cipolla	onion
fagiolini	string beans
melanzane	aubergines
patate	potatoes
peperoni	peppers
piselli	peas
spinaci	spinach

Fruit

arance	oranges
banane	bananas
ciliegie	cherries
fragole	strawberries
lampone	raspberries
mele	apples
pere	pears
pesche	peaches
uva	grapes

Glossary

Listed below are useful Italian terms. Some appear in the Venetian dialect (V). In a few instances, Italian words used only in Venice and, at the most, elsewhere in the Veneto have been identified (Vz). A couple of entries in French (F) and English (E) also appear. They are specialised terms that may not be familiar to all readers.

ACI – Automobile Club Italiano; Italian Automobile Club

acqua alta (s), **acque alte** (pl) – high water (flooding that occurs in Venice during winter, when the sea level rises)

affittacamere – rooms for rent (sometimes cheaper than a *pensione* and not part of the classification system)

AIG – Associazione Italiana Alberghi per la Gioventù; Italian Youth Hostel Association

albergo – hotel (up to five stars)

alimentari – grocery shop

alloggio – general term for lodging of any kind; not part of the classification system

alto – high

ambulanza – ambulance

anfiteatro – amphitheatre

appartamento – apartment, flat

apse – (E) domed or arched area at the altar end of a church

APT – Azienda di Promozione Turistica; provincial tourist office

arco – arch

ASL – Azienda Sanitaria Locale' provincial health agency

autobus – bus

autostazione – bus station/terminal

autostop – hitchhiking

autostrada (s), **autostrade** (pl) – motorway/highway

bacaro – (V) traditional Venetian bar or eatery

bagno – bathroom; also toilet

bancomat – ATM, or automated teller machine

basilica – (E) style of church, with a hall flanked by two aisles

battistero – baptistry

benzina – petrol

bicicletta – bicycle

biglietteria – ticket office

biglietto – ticket

binario – platform

bricola – (V) pylon marking navigable channel in Venetian lagoon

calle (s), **calli** (pl) – (Vz) street

camera – room

camera doppia – double room with twin beds

camera matrimoniale – double room with double bed

camera singola – single room

campanile – bell tower

campo – (Vz) square; equivalent to the piazza elsewhere in Italy

cappella – chapel

carabinieri – police with military and civil duties

carta marmorizzata – marbled paper

carta telefonica – phonecard

cartoleria – shop selling paper goods

cartolina (postale) – postcard

castello – castle

cattedrale – cathedral

cena – evening meal

centro – centre

centro storico – (literally 'historical centre') old town

chiaroscuro – (literally 'light-dark') the use of strong light and dark contrasts in painting to put the main figures in painting into stronger relief

chiesa – church

chiostro – cloister; covered walkway, usually enclosed by columns, around a quadrangle

cichetti – (Vz) traditional bar snacks eaten in bars and *osterie*

CIT – Compagnia Italiana di Turismo; Italian national travel agency

colazione – breakfast

colonna – column

comune – equivalent to a municipality or

county; town or city council; historically, a commune (self-governing town or city)
consolato – consulate
coperto – cover charge (in restaurant)
corte – (Vz) blind alley
CTS – Centro Turistico Studentesco e Giovanile; student/youth travel agency
cupola – dome

deposito bagagli – left luggage
digestivo – after-dinner liqueur
duomo – cathedral

ENIT – Ente Nazionale Italiano per il Turismo; Italian State Tourist Office
espresso – express mail; express train; short black coffee

farmacia – pharmacy, chemist's shop
farmacia di turno – late-night pharmacy
ferrovia – train station
festa – festival
fiume – river
fondamenta – (Vz) street beside a canal
fontana – fountain
forcola – (V) wooden support for gondolier's oar
foresto – (V) stranger, foreigner (non-Venetian)
foro – forum
francobollo – postage stamp
fresco – (E) the painting method in which watercolour paint is applied to wet plaster
FS – Ferrovie dello Stato; Italian State Railway
funicolare – funicular railway

gabinetto – toilet, WC
gettoni – telephone tokens
golfo – gulf

intarsia – inlaid wood, marble or metal

lago – lake
largo – (small) square; boulevard
lavanderia – laundrette
lavasecco – dry-cleaning
lettera – letter
lettera raccomandata – registered letter
lido – beach
locanda – inn, small hotel

loggia – covered area on the side of a building, porch
lungomare – seafront road, promenade

Maggior Consiglio – Grand Council; level of Venetian government (see History in the Facts about Venice chapter)
mare – sea
mercato – market
merceria – haberdashery shop
monte – mountain
motonave – big, inter-island ferry on Venetian lagoon
motorino – moped
motoscafo – motorboat; in Venice a faster, fully enclosed ferry
municipio – town hall

nave (s), **navi** (pl) – ship
necropoli – necropolis; (ancient) cemetery, burial site

oggetti smarriti – lost property
ombra – (Vz) small glass of wine
ospedale – hospital
ostello – hostel
osteria (s), **osterie** (pl) – traditional bar/restaurant

pacco – package, parcel
Pagine Gialle – Yellow Pages (telephone directory)
pala/pala d'altare – altarpiece; refers to a painting (often on wood) usually used as an ornament before the altar
palazzo (s), **palazzi** (pl) – palace, mansion; large building of any type, including an apartment block
panino (s), **panini** (pl) – bread roll with filling
parco – park
passeggiata – traditional evening stroll
passerelle – raised walkway
pasta – cake; pasta; pastry or dough
pasticceria – shop selling cakes, pastries and biscuits
pensione – guesthouse, small hotel
permesso di soggiorno – permit to stay for a period of time, residence permit
piazza – square
piazzale – (large) open square

pietà – (literally 'pity' or 'compassion') sculpture, drawing or painting of the dead Christ supported by the Madonna
pizzeria – pizza restaurant
polizia – police
poltrona – airline-type chair on a ferry
ponte – bridge
portico – portico; covered walkway, usually attached to the outside of buildings
porto – port
posta aerea – air mail
pronto soccorso – first aid, casualty ward
prosecco – lightly sparkling white wine

(La) Quarantia – (literally 'the 40') level of Venetian government (see History in the Facts about Venice chapter)
questura – police station

rifugio – shelter; mountain accommodation
rio (s), **rii** (pl) – (Vz) the name for most canals in Venice
rio terrà – (Vz) street following the course of a filled-in canal
riva – river bank
riva alta – high river bank
rivo – stream
rocca – fortress
rosso – red

salumeria – delicatessen
santuario – sanctuary
scalinata – staircase
scavi – excavations
servizio – service charge (in restaurant)
sestiere (s), **sestieri** (pl) – (Vz) term for the six 12th-century municipal divisions of Venice
Signoria – top level of Venetian government (see History in the Facts about Venice chapter)
soccorso stradale – highway rescue
sotoportego (s), **sotoporteghi** (pl) – (Vz) in Italian *sottoportico*; street continuing under a building (like an extended archway)

spiaggia – beach
spiaggia libera – public beach
squero – gondola-building and repair yard
stazione – station
stazione marittima – ferry terminal
stazione di servizio – service station, petrol station
strada – street, road
strada provinciale – main road; sometimes just a country lane
strada statale – main road; often multi-land and toll free

tabaccheria – tobacconist's shop
teatro – theatre
telegramma – telegram
tempio – temple
terme – thermal baths
tesoro – treasury
torre – tower
traghetto – small ferry; in Venice, the commuter gondolas that crisscross the Grand Canal
tramezzino – sandwich
trattoria (s), **trattorie** (pl) – fairly cheap restaurant
treno – train
trompe l'oeil – (F) painting or other illustration which is designed to 'deceive the eye', creating the impression that the image is real
tympanum – (E) vertical (often triangular) space above a doorway between lintel and arch

ufficio postale – post office
ufficio stranieri – foreigners' bureau (in police station)

vaporetto – ferry
via – street, road
via aerea – air mail
vigili urbani – traffic/local police
villa – town or country house; also the park surrounding the house

LONELY PLANET

Phrasebooks

Lonely Planet phrasebooks are packed with essential words and phrases to help travellers communicate with the locals. With colour tabs for quick reference, an extensive vocabulary and use of script, these handy pocket-sized language guides cover day-to-day travel situations.

- handy pocket-sized books
- easy to understand Pronunciation chapter
- clear & comprehensive Grammar chapter
- romanisation alongside script to allow ease of pronunciation
- script throughout so users can point to phrases for every situation
- full of cultural information and tips for the traveller

'...vital for a real DIY spirit and attitude in language learning'
– *Backpacker*

'the phrasebooks have good cultural backgrounders and offer solid advice for challenging situations in remote locations'
– *San Francisco Examiner*

Arabic (Egyptian) • Arabic (Moroccan) • Australian *(Australian English, Aboriginal and Torres Strait languages)* • Baltic States *(Estonian, Latvian, Lithuanian)* • Bengali • Brazilian • British • Burmese • Cantonese • Central Asia • Central Europe *(Czech, French, German, Hungarian, Italian, Slovak)* • Eastern Europe *(Bulgarian, Czech, Hungarian, Polish, Romanian, Slovak)* • Ethiopian (Amharic) • Fijian • French • German • Greek • Hebrew phrasebook • Hill Tribes • Hindi/Urdu • Indonesian • Italian • Japanese • Korean • Lao • Latin American Spanish • Malay • Mandarin • Mediterranean Europe *(Albanian, Croatian, Greek, Italian, Macedonian, Maltese, Serbian, Slovene)* • Mongolian • Nepali • Pidgin • Pilipino (Tagalog) • Quechua • Russian • Scandinavian Europe *(Danish, Finnish, Icelandic, Norwegian, Swedish)* • South-East Asia *(Burmese, Indonesian, Khmer, Lao, Malay, Tagalog Pilipino, Thai, Vietnamese)* • South Pacific Languages • Spanish (Castilian) *(also includes Catalan, Galician and Basque)* • Sri Lanka • Swahili • Thai • Tibetan • Turkish • Ukrainian • USA *(US English, Vernacular, Native American languages, Hawaiian)* • Vietnamese • Western Europe *(Basque, Catalan, Dutch, French, German, Greek, Irish)*

LONELY PLANET

Lonely Planet Journeys

J OURNEYS is a unique collection of travel writing – published by the company that understands travel better than anyone else. It is a series for anyone who has ever experienced – or dreamed of – the magical moment when they encountered a strange culture or saw a place for the first time. They are tales to read while you're planning a trip, while you're on the road or while you're in an armchair, in front of a fire.

These outstanding titles explore our planet through the eyes of a diverse group of international writers. JOURNEYS books catch the spirit of a place, illuminate a culture, recount a crazy adventure, or introduce a fascinating way of life. They always entertain, and always enrich the experience of travel.

MALI BLUES
Traveling to an African Beat
Lieve Joris (translated by Sam Garrett)

Drought, rebel uprisings, ethnic conflict: these are the predominant images of West Africa. But as Lieve Joris travels in Senegal, Mauritania and Mali, she meets survivors, fascinating individuals charting new ways of living between tradition and modernity. With her remarkable gift for drawing out people's stories, Joris brilliantly captures the rhythms of a world that refuses to give in.

THE GATES OF DAMASCUS
Lieve Joris (translated by Sam Garrett)

This best-selling book is a beautifully drawn portrait of day-to-day life in modern Syria. Through her intimate contact with local people, Lieve Joris draws us into the fascinating world that lies behind the gates of Damascus. Hala's husband is a political prisoner, jailed for his opposition to the Assad regime; through the author's friendship with Hala we see how Syrian politics impacts on the lives of ordinary people.

THE OLIVE GROVE
Travels in Greece
Katherine Kizilos

Katherine Kizilos travels to fabled islands, troubled border zones and her family's village deep in the mountains. She vividly evokes breathtaking landscapes, generous people and passionate politics, capturing the complexities of a country she loves.

'beautifully captures the real tensions of Greece' – *Sunday Times*

KINGDOM OF THE FILM STARS
Journey into Jordan
Annie Caulfield

Kingdom of the Film Stars is a travel book and a love story. With honesty and humour, Annie Caulfield writes of travelling in Jordan and falling in love with a Bedouin with film-star looks.

She offers fascinating insights into the country – from the tent life of traditional women to the hustle of downtown Amman – and unpicks tight-woven Western myths about the Arab world.

LONELY PLANET

Lonely Planet Travel Atlases

L onely Planet has long been famous for the number and quality of its guidebook maps. Now we've gone one step further and produced a handy companion series: Lonely Planet travel atlases – maps of a country produced in book form.

Unlike other maps, which look good but lead travellers astray, our travel atlases have been researched on the road by Lonely Planet's experienced team of writers. All details are carefully checked to ensure the atlas corresponds with the equivalent Lonely Planet guidebook.

- full-colour throughout
- maps researched and checked by Lonely Planet authors
- place names correspond with Lonely Planet guidebooks
- no confusing spelling differences
- legend and travelling information in English, French, German, Japanese and Spanish
- size: 230 x 160 mm

Available now: Chile & Easter Island • Egypt • India & Bangladesh • Israel & the Palestinian Territories • Jordan, Syria & Lebanon • Kenya • Laos • Portugal • South Africa, Lesotho & Swaziland • Thailand • Turkey • Vietnam • Zimbabwe, Botswana & Namibia

Lonely Planet TV Series & Videos

L onely Planet travel guides have been brought to life on television screens around the world. Like our guides, the programs are based on the joy of independent travel, and look honestly at some of the most exciting, picturesque and frustrating places in the world. Each show is presented by one of three travellers from Australia, England or the USA and combines an innovative mixture of video, Super-8 film, atmospheric soundscapes and original music.

Videos of each episode – containing additional footage not shown on television – are available from good book and video shops, but the availability of individual videos varies with regional screening schedules.

Video destinations include: Alaska • American Rockies • Argentina • Australia – The South-East • Baja California & the Copper Canyon • Brazil • Central Asia • Chile & Easter Island • Corsica, Sicily & Sardinia – The Mediterranean Islands • East Africa (Tanzania & Zanzibar) • Cuba • Ecuador & the Galapagos Islands • Ethiopia • Greenland & Iceland • Hungary & Romania • Indonesia • Israel & the Sinai Desert • Jamaica • Japan • La Ruta Maya • The Middle East (Syria, Jordan & Lebanon • Morocco • New York • Northern Spain • North India • Outback Australia • Pacific Islands (Fiji, Solomon Islands & Vanuatu) • Pakistan • Peru • The Philippines • South Africa & Lesotho • South India • South West China • South West USA • Trekking in Uganda • Turkey • Vietnam • West Africa • Zimbabwe, Botswana & Namibia

The Lonely Planet TV series is produced by: Pilot Productions
The Old Studio
18 Middle Row
London W10 5AT, UK

Lonely Planet On-line

Whether you've just begun planning your next trip, or you're chasing down specific info on currency regulations or visa requirements, check out Lonely Planet On-line for up-to-the minute travel information.

As well as mini guides to more than 250 destinations, you'll find maps, photos, travel news, health and visa updates, travel advisories, and discussion of the ecological and political issues you need to be aware of as you travel. You'll also find timely upgrades to popular guidebooks which you can print out and stick in the back of your book.

There's also an on-line travellers' forum where you can share your experience of life on the road, meet travel companions and ask other travellers for their recommendations and advice.

And of course we have a complete and up-to-date list of all Lonely Planet travel products including travel guides, diving and snorkeling guides, phrasebooks, atlases, travel literature and videos, and a simple on-line ordering facility if you can't find the book you want elsewhere.

Lonely Planet Diving & Snorkeling Guides

Beautifully illustrated with full-colour photos throughout, Lonely Planet's Pisces Books explore the world's best diving and snorkelling areas and prepare divers for what to expect when they get there, both topside and underwater.

Dive sites are described in detail with specifics on depths, visibility, level of difficulty, special conditions, underwater photography tips, and common and unusual marine life present. You'll also find practical logistical information and coverage on topside activities and attractions, sections on diving health and safety, plus listings for diving services, live-aboards, dive resorts and tourist offices.

LONELY PLANET

Guides by Region

Lonely Planet is known worldwide for publishing practical, reliable and no-nonsense travel information in our guides and on our Web site. The Lonely Planet list covers just about every accessible part of the world. Currently there are thirteen series: travel guides, shoestring guides, walking guides, city guides, phrasebooks, audio packs, city maps, travel atlases, diving and snorkeling guides, restaurant guides, first-time travel guides, healthy travel and travel literature.

AFRICA Africa – the South • Africa on a shoestring • Arabic (Egyptian) phrasebook • Arabic (Moroccan) phrasebook • Cairo • Cape Town • Cape Town city map• Central Africa • East Africa • Egypt • Egypt travel atlas • Ethiopian (Amharic) phrasebook • The Gambia & Senegal • Healthy Travel Africa • Kenya • Kenya travel atlas • Malawi, Mozambique & Zambia • Morocco • North Africa • South Africa, Lesotho & Swaziland • South Africa, Lesotho & Swaziland travel atlas • Swahili phrasebook • Tanzania, Zanzibar & Pemba • Trekking in East Africa • Tunisia • West Africa • Zimbabwe, Botswana & Namibia • Zimbabwe, Botswana & Namibia travel atlas
Travel Literature: The Rainbird: A Central African Journey • Songs to an African Sunset: A Zimbabwean Story • Mali Blues: Traveling to an African Beat

AUSTRALIA & THE PACIFIC Auckland • Australia • Australian phrasebook • Bushwalking in Australia • Bushwalking in Papua New Guinea • Fiji • Fijian phrasebook • Islands of Australia's Great Barrier Reef • Melbourne • Melbourne city map • Micronesia • New Caledonia • New South Wales & the ACT • New Zealand • Northern Territory • Outback Australia • Out To Eat – Melbourne • Papua New Guinea • Papua New Guinea (Pidgin) phrasebook • Queensland • Rarotonga & the Cook Islands • Samoa • Solomon Islands • South Australia • South Pacific Languages phrasebook • Sydney • Sydney city map • Tahiti & French Polynesia • Tasmania • Tonga • Tramping in New Zealand • Vanuatu • Victoria • Western Australia
Travel Literature: Islands in the Clouds • Kiwi Tracks • Sean & David's Long Drive

CENTRAL AMERICA & THE CARIBBEAN Bahamas, Turks & Caicos • Bermuda • Central America on a shoestring • Costa Rica • Cuba • Dominican Republic & Haiti • Eastern Caribbean • Guatemala, Belize & Yucatán: La Ruta Maya • Jamaica • Mexico • Mexico City • Panama • Puerto Rico
Travel Literature: Green Dreams: Travels in Central America

EUROPE Amsterdam • Amsterdam city map • Andalucía • Austria • Baltic States phrasebook • Barcelona • Berlin • Berlin city map • Britain • British phrasebook • Brussels, Bruges & Antwerp • Budapest city map • Canary Islands • Central Europe • Central Europe phrasebook • Corsica • Croatia • Czech & Slovak Republics • Denmark • Dublin • Eastern Europe • Eastern Europe phrasebook • Edinburgh • Estonia, Latvia & Lithuania • Europe • Finland • France • French phrasebook • Germany • German phrasebook • Greece • Greek phrasebook • Hungary • Iceland, Greenland & the Faroe Islands • Ireland • Italian phrasebook • Italy • Lisbon • London • London city map • Mediterranean Europe • Mediterranean Europe phrasebook • Norway • Paris • Paris city map • Poland • Portugal • Portugal travel atlas • Prague • Prague city map • Provence & the Côte d'Azur • Romania & Moldova • Rome • Russia, Ukraine & Belarus • Russian phrasebook • Scandinavian & Baltic Europe • Scandinavian Europe phrasebook • Scotland • Slovenia • Spain • Spanish phrasebook • St Petersburg • Switzerland • Trekking in Spain • Ukrainian phrasebook • Vienna • Walking in Britain • Walking in Ireland • Walking in Italy • Walking in Switzerland • Western Europe • Western Europe phrasebook
Travel Literature: The Olive Grove: Travels in Greece

INDIAN SUBCONTINENT Bangladesh • Bengali phrasebook • Bhutan • Delhi • Goa • Hindi/Urdu phrasebook • India • India & Bangladesh travel atlas • Indian Himalaya • Karakoram Highway • Kerala • Mumbai • Nepal • Nepali phrasebook • Pakistan • Rajasthan • Read This First: Asia & India • South India • Sri Lanka • Sri Lanka phrasebook • Trekking in the Indian Himalaya • Trekking in the Karakoram & Hindukush • Trekking in the Nepal Himalaya
Travel Literature: In Rajasthan • Shopping for Buddhas

LONELY PLANET

Mail Order

Lonely Planet products are distributed worldwide. They are also available by mail order from Lonely Planet, so if you have difficulty finding a title please write to us. North and South American residents should write to 150 Linden St, Oakland, CA 94607, USA; European and African residents should write to 10a Spring Place, London NW5 3BH, UK; and residents of other countries to PO Box 617, Hawthorn, Victoria 3122, Australia.

ISLANDS OF THE INDIAN OCEAN Madagascar & Comoros • Maldives • Mauritius, Réunion & Seychelles

MIDDLE EAST & CENTRAL ASIA Arab Gulf States • Central Asia • Central Asia phrasebook • Hebrew phrasebook • Iran • Israel & the Palestinian Territories • Israel & the Palestinian Territories travel atlas • Istanbul • Istanbul to Cairo • Jerusalem • Jordan & Syria • Jordan, Syria & Lebanon travel atlas • Lebanon • Middle East on a shoestring • Syria • Turkey • Turkish phrasebook • Turkey travel atlas • Yemen
Travel Literature: The Gates of Damascus • Kingdom of the Film Stars: Journey into Jordan

NORTH AMERICA Alaska • Backpacking in Alaska • Baja California • California & Nevada • Canada • Chicago • Chicago city map • Deep South • Florida • Hawaii • Honolulu • Las Vegas • Los Angeles • Miami • New England • New Orleans • New York City • New York city map • New York, New Jersey & Pennsylvania • Pacific Northwest USA • Puerto Rico • Rocky Mountain States • San Francisco • San Francisco city map • Seattle • Southwest USA • Texas • USA • USA phrasebook • Vancouver • Washington, DC & the Capital Region • Washington DC city map
Travel Literature: Drive Thru America

NORTH-EAST ASIA Beijing • Cantonese phrasebook • China • Hong Kong • Hong Kong city map • Hong Kong, Macau & Guangzhou • Japan • Japanese phrasebook • Japanese audio pack • Korea • Korean phrasebook • Kyoto • Mandarin phrasebook • Mongolia • Mongolian phrasebook • North-East Asia on a shoestring • Seoul • South-West China • Taiwan • Tibet • Tibetan phrasebook • Tokyo
Travel Literature: Lost Japan

SOUTH AMERICA Argentina, Uruguay & Paraguay • Bolivia • Brazil • Brazilian phrasebook • Buenos Aires • Chile & Easter Island • Chile & Easter Island travel atlas • Colombia • Ecuador & the Galapagos Islands • Latin American Spanish phrasebook • Peru • Quechua phrasebook • Rio de Janeiro • Rio de Janeiro city map • South America on a shoestring • Trekking in the Patagonian Andes • Venezuela
Travel Literature: Full Circle: A South American Journey

SOUTH-EAST ASIA Bali & Lombok • Bangkok • Bangkok city map • Burmese phrasebook • Cambodia • Hanoi • Healthy Travel Asia & India • Hill Tribes phrasebook • Ho Chi Minh City • Indonesia • Indonesia's Eastern Islands • Indonesian phrasebook • Indonesian audio pack • Jakarta • Java • Laos • Lao phrasebook • Laos travel atlas • Malay phrasebook • Malaysia, Singapore & Brunei • Myanmar (Burma) • Philippines • Pilipino (Tagalog) phrasebook • Singapore • South-East Asia on a shoestring • South-East Asia phrasebook • Thailand • Thailand's Islands & Beaches • Thailand travel atlas • Thai phrasebook • Thai audio pack • Vietnam • Vietnamese phrasebook • Vietnam travel atlas

ALSO AVAILABLE: Antarctica • The Arctic • Brief Encounters: Stories of Love, Sex & Travel • Chasing Rickshaws • Lonely Planet Unpacked • Not the Only Planet: Travel Stories from Science Fiction • Sacred India • Travel with Children • Traveller's Tales

LONELY PLANET

FREE Lonely Planet Newsletters

We love hearing from you and think you'd like to hear from us.

Planet Talk

Our FREE quarterly printed newsletter is full of tips from travellers and anecdotes from Lonely Planet guidebook authors. Every issue is packed with up-to-date travel news and advice, and includes:

- a postcard from Lonely Planet co-founder Tony Wheeler
- a swag of mail from travellers
- a look at life on the road through the eyes of a Lonely Planet author
- topical health advice
- prizes for the best travel yarn
- news about forthcoming Lonely Planet events
- a complete list of Lonely Planet books and other titles

To join our mailing list, residents of the UK, Europe and Africa can email us at go@lonelyplanet.co.uk; residents of North and South America can email us at info@lonelyplanet.com; the rest of the world can email us at talk2us@lonelyplanet.com.au, or contact any Lonely Planet office.

Comet

Our FREE monthly email newsletter brings you all the latest travel news, features, interviews, competitions, destination ideas, travellers' tips & tales, Q&As, raging debates and related links. Find out what's new on the Lonely Planet Web site and which books are about to hit the shelves.

Subscribe from your desktop: www.lonelyplanet.com/comet

Index

Text

D

Bold indicates maps.

Boxed Text

VENICE
MAPS

MAP 2 VENICE (VENEZIA)

to Mestre

Isola di
San Secondo

Ponte della Libertà

Canale delle Sacche

Canale delle Navi

Parco
Groggia

2
S. Canale

MAP 3

CANNAREGIO

Isola del
Tronchetto

P 3

Parco
Savorgnan

Stazione di
Santa Lucia
(Ferrovia)

Canal Grande

(Grand Canal)

Ponte dei
Scalzi

SANTA CROCE

Stazione
Merci

Stazione
Marittima
(Merci)

Bus Station

Piazzale
Roma

Giardino
Papadopoli

SAN POLO

Ponte di
Rialto

Canal Grande (Grand Canal)

Bacino della Stazione Marittima

Canale Scomenzera

Santa
Marta

Stazione
Marittima

DORSODURO

Ponte dell'
Accademia

Canale di Fusina

MAP 5

Sacca Fisola

Canale   della

Sacca
San
Biagio

5

MAP 9

0   150   300 m

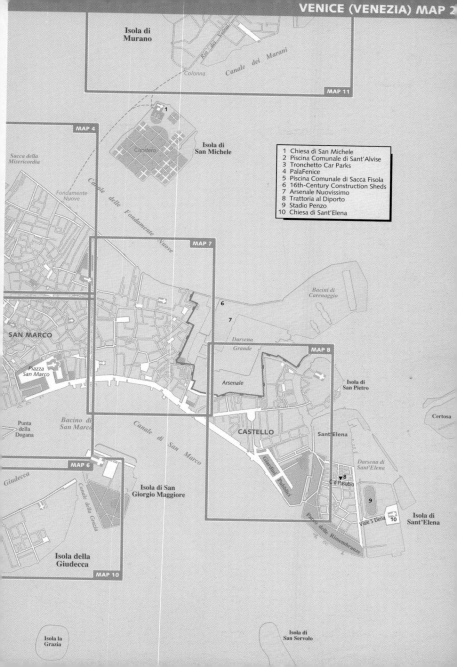

Isola di
Murano

MAP 11

Isola di
San Michele

Cimitero

1 Chiesa di San Michele
2 Piscina Comunale di Sant'Alvise
3 Tronchetto Car Parks
4 PalaFenice
5 Piscina Comunale di Sacca Fisola
6 16th-Century Construction Sheds
7 Arsenale Nuovissimo
8 Trattoria al Diporto
9 Stadio Penzo
10 Chiesa di Sant'Elena

Sacca della
Misericordia

MAP 4

Fondamente
Nuove

Canale delle Fondamente Nuove

MAP 7

Bacini di
Carenaggio

SAN MARCO

Darsena
Grande

MAP 8

Piazza
San Marco

Arsenale

Isola di
San Pietro

Certosa

Punta
della
Dogana

Bacino di
San Marco

Canale di San Marco

CASTELLO

Sant'Elena

Darsena di
Sant'Elena

MAP 6

Giudecca

Canale della Grazia

Isola di San
Giorgio Maggiore

Giardini
Pubblici

Ca' di Pisubio

8

9

Viale S'Elena

Isola di
Sant'Elena

10

Isola della
Giudecca

MAP 10

Isola la
Grazia

Isola di
San Servolo

MAP 3

MAP 5

MAP 5

Ponte Moro

Fondamenta Carlo Coletti

Rio di San Girolamo

Fondamenta di San Giobbe

Calle Guidiana

Calle Ferau

Calle del Ferner

Calle del Forno

Fondamenta Cres Nuove

Fondamen

Calle de la Coquescia

Calle Tintoria

Fondamenta del Batello

Rio del Batello

Calle delle Beccarie

Calle del Scalatto

Calle dei Cobeti

Calle del Magazzen

Calle dei Tinton

Calle delle Canne

Calle di Bisacetella

Calle della Cerenis

Ponte di Tre Archi

Ponte Saponello

Campo San Giobbe

Calle della Madonna

Fondamenta di Cannaregio

Calle delle Sotto Seren

Canale di Cannaregio

Rio di San Giro

Fondamenta Savorgnan

Fondamenta

Rio Terre della Crea

Calle Batello

Calle Riello

Rio della Crea

Canale Colombola

Parco Savorgnan

Rio di San Giobbe

Calle Priuli, detta dei Cavalletti

Calle della Misericordia

Calle Pesaro

Rio Terà lista di Spagna

Rio Terà di Saldoni

Fond. Crotta

Ponte della Libertà

Ponte della Libertà

Canal Grande

Rio della Croce

Stazione di Santa Lucia (Ferrovia)

Ferrovia Scalzi

Fondamenta dei Scalzi

Ponte dei Scalzi

Campiello Simeon Gran

Calle Lunga Chioverette

Rio Marin

Fondamenta di Santa Lucia

Ferrovia Santa Lucia

Clio di Comare

Calle del Traghetto di Santa Lucia

Calle Bergamaschi

Ramo Chioverette

Corte Canal

Piazzale Roma Scorrienzera

Piazzale Roma Parisi

Stazione Merci

Fondamenta Santa Simeon Piccolo

Fond. del Croce

Corte de Case Nuove

Campo della Lana

Calle della

Piazzale Roma Santa Chiara

Giardini Papadopoli

Fondamenta di Santa Chiara

C. Volto

Fondamenta di Santa Chiara

Canale di Santa Chiara

Campo di S Andrea

Garage Comunale P

Piazzale Roma

0   50   100 m

1
2
3
4
53
54
55
56
57
58
59
60
61
62
63
64
65
66
67
68
69
70
71
72
73
75
76
77
78
79
80
81
14

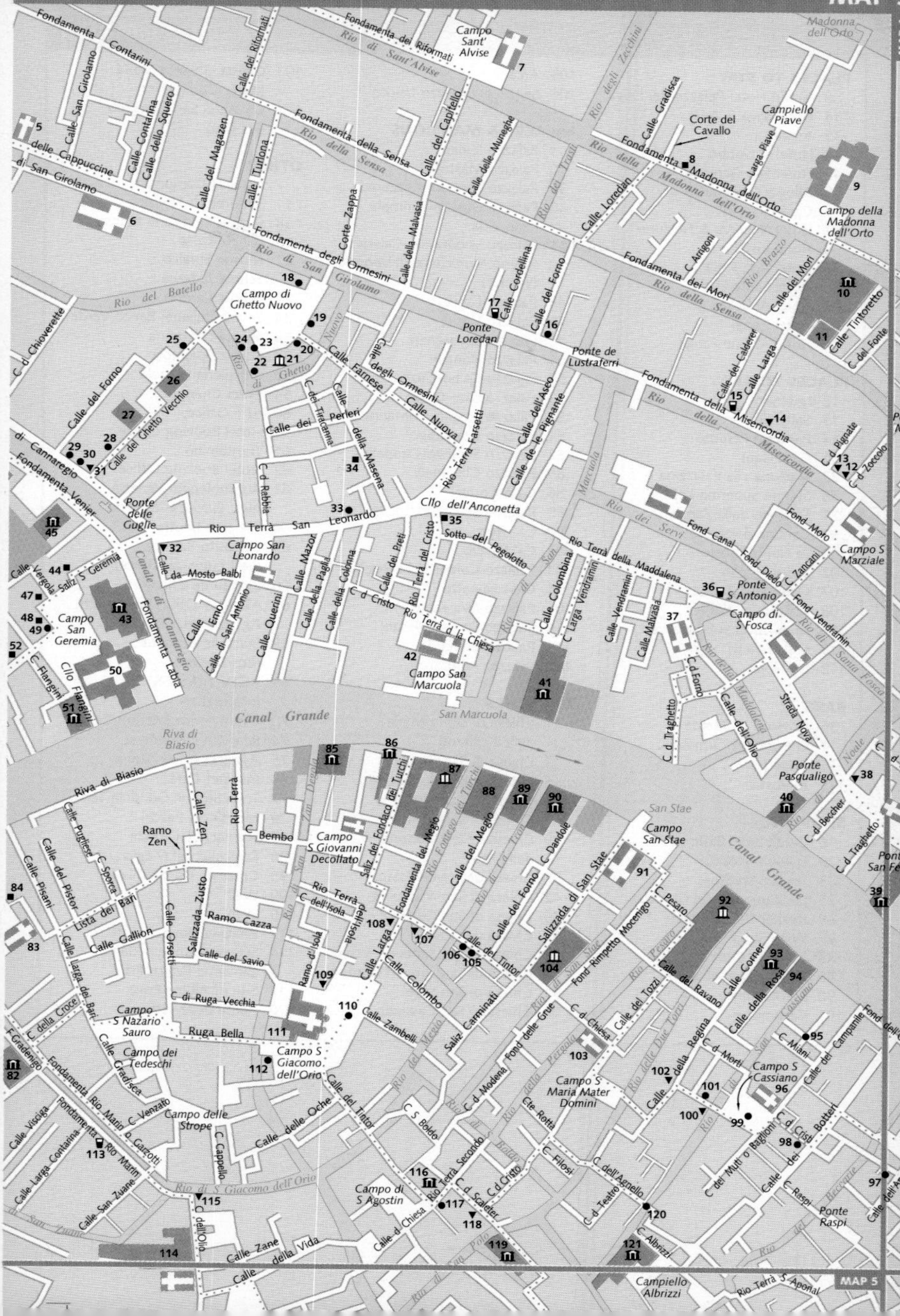

Fondamenta Contarini

Calle San Girolamo
Calle della Squero
Calle Contarina
Calle del Magazen

Calle dei Riformati
Fondamenta dei Riformati
Rio di Sant'Alvise

Campo Sant'Alvise 7

Madonna dell'Orto

Corte del Cavallo 8

Campiello Piave

delle Cappuccine 5

di San Girolamo

6

Fondamenta della Sensa
Rio della Sensa
Calle Turlona
Calle del Capitello
Calle delle Munghe
Calle Loredan
Fondamenta della Madonna dell'Orto

Madonna dell'Orto 8

Campo della Madonna dell'Orto 9

Calle dei Mori 10

11 Tintoretto

Rio del Batello
Rio di San Girolamo
Fondamenta degli Ormesini

Campo di Ghetto Nuovo 18

19

20
21
22
23
24

25
26
27
28
29 30
31

Calle del Forno
Calle del Ghetto Vecchio

Calle Farnese
Calle degli Ormesini
Calle Nuova
Calle dell'Aseo
Calle de la Masena
Calle de la Pasina

17
16
Ponte Loredan
Ponte de Lustraferri

Fondamenta dei Mori
Rio della Sensa
Calle dei Caldera
Calle dei Forno
Calle dell'Aseo

Calle dei Mori

15
14
13
12

Ponte delle Guglie
Rio Terrà San Leonardo

Calle de la Malvasia
Corte Zappa

Calle del Forno

Ponte de Donna Onesta

Campo San Leonardo
Sotto del Pegolotto

32
33
34
35

42

Campo San Marcuola

41

San Marcuola

Canal Grande

Riva di Biasio

Rio Terrà della Maddalena
Ponte S Antonio
36

Campo di S Fosca

37

Campo S Marziale

Campo San Geremia 43
Verso Santi S Geremia
44
45
46
47
48 49
50
51
52

Ponte Pasqualigo 38

40

39

85
86
87
88
89
90
91

Campo S Giovanni Decollato
Campo San Stae

92
93
94
95

Ramo Zen
Bembo

Rio Terrà dell'Isola

83
84

108
107
106
105
104
109
110
111
112
113

Campo S Nazario Sauro
Campo dei Tedeschi
Campo S Giacomo dell'Orio
Campo delle Strope

82

Campo S Maria Mater Domini

102
101
100
99
98
96
97

Campo S Cassiano

Campo S Agostin

114
115
116
117
118
119
120
121

Campiello Albrizzi

MAP 5

MAP 3

PLACES TO STAY

- 8 Grand Hotel Palazzo dei Dogi
- 34 Hotel Silva & Ariel
- 35 Archies
- 44 Hotel al Gobbo
- 47 Hotel San Geremia
- 48 Alloggi Calderan & Casa Gerotto
- 52 Hotel Minerva & Nettuno
- 53 Hotel Rossi
- 55 Hotel Villa Rosa
- 56 Hotel Santa Lucia
- 57 Hotel Abbazzia
- 72 Hotel Canal
- 84 Hotel Ai Due Fanali

PLACES TO EAT

- 12 Iguana
- 13 Sahara
- 14 Paradiso Perduto
- 31 Gam Gam
- 32 Trattoria alla Palazzina
- 38 Standa Supermarket
- 71 Trattoria dalla Zanze
- 97 Cantina do Spade
- 100 Al Nono Risorto
- 102 Vecio Fritolin
- 107 Osteria La Zucca
- 108 Trattoria al Ponte
- 109 Mini-Coop Supermarket
- 115 Shri Ganesh
- 118 Da Fiore

BARS

- 15 Le Notti d'Oriente
- 17 Osteria agli Ormesini
- 36 Wine Bar
- 113 Ai Postali

SHOPPING

- 16 Cantina del Baffo
- 20 David's Shop
- 23 Jewish Art Store
- 25 La Stamperia del Ghetto
- 28 Kosher Delicatessen
- 29 Wine Shop
- 33 Nave de Oro
- 49 Libreria Demetra
- 98 L'Arlecchino
- 101 Ceramiche

- 105 Arca
- 106 Segno di Lorenzo Usicco

PALACES & MANSIONS

- 4 Palazzo Surian
- 10 Palazzo Mastelli
- 39 Palazzo Fontana-Rezzonico
- 40 Palazzo Gussoni-Grimani della Vida
- 41 Palazzo Vendramin-Calergi; Casinò Municipale di Venezia (Winter)
- 43 Palazzo Labia
- 45 Palazzo Venier
- 46 Palazzo Savorgnan
- 51 Palazzo Flangini
- 58 Palazzo Calbo-Crotta
- 73 Palazzo Emo-Diedo
- 80 Palazzo Foscari-Contarini
- 81 Palazzo Gradenigo
- 82 Palazzo Soranzo-Cappello
- 85 Palazzo Giovanelli
- 86 Casa Correr
- 89 Palazzo Belloni Battaglia
- 90 Ca' Tron
- 92 Ca' Pesaro
- 93 Palazzo Corner della Regina
- 94 Casa Favretto
- 104 Palazzo Mocenigo
- 116 Palazzo Soranzo-Pisani
- 119 Palazzo Bernardo
- 121 Palazzo Albrizzi

CHURCHES

- 1 Chiesa di Santa Maria delle Penitenti
- 3 Chiesa di San Giobbe
- 5 Chiesa delle Cappuccine
- 6 Chiesa di San Girolamo
- 7 Chiesa di Sant'Alvise
- 9 Chiesa della Madonna dell'Orto
- 37 Chiesa della Maddalena
- 42 Chiesa di San Marcuola
- 50 Chiesa di San Geremia
- 59 Chiesa dei Scalzi
- 78 Chiesa di San Simeon Piccolo
- 83 Chiesa di San Simeon Grande
- 91 Chiesa di San Stae
- 96 Chiesa di San Cassiano

- 103 Chiesa di Santa Maria Mater Domini
- 111 Chiesa di San Giacomo dell'Orio

OTHER

- 2 Macello Comunale
- 11 Tintoretto's House
- 18 Casa Israelitica di Riposo
- 19 Banco Rosso
- 21 Museo Ebraico; Schola Tedesca
- 22 Schola Canton
- 24 Schola Italiana; Banco Verde
- 26 Schola Levantina
- 27 Schola Spagnola
- 30 Cartoleria Gianola
- 54 Exact Change
- 60 APT Office; Hotel Booking Office
- 61 Transalpino
- 62 Hotel Booking Office
- 63 Autonoleggio Venezia, Avis, Europcar & Hertz
- 64 Telecom Booth
- 65 Deposito Bagagli (Left Luggage Office)
- 66 Bureau de Change
- 67 ATVO & Other Bus Tickets; Agenzia Brusutti
- 68 Stazione Autobus (Bus Station)
- 69 ACTV Tickets & Information
- 70 Omniservice Internet Café
- 74 Bea Vita Lavanderia
- 75 Agenzia Arte e Storia
- 76 Internet Café
- 77 Train Station Gondola Service
- 79 Monte dei Paschi
- 87 Fondaco dei Turchi
- 88 Deposito del Megio
- 95 Corte de Ca' Michiel
- 99 Well
- 110 Well
- 112 ArciGay Nove
- 114 Scuola Grande di San Giovanni Evangelista
- 117 Site of Aldine Press
- 120 Ponte delle Tette

MAP 4

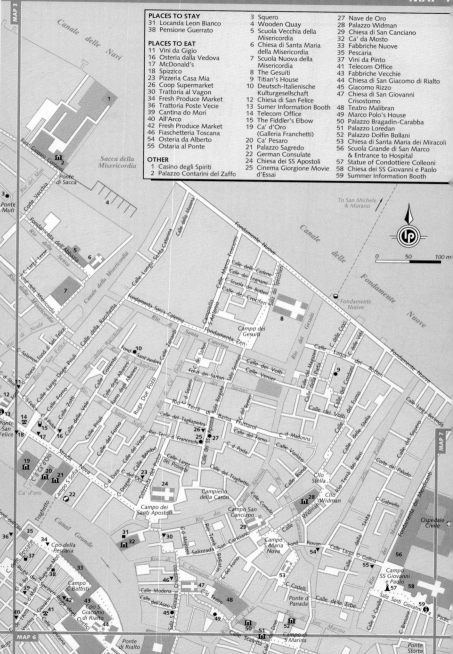

MAP 3

PLACES TO STAY
31 Locanda Leon Bianco
38 Pensione Guerrato

PLACES TO EAT
11 Vini da Gigio
16 Osteria dalla Vedova
17 McDonald's
18 Spizzico
23 Pizzeria Casa Mia
26 Coop Supermarket
30 Trattoria al Vagon
34 Fresh Produce Market
36 Trattoria Poste Vecie
39 Cantina do Mori
40 All'Arco
42 Fresh Produce Market
46 Fiaschetteria Toscana
54 Osteria da Alberto
55 Ostaria al Ponte

OTHER
1 Casino degli Spiriti
2 Palazzo Contarini del Zaffo

3 Squero
4 Wooden Quay
5 Scuola Vecchia della
  Misericordia
6 Chiesa di Santa Maria
  della Misericordia
7 Scuola Nuova della
  Misericordia
8 The Gesuiti
9 Titian's House
10 Deutsch-Italienische
   Kulturgesellschaft
12 Chiesa di San Felice
13 Telecom Office
14 Sumer Information Booth
15 The Fiddler's Elbow
19 Ca' d'Oro
   (Galleria Franchetti)
20 Ca' Pesaro
21 Palazzo Sagredo
22 German Consulate
24 Chiesa dei SS Apostoli
25 Cinema Giorgione Movie
   d'Essai

27 Nave de Oro
28 Palazzo Widman
29 Chiesa di San Canciano
32 Ca' da Mosto
33 Fabbriche Nuove
35 Pescaria
37 Vini da Pinto
41 Telecom Office
43 Fabbriche Vecchie
44 Chiesa di San Giacomo di Rialto
45 Giacomo Rizzo
47 Chiesa di San Giovanni
   Crisostomo
48 Teatro Malibran
49 Marco Polo's House
50 Palazzo Bragadin-Carabba
51 Palazzo Loredan
52 Palazzo Dolfin Bollani
53 Chiesa di Santa Maria dei Miracoli
56 Scuola Grande di San Marco
   & Entrance to Hospital
57 Statue of Condottiere Colleoni
58 Chiesa dei SS Giovanni e Paolo
59 Summer Information Booth

0   50   100 m

To San Michele
& Murano

MAP 7

MAP 6

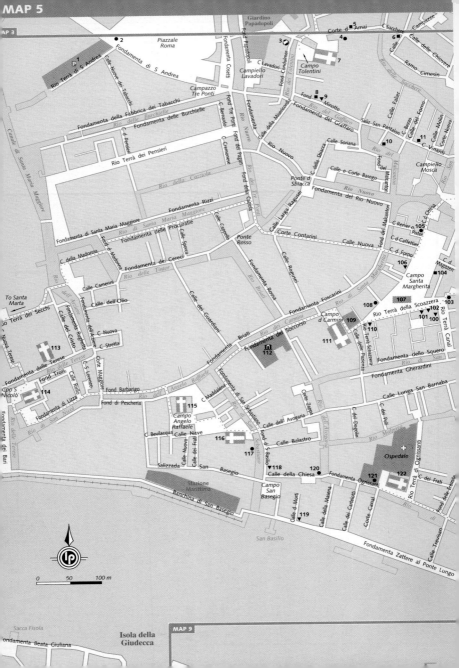

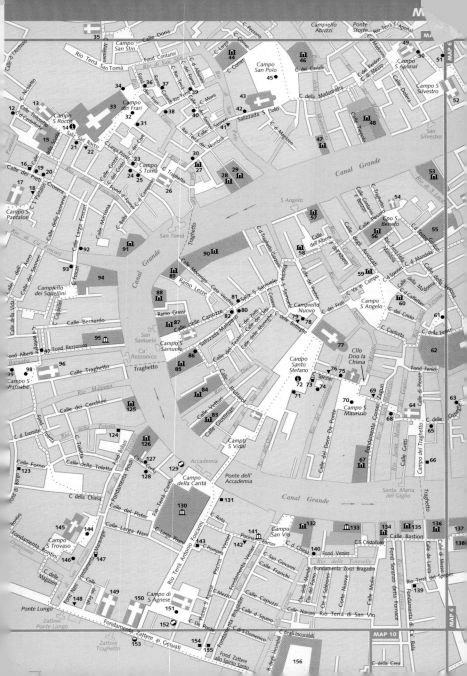

MAP 5

PLACES TO STAY
5 Hotel al Gallo
6 Domus Civica
8 Locanda Salieri
10 Hotel dalla Mora
11 Albergo Casa Peron
66 Gritti Palace Hotel
78 Locanda Fiorita
104 Albergo Antico Capon
123 Antica Locanda Montin
124 Albergo Accademia
  Villa Maravege
131 Hotel Galleria
139 Hotel Messner
143 Albergo agli Alboretti
154 La Calcina
155 Pensione Seguso

PLACES TO EAT
9 Brodo di Giuggiole
18 Arca
22 Gelateria Millefoglie da Tarvisio
41 Osteria alla Patatina
69 Tavernetta San Maurizio
76 Pasticceria Marchini
79 Trattoria Fiore
100 L'Incontro
101 Green Pub
102 Gelateria il Doge
106 Caffè
110 Al Sole di Napoli
118 Osteria da Toni
119 Billa Billa Supermarket
142 Trattoria ai Cugnai
148 Gelati Nico

BARS
16 Caffè Blue Music
73 Morozi
147 Cantinone Già Schiavi

SHOPPING
21 Graffiti
24 Il Baule Blu; Teddy Hospital
25 Argenteria
30 Tragicomica
31 Legatoria Polliero
36 La Zanze Veneixana
37 Laboratorio Artigianale di
  Decorazione Artistica
38 Atelier Pietro Longhi
39 A Mano
40 Gilberto Penzo
42 La Viola
50 BAC Art Studio
51 Manuela Calzature
63 Libreria Cassini
65 Galleria Traghetto
68 Legatoria Piazzesi
71 Fiorella Gallery
74 Nalesso

75 Il Papiro
80 Livio de Marchi
82 Galleria Marina Barovier
97 Ca' Macana
99 Legno e Dintorni
105 Nave de Oro
108 Loris Marazzi
140 Il Pavone

PALACES & MANSIONS
27 Palazzo Centani
28 Palazzo Tiepolo
29 Palazzo Pisani-Moretta
44 Palazzo Corner
46 Palazzi Soranzo
47 Palazzo Bernardo
48 Palazzo Papadopoli
53 Palazzo Grimani
56 Palazzo Fortuny
57 Palazzo Corner-Spinelli
58 Casa Nardi
59 Palazzo Gritti
60 Palazzo Duodo
67 Palazzo Corner (Ca' Granda)
83 Palazzo Giustinian-Lolin
84 Ca' del Duca
85 Palazzo Malipiero
87 Palazzo Grassi
88 Palazzo Moro-Lin
89 Palazzo Contarini dalle Figure
90 Palazzi Mocenigo
91 Palazzo Balbi
94 Ca' Foscari (University)
95 Ca' Rezzonico (Museo del
  Settecento Veneziano)
112 Palazzo Zenobio
125 Palazzo Loredan
  dell'Ambasciatore
126 Palazzo Contarini degli Scrigni
132 Palazzo Barbarigo
134 Palazzo Dario
135 Palazzo Salviati
136 Palazzo Genovese

CHURCHES
7 Chiesa di San Nicolò
  da Tolentino
13 Chiesa di San Rocco
17 Chiesa di San Pantalon
26 Chiesa di San Tomà
33 Chiesa di Santa Maria
  Gloriosa dei Frari
35 Chiesa di San Giovanni
  Evangelista
43 Chiesa di San Polo
49 Chiesa di Sant'Aponal
52 Chiesa di San Silvestro
54 Chiesa di San Beneto
64 Chiesa di Santa Maria del Giglio
77 Chiesa di Santo Stefano
96 Chiesa di San Barnaba

111 Chiesa dei Carmini
113 Former Chiesa di Santa Teresa
114 Chiesa di San Nicolò dei
  Mendicoli
115 Chiesa di Angelo Raffaele
116 Chiesa di San Sebastiano
122 Former Chiesa di Ognissanti
138 Former Chiesa di San Gregorio
145 Chiesa di San Trovaso
149 Chiesa di Santa Maria
  della Visitazione
150 Chiesa dei Gesuati

OTHER
1 Parking San Marco
2 Hotel Booking Office
3 Austrian Consulate
4 IUAV
12 Associazione Italiana Alberghi
  per la Gioventù
14 Summer Information Booth
15 Scuola Grande di San Rocco
19 Play the Game
20 Café Noir
23 Scuola dei Caleghei
32 Well
34 Archivio di Stato
45 Well
55 Cinema Rossini
61 Campiello della Fenice
62 Teatro La Fenice
70 Well
72 Summer Information Booth
81 Casa del Veronese
86 Casanova's Birthplace
92 Università Ca' Foscari
  Notice Boards
93 CTS
98 Well
103 Istituto Zambler
107 Scuola Varoteri
109 Scuola Grande dei Carmini
117 Università Ca' Foscari
  Notice Boards
120 Squero
121 Consultorio Familiare
127 Piccolo Mondo
128 Cinema Accademia d'Essai
129 UK Consulate
130 Gallerie dell'Accademia
133 Peggy Guggenheim Collection
  (Palazzo Venier dei Leoni)
137 Abbazia di San Gregorio
141 Galleria di Palazzo Cini
144 Well
146 Squero di San Trovaso
151 Well
152 Swiss Consulate
153 Alilaguna Boat to Airport;
  LineaFusina Vaporetto
156 Ospedale degli Incurabili

Giudecca waterfront view

Streets meet in Castello.

Savour the calm and charm of Venice off the beaten track.

Università Ca' Foscari is housed in a 15th-century palazzo.

Taking a moment out

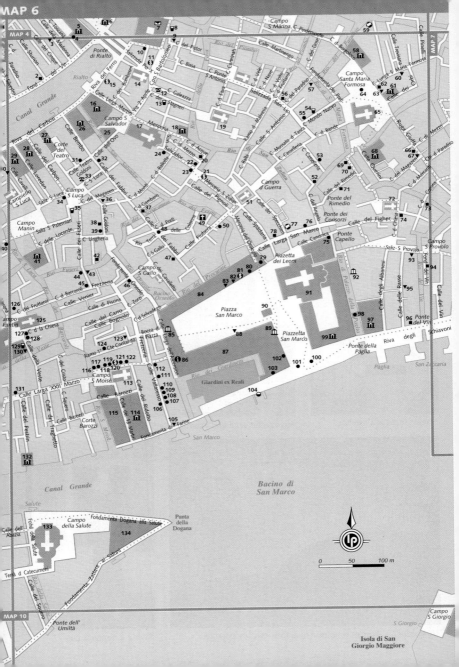

MAP 6

MAP 4

MAP 7

MAP 10

Canal Grande

Ponte di Rialto

Rialto

Campo S Salvador

Mercera

Campo S Paternian

Campo Manin

Campiello S Luca

Corte del Teatro

Campo d'Guerra

Campo S Gallo

Bacino Orseolo

Piazza San Marco

Piazzetta dei Leoni

Piazzetta San Marco

Giardini ex Reali

San Marco

Ponte del Rimedio

Ponte dei Consorzi

Ponte Capello

Campo S Provolo

Ponte del Vin

Ponte della Paglia

Riva degli Schiavoni

San Zaccaria

Paglia

Campo Santa Maria Formosa

Campo S Marina

Ruga Giuffa

Bacino di San Marco

Canal Grande

Salute

Campo della Salute

Fondamenta Dogana alla Salute

Punta della Dogana

Terà di Catecumeni

Ponte dell' Umiltà

S Giorgio

Isola di San Giorgio Maggiore

0   50   100 m

MAP 6

PLACES TO STAY

- 2 Locanda Sturion
- 20 Pensione al Gazzettino
- 37 Al Gambero
- 38 Serenissima
- 42 Locanda Casa Petrarca
- 47 Hotel Noemi
- 52 Hotel Riva
- 56 Hotel da Bruno
- 62 Hotel Scandinavia
- 66 Locanda al Piave
- 69 Locanda Silva
- 70 Locanda Canal
- 71 Locanda Remedio
- 73 Albergo Corona
- 74 Hotel Bridge
- 78 Hotel ai do Mori
- 94 Hotel Doni
- 96 Hotel Danieli
- 115 Bauer Grünewald & Grand Hotel

PLACES TO EAT

- 3 Trattoria alla Madonna
- 9 Ai Rusteghi
- 30 Enoteca Il Volto
- 36 Standa Supermarket
- 43 Ristorante da Ivo
- 57 Ristorante ai Barbacani
- 60 Osteria al Mascaron
- 63 Pizzeria da Egidio
- 67 Trattoria agli Artisti
- 82 Lavena
- 83 Caffè Quadri
- 88 Caffè Florian
- 93 Alla Rivetta
- 95 Al Vecchio Penasa
- 105 Harry's Bar
- 123 Osteria da Carla
- 130 Vino Vino

BARS

- 8 Bacaro Jazz
- 13 Devil's Forest
- 35 Black Jack Bar
- 54 Irishark
- 129 Martini Scala

SHOPPING

- 1 L'Arlecchino (2)
- 4 Color Team
- 10 Libreria al Fontego
- 24 Jesurum
- 32 Libreria Goldoni
- 39 Libreria Emiliana
- 40 Libreria al Ponte
- 45 Kenzo
- 46 Daniele Bardella
- 48 Armani
- 50 Valese
- 53 Editore Filippi
- 55 Nave de Oro
- 75 San Marco Studium
- 76 Veneziartigiana
- 107 Gucci
- 108 Roberto Cavalli
- 109 Dolce & Gabbana
- 110 Missoni
- 111 Agnona
- 112 Bruno Magli
- 116 Louis Vuitton
- 117 Versace
- 118 Prada
- 119 L'Isola
- 121 Valentino
- 122 Fendi
- 127 Bugno Samueli Art Gallery
- 128 Studio Aoristico di Matteo Lo Greco
- 131 Laura Bigiotti

PALACES & MANSIONS

- 5 Palazzo dei Dieci Savi
- 6 Palazzo dei Camerlenghi
- 16 Palazzo Dolfin-Manin
- 18 Palazzo Giustinian-Faccanon
- 26 Palazzo Bembo
- 27 Palazzo Dandolo
- 28 Palazzo Loredan
- 29 Ca' Farsetti
- 41 Palazzo Contarini del Bovolo
- 58 Palazzi Donà
- 61 Palazzo Vitturi
- 68 Palazzo Querini-Stampalia
- 97 Palazzo dei Prigioni (Prigioni Nuovi)
- 99 Palazzo Ducale
- 114 Palazzo Giustinian
- 132 Palazzo Contarini-Fasan

CHURCHES

- 14 Chiesa di San Bartolomeo
- 17 Chiesa di San Salvador
- 19 Chiesa di Santa Maria della Fava
- 49 Chiesa della Santa Croce degli Armeni
- 51 Chiesa di San Zulian
- 65 Chiesa di Santa Maria Formosa
- 72 Chiesa di San Giovanni Novo
- 91 Basilica di San Marco
- 113 Chiesa di San Moisè
- 125 Chiesa di San Fantin
- 133 Chiesa di Santa Maria della Salute

OTHER

- 7 Fondaco dei Tedeschi & Main Post Office
- 11 Exact Change
- 12 Telephones
- 15 Thomas Cook
- 21 Exact Change
- 22 Alliance Française
- 23 Agenzia Kele & Teo
- 25 Scuola Grande di San Teodoro
- 31 Teatro Goldoni
- 33 Telecom Office
- 34 Cassa di Risparmio di Venezia (Tickets for La Fenice)
- 44 ACTV Office
- 59 French Consulate
- 64 Well
- 77 Dutch Consulate
- 79 Torre dell'Orologio
- 80 Intras Travel
- 81 Thomas Cook
- 84 Procuratie Vecchie
- 85 Museo Correr (Ala Napoleonica)
- 86 APT Office
- 87 Procuratie Nuove
- 89 Museo Archeologico
- 90 Campanile
- 92 Museo Diocesano d'Arte Sacra
- 98 Ponte dei Sospiri (Bridge of Sighs)
- 100 Column with Lion of St Mark
- 101 Column with Statue of San Teodoro
- 102 Libreria Nazionale Marciana
- 103 La Zecca
- 104 Alilaguna Boat to Airport
- 106 Teatro al Ridotto
- 120 American Express
- 124 Assessorato alla Gioventù
- 126 Ateneo Veneto
- 134 Dogana da Mar

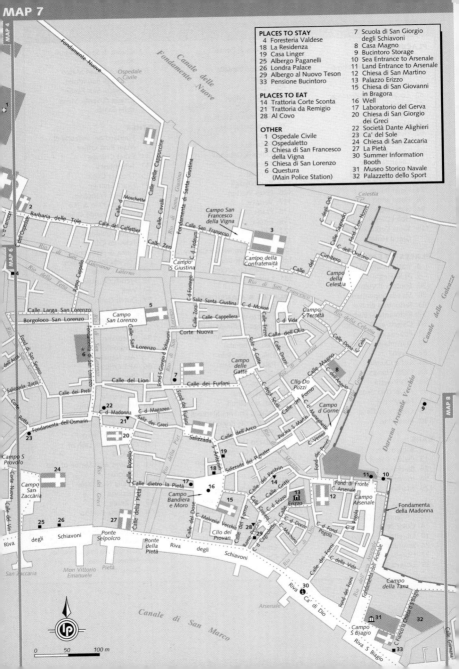

MAP 7

PLACES TO STAY
4 Foresteria Valdese
18 La Residenza
19 Casa Linger
25 Albergo Paganelli
26 Londra Palace
29 Albergo al Nuovo Teson
33 Pensione Bucintoro

PLACES TO EAT
14 Trattoria Corte Sconta
21 Trattoria da Remigio
28 Al Covo

OTHER
1 Ospedale Civile
2 Ospedaletto
3 Chiesa di San Francesco
  della Vigna
5 Chiesa di San Lorenzo
6 Questura
  (Main Police Station)

7 Scuola di San Giorgio
  degli Schiavoni
8 Casa Magno
9 Bucintoro Storage
10 Sea Entrance to Arsenale
11 Land Entrance to Arsenale
12 Chiesa di San Martino
13 Palazzo Erizzo
15 Chiesa di San Giovanni
   in Bragora
16 Well
17 Laboratorio del Gerva
20 Chiesa di San Giorgio
   dei Greci
22 Società Dante Alighieri
23 Ca' del Sole
24 Chiesa di San Zaccaria
27 La Pietà
30 Summer Information
   Booth
31 Museo Storico Navale
32 Palazzetto dello Sport

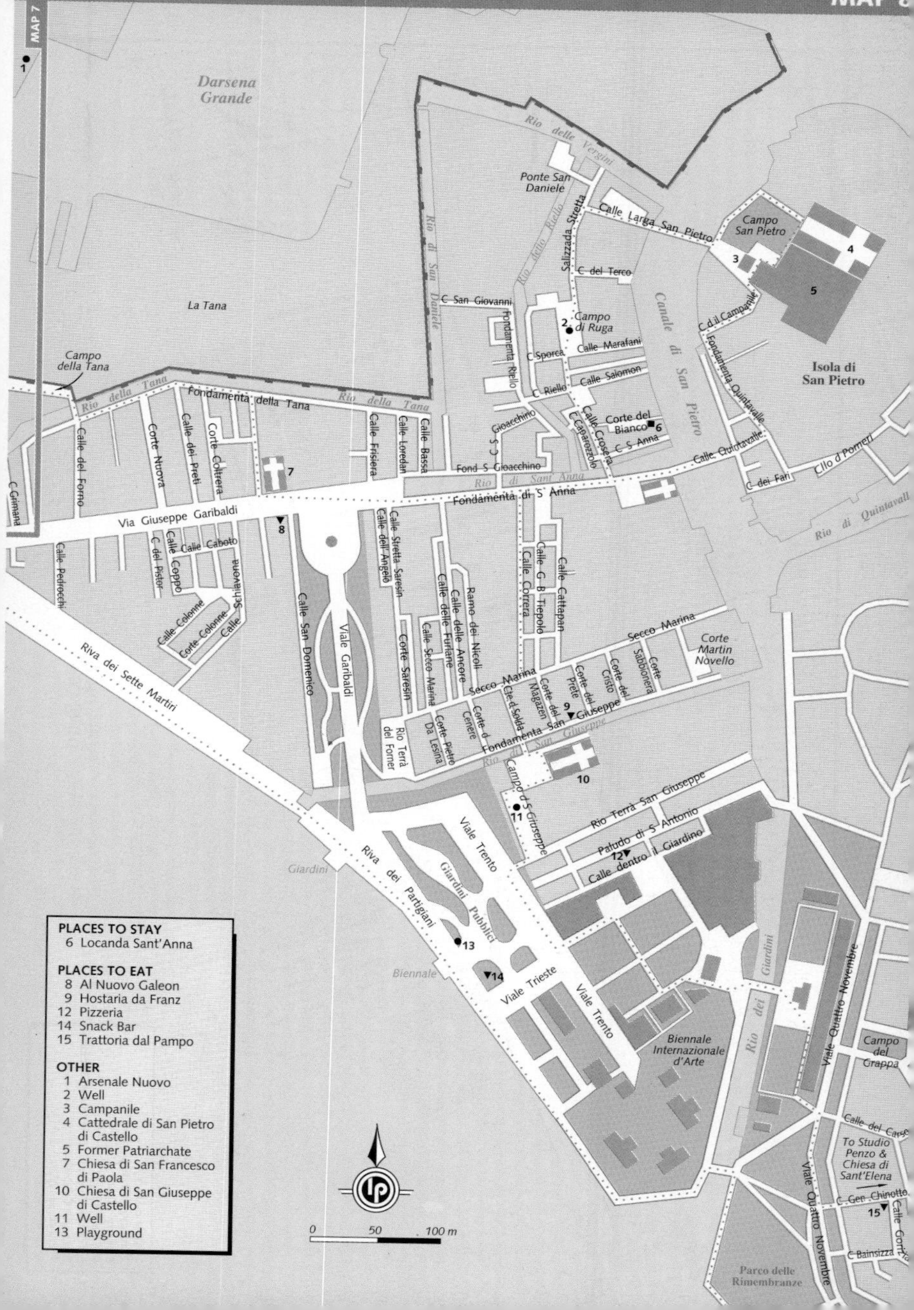

MAP 8

MAP 7

Darsena
Grande

La Tana

Campo
della Tana

Rio della Tana   Rio della Tana

Fondamenta della Tana

Via Giuseppe Garibaldi

Riva dei Sette Martini

Ponte San
Daniele

Calle Larga San Pietro

Campo
San Pietro

C del Terco

Salizzada Stretta

Rio di San Daniele

C San Giovanni

Fondamenta Riello

Campo
di Ruga

C Sporca

Calle Marafani

C Riello

Calle Salomon

Gioacchino

Corte del
Bianco

Fond S Gioacchino

C S Anna

Calle Crutchavalle

Fondamenta di S Anna

Canale di San Pietro

Isola di
San Pietro

Fondamenta Quintavalle

C d'Al Campanile

C dei Fari

Cllo d'Poneri

Rio di Quintavalle

Calle Colonna

Calle dell'Angelo

Calle Stretta Sarasin

Calle G B Tiepolo

Calle Cattanin

Secco Marina

Corte
Martin
Novello

Calle delle Ancore

Calle Orseolo

Calle Sesto Marina

Corte Sarasin

Rio Terrà
del Forner

Secco Marina

Ramo dei Nicoli

Corte San
Giuseppe

Corte dei
Prede

Corte del
Cristo

Corte
Sabbioneta

Calle Pietro
Cenami

Corte dei
Nazareni

Fondamenta San Giuseppe

Rio Campo S Giuseppe

Calle San Domenico

Viale Garibaldi

Calle Pedrocchi

Corte Colonne

Corte Celomal

Calle Caboto

C del Pestor

Calle Coppo

Calle Nuova

Corte del
Forno

Calle dei Preti

Calle del Fresiera

Calle Bassa

Calle Loredan

Calle Frisiera

C Grimani

Campo
della Tana

Rio Terrà San Giuseppe

Palludo di S Antonio

Calle dentro

I Giardino

Viale Trento

Viale Trento

Giardini
Pubblici

Giardini
dei
Partigiani

Riva dei Sette Martiri

Giardini

Biennale

Viale Trieste

Biennale
Internazionale
d'Arte

Rio dei Giardini

Campo
del
Grappa

Viale Quattro Novembre

Viale Quattro Novembre

To Studio
Penzo &
Chiesa di
Sant'Elena

Calle del Cases

C Gen Chinotto

C Bainsizza

Parco delle
Rimembranze

1
2
3 4
5
6
7
8
9
10
11
12
13
14
15

PLACES TO STAY
6 Locanda Sant'Anna

PLACES TO EAT
8 Al Nuovo Galeon
9 Hostaria da Franz
12 Pizzeria
14 Snack Bar
15 Trattoria dal Pampo

OTHER
1 Arsenale Nuovo
2 Well
3 Campanile
4 Cattedrale di San Pietro
   di Castello
5 Former Patriarchate
7 Chiesa di San Francesco
   di Paola
10 Chiesa di San Giuseppe
   di Castello
11 Well
13 Playground

0   50   100 m

Lp

MAP 9
MAP 10
MAP 10
MAP 10
MAP 5

Former Ospedale degli Incurabili

Zattere allo Spirito Santo

Zattere ai Gesuati · Fondamenta

Zattere Traghetto

Calle dei Frati
Calle degli Orti
Calle del Principe
Calle del Pesce
Calle dell'Albero
Calle San Giacomo

Campo San Giacomo

Fondamenta di San Giacomo

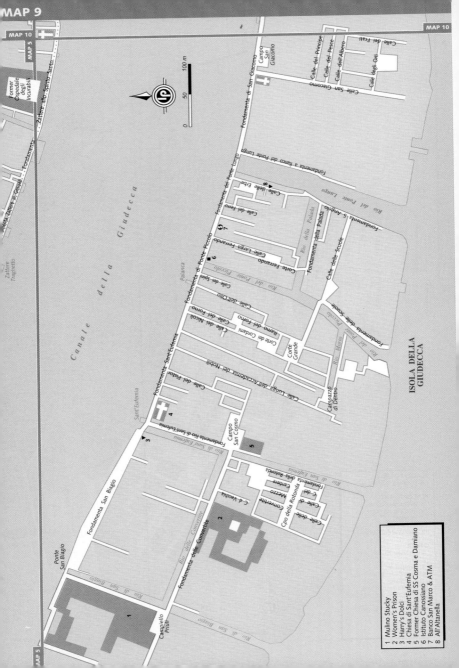

C a n a l e   d e l l a   G i u d e c c a

G i u d e c c a

100 m
50
0

Fondamenta a fianco del Ponte Lungo

Fondamenta del Ponte Lungo

Calle delle Erbe

Rio del Ponte Lungo

Fondamenta S. Angelo

Rio della Palada

Fondamenta della Palada

Fondamenta delle Scuole

Calle delle Scuole

Calle del Forno

Calle Larga Fernando

Corte Ferrando

Palanca

Fondamenta di Ponte Piccolo

Calle dei San Piccolo

Rio del Ponte Piccolo

Calle dell'Olio

Ramo del Forno

Calle dei Nicoli

Calle del Forno

Corte dei Cordami

Corte Grande

Rio del Ponte Piccolo

Fondamenta delle Scuole

Rio Morto

Canazzo di Dentro

ISOLA DELLA GIUDECCA

Fondamenta Sant'Eufemia

Calle Lunga dell'Accademia dei Nobili

Calle del Pistor

Sant'Eufemia

Fondamenta Rio di Sant'Eufemia

Rio di Sant'Eufemia

Campo San Cosmo

C. d Vecchia

Rio delle Convertite

Fondamenta delle Convertite

Fondamenta San Biagio

Ponte San Biagio

Campiello Priuli

Rio di San Biagio

Convertite

Cpo della Rotonda

Calle delle Mezzo

Calle del Cantiere

Fondamenta della Rotonda

Rio di San Eufemia

1 Mulino Stucky
2 Women's Prison
3 Harry's Dolci
4 Chiesa di Sant'Eufemia
5 Former Chiesa di SS Cosma e Damiano
6 Istituto Canossiano
7 Banco San Marco & ATM
8 All'Altanella

MAP 10

1 Saloni Ex-Magazzini del Sale
2 Chiesa di Spirito Santo
3 Chiesa del Redentore
4 Former Chiesa della Croce
5 Ostello Venezia
6 Los Murales
7 Università Internazionale dell'Arte
8 Ai Tre Scaini
9 Chiesa delle Zitelle
10 Hotel Cipriani
11 Fondazione Cini
12 Chiesa di San Giorgio Maggiore
13 Teatro Verdi (Closed)

Isola di San
Giorgio Maggiore

Campo San
Giorgio

MAP 6

Canale della Grazia

Campo Nani
e Barbaro

Fondamenta San Giovanni

Zitelle

Fondamenta delle Zitelle

Campiello
Ospizio

Calle dell'Asia Minore

Calle Esterna

Calle Michelangelo

Calle Larga della Crocefissa

Calle dell'Asia Maggiore

Calle dietro la Croce

Calle del Gran

Calle dello Squero

Canale della Giudecca

ISOLA DELLA
GIUDECCA

Calle della Croce

Fondamenta della Croce

Calle della Croce

Campo del
Redentore

Rio della Croce

Fondamenta al Rio della Croce

Redentore

Fond di Ca' Bala

Fondamenta S. Giacomo

Cte di Sant

MAP 9

0   50   100 m

S

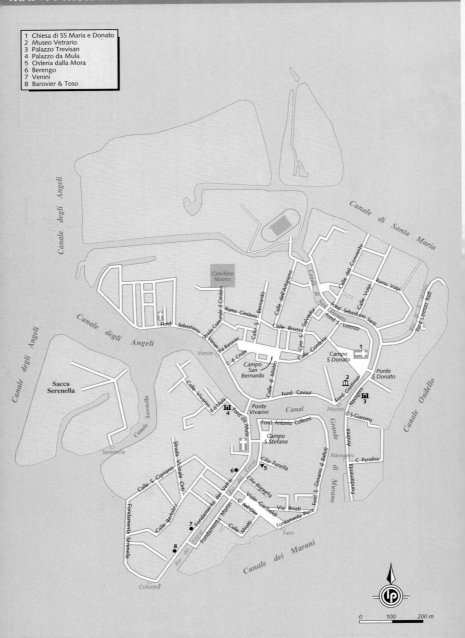

MAP 11 MURANO

1 Chiesa di SS Maria e Donato
2 Museo Vetrario
3 Palazzo Trevisan
4 Palazzo da Mula
5 Osteria dalla Mora
6 Berengo
7 Venini
8 Barovier & Toso

Canale degli Angeli

Canale di Santa Maria

Canale degli Angeli

Canale degli Angeli

Cimitero Nuovo

Fond. Sebastiano

Strada Comunale d'Cimitero

Ramo Cimitero

Ramo Venier o Via Barovier

Venier o Via Barovier

Calle dell'Artigiano

Calle S Bernardo

Calle Brussa

Campo del Convento

Calle del Convento

Ramo Volpi

Calle Volpi

Fond. Sebastiano Sinti

Fond. S Lorenzo

Tor. Lorenzo Radi

Fond. S Salvador

Lepo S Salvador

Calle Corrette

C. d' Cristo

Campo San Bernardo

Calle d-Aliotto

Fond Cavour

Campo S Donato

Ponte S Donato

Museo-Navagero

Fond. Giustinian

C.S Giacomo

C.S Andrea

C. Paradiso

Sacca Serenella

Canale Serenella

Serepella

Calle Vivarini

Ponte Vivarini

R d/ Mula

Fond da Mula

Fond Antonio Coleoni

Campo S Stefano

Clio Turella

Clio Bigaglia

Canale Ondello

Canal

Grande

di

Murano

Fond S Giovanni d' Batttti

Via Briati

Fondamenta Piave

Faro

Calle S Cipriano

Strada V Chiale Orti

Calle Bertolini

Fondamenta dei Vetrai

Fondamenta Manin

Rio dei Vetrai

Viale Garibaldi

C dell'Olio

Calle Miotti

Fondamenta Serenella

Colonna

Canale dei Marani

6

7

8

5

4

2

3

1

0   100   200 m

1 Museo di Torcello (Palazzo del Consiglio)
2 Palazzo dell'Archivio
3 Cattedrale di Santa Maria Assunta
4 Chiesa di Santa Fosca
5 Locanda Cipriani
6 Osteria al Ponte del Diavolo
7 Ristorante al Trono di Atilla
8 Post Office
9 Museo del Merletto
10 Chiesa di San Martino
11 Ristorante Galuppi
12 Locanda al Raspo de Ua
13 Chiesa di Santa Caterina

Canale di Torcello

Piazza
Torcello

TORCELLO

Fondamenta Borgognoni

Torcello

Canale Borgognoni

Canale Sant'Antonio

Palude dei Laghi

Canale di Burano

Burano

Mazzorbo

Fondamenta di Santa Caterina

Strada del Cimitero

Canale di Mazzorbo

Mazzorbo

Fondamenta di Santa Caterina

Cimitero

Strada di Corte Comare
Strada S. Mauro
Calle di Sulei
Fond S. Mauro
Fond Spolverin
Fond Portuiello
Fond di Cao di Rio
Vigna
Moleca
Calle Pittona
Via Galuppi
Via
Corte Comare
Fondamenta Cao
Fond della Giudecca
Fond della Pescheria
Terra del Pizzo
Piazza Galuppi
Fond di Terranova

BURANO

0   100   200 m

MAP 13 LIDO DI VENEZIA

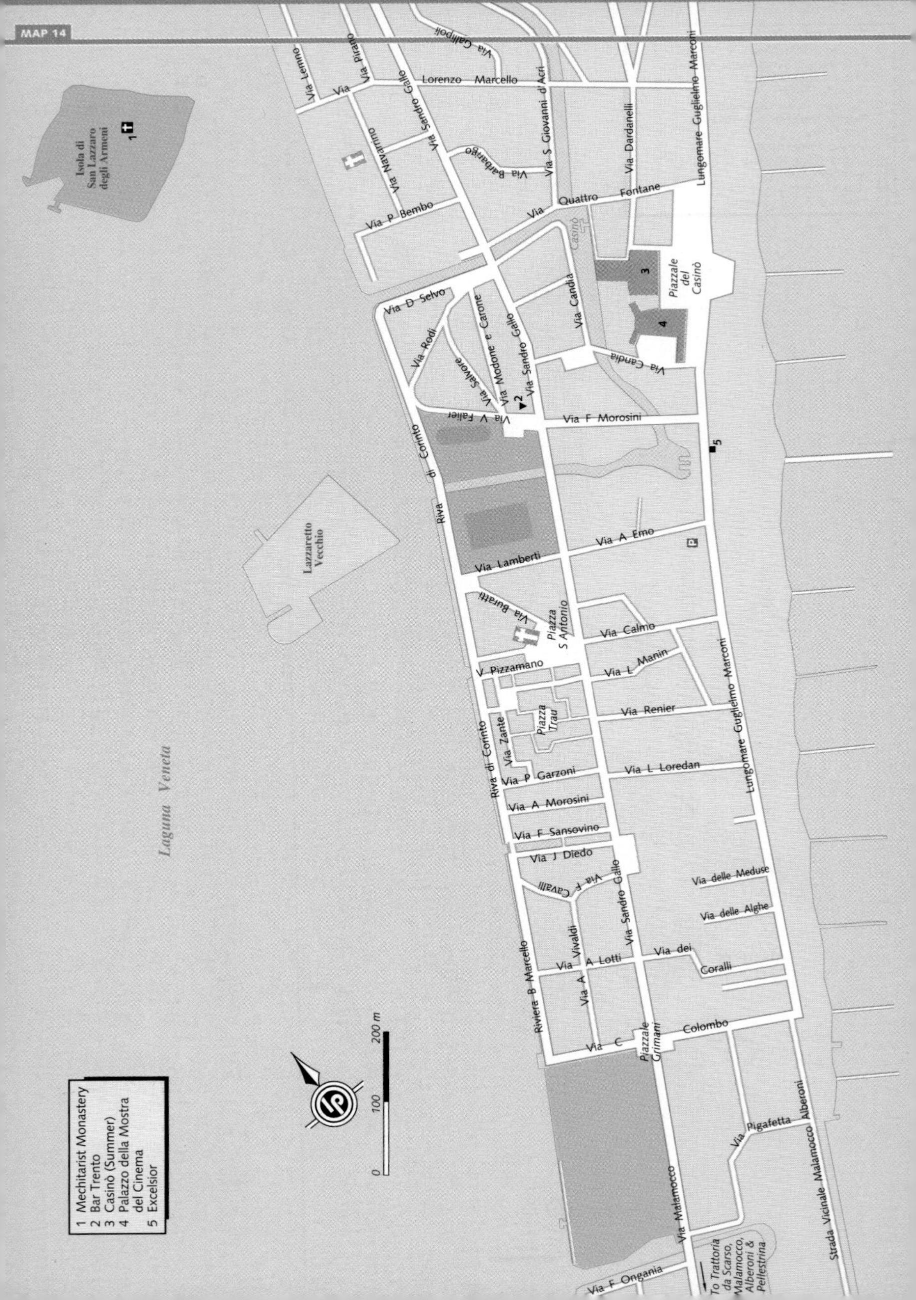

MAP 14

Map Legend

1 Mechitarist Monastery
2 Bar Trento
3 Casinò (Summer)
4 Palazzo della Mostra del Cinema
5 Excelsior

Isola di San Lazzaro degli Armeni

Lazzaretto Vecchio

Laguna Veneta

0   100   200 m

Via Lemmo
Via Pilastro
Via Galiffoli
Lorenzo Marcello
Via Sandro Gallo
Via Balneario
Via S. Giovanni d'Acri
Via Dardanelli
Via Havarino
Lungomare Guglielmo Marconi
Via P. Bembo
Quattro Fontane
Via D. Selvo
Via Candia
Piazzale del Casinò
Via Rodi
Via Modone e Corone
Via Sandro Gallo
Via V. Faller
Via della Salute
Via Candia
Via F. Morosini
Riva di Corinto
Via A. Emo
Via Lamberti
Via Buratti
Piazza S Antonio
Via Calmo
V. Pizzamano
Via L Manin
Riva di Corinto
Piazza Trau
Via Renier
Via Zante
Via P. Garzoni
Via L Loredan
Via A. Morosini
Via F. Sansovino
Lungomare Guglielmo Marconi
Via J. Diedo
Via F. Cavalli
Via Sandro Gallo
Via delle Meduse
Via delle Alghe
Via Vivaldi
Via A. Lotti
Via dei Coralli
Riviera B. Marcello
Via C.
Piazzale Grimani
Colombo
Via Malamocco
Via Pigafetta
Via F. Ongania
Strada Vicinale Malamocco-Alberoni
To Trattoria da Scarso, Malamocco, Alberoni & Pellestrina

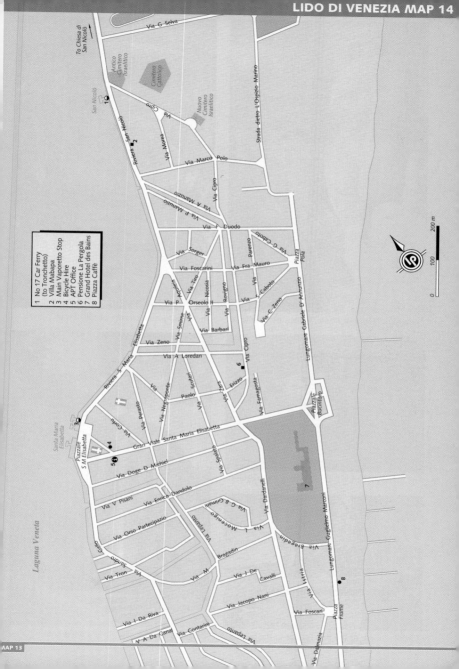

1 No 17 Car Ferry
   (to Tronchetto)
2 Villa Mabapa
3 Main Vaporetto Stop
4 Bicycle Hire
5 APT Office
6 Pensione La Pergola
7 Grand Hotel des Bains
8 Piazza Caffè

To Chiesa di San Nicolò

Via G. Selva

Antico Cimitero Israelitico

Cimitero Cattolico

Nuovo Cimitero Israelitico

San Nicolò

Strada dietro L'Ospizio Marino

Riviera S. Nicolò

Via Morea

Via Marco Polo

Via Cipro

Via A. Manuzio

Via G. Duodo

Via G. Cabotto

Piazza Pola

Via Sorger

Via Foscarini

Parenzo

Via Fra Mauro

Artiglieria

Via Tiro

Via Nicosia

Rovigno

Via S. Cabotto

Via P. Orseolo II

Via C. Zeno

Lungomare Gabriele D'Annunzio

Via Smirne

Via Barbari

Elisabetta

Via Zeno

Via A. Loredan

Via Cipro

6

Riviera S. Maria Elisabetta

Via

Scutari

Paolo

Via Negroponte

Via Zara

Via Erizzo

Via Famagosta

Piazzale Bucintoro

Santa Maria Elisabetta

Via Perasto

Via Corfù

3

4

5

Gran Viale Santa Maria Elisabetta

Piazzale S M Elisabetta

Via Doge D. Michiel

Via V. Pisani

Via Enrico Dandolo

Via Orso Partecipazio

Via L. Mocenigo

Via B. Grimani

Via Lepanto

Via Dardanelli

Via Brasadin

Lungomare Guglielmo Marconi

7

Via V. Sandro

Via Colfo

Via Tron

Via M.

Bragadin

Via J. De
Cavalli

Via I. Da Riva

V. A. Da Canal

Via Contarini

Via Lepanto

Via Jacopo Nani

Via Foscari

Piazza Fiume

8

Via Dalmazia

Laguna Veneta

200 m

0   100

MAP 13

The grounds of Villa Pisani, Riviera del Brenta

The sumptuous ballroom of Villa Pisani

The island and church of San Giorgio Maggiore

Torcello, home of the first settlers in the lagoon

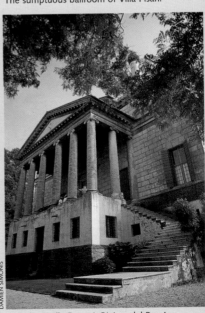
Palladio's Villa Foscari, Riviera del Brenta

PLACES TO STAY
5 Hotel Vivit
15 Hotel Monte Piana
16 Albergo Roberta
19 Hotel Giovannina
21 Hotel Tritone

PLACES TO EAT
8 Brek
14 Osteria La Pergola
17 Da Bepi Venesian

OTHER
1 Castello
2 Metrò
3 Clipper Viaggi
4 Le Barche Shopping
  Complex
6 Chiesa di San Lorenzo
7 Telecom Office
9 Post Office
10 ACTV Office
11 CTS
12 APT Office
13 Laundrette
18 Cinema Dante d'Essai
20 Serenissima Parking
22 ATVO Bus Tickets
23 ACTV Buses to Venice
   (No 2; Night Bus No N1)
24 Train Station

MAP LEGEND

BOUNDARIES

.................International
.................Provincial
.................Regional

HYDROGRAPHY

.................Coastline, Lake
.................River, Creek
.................Canal
.................Swamp

ROUTES & TRANSPORT

.................Freeway
.................(under construction)
.................Highway
.................Major Road
.................Minor Road
.................Unsealed Road
.................City Freeway
.................City Highway
.................City Road

.................City Street, Lane
.................Pedestrian Mall
.................Tunnel
.................Train Route & Station
.................Metro & Station
.................Cable Car or Chair Lift
.................Walking Track
.................Walking Tour
.................Ferry Route

AREA FEATURES

.................Park, Gardens
.................Cemetery

.................Building
.................Urban Area

.................Market
.................Beach, Desert

MAP SYMBOLS

○ **ROMA** ....National Capital
◉ **MILANO** ....Provincial Capital
● La Spezia ....City
● Varazze ....Town
● Arenzano ....Village

● ....Point of Interest
■ ....Place to Stay
▲ ....Camp Site
☞ ....Caravan Park
⌂ ....Hut or Chalet
▼ ....Place to Eat
☗ ....Pub or Bar

.................Airport
.................Ancient or City Wall
.................Archaeological Site
.................Bank
.................Beach
.................Castle or Fort
.................Cave or Grotto
.................Cathedral, Church
.................Cliff or Escarpment
.................Embassy or Consulate
.................Hospital
.................Lookout
.................Monument
▲ ....Mountain or Hill
.................Mountain Range

.................Museum
.................National Park
.................Parking
)(.................Pass
.................Petrol Station
★ ....Police Station
.................Post Office
.................Stately Home
.................Synagogue
☎ ....Telephone
.................Temple
.................Tomb
.................Tourist Information
.................Transport
.................Zoo

Note: not all symbols displayed above appear in this book

LONELY PLANET OFFICES

Australia
PO Box 617, Hawthorn, Victoria 3122
☎ 03 9819 1877 fax 03 9819 6459
email: talk2us@lonelyplanet.com.au

USA
150 Linden St, Oakland, CA 94607
☎ 510 893 8555 TOLL FREE: 800 275 8555
fax 510 893 8572
email: info@lonelyplanet.com

UK
10a Spring Place, London NW5 3BH
☎ 020 7428 4800 fax 020 7428 4828
email: go@lonelyplanet.co.uk

France
1 rue du Dahomey, 75011 Paris
☎ 01 55 25 33 00 fax 01 55 25 33 01
email: bip@lonelyplanet.fr
www.lonelyplanet.fr

World Wide Web: www.lonelyplanet.com *or* AOL keyword: lp
Lonely Planet Images: lpi@lonelyplanet.com.au